Reading Keys

Fourth Edition

Laraine E. Flemming

WADSWORTH
CENGAGE Learning·

Australia • Brazil • Japan • Korea • Mexico • Singapore • Spain • United Kingdom • United States

WADSWORTH
CENGAGE Learning

Reading Keys, Fourth Edition
Laraine Flemming

Director of Developmental Studies:
Annie Todd

Executive Editor: Shani Fisher

Senior Development Editor:
Kathy Sands-Boehmer

Editorial Assistant: Erin Nixon

Media Editor: Christian Biagetti

Brand Manager: Lydia LeStar

Market Development Manager:
Erin Parkins

Marketing Communications Manager:
Linda Yip

Senior Content Project Manager:
Aimee Chevrette Bear

Art Director: Faith Brosnan

Print Buyer: Betsy Donaghey

Rights Acquisition Specialist:
Ann Hoffman

Production Service: Books By
Design, Inc.

Text Designer: Books By Design, Inc.

Cover Designer: Saizon Design

Cover Image: shutterstock.com
© Andromed

Compositor: S4Carlisle Publishing
Services

For product information and technology assistance, contact us at
Cengage Learning Customer & Sales Support, 1-800-354-9706

For permission to use material from this text or product, submit all requests online at **www.cengage.com/permissions**.
Further permissions questions can be e-mailed to
permissionrequest@cengage.com.

Library of Congress Control Number: 2012946774
ISBN-13: 978-1-133-58995-2
ISBN-10: 1-133-58995-2

Wadsworth
20 Channel Center Street
Boston, MA 02210
USA

Cengage Learning is a leading provider of customized learning solutions with office locations around the globe, including Singapore, the United Kingdom, Australia, Mexico, Brazil, and Japan. Locate your local office at **international.cengage.com/region**.

Cengage Learning products are represented in Canada by Nelson Education, Ltd.

For your course and learning solutions, visit **www.cengage.com**.

Purchase any of our products at your local college store or at our preferred online store **www.cengagebrain.com**.

Instructors: Please visit **login.cengage.com** and log in to access instructor-specific resources.

Printed in the United States of America
2 3 4 5 6 7 17 16 15 14

Contents

4   Identifying Topics, Main Ideas, and Topic Sentences   157

5   Working Together: Topic Sentences and Supporting Details   220

6   Drawing Inferences About Implied Main Ideas   285

7   Recognizing Patterns of Organization   332

9   Analyzing Arguments   464

Combining Your Skills   528

Answer Key: Reviewing the Key Points   571

Preface

Instructors who have used previous editions of *Reading Keys* will be happy to hear that the fourth edition has many of the same features that encouraged them to choose the book initially. In this new edition, *Reading Keys* still uses a carefully scaffolded chapter sequence that shows readers how to build new skills upon previous ones, thereby ensuring that students never feel overwhelmed by new concepts and applications. Instead, through the acquisition of each new skill, they become more independent and confident readers. As in previous editions, the first chapter identifies and models study strategies that lead to in-depth learning and remembering. The remaining chapters take students step by step through reading paragraphs to understanding and evaluating longer, multi-paragraph readings.

While many elements of *Reading Keys* remain the same, there is much that is new to this edition.

Here's What's New in the Fourth Edition

◆ More Visual Instruction

Because so much new research in cognitive science suggests that information makes its way into the brain by several distinct neural pathways, this edition includes many more diagrams and photos, which provide visual illustrations of the verbal explanations. The goal of this dual instruction, visual and verbal, is to double students' chances of retaining in long-term memory the concepts, skills, and topics this text introduces.

◆ Research-Based Advice on Learning Strategies

Many of the study skills suggestions in Chapter 1, **Getting into a Textbook State of Mind**, have been revised to take into account new research on how the brain learns best. Students are encouraged, for instance, to interrupt their study sessions and take walking breaks in which they move around a bit and change rooms before resuming their reading. This advice acknowledges the results of cognitive research showing that changes in location encourage the brain to re-process newly learned information.

◆ A Revised Chapter on Sentence Relationships

At the request of reviewers, this edition of *Reading Keys* brings back the chapter on sentence relationships originally included in the second edition. Re-titled **Understanding Sentence Relationships**, the chapter has been revised from first page to last. Clearly and concisely, it identifies and illustrates the underlying relationships that most commonly structure a writer's thoughts. It also shows students how to recognize those relationships and use them to better understand the author's meaning.

◆ "Class Action" Now Includes the Web

Since the first edition, *Reading Keys* has included a "Class Action" feature that encourages students to collaborate in their response to questions posed in the text. This edition expands that feature to include a question (or questions) to be answered through Web research. The goal of the revision is to give students practice doing Web research while encouraging them to talk among themselves about their results. That way they can compare notes not just on their conclusions but also on the Web sources they used as the basis of their response.

◆ New Discussion of How to Select and Evaluate Websites

Research on how students use the Web shows that students, even grad students, are not especially savvy about how they select and evaluate websites. In an effort to make your students use the Web with both speed and efficiency, this edition of *Reading Keys* offers a completely revised discussion of how to formulate a search term and *evaluate* the results that search term produces.

◆ Expanded Discussion of Summarizing

Summarizing is a key academic skill that's required in most college courses. Yet very few students know how to go about writing a summary. To remedy that academic deficit, this edition of *Reading Keys* has enlarged the discussion of summarizing to make it more concrete and provide more practice with summary writing than the previous edition. A new six-point chart, *Pointers on Summary Writing* in Chapter 5, tells students how to look at the text to be summarized and decide which ideas should be retained and which ones left out.

◆ Marginal Think-Alouds Model the Responses of Skilled Readers

Marginal notes throughout the chapters illustrate how skilled readers typically respond to text features, providing students with models of how experienced readers make and confirm predictions, infer connections and references, and just generally stay connected to the author's train of thought.

◆ Plenty of New Readings

At least 50 percent of the readings in this edition are new and at least one-quarter of those are from textbooks. Instructors have said that they want their students to have more exposure to textbook conventions, and this edition aims to fulfill that request. However, as in the past, *Reading Keys* includes a variety of readings that will stimulate your students' interest and motivate them to read. As they work their way through the book, students will learn, among other things, about the cave towns of Africa's Tunisia, the dangers of too much charisma, the tragic story of the Elephant Man, and the bravery of Afghani schoolgirls, who won't be scared into giving up their right to an education.

◆ New Vocabulary Tests

Users of *Reading Keys* wanted to have vocabulary quizzes that move beyond simple fill-in-the-blank exercises. In response to this request, *Reading Keys* now provides two different types of tests. In the first, students are asked to provide more academic versions of familiar words. In the second, they have to choose the one sentence out of three that uses the new word correctly. These two new test formats are guaranteed to make your students think more deeply about the words they are learning, which is another way of saying they will remember the words long after they have finished reading this book.

Supplements Package

Available both in print and online, the robust Instructor's Manual and Test Bank features Answer Keys for Chapters 1–9 and *Combining Your Skills*. It also includes additional quizzes with a corresponding answer key, along with a midterm and final exam. Instructors who want a print copy of the manual and test bank should request it from their Cengage representative. Instructors using an online version should go to login .cengage.com and use the access code provided by their Cengage representative.

◆ Companion Websites

The **Instructor's Companion Website** features a variety of teaching tools including the **Instructor's Manual and Test Bank** along with key concept **PowerPoint** slides. The PowerPoint slides define all the terms critical to the chapter explanations. Both the manual and the Power-Point slides are available at login.cengage.com, which requires an access code provided by your Cengage representative.

The **Student Companion Website** available at www.cengagebrain .com offers resources to help students succeed using *Reading Keys*, including interactive practice quizzes, a Guide to Phonics, and new to this edition are vocabulary flashcards for all of the academic vocabulary words that appear at the end of every chapter.

Aplia for *Reading Keys* offers students a seamless, interactive learning experience, ensuring that students stay on top of their coursework with regularly scheduled assignments and interactive learning tools. Aplia also features **Diagnostic Testing** and **Individualized Study Plans** that tailor instruction to the specific needs of students and provide instructors with powerful analytic tools that demonstrate real learning progress. For a demo of Aplia, visit www.aplia.com/developmentalenglish.

Acknowledgments

Once again, I have been lucky to have a wonderful group of reviewers, whose comments and suggestions gave me a blueprint for this revision. My thanks go to Elaine Bush, Darton College; Debbie Felton, Cleveland State Community College; Doug Holland, Pima Community College; Kelly Humphries, Snead State Community College; Robbi Muckenfuss,

Durham Technical Community College; Dee (Diana) Robbins, Black Hawk College; Melanie Thornton, Darton College; and Jenni Wessel-Fields, Black Hawk College.

In addition to reviewers, I am indebted to my acquisitions editor Shani Fisher, who took a close look at *Reading Keys* and offered wise advice about how best to meet the needs of today's college students. My development editor Kathy Sands-Boehmer kept me on schedule during the writing of this edition, and for that I am deeply grateful. As she has for years now, Nancy Benjamin of Books By Design gave meticulous attention to every aspect of the book, while Mary Schnabel, thankfully, caught every typo and spelling error I missed. And last, but certainly not least, I need to thank Ulrich Flemming, whose gorgeous photos are a hugely important new feature of this, the fourth edition of *Reading Keys*.

Getting into a Textbook State of Mind

1

IN THIS CHAPTER, YOU WILL LEARN

- how to develop and maintain concentration.
- how to read textbook assignments using *SQ3R*.
- how to take marginal notes.
- how to remember what you read by paraphrasing, or exchanging your words for the author's.
- how using the Web for background knowledge can improve reading comprehension.

"Students learn and remember more when they can connect information in meaningful ways...."
—Susan Ambrose et al., *How Learning Works,* p. 57

By some mystery that can't really be explained, some stories just capture our imagination. Without conscious effort, we get absorbed in them and stay focused on how the story unfolds. Textbook reading, however, is altogether different.

With textbooks, the subject matter and the vocabulary are often unfamiliar. The writing style is also usually more complicated or involved than we are used to from, say, novels or magazines and newspapers. No wonder, then, that textbook reading requires a state of mind quite different from the one that spontaneously emerges when we read novels, short stories, or articles that we ourselves have selected.

Because there are differences between how one reads a narrative, or story, and how one reads a textbook, the goal of this chapter is to show you how to concentrate and stay focused when reading textbooks, even if you're feeling something other than spontaneous enjoyment.

Learn How to Develop and Maintain Concentration

With textbooks, focused concentration won't just come naturally, without effort. For precisely that reason, you need to plan and organize your study sessions very carefully. Here are some general tips to help you maintain concentration while reading.

Pointers for Developing and Maintaining Concentration
◆

1. **Set aside specific times to study.** Your goal here is to use repetition to create a habit that's hard to break. What you need to do, then, for several weeks running is to start studying at the same time every day, say six o'clock. You also need to set yourself up in the same place, for instance, the first workstation on the first floor of the library, or, if you hate the library, your kitchen table.

   Odd as it sounds, your goal is to make yourself feel guilty if you are not sitting at your work table or desk, at home or in school, at six o'clock on the days you have set aside for studying. However, don't think you have to stay in the same place while you study. On the contrary, take regular breaks and feel free to change your location when you do.

2. **Take frequent walk-around breaks.** One of the hardest things about studying is sitting still for long periods of time. Well, there's some good news on that front. The latest research done by cognitive psychologists, the people who spend their lives figuring out how we think and learn most effectively, says that moving from place to place is useful for storing new information in long-term memory.[1]

---

[1]Benedict Carey, "Forget What You Know About Good Study Habits," *New York Times*, September 6, 2010, p. D-1.

That truly amazing organ, your brain, re-processes new information every time the background changes. While it's processing the change in background—Hmm, the walls are green in this room—it also re-processes whatever it is you are thinking about as you change locations. So let's say you are studying American history and you are trying to remember the Bill of Rights, both its meaning and content. Start by **paraphrasing**, or putting into your own words, what it was and how it came about while you are still at your desk, for example: "The Bill of Rights," written by James Madison and strongly supported by Thomas Jefferson, comprised the first ten amendments to the Constitution. The Bill of Rights guaranteed things like freedom of speech. It also guaranteed the right to bear arms and be judged by independent courts.

Once you finish your first paraphrase, take a break and stroll into the kitchen to get a drink of water. On your way, recite as many of the amendments as you can. Preferably, recite them out loud. Listening to yourself think aloud will increase your chances of long-term remembering.[2]

On your way back to your desk, try to remember why Madison and Jefferson thought the Bill of Rights was necessary. In each location, your brain is going to review the Bill of Rights from a slightly different perspective.

Think you are still shaky on this subject? Make it the topic of your next walking break. Throughout the course of your study session, make a list of things you need to review when you are *not* sitting at your desk.

3. **Be sure to have everything you need *before* you start to study.** Learning to stay focused is not easy in the beginning. Initially, we all try to distract ourselves so that we can avoid settling down to work. Don't let that happen. Have your book, laptop, passwords, pens, pencils, paper, etc., all set up and ready so that you can get right to work.

4. **Eliminate distractions.** Turn off your cell phone and anything else that might distract you, like television or radio. Tell yourself (and mean it) that checking e-mail, text messaging, and tweeting are not allowed during the times you've allotted to study.

5. **Forget multitasking.** Do you think you are one of those gifted multitaskers who can text a few friends, reorganize your notebook, make a couple of phone calls, *and* read your sociology

---

[2]See the blog *Workplace Psychology*, for just one example, http://workplacepsychology .net/2011/04/04/multitasking-doesnt-work.

chapter all at the same time? Well, you might be. But then you are as rare as a unicorn because the research says multitaskers who perform at a high level don't exist. Several studies, some of them a good ten years old, show that multitaskers only think they are getting the job done.[3] In fact, they repeatedly underperform compared to people who are doing one thing at a time.

6. **Have a plan in mind for what you expect to accomplish.** In a two-hour study session, you might, for instance, plan to read ten pages from the assignment in your criminal justice textbook, use the Web to get background knowledge about your reading assignment in sociology, and review four or five terms from your introduction to a programming course.

7. **Be prepared for days when your motivation wavers.** No matter how motivated you are, there will be days when you just don't feel like getting to work. Be prepared for those days with success statements. **Success statements** identify your future goals and relate them to current assignments—for example, "Someday I'll have a great job as an x-ray technician and this assignment is a step on the way to achieving my goal"; "In ten years, I'm going to own my own landscaping business, but I need to understand the ins and outs of botany and accounting to get to that point, so I don't care if I don't like this assignment, I'm doing it."

Useful too are motivational mottos like the ones listed below. You'd be surprised at how effective they can be when you are ready to give up because you are tired or the reading is hard to finish.

Motivational Mottos
◆

1. The biggest risk is a missed opportunity.
2. Your reach should exceed your grasp.
3. Champions keep playing until they get it right (tennis player Billie Jean King).
4. You are the handicap you must face. You are the one who must choose your place (novelist James Lane Allen).
5. Most people never run far enough on their first wind to find out if they've got a second. Don't be one of them.

---

[3]See, for example, Richard Evans, "Information Overload and Why Multitasking Doesn't Work." *Los Angeles Times*, April 11, 2010, http://articles.latimes.com/2010/apr/11/business/la-fi-books11-2010apr11.

◆ **EXERCISE 1**   **Keeping Yourself Motivated**

DIRECTIONS   Read the following quotes. Then explain what you think
each one means. Pick one you think would work for you. Explain why
you picked it.

1. *Luke Skywalker*: I don't believe it. *Yoda*: That is why you fail.

   <u>Believe in yourself.</u>

   _____

2. Confidence is rooted in challenges met.

   <u>have confidence to meet</u>
   <u>chalenges.</u>

3. Don't let the perfect become the enemy of the good.

   <u>Nothing has to be Perfect</u>

   _____

4. If failure were fatal, we'd all be dead.

   <u>everybodyfails</u>

   _____

5. Success seems to be largely a matter of hanging on after others have
   let go (William Feather).

   <u>Never give up Never</u>
   <u>give in.</u>

Can you create some motivational quotes of your own?

having confidence,

Study Skills Checklist

DIRECTIONS   Here's a checklist of good study habits. Your answer for
each one should be *yes*. Circle the ones that got a *no* answer and ask
yourself why you don't have these particular habits. Think about what
you can do to acquire them.

	No	Yes
1. Do you have a clear sense of your long-term personal and professional goals?	☐	☑
2. Do you have a particular time set aside for studying?	☒	☐
3. Do you eliminate possible distractions beforehand and make sure you have everything you need before you sit down?	☐	☒
4. When you sit down to study, do you know what assignments you intend to complete and approximately how much you want to get done for each one?	☐	☒
5. If you don't own a laptop or tablet, do you work in a place that gives you easy access to a computer?	☐	☑
6. Do you go online to get information about unfamiliar topics *before* you begin your assignments?	☐	☒
7. Do you preview assignments to get a sense of the content and the author's writing style?	☒	☐
8. Do you vary the number of pages you plan to study based on the difficulty of the text, allotting fewer pages for complex material and more for easier assignments?	☐	☒
9. Do you take regular walk-around breaks while you study and during that time do you go over in your mind the material you have just studied?	☐	☒
10. Do you use chapter headings to formulate questions about each chapter section?	☐	☒
11. Do you monitor, or check, your comprehension by seeing how much you can remember after completing a chapter section?	☐	☒
12. Do you mark and re-read passages that give you trouble?	☐	☒
13. Do you highlight, underline, and write in the text you are studying?	☐	☒
14. Do you make personal connections between what you read and what you already know?	☐	☒
15. When you finish an assignment, do you leaf through the pages to see if you have a grasp of both the content covered and the author's approach to that content?[4]	☐	☒

[4]Many of the pointers on this checklist were inspired by Sharon Benge Kletzien, "Strategy Use by Good and Poor Comprehenders Reading Expository Text of Differing Levels," *Reading Research Quarterly*, 25(1), 67–85.

🔑 READING KEYS

- ◆ Getting yourself concentrated or focused to study doesn't just happen; it's something you have to actively prepare for.
- ◆ Form a habit of studying in a particular place and at a particular time. Just remember you don't have to stay in one place to do the work. Take walking breaks and review while you move from place to place. Go back to the original spot you started in, but you don't have to. You can also continue working on the assignment in another room.
- ◆ Moving around while studying, as long as you review while you are on the move, is probably a better way to remember new information long term than sitting still in the same spot for two hours.
- ◆ Use success statements and motivational mottos to keep you going when you want to quit.

"Your brain is like a sponge that absorbs knowledge, but that's not exactly how it's done."

◇ Use or Develop a System for Study Reading

This next section describes a study system called *SQ3R*. Developed by an educational psychologist named Francis Robinson, the system has been in use for decades. Over the years, numerous studies have provided support for its effectiveness.[5] Studies show that, *when used consistently*, *SQ3R* does work. Students who use it regularly do remember more of what they read. The trick, though, is to be both consistent and flexible. Use it regularly, but modify it when you need to. Robinson never intended users of his system to follow it rigidly.

Here are the individual steps you can modify to suit your assignments. For instance, surveys of articles will undoubtedly be briefer than surveys of whole chapters.

S Is for Survey

Before you start reading, survey or preview the chapter you are about to read. Seeing the big picture *before* you begin reading will help you figure out how the specific parts of the chapter relate to and develop one another. A good chapter preview usually requires the following steps.

Steps in a Survey
◆

1. Read the title and all introductory material. In addition to the opening paragraphs, you should also read lists of objectives and questions.

2. Look at all the headings (1) to get a sense of how deeply the author goes into the topic addressed in the chapter and (2) to better understand the relationship among the chapter topics.

3. If the headings don't clarify the relationship of topics in the chapter, read the first sentence of every paragraph.

4. Read concluding sections with titles such as "Summary," "Review," or "Summing Up." Here's where you will find the meat of the chapter. In fact, these concluding sections are where the author (or authors) tell you: "This is what you need to know as a result of reading what I wrote."

---

[5]For one good example, see Dolores Fadness Tadlock, "SQ3R: Why It Works Based on an Information Processing Theory of Learning," *Journal of Reading*, 22(2), 110–12.

RE...

...r *before* you begin
...pter together *while*

...for instance, there
...aph.

◆ **EXERCISE 2**   **Su...**

D... sentence of every
pa... ...rmation of Native
Cu... you finish, answer
the... or the letter of the
co...

[Handwritten note:]
Page 9
1. B   done
2. False
3 True
4. True   review pg 40 text
5. True

1. Based on the title, headings, and opening sentences, which one
   of these statements would you say accurately sums up the chapter
   section?
   a. Native American culture was forever altered due to the over-
      hunting and the resulting extinction of buffalo herds.
   b. Native American culture was largely destroyed by the invasion
      of white settlers.
   c. Native American culture was destroyed because Indians were
      not united by a tribal identity.

2. *True* or *False*. In the authors' description of frontier culture, white
   men are the only ones who resort to violence.

3. *True* or *False*. The authors seem surprised that Native Americans
   did not fight back when they were forced onto reservations.

4. *True* or *False*. In the nineteenth century, reformers were convinced
   that they needed to civilize Native Americans.

5. *True* or *False*. The U.S. government didn't like the idea that Native
   American women were, in certain ways, the equal of men.

Q Is for Question

Prior to reading, try to come up with several questions about the chapter. Then read to find answers. Having questions in mind while you read will help you maintain concentration. Questions based on the headings will also guide your attention so that you know which passages in the chapter are the most significant.

The questions can be from your own personal experience, for example, "How accurate are movie versions of Native American life?" They can also be based on the headings. Headings can be turned into questions using words and phrases like *why*, *how*, and *in what way*, such as "How did Native Americans react to attempts to confine them to reservations?" You can also use the questions that appear in the summary sections of chapters.

O━ READING KEY

◆ Before you start reading, develop some questions that you want to answer about the chapter. The questions will help keep you focused. Questions based on the headings will also direct your attention to key points in the chapter.

R-1 Is for Read Strategically

As the name implies, **reading strategically** is reading with a strategy, or plan. It's using advance, or prior, knowledge to generally predict what the author will say and then reading to confirm or revise that prediction. (Learn how to get advance knowledge from the Web on pages 22–30.)

Reading strategically also means that you don't give every single detail the same amount of attention. Instead you evaluate the material as you read, speeding up or slowing down as soon as you recognize the significance of the words. If the text seems familiar, maybe even offers little more than common sense, feel free to whiz through it. But if you find a passage confusing, or it has several marginal annotations signaling that the author thinks the material is important, slow down. Read it twice. Read it aloud even.

Strategic readers also read chapter sections with a specific question (What does habeas corpus[†] mean?) or prediction (The author is going to describe how the Texas "two-step" primary works.) in mind.

[†]habeas corpus: a petition whereby a person who has been imprisoned can request a court hearing to determine if the imprisonment was illegal.

Strategic readers base their questions and predictions on the textual clues provided by the author. Headings, for instance, provide clues to both importance and meaning, but so, too, do pictures, visual aids, marginal notes, boldface type, and highlighting devices, such as color ink and icons (the keys in this text are examples of icons).

READING KEY

◆ To read strategically is to read with a plan. It's reading with questions and predictions in mind that are then answered, confirmed, or revised.

R-2 Is for Recall

"One of the best ways to learn anything is to teach it to someone else."

—Dave Ellis, *Becoming a Master Student*

When the author's words are in front of you, you are likely to think you understand everything you just read. But often if you look away from the page and try to recall, in your own words, the passage you just finished reading, you will be in for a surprise. You'll discover that your understanding is a little foggier than you supposed. That's why recalling what you've read right after completing a difficult paragraph or chapter section is so important. The recall step of *SQ3R* will tell you what parts of the reading are still a little fuzzy.

Here's a list of different ways you can complete this critical step:

1. **Mentally recite the key elements of any paragraph or passage.** Most textbook paragraphs consist of a general main idea or point and several specific supporting details. (Read more on this subject in Chapters 4–8.) When you finish a chapter section, ask yourself, "What was the point of this reading?" How did the author make that point convincing?" If you come up blank in response to both questions, mark the passage for a second reading, e.g., write "RR" or "x2" in the margin.

2. **Write out answers to questions about headings.** If you posed a question based on the heading, see if you can write out an answer once you finish the chapter section.

3. **Make a diagram or draw a picture.** If what you are reading about is a concrete process or series of events, i.e., something that can be physically seen, try making a picture or diagram. Draw the part of the eye or a flower. Make a diagram of what happens as some proposed piece of legislation becomes a law. Here, for

example, is the kind of *very rough* drawing you might make if you were reading about the two kinds of lenses that are in your eyes, eyeglasses, contacts, microscopes, or cameras:

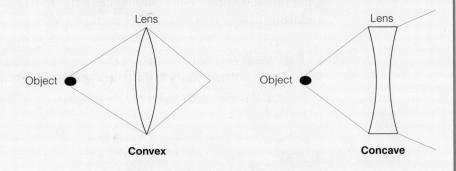

4. **Work with a study companion.** Work with someone else in the class. Take turns reading sentences aloud and answering questions like, What did the author mean with this sentence? Why does the author mention this? What does it have to do with the overall point of the chapter section? Is it important or not?

"By God, for a minute there it suddenly all made sense!"

R-3 Is for Review Globally

Once you have finished a chapter in its entirety, make a list of all the major headings that introduce new topics or issues. Underneath each one, write down whatever you can remember about each chapter section. Put a check mark or an "x" next to those headings that call up the least amount of information. These are the chapter sections that will need more reviews. What you want to know at this point is where the weak spots are in your understanding of the chapter.

Try as well to get a sense of how the individual chapter sections fit together. Do they each cover a series of individual events that led up to one major event like the Civil War? Or does the author focus on individual events that occurred over the course of a decade?

Consider, too, if you see any evidence of **bias**, or favoritism, for or against a particular point of view. Do the headings, for instance, suggest the author's personal judgment? There is big difference, after all, in headings that simply introduce the subject matter, e.g., "The Warren Court Decisions," versus headings that already evaluate the material, "The Great Society: A Failed Dream."

A Word About Spacing Your Reviews

"Larger gaps between study sessions result in better recall of facts."
—Nicholas Cepeda and Doug Rohrer, learning researchers from the University of California

Reviewing right after completing a chapter will help you understand how the chapter sections fit together. It will also help you remember more of what you've read. *But don't think that one review will prepare you for exams.* Just about every piece of research on test taking confirms what Hermann Ebbinghaus, the first person to study human memory, discovered in the late nineteenth century: **Reviews spaced out over an extended period of time are the key to long-term remembering.**

Timing Really Is Everything

If you want to excel academically, you need to get started on midterms and finals early on in the semester. You need, that is, to set aside time for spaced reviews that force you to re-process the same material several different ways.

Initially, review just to make sure you understood everything covered by your assignments. However, by the time exams arrive, be ready to recall big chunks of information from just a few stimulus, or trigger, words. For instance, start by reviewing a paragraph that's been underlined and marked like this. Focus mainly on what's been noted or underlined.

> In the (1870s) and (1880s) <u>reformers</u> and <u>government officials</u> sought to ("civilize") Native Americans <u>through landholding and education</u>. For some, this meant <u>outlawing customs deemed savage</u> and pressuring Indians <u>to adopt American values</u> of ambition, thrift, and materialism."* In doing so, the United States copied other nations' imperialistic* policies, such as France, which banned native religious ceremonies in its Pacific island colonies. Others argued for <u>sympathetic…treatment</u>. Writers George Manypenny (*Our Indian Wards*, 1880) and Helen Hunt Jackson (*A Century of Dishonor*, 1882) aroused the American conscience.
> (Adapted from Mary Beth Norton et al., *A People and a Nation*, 9th ed., p. 438. © Cengage Learning.)

Example of opposing viewpoint on treatment of Indians.

But the closer you get to exams, the more your review notes should be nothing more than **recall clues**. These are words and phrases that have a cluster of meanings attached to them. Notes based on recall clues should separate the recall clue from the meanings they represent. That way you can look at the clue and see if you call up the right associations. Here, for example, is a note card about nineteenth-century Indian reform that you could create with actual index cards or online flash cards.

2 sides of 19th century Indian reform

---

*materialism: placing value on money and products over inner well-being.
*imperialistic: assuming control of other countries.

On the back of your index card or on the next screen, if you are using online flash cards, there should be a list of the key details related to Indian reform.

---

1. Some reformers insisted on civilizing Native Americans.
   a. make them value what white people valued
   b. make them materialistic
2. Others like Helen Hunt Jackson and George Manypenny tried to waken the American conscience to the need for respect and better treatment.

Your goal is to get to the point where looking at the recall clue calls up in your mind all of the related information on the back of the card.

◆ Making Marginal Notes

"Reading involves a fair measure of push and shove. You make your mark on a book and it makes its mark on you."

—David Bartholomae and Anthony Petrosky, *Ways of Reading*

Marginal annotations, or notes written into the margins—if you are working with an e-book, make use of pop-up note-taking boxes—are probably the best way to understand and remember what you read. That's because your notes require you to abbreviate and paraphrase the author's original language. Both activities—abbreviating and paraphrasing—ensure that your mind is actively working on the material. This is the kind of active processing of information you need to do in order to avoid a common mistake: assuming that just looking at the words means you have understood them.

Being Selective

When you abbreviate information, be **selective**. First figure out what sentences are central to the author's point. Then determine what parts of those sentences can help you convey the writer's overall meaning. In other words, you have to really think about the material to decide what you absolutely need for your notes and what can be left out. It's this kind of **analysis**, or breaking into parts, that makes the author's words mean something to you and stay in your memory over time.

For subjects you find not too difficult, you can probably get away with just taking marginal notes while underlining and highlighting other portions of the text. But for key subjects, the ones your future depends on, you would be better off turning textbook paragraphs into more detailed notes. Here's an illustration, starting with the original text and then the notes:

> President Theodore Roosevelt's love for the outdoors inspired lasting contributions to resource conservation.* Government establishment of national parks began in the late nineteenth century. Roosevelt advanced the movement by favoring *conservation* over *preservation*. He exercised presidential power to protect such natural wonders as the Grand Canyon in Arizona by declaring them national monuments. He also backed a policy of "wise use" of forests, waterways, and other resources. Previously, the government had transferred ownership of natural resources on federal land to the states and private interests. Roosevelt, however, believed efficient resource conservation demanded federal management over lands in the public domain. (Mary Beth Norton et al., *A People and a Nation*, 9th ed., p. 558. © Cengage Learning.)

Outdoors-lover Roosevelt advanced the conservation movement's goals.

1. protected natural resources like the Grand Canyon by categorizing them as national monuments.
2. favored conservation over preservation, emphasizing "wise use."
   —Wise use relied on federal management over lands put into the public domain.
   —R. wasn't willing to turn over natural resources to states or private interests.

---

*conservation: protection and restoration of the environment.

Paraphrasing and Memory

Paraphrasing, or exchanging the author's words for your own without altering the original meaning, is one of the best things you can do to aid memory and comprehension. As you look for words you can use to replace the author's, you are forced to process the meaning of each word in the original text.

The Reading Paraphrase versus the Writing Paraphrase

Keep in mind that paraphrasing key points in the margins of your texts is not the same as paraphrasing for a term paper. When you paraphrase for a paper, you have to make sure you retain *all of* the original meaning. Here, for instance, is an original piece of text followed by a paraphrase that would be appropriate for a term paper.

Original   The extent of religious intermarriage in the United States depends in good part on the particular religion being considered. Among the Old Order Amish, mate selection outside the group is practically nonexistent. However, intermarriage among the various Protestant denominations—Episcopalians, Baptists, Lutherans, Presbyterians, Methodists, and others—seems to be quite common.

Paraphrase
for a Paper   In the United States, the degree of intermarriage allowed among members of a religious group varies according to the religion. Marrying outside the group is all but unheard of among the Amish. However, among the Protestant denominations, it's quite common.

Now here's a paraphrase that would be appropriate for marginal notes:

Paraphrase
for Reading Notes   Acceptance of intermarriage varies with religion.—Amish don't; Protestants do.

See the difference?

The Purpose of Paraphrasing

Paraphrasing while reading is a crucial part of learning from textbooks. It helps you remember what you read and identifies those portions of text you haven't completely understood. Any time you can't paraphrase, the chances are good that you haven't truly understood the material. If you want to ensure your success as a student, make paraphrasing while reading a regular practice.

Later chapters will go into more detail about how to paraphrase both formally for papers and informally for reading notes. But you can get started on paraphrasing immediately. You'll only get better at paraphrasing if you practice it yourself in an informal fashion and then learn more about how readers and writers create more formal paraphrases when they need to.

How to Paraphrase for Reading Notes
◆

1. When you finish reading the paragraph or passage, ask yourself, without looking back at the page, what general point the author wants to get across. If you don't have an answer, re-read the passage.

2. If the point is still not completely clear, ask yourself what people, places, events, or ideas come up repeatedly in the selection.

3. Look for a sentence that seems to get more attention than other sentences in the paragraph. See if it sums up the relationship among the people, places, events, or ideas repeatedly referred to in the paragraph. If it does, that sentence is the main point of the paragraph or passage.

4. Using as many of your own words as possible, paraphrase that general summary sentence. If no sentence like that appears, make up your own sentence to sum up the paragraph.

5. Make your paraphrase as brief as possible, even if the result is not a grammatical sentence. Think of your paraphrase as a headline for the passage, e.g., "Even extinct volcanoes erupt"; "Alfred Wegener, father of continental drift"; "Ideas about being right-brained or left-brained not scientific." When it comes to reading notes, your paraphrase, as you can see from the examples, need not be a complete sentence.

6. Decide if you should also abbreviate and paraphrase one or two specific sentences used to explain the general one. If the specific details are not too complex in themselves, you can also just number them or give them labels such as *Ex* (for *example*) or *R1, R2, R3* (for *reasons*).

Marking Up the Text

In addition to paraphrasing, get into the habit of marking your text by underlining, highlighting, starring, and bracketing important material. Like paraphrasing, marking pages forces you to think about the author's words. In the process of figuring out what to mark and what not to mark, you are actually re-processing what you've read, and that leads to improved comprehension and remembering.

Some Symbols for Marking Pages in Your Textbook ♦		
	Brackets or vertical lines for key passages	[ ] | |
	Underlining for important points	___ ___ ___
	Abbreviations to show the type of support: examples, studies, reasons, exceptions, statistics	Ex, Stu, R, Exc, Stat
	Numbers to itemize examples, reasons, steps, or studies	1, 2, 3
	Stars for particularly important statements or quotations	★ ★
	Boxes for key terms	☐
	Circles for important names, dates, or terms	◯
	Exclamation points to show surprise	!!
	Question marks to indicate an unclear sentence or passage	??
	Connected arrows to highlight related statements	✐
	Marginal notes to record personal comments and questions	I don't believe this.

◆ EXERCISE 3   Taking Marginal Notes

DIRECTIONS   Read each passage. Then select the appropriate letter to identify which set of marginal notes on the paragraph better sums up the key points.

EXAMPLE   Ever since 1989, the first year in which DNA testing resulted in the release of an innocent prisoner, the public has been repeatedly confronted with evidence that far from being an impossibility, convicting the innocent is much more common than we feared. The Innocence Project, founded by Barry Scheck and Peter J. Neufeld, keeps a running record on its website of the hundreds of men and women imprisoned for murder or rape who have been cleared. They have been cleared most often by DNA testing but also by other kinds of evidence, such as mistaken eyewitness identifications. Death-row exonerations, of course, get the greatest public attention, but the number of wrongful convictions for lesser crimes is also alarming. (Carol Tavris and Eliot Aronson, *Mistakes Were Made*, Mariner Books, 2008, p. 130.)

Marginal Notes   a. DNA has proven that half the people on death row shouldn't be.
   1. Barry Scheck and Peter J. Neufeld
   2. Cleared by DNA testing

b. Since 1989, DNA evidence has exonerated hundreds of men and women.
   1. Innocence Project keeps track of people cleared
   2. Mistaken eyewitnesses also wrongfully convict

EXPLANATION   Answer *a* won't work because the passage as a whole doesn't talk just about people on death row. The authors make a point of mentioning people convicted of other kinds of crimes. Answer *b* is correct because the opening sentence comes closer to summing up the main idea or point of the paragraph. It takes into account people on death row and other people in prison. It also makes clear the role of the Innocence Project.

1. In 1978, when a Boeing 747 with 213 people aboard plunged into the Arabian Sea, people speculated about political terrorism. But as the Indian navy began to salvage pieces of the airplane, the investigators found no signs of fire, heat, or in-flight breakup. The airplane's crash-proof black boxes and cockpit voice recorders were

intact. They indicated that the airplane's engines and controls had functioned normally, but that something in the cockpit had gone terribly wrong. The fault appeared to be the pilot's. On a quiet night, after twenty-two years of steady service, he had flown a perfectly sound airplane into the water.

Marginal Notes

a. Even in 1978, if a plane crashed, there was speculation about political terrorism.
   1. Plane crashed into Arabian Sea
   2. Evidence showed plane functioning fine

b. On a quiet night, no one expected plane to crash into the sea.
   1. It was the Arabian Sea
   2. Indian navy salvaged wreckage

2. In 1954, twenty-two well-adjusted, eleven-year-old boys participated in a three-week study conducted by social psychologist Muzafer Sherif and his colleagues at a campsite in Robbers Cave State Park in Oklahoma. On arrival, the boys were immediately assigned to one of two groups. Each group stayed in its own cabin. The cabins were located quite a distance apart in order to reduce contact between the two groups. The distance was also meant to encourage bonding within each group. After about a week, the researchers set up a series of competitive activities in which the two groups were pitted against each other so that either group lost or won. It didn't take long before group members were hostile toward those outside their own group, suggesting that group membership, for all its benefits, can create conflict. (Adapted from James Waller, *Becoming Evil.* Oxford University Press, 2005, p. 238.)

Marginal Notes

a. Muzafer Sherif's research suggests that among preteen boys there's bound to be aggression and hostility.
   1. Two groups of eleven-year-olds
   2. Kids couldn't stand one another

b. Muzafer Sherif's research highlights conflicts stemming from group bonding.
   1. Eleven-year-old boys kept in two groups that engage in competitive games
   2. Each group starts disliking other

⊙━ᴍ READING KEYS

♦ Whenever you spend time thinking about the author's words in order to abbreviate or paraphrase them, you are giving your brain the time it needs to understand what those words mean.

♦ Paraphrasing for reading notes and paraphrasing for term papers are two different things. Reading notes don't require the same level of formality, completeness, or grammatical correctness.

Turning to the Web for Background Knowledge

Reading research has repeatedly shown that background knowledge aids comprehension.[6] Fortunately, thanks to the Web, everyone can put that insight to use.

For instance, imagine that you're surveying a history chapter assignment and see the heading "Iranian Hostage Crisis." If that heading doesn't call up anything in your mind when you see it, then use the Web to look up the topic it mentions *before* reading the chapter section.

Use a Precise Search Term

Search terms need to be precise. They need to exclude, as much as possible, the events and ideas you don't want to learn about. In other words, if you want to know more about how the Taliban is faring in Afghanistan currently, you need to type "Taliban Afghanistan 2012" into the search box, rather than just "Taliban."

Fortunately, headings of chapter sections are supposed to tell readers what each chapter section is about. Thus they tend to be precise and don't usually need much modification, or refining. Look up "Iranian Hostage Crisis," and a list like this one will come up if you are using Google.

---

[6]Peter P. Afflerbach, "The Influence of Prior Knowledge on Expert Readers' Main Idea Construction Strategies," *Reading Research Quarterly, 25*(1), 31–45.

| Search | Images | Maps | Play | YouTube | News | Gmail | Documents | Calendar | More ▼ |

Google   Iranian Hostage Crisis   🔍   Sign in

Advanced search

Web   About 1,350,000 results (0.28 seconds)

[1] **Iran hostage crisis** - Wikipedia, the free encyclopedia
en.wikipedia.org/wiki/**Iran_hostage_crisis**
The **Iran hostage crisis** was a diplomatic crisis between Iran and the United
States where 66 Americans were held hostage for 444 days from November 4,
1979 ...
↳ Start - Planning - 444 days hostage - Aftermath

[2] The **Iranian Hostage Crisis** . Jimmy Carter . WGBH American ...
www.pbs.org/wgbh/americanexperience/.../carter-**hostage**-**crisis**/
An article on the **Iranian Hostage Crisis**, from the Jimmy Carter documentary
from AMERICAN EXPERIENCE. November 1979 - January 1981. On
November 4 ...

[3] **Iran Hostage Crisis**
www.u-s-history.com/pages/h2021.html
Foreign Affairs, November 4, 1979 to January 20, 1981. Two American
hostages. On November 4, 1979, an angry mob of some 300 to 500 "students"
who called ...

[4] **Iran hostage crisis** — Infoplease.com
www.infoplease.com/ce6/history/A0825448.html
Iran hostage crisis. **Iran hostage crisis**, in U.S. history, events following the
seizure of the American embassy in Tehran by Iranian students on Nov. 4, 1979.

[5] The **Hostage Crisis** in **Iran**
www.jimmycarterlibrary.gov/documents/**hostages**.phtml
The **Hostage Crisis** in **Iran**. On November 4, 1979, **Iranian** militants stormed
the United States Embassy in Tehran and took approximately seventy
Americans ...

[6] BBC NEWS | In pictures: **Iran hostage crisis**
news.bbc.co.uk/2/shared/spl/hi/.../04/...**Iran_hostage_crisis**/.../1.stm
On 4 November 1979, revolutionary students stormed the United States
embassy in Tehran taking dozens of US staff **hostage**. Thousands of other
protesters ...

[7] The History Guy: **Iran**-U.S. **Hostage Crisis** (1979-1981)
www.historyguy.com/**Iran**-us_**hostage_crisis**.html
Dec. 3, 2011 – Description of the **hostage crisis** between the United States
and **Iran**.

[8] **Iran hostage crisis** (United States history) – Britannica Online ...
www.britannica.com/EBchecked/topic/272687/**Iran**-**hostage**-**crisis**
Iran hostage crisis (United States history), international crisis (1979–81) in
which militants in Iran seized 66 American citizens at the U.S. embassy in
Tehran, ...

Comparing Search Engines

"Perhaps the greatest of all pedagogical fallacies[†] is the notion that a person learns only what he is studying at the time."

—John Dewey

When you are searching for background knowledge, it's a good idea to compare the results from two different search engines. Different search engines do sometimes bring up different results. Thus it pays to do two different searches with, for instance, Google and Bing.

Comparing search engine results while you are looking for background knowledge is useful even if two different search engines turn up almost exactly the same list of sites. Without realizing it, you will be engaging in incidental learning while you browse the sites, deciding which one to choose. **Incidental learning** occurs without any conscious effort while you are doing something else. In this case, just from looking over the lists of websites, you are bound to pick up some information about a crisis that drove then President Jimmy Carter from office.

Selecting the Right Site

When your search engine brings up a list of websites, whatever you do, *don't click on the first website assuming that it's the best site because it's the first.* Exactly how search engines pick the sites they list is somewhat mysterious because the algorithm, or formula for decision making, is top secret. Much of the time, the first site is the most popular. But it's probably the most popular *because* it's the first site. It's the one people turn to first *because they mistakenly trust in their search engine to order the sites selected according to quality.*[7] But nothing could be further from the truth. Search engines do not evaluate the websites for quality. That's your job.

Don't Automatically Turn to Wikipedia

Precisely because of its popularity, Wikipedia is often the first site to come up when you use a search engine. But using Wikipedia for background knowledge is not necessarily the right choice. And that's not because it's had some problems with posting inaccurate information in the past. When it comes to getting the facts right, Wikipedia has taken

---

[†]pedagogical fallacies: errors in logic related to teaching. John Dewey was an extremely influential psychologist and philosopher, who wanted to change the American educational system.

[7]Exzter Hargittai et al., "Trust Online: Young Adults' Evaluation of Web Content," *International Journal of Communication*, 4, 468–94.

measures to be more reliable than it once was. However, it's an open source site, meaning that those who wish to can keep adding information to an entry. This adds to entry length. Thus, when it comes to getting background knowledge for your reading, using this site is like lighting up a stick of dynamite to get rid of a fly in the room. There's too much information to wade through.

Above all, there are too many links to other sources that are not particularly **relevant**, or related, to your search. But relevant or not, they can distract you from your goal: to get a quick overview of the issue addressed in your text.

What you are looking for at this point in your reading is a short, readable explanation of the topic or issue you are about to study. Preferably you want one with several pictures so that your brain can process the information both verbally and visually.

Captions Reveal a Lot

Read the caption for each website carefully before you hit the link. Are the exact words from the heading used in the website's caption? That's a good sign. It strongly suggests that the site will give you the information you are looking for.

Commercial News Sites Can Prove Rewarding

When you are looking for basic background knowledge, websites linked to commercial news publishers or broadcasters, such as the *New York Times*, *Time Magazine*, and the Public Broadcasting Company (PBS), are usually a good choice. Managers of news sites generally recognize that their readers don't want to scroll a lot. For that reason, they keep their online articles fairly short.

They also know they have to keep their readers interested or they will go someplace else. Thus writers for news sites try to inject as much color and energy into their writing as possible. However, they also try to remain fairly **objective**, or personally neutral, toward the ideas under discussion. Based on these criteria, or standards, the Public Broadcasting System (PBS) website that turned up in the Google search (p. 23) would be a good choice for background knowledge about the Iranian hostage crisis.

Educational and Government Sites Can Also Provide Background Knowledge

If no news sites come up on your list, try a website associated with a school. The URL[†] for these sites usually ends in *edu*. If there's a choice between high school and university sites, go with the high school site, which is likely to have shorter entries. It's also unlikely that the person in charge of the site would post information that has not been checked for accuracy.

Government sites end in *gov*. They, too, can prove useful. Just check the caption carefully and avoid any that emphasize official documents. Government documents can be lengthy and difficult to read.

Consider the Internet Archive

The Internet Archive is a digital library funded by several different institutions, among them the National Science Foundation and the Library of Congress. The site stores articles and video clips posted on the Web since 1996. It's a great place to get up-to-date on any number of topics.

A word of caution, though: If you use the Internet Archive, you are better off focusing on videos from news sites. You can find information on just about any topic, past or present, on the Internet Archive. But it can send you to sites like the Web-based Project Gutenberg, which gives you access to free books. However, whole books are not what you need when you are looking for background knowledge about a single chapter section.

Compare Sites

Even with sites that seem highly trustworthy, get into the habit of double-checking one site against another. Do the two sites mention similar dates and the same names? Do they use different photos? Are they similar in terms of how they report on the issue? Does one seem more biased than the other? Fact checking on the Web is not as consistent as it is in print.[8] Thus even highly reputable, or respected, sites don't always get high marks for fact checking. If two sites differ greatly in the

---

[†]URL: uniform resource locator; basically, a website's address.
[8]See the *Columbia Journalism Review* study conducted in 2009 by Victor Navasky and Evan Lerner titled "Magazines and Their Web Sites" available online. For a summary of the report, see Stephanie Clifford, "Survey Finds Slack Editing on Magazine Web Sites," *New York Times*, February 28, 2010, p. B-6.

information they provide, you need to check a third site to see which actually got it right.

Think Twice About Advocacy Sites

Advocacy sites usually end with *org*. As their name implies they advocate, or show support for, particular ideas or activities. Here are several examples:

- Amnesty International (www.amnesty.org)

- Greenpeace (www.greenpeace.org)

- Jane Goodall Institute (www.janegoodall.org)

- Natural Resources Defense Council (www.nrdcwildplaces.org)

- Sierra Club (www.sierraclub.org)

- People for the Ethical Treatment of Animals (www.peta.org)

When you are ready to do a term paper, advocacy sites can serve you well because they identify specific points of view. Thus, you can use them to develop a sense of how people differ in their attitude toward a topic. Advocacy groups on the same subject, like environmentalism, don't always hold the same point of view. Thus, reading different advocacy sites on the same issue can give you a sense of the various positions people take on the subject.

But when your objective is background knowledge, these sites might not serve you as well. They represent groups that have a bias, or inclination, in favor of a particular position, one that might not be generally shared. When you are looking for basic background knowledge, your goal is to get information that is as unbiased as possible.

Leave Blogs for Later

What you want at this point is a website that tells you what's commonly known and believed about the hostage crisis. You don't want a strongly personal interpretation. Blogs specialize in giving you one person or group's particular point of view. That's fine. In fact when you are looking for research topics, blogs can sometimes provide an original slant on the topic you want to write about. However, when you are just trying to get a general impression of the topic, you want a more mainstream, or generally held, point of view.

Pay Attention to Both Language and Images

When general background knowledge is your purpose, avoid sites that appear to have a personal or political agenda. If, for instance, you are looking for information on anorexia, you should avoid sites that are—and some are—promoting what is a serious, sometimes fatal medical condition. If the website does have a strong bias, you can usually tell from the language used. A website that describes the disease this way is what you are looking for:

Anorexia nervosa is characterized by:

- Extreme thinness (emaciation)
- A relentless pursuit of thinness and unwillingness to maintain a normal or healthy weight
- Intense fear of gaining weight
- Distorted body image, a self-esteem that is heavily influenced by perceptions of body weight and shape, or a denial of the seriousness of low body weight
- Lack of menstruation among girls and women
- Extremely restricted eating

Many people with anorexia nervosa see themselves as overweight, even when they are clearly underweight. Eating, food, and weight control become obsessions. People with anorexia nervosa typically weigh themselves repeatedly, portion food carefully, and eat very small quantities of only certain foods. Some people with anorexia nervosa may also engage in binge-eating followed by extreme dieting, excessive exercise, self-induced vomiting, and/or misuse of laxatives, diuretics, or enemas. (Source: www.nimh.nih.gov/health/publications/eating-disorders/complete-index.shtml.)

What you don't want is a website that describes the disease in **loaded language**. This is language that carries with it positive or negative **connotations**, or associations. It is meant to influence you by encouraging you to think positively or negatively about the person or issue discussed.

In the illustration below, the language makes anorexia sound not so bad. It's presented as a lifestyle choice, rather than a dangerous and sometimes deadly disease.

Looking for Thinspiration?
◆

Here are some tips and tricks for maintaining your ideal weight. And remember some people might consider your ideal weight to be excessive and might label you anorexic. But that's all the name is, just a label. We here on this site know that thin is beautiful, and we have nothing to be ashamed of. So next time you are thinking about packing on those pounds, try some of these tips:

1. Pick a food you can divide up, like an apple. Cut it into four quarters and munch on it for breakfast, lunch, and dinner, and finally for a bed time snack. If you feel like eating more, imagine how gorgeous you will be when you drop just a few more pounds.

2. Take a picture of yourself and print it out. Circle all the places on your body that are too fat. Look at that picture every time you want to eat something.

3. Put a rubber band around your wrist. Every time you want to get a snack, snap the band and remind yourself that your goal in life is to have pounds melt away, not pack on more fat.

© iStockphoto.com/PhotoGraphyKM

(The tips here are based on a real pro anorexia site.)

Probably few sites are completely unbiased. After all, even the *selection* of facts or figures can reflect a bias. But particularly for the purpose of gathering background knowledge before reading, avoid sites where the language and/or images make it clear that the person or group posting the information has an agenda.

And keep in mind that pictures can be as persuasive as language. If, for instance, you are doing a paper on the Rosenberg spy case of the 1950s and land on a site featuring pictures of Julius and Ethel Rosenberg at their wedding and surrounded by family and friends, you should look elsewhere for information. Those photos reflect a bias, i.e., the Rosenbergs were innocent victims. For basic background knowledge prior to reading, you need sites not inclined to focus on one train of thought and exclude all others.

READING KEYS

◆ The Web can usually give you the background knowledge you need to get the most out of your textbooks.

◆ To get your search term to come up with the information you need, make it as precise as possible, using phrases more often than single words.

◆ It's a good idea to use your search term with two different search engines because one might give you better results than another. And even if both search engines turn up the same results, you will still learn something about the topic you are researching via incidental learning.

◆ When a list of websites appears on your screen, don't assume that a site's position in the list is an indication of quality. The site at the top of the list is often popular but might not be that informative for your purposes.

◆ Commercial news sites might serve you better than Wikipedia, which has very long entries for most topics and issues covered. Websites linked to television or print news are less likely to overwhelm you with information, and the writing will be livelier.

◆ For purposes of background knowledge, stay away from websites with connotative, or emotionally loaded, language. Your goal is to get a sense of what is commonly believed or known about your topic.

◆ What you don't want at this stage is a personal opinion that deviates, or differs, wildly from traditional opinion. At this point, in fact, what you want is the traditional point of view, although you might well start to disagree with it once you know more.

◆ Keep in mind that photos can be as persuasive as words.

◆ **EXERCISE 4** **Creating Search Terms**

DIRECTIONS   For each search goal, come up with a search term that you think would get you the information in the shortest amount of time.

1. Sinkholes are yawning holes that develop in backyards, sometimes swallowing up entire houses.

    Search Goal: You want to discover if there are different kinds of sinkholes and what causes them. What search term will you use?

    What kind of Sinkholes are there?

2. Watergate was the name of a hotel where a historic break-in took place. The scandal that followed from that break-in became known as "Watergate" and had numerous and far-reaching effects on the country.

    Search Goal: You want to know how and why Watergate affected journalism. What search term will you use?

    How did watergate affect Journalism?

3. Hurricanes are all assigned, in alphabetical order, the names of people.

    Search Goal: You want to know when this tradition started and how the names are assigned. What search term will you use?

    how did hurricanes get their names?

◆ **EXERCISE 5** **Using the Web for Background Knowledge**

DIRECTIONS   Type each search term into a search engine box. Pick two sites to look at for each topic. See how quickly you can answer the questions about these important events in American history.

1. *Search Term*: **Woodrow Wilson League of Nations**

    Who was Woodrow Wilson, and what did he think about the League of Nations?

    president

    a good Idea

What senator opposed him and won?

Henry cabot lodge

2. *Search Term*: **Herbert Hoover Bonus Army**

What issue brought the Bonus Army into being?

to Help the Veterans

How did President Herbert Hoover respond to the Bonus Army?

He told his men to destroy the campsite

3. *Search Term*: **Harry Truman Versus Thomas Dewey 1948**

What surprised everyone in this election?

The newspaper got it wrong

4. *Search Term*: **Maslow's Hierarchy Diagram**

What shape does the diagram associated with Maslow's hierarchy, or ranking, of needs usually have?

Triangle

What kinds of needs are at the bottom?

Physiological and Safety

What kinds are at the top?

Self Actualization and

5. *Search Term*: **Rosie Ruiz Boston Marathon**

What did Rosie Ruiz achieve in the Boston Marathon?

it looked like She Won.

How did she accomplish that feat?

She Cheated.

Building a Textbook Vocabulary

The language of textbooks differs from the language we hear in casual conversation. Words that don't regularly turn up when we chat with family and friends appear all the time in textbook writing. How often, for instance, have you used the word *cognition*—the mental process of knowing something through reason, awareness, or judgment—in everyday conversation? You probably haven't used the word much. Yet if you read a psychology textbook, you'll see the word repeatedly.

Although it is partially true that the more-common-in-conversation word *thinking* could be used as a substitute for *cognition*, that word choice would oversimplify what *cognition* stands for in the **context**, or setting, of psychology. Psychology texts, like almost all textbooks, describe and discuss the world in deeper and more complicated terms than you and I do when chatting with our friends. Thus, textbooks require a **specialized vocabulary**, or a body of words appropriate to the subject matter. Health and psychology texts, for instance, don't study the aging of one person; they study the aging of entire populations. The word for this is *gerontology*—studying the psychological, social, and biological effects of aging.

To help you develop a vocabulary of words typical for textbooks, each chapter in *Reading Keys* ends with ten new words to add to your textbook vocabulary. (See p. 37 for this chapter's ten.) Your job is to learn these words in preparation for textbook assignments.

If the Margins Don't Tell You Enough, Check the Glossary

If a word or phrase is defined in the margins of your textbook, it probably belongs to the specialized vocabulary of the subject under discussion. However, if you are still unsure of the word's meaning after reading the marginal note, turn to the back of the book. Most textbooks have **glossaries**, or lists of key definitions, in their final pages.

It's Not Just Specialized Vocabulary That Matters

To avoid word repetition while keeping the same topic or topics before the reader's eyes, writers have to vary the words they use. If they didn't, readers would find the repetition so tiresome, they'd stop reading. It's no surprise, then, that textbook writers (and writers of other kinds of books as well) make use of an extensive vocabulary.

Take, for example, a writer discussing Winston Churchill, England's prime minister during World War II. Churchill was famous for his bouts of deep depression. To provide an extended discussion of how these moods affected Churchill's behavior, the writer would need some **synonyms,** or words similar in meaning, for the word *depressed.* When describing Churchill, the writer might use synonyms such as *morose, melancholy,* and *dour.*

Because words like these are less common in casual conversation, you might have to struggle a bit to discover the author's meaning. But the larger your general vocabulary is, the easier it will be to read your textbooks without hesitation, which means it's in your interest to make regular vocabulary study part of your schedule. At least three times a week, spend a half hour to forty-five minutes learning new words. To help you get started, Chapter 1 will supply ten words that are essential to academic reading.

Don't Forget Idioms

Idioms are expressions common to one language and difficult or impossible to translate into another. When idioms are translated, they don't seem to make sense or fit the context. A non-native speaker, for instance, might be puzzled by the following sentence, which uses the idiom *whistle blower:* "Perhaps the most famous *whistle blower* of all time was John Dean, who helped bring down Richard Nixon's presidency."[†]

Someone from another country might, initially at least, wonder how a person blowing a whistle could destroy a president's career. The person's confusion would stem from not knowing the idiom *whistle blower.* The term refers to someone who informs the press or legal officials about crimes committed by a company or an institution to which he or she belongs. It has nothing to do with a real whistle or the sound of a whistle.

Idioms are most common in ordinary speech. However, they do make their appearance in textbooks. *Whistle blower,* for instance, is a common term in business and legal textbooks. In fact, there is even whistle blowing legislation, designed to protect those who reveal the ethical lapses of those they work for.

Because idioms do appear in textbooks, it's a good idea to make them part of your vocabulary building To help you do that, the chapters in this text will periodically introduce an important idiom under the heading "Idiom Alert." If you don't already know the idiom, make a note of it in your vocabulary file,[†] notebook, or card.

[†]Dean provided evidence showing that Richard Nixon had known about members of his administration approving breaking and entering in order to gather information about the opposing party.
[†]Online notebooks like Evernote or Springpad are great for this purpose. There are a host of them available, most of them for free if your files don't get too huge.

ROUNDING UP THE KEYS

Here is a list of all the reading keys introduced in the chapter. Use them to review for the test on page 45. If a particular reading key doesn't make sense on its own, go back to the page where it appeared and review the section preceding it.

🔑 **READING KEYS: Learn How to Develop and Maintain Concentration**

- ◆ Getting yourself concentrated or focused to study doesn't just happen; it's something you have to prepare for. (p. 7)
- ◆ Form a habit of studying in a particular place and at a particular time. Just remember you don't have to stay there. Take walking breaks and review while you move from place to place. Go back to the original spot you started in, but you don't have to. You can also continue working on the assignment in another room. (p. 7)
- ◆ Moving around while studying, as long as you review while you are on the move, is probably a better way to remember new information long term than sitting still in the same spot for two hours. (p. 7)
- ◆ Use success statements and motivational mottos to keep you going when you want to quit. (p. 7)

SQ 3R's

🔑 **READING KEYS: *S* is for Survey**

- ◆ Getting an overall picture of what's in a chapter *before* you begin reading makes it easier to fit the pieces of the chapter together *while* you are reading. (p. 9)
- ◆ Survey steps should vary to suit the material. If, for instance, there are no headings, read the first line of every paragraph. (p. 9)

🔑 **READING KEY: Develop Questions**

- ◆ Before you start reading, develop some questions that you want to answer about the chapter. The questions will help keep you focused. Questions based on the headings will also direct your attention to key points in the chapter. (p. 10)

🔑 **READING KEY: Read Strategically**

- ◆ To read strategically is to read with a plan. It's reading with questions and predictions in mind that are then answered, confirmed, or revised. (p. 11)

READING KEYS: Paraphrasing and Memory

◆ Whenever you spend time thinking about the author's words in order to abbreviate or paraphrase them, you are giving your brain the time it needs to understand what those words mean. (p. 22)

◆ Paraphrasing for reading notes and paraphrasing for term papers are two different things. Reading notes don't require the same level of formality, completeness, or grammatical correctness. (p. 22)

READING KEYS: Turning to the Web for Background Knowledge

◆ The Web can usually give you the background knowledge you need to get the most out of your textbooks. (p. 30)

◆ To get your search term to come up with the information you need, make it as precise as possible, using phrases more often than single words. (p. 30)

◆ It's a good idea to use your search term with two different search engines because one might give you better results than another. And even if both search engines turn up the same results, you will still learn something about the topic you are researching via incidental learning. (p. 30)

◆ When a list of websites appears on your screen, don't assume that a site's position in the list is an indication of quality. The site at the top of the list is often popular but might not be that informative for your purposes. (p. 30)

◆ Commercial news sites might serve you better than Wikipedia, which has very long entries for most topics and issues covered. Websites linked to television or print news are less likely to overwhelm you with information, and the writing will be livelier. (p. 30)

◆ For purposes of background knowledge, stay away from websites with connotative, or emotionally loaded, language. Your goal is to get a sense of what is commonly believed or known about your topic. (p. 30)

◆ What you don't want at this stage is a personal opinion that deviates, or differs, wildly from traditional opinion. At this point, in fact, what you want is the traditional point of view, although you might well start to disagree with it once you know more. (p. 30)

◆ Keep in mind that photos can be as persuasive as words. (p. 30)

Ten Words for Your Academic Vocabulary

To get you started working on your academic vocabulary, here are ten words you absolutely must know to read textbooks from just about *any* discipline. Each word is followed by a textbook example. These words, however, can be found in a wide variety of disciplines. They are not limited to the subject of the textbook illustration.

1. **facilitate:** to make easier

    To fully *facilitate* coverage of political campaigns, staffers supply the media with daily schedules, advance copies of speeches, and access to telephone and fax machines. (Alan Gitelson et al., *American Government*, 8th ed., p. 287. © Cengage Learning.)

2. **innovations:** new ideas or products

    Four *innovations* in Adjustable Rate Mortgages have been developed. (Thomas E. Garman and Raymond E. Forgue, *Personal Finance*, 2nd ed., p. 302. © Cengage Learning.)

3. **stimulant:** something that provokes an action or a response

    As a *stimulant*, nicotine speeds up the heart rate, dampens appetite, and produces a mild rush or psychological kick. (Jeffrey S. Nevid, *Psychology: Concepts and Applications*, 3rd ed., p. 167. © Cengage Learning.)

4. **repercussion:** consequence, result, often negative

    By empowering employees to make their own decisions and try new ideas without *repercussions* and by treating them as people, not merely workers, managers strive to make working at Southwest a positive experience for all employees. (William M. Pride, Robert J. Hughes, and Jack R. Kapoor, *Business*, 10th ed., p. 205. © Cengage Learning.)

5. **dearth:** scarce supply

    For many years, the parents of daughters complained about the *dearth* of toys available to them; other than Barbie, what was there? (William William Boyes and Michael Melvin, *Fundamentals of Economics*, 2nd ed., p. 123. © Cengage Learning.)

6. **imminent:** about to happen or occur

    Whether a volcano poses an *imminent* threat to human life and property cannot always be readily determined. (Adapted from Stanley Chernicoff and Hayden A. Fox, *Essentials of Geology*, 2nd ed., p. 62. © Cengage Learning.)

7. **derive:** come or stem from

In German, the word "schadenfreude" refers to pleasures *derived* from another's misfortunes. (Matsumoto, *People,* p. 120.)

8. **components:** parts or elements

There are several important *components* involved in the prevention of child abuse. (Kathleen D. Mullen et al., *Connections for Health,* 4th ed., p. 335. New York: McGraw-Hill.)

9. **advocate:** supporter

Alexander Hamilton was an early *advocate* of a strong central government. (Adapted from Carol Berkin et al., *Making America,* 5th ed., p. 208. © Cengage Learning.)

10. **annihilated:** destroyed

In sub-Saharan Africa, so many adults have been *annihilated* by HIV/AIDS that an entire generation of children is now without parents. (Jeffrey S. Nevid, *Psychology: Concepts and Applications,* 3rd ed., p. 451. © Cengage Learning.)

◆ **EXERCISE 6**   **Making Academic Vocabulary Familiar**

DIRECTIONS   Each sentence uses a more conversational or simpler version of one of the academic words listed below. At the end of the sentence, fill in the blank with the more academic word that could replace the underlined word in the sentence.

annihilate imminent facilitate   repercussions derives
advocate   dearth   components   stimulant   innovations

1. As a <u>supporter</u> of states' rights, John C. Calhoun insisted that an individual state government could refuse legislation imposed by the national government. advocate

2. The <u>immediate</u> arrival of the presidential candidate had reporters in a frenzy. imminent

3. The development of the birth control pill had enormous social consequences. repercussions

4. Currently, there is a serious <u>lack</u> of part-time jobs for college students, and many students, who use their summer earnings for school, are worried. _dearth_

5. The chemicals used to <u>kill</u> the mosquitoes causing malaria ended up killing beneficial insects as well. _Annihilate_

6. The person appointed to <u>guide</u> the discussion between opponents was highly ineffective, and it didn't take long for the discussion to become an angry free-for-all. _facilitate_

7. A good speech has to have three <u>parts</u>: a catchy introduction, a point, and a rousing conclusion. _Components_

8. The big new <u>changes</u> in teacher training were supposed to reap large rewards; but after a year, the university went back to more traditional methods. _innovations_

9. The company <u>gets</u> most of its profits from overseas sales. _derives_

10. For most people, coffee is a strong <u>pick-me-up</u>. _Stimulant_

DIGGING DEEPER

The Transformation of Native Cultures

Looking Ahead   This reading describes the changes that took place in Native American culture during the nineteenth century.

1   Buffalo slaughter and salmon reduction undermined Indian culture in the nineteenth century. But population shifts also contributed. Throughout the nineteenth century, white migrants were overwhelmingly young, single males in their twenties and thirties, the age when they were most prone to violent behavior. In 1870, white men outnumbered white women by three to two in California, two to one in Colorado, and two to one in Dakota Territory. By 1900, a high proportion of men remained throughout these places. As a result, Indians were more likely to come into contact first with white traders, trappers, soldiers, prospectors and cowboys—almost all of whom owned guns and would use them on animals and humans who got in their way.

2   **Attitudes of Western Men**   Moreover these men subscribed to prevailing attitudes that Indians were primitive, lazy, and devious. Such contempt made exploiting and killing natives easier, further justified by claims of threats to life and property. When Indians raided white settlements, they sometimes mutilated bodies, burned buildings, and kidnapped women, acts that were embellished in campfire stories and popular fiction to portray Indians as savages. In saloons and cabins, men boasted about fighting Indians and showed off scalps and other body parts from victims.

3   Indian warriors, too, were young, armed, and prone to violence. Valuing bravery, they boasted of fighting white intruders. But Indian communities contained excesses of women, the elderly and children, making native bands less mobile and more vulnerable. They also were susceptible to bad habits of bachelor white society, copying their binges on cheap whiskey and prostitution. The syphilis and gonorrhea that Indian men contracted from Indian women infected by white men killed many and hindered reproduction, which their populations, already declining from smallpox and other white diseases, could not afford. Thus the age and gender structure of the white frontier population, combined with racist contempt, further threatened western Indians' existence.

4   **Government Policy and Treaties**   Government policy reinforced efforts to remove Indians. North American natives were organized not into tribes as whites believed, but into bands, confederacies,* and villages. Two

---

*confederacies: loosely connected groups; the United States, for instance, started out as a confederacy of states.

hundred languages and dialects separated these groups. This made it difficult for Indians to unite against white invaders. Although a language group
could be defined as a tribe, separate bands and clans had different leaders,
and seldom did a chief hold widespread power. Moreover, bands often
spent more time battling among themselves than with white settlers.

5   Nevertheless, the U.S. government needed some way of categorizing
Indians. After 1795, American officials considered Indian tribes as nations
with which they could make treaties ensuring peace and land boundaries.
This was a faulty assumption because chiefs who agreed to a treaty did not
always speak for the whole band....Moreover, whites seldom accepted treaties as guarantees of Indians' land rights. On the Plains, whites settled wher-
ever they wished, often commandeering choice farmland. In the Northwest,
whites considered treaties protecting Indians' fishing rights on the Columbia
River to be nuisances and ousted Indians from the best locations.

6   **Reservation Policy**   Prior to the 1880s, the federal government tried to
force western Indians onto reservations, where they might be "civilized."
Reservations usually consisted of areas in the group's previous territory
that were least desirable to whites. The government promised protections
from white invasion, along with food, clothing, and other necessities.

7   Reservation policy helped make way for the market economy. In the
early years, trade had benefited Indians and whites equally. Indians acquired clothing, guns, and horses in return for furs, jewelry, and sometimes, military assistance against other Indians. Over time, Indians became
more dependent, and whites increasingly dictated trade. For example,
white traders persuaded Navajo weavers in the Southwest to produce
heavy rugs for eastern customers and to change designs and colors to
boost sales. Meanwhile, Navajos raised fewer crops and were forced to buy
food. Soon they were selling land and labor to whites, and their depen-
dency made it easier to force them onto reservations.

8   Indians had no say over their affairs on reservations. Supreme Court decisions in 1884 and 1886 defined them as wards (like helpless children under
government protection) and denied them U.S. citizenship. Thus, they were
unprotected by the Fourteenth and Fifteenth Amendments, which extended
citizenship to African Americans. Second, pressure from white farmers, miners, and herders who sought Indian lands made it difficult for the government to preserve reservations intact. Third, the government ignored native
history, even combining on one reservation enemy bands. Rather than serv-
ing as civilizing communities, reservations weakened Indian culture.

9   **Native Resistance**   Not all Indians succumbed to market forces and reservation restrictions. Apaches in the Southwest battled whites even after being

forced onto reservations. Pawnees in the Midwest resisted disadvantageous deals from white traders. In the Northwest, Nez Percé Indians escaped reservations by fleeing to Canada in 1877. They eluded U.S. troops until 1,800 miles later in Montana. Their leader, Young Joseph, recognized they could not succeed and ended the flight. Sent to a reservation, Joseph unsuccessfully petitioned the government to return his people's ancestral lands.

10   Whites responded to western Indian defiance militarily. In 1860, Navajos reacted by raiding Fort Defiance in Arizona Territory. The army then attacked and starved the Navajo into submission, and in 1863–1864 forced them on a "Long Walk" from their homelands to a reservation at Bosque Redondo in New Mexico. In the Sand Creek region of Colorado in 1864, a militia commanded by Methodist minister John Chivington attacked Cheyennes led by Black Kettle, killing almost every Indian. In 1879, four thousand U.S. soldiers forced surrender from Utes who were resisting further land concessions.

11   The most publicized battle occurred in June 1876, when 2,500 Lakotas and Cheyennes led by Chiefs Rain-in-the-Face, Sitting Bull, and Crazy Horse annihilated 256 government troops led by the rash Colonel George A. Custer near the Little Big Horn River in southern Montana. Although Indians demonstrated military skill, supply shortages and relentless pursuit by U.S. soldiers eventually overwhelmed armed Indian resistance. Native Americans were not so much conquered as they were harassed* and starved into submission. (Adapted from Mary Beth Norton et al., *A People and a Nation,* 9e (Brief Edition). © Cengage Learning.)

Sharpening Your Skills

DIRECTIONS   Answer the following questions by circling the letter of the correct response or filling in the blanks.

1. Opening paragraphs tend to set the stage for what's to follow. What does the first paragraph in this reading suggest about the relationship between white and Indian cultures in the nineteenth century?

    a. Native Americans used violent means to retaliate against the invasion of white settlers.

    b. Native Americans were opposed to violence and only took up arms when they were attacked.

    c. Male settlers with a tendency toward violence were the first white people that Native Americans encountered in the old West.

---

*harassed: tormented.

2. In paragraph 2, what do you think *embellished* means in the following sentence: "When Indians raided white settlements, they sometimes mutilated bodies, burned buildings, and kidnapped women, acts that were *embellished* in campfire stories and popular fiction to portray Indians as savages."

   Made the Story seem true.

3. According to the authors, what did young Indian men learn from white settlers?

   Killing and Kidnapping.

4. According to the authors, how did what they learned contribute to the destruction of their way of life?

   They got Deseases.

5. According to the reading, how did being organized into "bands, confederacies, and villages" hinder the Indians' ability to fight the invasion of white settlers?

   their Dialects and languages

6. The heading for paragraph 6 is "Reservation Policy." Which statement best sums up the point made under this heading?

   a. Reservations were a way of protecting Indians from the white settlers who surrounded them.

   b. Through creating reservations, the government found a way of exploiting and controlling Indians without resorting to violence.

   c. Through reservations, the government tried to make up to Indians what had been taken away from them when white settlers came West.

7. Paragraph 9 opens with the heading "Native Resistance." What point do the authors make about that heading?

   They were Battling white men to Protect.

8. Paragraph 9 describes how some Indians responded to attempts to push them onto reservations. What does paragraph 10 add to that discussion?

   White men went to the military.

9. The following three sentences open paragraph 10.

   "Whites responded to western Indian defiance militarily. In 1860, Navajos reacted by raiding Fort Defiance in Arizona Territory. The army then attacked and starved the Navajo into submission, and in 1863–1864 forced them on a 'Long Walk' from their homelands to a reservation at Bosque Redondo in New Mexico."

   What phrase from the first sentence does the second sentence help clarify? *reacted by raiding* What word from the first sentence does the third sentence help explain? *the Army then Attacked*

10. Which statement best describes the authors' bias?

    a. The authors try to remain objective and not reveal any personal judgment of the events they describe.
    b. The authors are unsympathetic to the plight of the Indians and feel that white settlers did what they had to in order to make a new life on the frontier.
    c. The authors believe that the Indians were badly treated by both the white settlers and the government that represented those settlers.

▶ **SHARE YOUR THOUGHTS**

In 1976, the Supreme Court issued a decision making Indian reservations free of state taxation and regulation. As a result, some Indian groups have successfully opened and run gambling casinos without paying any state taxes. Many argued that the decision was a fair one. In their eyes, the Supreme Court's decision functioned as a form of reparation, or compensation, for the harm that had been done to Indians when white settlers moved west. Others were furious. They claimed that the Indians, particularly those running successful gaming businesses, should be taxed like anyone else. What do you think?

Shouldn't Be taxed

▶ **TEST 1**   **Reviewing the Key Points**

DIRECTIONS   Answer the following questions by circling *T* (true) or *F* (false). *Note*: Read the questions carefully. Part of a question may be true and part may be false, making the whole sentence false.

T *F*   **1.** The ability to concentrate comes naturally if you just place yourself in the right setting.

T *F*   **2.** Success statements identify future goals and connect them to current assignments.

T *F*   **3.** There is no such thing as a good habit. All habits interfere with spontaneous and creative thoughts.

T *F*   **4.** Previewing a chapter before reading is important mainly because it helps the reader figure out how long the chapter will take to read.

T *F*   **5.** Making your Internet search term as precise and focused as possible is the key to getting useful background information about the topics covered in a reading assignment.

T *F*   **6.** If you paraphrase while reading, there's no need to mark pages while reading.

T *F*   **7.** Textbooks never reveal a personal bias.

T *F*   **8.** Small changes in the original meaning are acceptable when the reader is paraphrasing just to take marginal notes.

T *F*   **9.** When paraphrasing for reading notes, it's important to maintain standards of formal grammar exactly as if you were paraphrasing for a term paper.

T *F*   **10.** Idioms are expressions that develop over time within a given language and cannot be translated word for word; thus, they are often puzzling to non-native speakers.

To correct your test, turn to page 587. If one or more of your answers is incorrect, re-read the Rounding Up the Keys section of the chapter to find out where your mistake might be.

▶ **TEST 2** **Enlarging Your Academic Vocabulary**

DIRECTIONS Circle the letter of the sentence that uses the opening word correctly.

1. **facilitate**

   a. As a preacher, the Reverend Martin Luther King was very *facilitate* with words.

   b. In order to *facilitate* the beginning of construction, some projects start before the design has been completed.

   c. One cannot *facilitate* a narrow, winding road with a wide trailer.

2. **innovation**

   a. The cell phone is an *innovation* that profoundly changed the way people conduct business.

   b. My opponent's speech has been riddled with *innovations* too numerous to be refuted one-by-one.

   c. The word *ingrate* refers to someone who is not grateful; similarly, an *innovation* is something that is not new.

3. **stimulant**

   a. The bouncy beat of the music worked as a *stimulant* for people to start dancing.

   b. He was such a good *stimulant* that he could always convince his boss he was sick when he wanted to get out of an assignment.

   c. Basil is a common *stimulant* in Italian dishes.

4. **repercussion**

   a. In order to *repercussion* the effects of a bad economy, the governor proposes to lower the state income tax.

   b. As a *repercussion*, the company paid its top managers a hefty bonus at the end of the year.

   c. The *repercussions* of the earthquake of 2011 are still felt in Japan.

5. **dearth**

   a. Improving the city roads is a goal *dearth* to the mayor's heart.

   b. The incumbent stated repeatedly that *dearth* was missing in her opponent's arguments.

   c. A *dearth* of jobs in their own country leads many qualified workers to seek employment abroad.

6. **imminent**

   a. The student basked in the praise her dissertation received from the *imminent* scholar.

   b. The cult leader had convinced his followers that the end of the world was *imminent*.

   c. When asked about the president's proposal, the senator's *imminent* reply was that he had mixed feelings about it.

7. **derive**

   a. The defensive captain *derived* his teammates for their sloppy coverage.

   b. Longer and fancier-sounding English words are often *derived* from Latin or French terms.

   c. In order to *derive* at a balanced budget, tough choices need to be made.

8. **components**

   a. Caring for a sick child is an unavoidable *component* of parenthood.

   b. Robin Hood and his *components* roamed the forests around Nottingham in medieval England.

   c. After a long debate, some opponents of the bill turned into *components*.

9. **advocate**

   a. Tax reform is difficult to accomplish because its *advocates* have vastly different motivations.

   b. Italian words are easy to *advocate*, even by people who do not know how they are supposed to be pronounced.

   c. As an *advocate* for PETA, People for the Ethical Treatment of Animals, the scientist complained bitterly about the organization's positions and policies.

10. **annihilate**

   a. Research has shown that tobacco is dangerous even for people who *annihilate* secondhand smoke.

   b. If one species gets *annihilated*, others may suffer, too, because their food supply may have disappeared.

   c. The country needs a large investment to *annihilate* new bridges.

More on Words and Meanings

2

IN THIS CHAPTER, YOU WILL LEARN

- how context clues can suggest word meaning.
- how the context of a word can alter its meaning.
- how knowledge of word parts can help you define unfamiliar words.

> *"Words mean more than what is set down on paper."*
> —*Maya Angelou*

Chapter 1 introduced several study strategies for textbooks. However, the best reading strategies in the world will be of little use if you are having trouble recognizing word meaning. Thus, this chapter shows you how to continue what you started at the end of Chapter 1—improving your academic vocabulary. It also provides some tips on what to do when you don't know what a word means. Sure, you can look the word up. But if you do that too often, it can become a distraction.

Too many interruptions to check the dictionary, whether online or in print, can interrupt your concentration. The problem is, however, that you can't just ignore unfamiliar words. Ignoring them can undermine comprehension.

The good news is that other strategies exist. This chapter describes two of the most useful ones. It also encourages you to start a notebook or file in which you record words common to textbooks. Then you can review these words on a regular basis until they are part of your vocabulary.

Using Context Clues

Frequently, the context—the sentence or passage in which an unfamiliar word appears—offers a clue to its meaning. Armed with that clue, you can usually figure out an **approximate definition**. An approximate definition is usually not the same as the dictionary definition. However, it will be close enough to let you make sense of the passage. The most common kinds of context clues are (1) restatement, (2) contrast, (3) example, and (4) general knowledge.

○━ READING KEY
- Approximate definitions derived from context allow you to keep reading without interruption.

Restatement Clues

If a word or phrase is unfamiliar, don't just ignore it. Instead, scan the rest of the sentence. Look as well at the sentence that follows. You may find a **synonym** or simpler rephrasing of the unknown word. Look, for example, at the restatement clue in the following passage. Can you use context to figure out the meaning of *decipher*?

> During World War II, the British repeatedly tried to *decipher* the Germans' code. However, they couldn't figure it out until mathematician Alan Turing[†] broke the code.

Did you recognize the restatement clue "figure it out" and come up with a meaning? If you did, you realized that definitions such as "figure it out," "determine," and "broke the code" would be appropriate substitutes for the word *decipher*.

[†]Alan Turing is widely considered to be the father of computer science.

Restatement Clues and Specialized Vocabulary

Textbooks make heavy use of restatement clues. This is particularly true when the author is dealing with **specialized vocabulary**, or the words that are essential to understanding a particular subject matter. Note, for instance, how the author of the following passage first highlights the term *social mobility*. Then he follows it with a definition.

> In almost all societies there is some **social mobility**, movement from one social standing to another. (Adapted from Alex Thio, *Society: Myths and Realities*, 4th ed., p. 218. © Cengage Learning.)

Although textbook authors commonly put key words or terms into boldface or italics, be prepared as well for restatement clues to be introduced by colons, parentheses, dashes, and the letters *i.e.* See the following list for some examples:

1. In an average person, the *vital capacity*—maximum amount of air you can inhale and exhale—is about 4.5 liters (8.4 pints). (James H. Otto and Albert Towle, *Modern Biology*, 3rd ed., p. 24. New York: Holt, Rinehart and Winston.)

2. The process of globalization (the rapid movement of goods, capital, labor, technology, and ideas) has been met with mixed reactions. (Gary Ferraro and Susan Andreatta, *Cultural Anthropology*, p. 202. © Cengage Learning.)

3. Sherron Watkins, a vice president at Enron Corporation, was one of the more prominent whistle blowers—people who disclose wrongdoing to parties who can take action—of the last two decades. She wrote an anonymous letter exposing unsound, if not dishonest, financial reporting and dropped the letter off at company headquarters. (Adapted from Andrew J. Dubrin, *Leadership*, 6th ed., p. 187. © Cengage Learning.)

4. Swans are famous for being monogamous, i.e., they mate for life.

🔑 READING KEYS

◆ Restatement clues are the most common context clues in textbooks.
◆ In addition to boldface and italics, colons, dashes, parentheses, and the letters *i.e.* can also signal the presence of restatement clues.

◆ **EXERCISE 1** **Recognizing Restatement Clues**

DIRECTIONS Use the underlined restatement clues to determine the approximate meaning for the italicized words.

EXAMPLE The lawyer claimed that the police had no *valid* evidence linking her client to the crime. She argued that the only <u>sound</u> evidence they had related to her client's character rather than his crime.

a. visual
b. secondary
(c.) trustworthy
d. unusual

EXPLANATION In the first sentence, the author uses the word *valid* to describe the evidence. In the second, he uses the word *sound*, meaning trustworthy or reliable. The restatement clue points to *trustworthy* as the best answer.

1. In addition to women, Asians are also victims of the *glass ceiling*—the <u>barrier that keeps minority professionals from holding leadership positions.</u> (Adapted from Alex Thio, *Society: Myths and Realities*, 4th ed., p. 245. © Cengage Learning.)
   a. insult
   b. ridicule
   c. obstacle
   d. demote

2. His *recollections* of the past were hazy at best; <u>thoughts of the past</u> were so depressing he did not wish to dredge them up.
   a. words
   b. insults
   c. purchases
   d. memories

3. Jacob Riis's pictures of the *urban* poor suggested that life <u>in the city</u> was a living hell for those without money.
   a. having to do with cities
   b. related to the country
   c. showing signs of starvation
   d. foreign

4. His patients thought of the doctor as *altruistic*. However, the nurses he worked with did not see him as <u>selfless</u>.

 a. selfish

 b. giving

 c. impatient

 d. religious

5. Police must have a reasonable suspicion that a suspect is armed and dangerous in order to *frisk*, or <u>pat down the outer clothing</u>, for concealed weapons. (Adapted from Russell Adler et al., *Criminal Justice*, p. 209. © Cengage Learning.)

 a. jail

 b. search

 c. handcuff

 d. hold

◆ EXERCISE 2   Recognizing Restatement Clues

DIRECTIONS   Use the restatement clues to determine the approximate meaning for the italicized words.

EXAMPLE   The ease and speed with which children acquire language have caused some researchers to conclude that children are born with a *predisposition*, or built-in tendency, to learn language. (Adapted from Kelvin Seifert and Robert J. Hoffnung, *Child and Adolescent Development*, 5th ed., p. 42. Boston: Houghton Mifflin.)

Predisposition means ___having an inborn ability___.

EXPLANATION   In this case, the comma followed by the word *or* is a signal that a restatement will follow, as indeed it does. *Predisposition* means having a built-in or an inborn tendency or ability.

1. Concern over the *escalating*, some would even say <u>skyrocketing</u>, influence of wealthy special interests in campaigns has led some reform groups like Common Cause to call for stricter regulation of campaign contributions by individuals and groups.

 Escalating means ___going up___.

2. In the middle of a tantrum, the child could not be *appeased*; no matter what his mother did, he would not calm down.

   Appeased means ___To be quiet___.

3. The candidate was known for his *volatile* temper. It was so explosive, in fact, that even his closest aides feared angering him.

   Volatile means ___Quick tempered___.

4. A *staunch* opponent of capital punishment, the writer became even more passionate in her conviction after the state executed a young man with a serious learning disability.

   Staunch means ___to Believe a lot___.

5. How we *appraise,* or look at, events can depend on what the events mean to us personally. The exact same event, such as pregnancy or job change, can lead to feelings of joy, fear, or even anger, depending on the individual. (Adapted from Jeffrey S. Nevid, *Psychology: Concepts and Applications*, 3rd ed., p. 332. © Cengage Learning.)

   Appraise means ___See___.

Contrast Clues

As you might expect, contrast clues tell you what a word *doesn't* mean. Armed with the *antonym*—a word or phrase opposite in meaning—you can often develop a good approximate definition. Look, for example, at how the term *tongue-tied* offers a clue to the meaning of *articulate*.

> As a young man, he had lacked confidence and became tongue-tied when he had to talk in a group, but as he grew older and more confident, he was relaxed and *articulate*, even in a crowd.

Based on the contrast clue "tongue-tied," what do you think *articulate* means? Would you vote for "gifted with words," "well-spoken," or "expressive"? If so, you have made good use of the contrast clue.

Contrast clues are likely to appear whenever the author points out differences between two topics. They are also likely to appear following the transitional words and phrases such as *however, but, in contrast, whereas*, and *while*. **Transitions** are verbal bridges that identify relationships and allow readers to move easily from thought to thought. The transitions identified here, called **contrast** or **reversal transitions**, signal a shift or change from the point of the previous sentence. Anytime you are trying to determine the meaning of an unfamiliar word and spot a contrast or reversal transition, be aware that the sentence might also contain a contrast clue to word meaning.

IDIOM ALERT: Old hat

The phrase was already used in the early part of the twentieth century to refer to something that was out-of-date and old-fashioned. The origins of the expression, however, are unknown. "Directories[†] began to seem **old hat**: Why bother compiling lists of lawyers in New Hampshire or plumbers in Nashua when a Web search might find them?—*Nashua Telegraph* (12/11/2011)."[1]

READING KEYS

- ◆ Contrast clues tell you what a word doesn't mean.
- ◆ Look for contrast clues when the author describes differences between two people, things, or ideas.
- ◆ Transitional words like *however*, *whereas*, and *yet* also signal the presence of contrast clues.

◆ EXERCISE 3 Recognizing Contrast Clues

DIRECTIONS Use the underlined contrast clues to determine approximate meanings for the italicized words.

EXAMPLE The programmer thought his new phone application was *ingenious* but when he played it with his teenage nephews, he realized it was <u>old hat</u> to them.

a. simple and popular

b. silly and boring

c. true

(d.) clever and new

[†]The word *directories* refers to Web directories that collect and categorize information found on the Web. Usually the sifting and sorting of information is done by real people, rather than by an algorithm, or mathematical formula.
[1]From the website idiomsinthenews.com.

EXPLANATION   In this sentence, the word *ingenious* is the opposite of the idiom *old hat*, meaning out-of-date. Thus, definition *d* makes the most sense.

1. Unlike most pop singers whose careers last only a few years, Madonna's career has had unusual *longevity*.
   a. popularity
   b. huge success
   c. extended life
   d. international fame

2. People who are successful in life *persevere* in the face of obstacles, rather than give up.
   a. cheer up
   b. persist
   c. turn away
   d. turn inward

3. The French soldiers were unable to *pacify* the Ivory Coast rebellion; if anything, the rebels were increasing in both strength and violence.
   a. challenge
   b. excite
   c. calm
   d. portray

4. Despite the poor lighting, the photographs captured the scene exactly, with almost no *distortion*.
   a. error
   b. beauty
   c. exaggeration
   d. addition

5. The police were supposed to keep the witness's house under *surveillance* twenty-four hours a day, but somehow the order did not go through and the house was left unobserved during daylight.

    a. observation

    b. wraps

    c. construction

    d. misunderstanding

◆ EXERCISE 4   Recognizing Contrast Clues

DIRECTIONS   Use the contrast clues to determine approximate meanings for the italicized words.

EXAMPLE   People used to believe that mental illness was caused by evil spirits. But, thankfully, that is no longer the *prevailing* opinion.

Prevailing means <u>current, up-to-date, widespread</u>.

EXPLANATION   In this passage, the *prevailing* opinion is contrasted with an opinion held in the past. Thus, "current," "up-to-date," and "widespread" make good approximate definitions.

1. The painting may not be the real thing, but it is an excellent *facsimile*.

   Facsimile means ___False___.

2. That story appeared on the front page of the newspaper, but it was still more *fiction* than reality.

   Fiction means ___Not true___.

3. Although the singer wore *flamboyant* costumes onstage, offstage his clothes were plain and unremarkable.

   Flamboyant means ___Normal___.

4. Just when the wheat seemed to be thriving, a plague of locusts arrived and *ravaged* the farmers' fields.

   Ravaged means ___shrinking___.

5. The bouncer had only glanced at her older companion's I.D., but he *scrutinized* the teenager's fake driver's license very carefully.

   Scrutinized means ___staring___.

Example Clues

Context can also provide you with examples of the behavior or activity related to the word you don't know. For an illustration, read the following sentence:

> Jay's feelings about rap music were *ambivalent*. He admired the clever rhyming lyrics but detested the thoughts they conveyed.

Notice how Jay felt both admiration and dislike. Because this is an example of conflicted feelings, it's safe to say that *ambivalent* probably means something like "contradictory," "contrary," or "conflicted."

With example clues, you may have to ask yourself, "What kind of event, behavior, or experience does this example illustrate?" Once you answer that question, you also have your approximate meaning.

Particularly in textbooks, examples are often introduced by transitions like "for instance," "for example," "more specifically," and "more precisely." These phrases are more likely to follow the words they illustrate than to precede them.

◆ EXERCISE 5   **Recognizing Example Clues**

DIRECTIONS   Use the example clues to determine approximate meanings for the italicized words.

EXAMPLE   The British *aristocracy* doesn't generally have a way with ordinary people. The party-loving, free-spirited Princess Diana was a spectacular exception to that rule.

    a. theater

    (b.) nobility

    c. kings

    d. folks

EXPLANATION   In this sentence, Princess Diana is an example of the *aristocracy*. Thus, the only answer that makes sense is *b*, nobility.

1. Joan of Arc was *valiant* to the end, refusing to show any fear as men with torches prepared to burn her at the stake.

    a. mad

    b. brave

c. quiet

d. outraged

2. As a child, she had been *vulnerable* to all kinds of illnesses; in addition to the normal childhood diseases like mumps and measles, she had also had scarlet and rheumatic fever, bronchitis, and pneumonia.

   a. protected from

   b. expecting

   c. open to attack

   d. untouched

3. According to one of the *provisions* in the Versailles Treaty that ended World War I, the Germans were not allowed to use the coal mined from their coal-rich Saar region; instead, coal coming from the Saar region would be used by France.

   a. exceptions

   b. insults

   c. clues

   d. sections

4. The 1862 Homestead Act, designed to give free land to the poor, produced a lot of *fraudulent* activity. For instance, large landowners would send their employees to apply for deeds to the free land; then the landless employees would sign over the deeds to their wealthy employers.

   a. unusual

   b. brilliant

   c. illegal

   d. amusing

5. The candidate promised full *disclosure* and she kept her word. That same day, she produced the last five years of tax returns and a list of her campaign contributors.

   a. contradiction

   b. decision

   c. indication

   d. exposure

○━┓ **READING KEY**

 ◆ Example clues usually follow the words they illustrate, but they can also precede them.

IDIOM ALERT: Take with a grain of salt

To *take with a grain of salt* means to be skeptical, to not take something too seriously—for instance: Ads promoting miraculous skin creams that can reverse aging need to be *taken with a grain of salt* because the goal of the ad is to increase sales of the cream.

WEB QUEST/CLASS ACTION

Use the Web to find at least two other idioms that mention something people eat, e.g., *salt*, *meat*, *bread*, *butter*, *pie*, and *apples*. Come to class ready to use them in sentences so your classmates can guess their meaning.

◆ **EXERCISE 6**   **Recognizing Example Clues**

DIRECTIONS   Use the example clues to determine approximate meanings for the italicized words.

EXAMPLE   His face showed how *traumatic* the experience had been. Both his wife and his child had died in the plane crash.

Traumatic means <u>miserable, painful, tragic   </u>.

EXPLANATION   The example of a man suffering from the loss of his wife and child tells how painful a *traumatic* experience is.

1. This novel is filled with *personification*. Computers cough and tables groan while the wind cries and howls in the night.

   Personification means <u>Acting like a perso</u>.

2. The results of polls need to be taken with a grain of salt. The phrasing of the questions asked can *skew* the responses and allow the pollster, rather than the respondents, to decide the results.

   Skew means <u>Confuse</u>.

3. The threat of detention was a quick *antidote* to the class's unruly behavior. As soon as the substitute teacher uttered the words "staying after school," the shouting stopped and quiet reigned.

   An *antidote* is a ___Cure___.

4. Supreme Court Justice Oliver Wendell Holmes Jr. was known as the Great *Dissenter*. On occasion, Holmes even challenged his own previous rulings.

   A *dissenter* is ___Thinking about himself___

5. Psychologist Robert Sternberg proposes a model of love that has three basic *components*: intimacy, passion, and commitment. (Adapted from Jeffrey S. Nevid, *Psychology: Concepts and Applications*, 3rd ed., p. 333. © Cengage Learning.)

   Components are ___Parts___.

General Knowledge Clues

In textbooks, restatement clues are probably the most common clues. However, when you read a newspaper or an essay, you are more likely to encounter general knowledge clues. These are clues that draw on your experience. Because you know something about the situation described on the page, determining word meaning becomes easier.

For example, in the following paragraph you can probably determine the meaning of *bungled* because you understand what inspections of anything, from airplanes to cars, are supposed to accomplish. You can also tell that, in this case, the inspections performed by American Airlines were not successfully completed.

> American Airlines grounded 300 jets and disrupted travel for 50,000 passengers Tuesday after federal regulators found that the airline *bungled* inspections required to prevent fires or fuel tank explosions, according to the government and the airline. (*USA Today,* April 9, 2008, p. 1.)

If you inferred that *bungled* means "mismanaged" or "handled badly," you have drawn the right conclusion from the general knowledge clues supplied by the passage.

READING KEY

◆ General knowledge clues draw on what you already know about the experience described on the page.

◆ EXERCISE 7   Recognizing General Knowledge Clues

DIRECTIONS   Use your knowledge of the situation described to determine the approximate meanings for the italicized words.

EXAMPLE   Over the years, all of Danielle's teachers had suggested that she had enormous *potential*; what seemed to be missing was a desire to be successful.

a. anger

(b.) possibility

c. wildness

d. shyness

EXPLANATION   We all know people who have the *potential*, or possibility, of achieving something but just never quite seem to get there. Thus, Danielle's situation is a familiar one, making it easier to come up with an approximate definition for *potential*.

1. Prison was once meant to *rehabilitate* those convicted of a crime. But that is hardly what happens in today's overcrowded prisons, where violent and nonviolent criminals are thrown together under crowded conditions.

   a. reform

   b. reveal

   c. discourage

   d. punish

2. Staring out the window of a train, Max Wertheimer[†] observed a *phenomenon* that would alter his life and launch a new movement in psychology.

[†]Max Wertheimer: one of the founders of Gestalt psychology, which emphasizes the brain's tendency to organize individual pieces of information into connected forms or gestalts.

a. struggle

b. conflict

c. happening

d. disaster

3. Raised in a household where violence was the *norm*, he didn't know how to respond to the world except with his fists. That's all he had ever learned.

a. typical experience

b. odd event

c. consequence

d. outcome

4. Asked a difficult question by a student at the rally, the senator *pondered* a bit before answering.

a. muttered

b. wrote

c. laughed

d. thought

5. In the nineteenth century, few protections were in place for workers, who faced long hours and daily *hazards* on the job.

a. distances

b. rejections

c. dangers

d. improvements

◆ **EXERCISE 8** **Recognizing General Knowledge Clues**

DIRECTIONS Use your knowledge of the events described to determine approximate meanings for the italicized words.

EXAMPLE When John Muir first visited the forests of California, he was *awestruck*. The huge gray mountains against a brilliant blue sky, and the towering redwoods, were like nothing he had ever seen before. After his first sight of what would one day become Yosemite National Park, Muir dedicated himself to protecting the wilderness.

Awestruck means <u>full of wonder; impressed; overwhelmed; stunned</u>.

EXPLANATION   Given what Muir was responding to—towering redwoods and huge mountains—it makes sense to define *awestruck* as "full of wonder," "impressed," "overwhelmed," or "stunned."

1. The young climber's friends and family tried to *dissuade* her from climbing Mount Everest. But she would not listen. Determined to be the first Brazilian woman to reach the top, she was deaf to everything they said.

   Dissuade means <u>Stop her from doing.</u>

2. Across the room, the two strangers caught each other's eye. He smiled and so did she. But when she lifted a cigarette to her lips, he *grimaced* and turned away.

   Grimaced means <u>frowned at</u>.

3. He had studied Spanish for years, faithfully reading every assignment and doing all the homework. But the only time he spoke the language was in class. It wasn't until he lived in Mexico for several months that he became *fluent* in Spanish.

   Fluent means <u>Very Good at</u>.

4. Because of their shared interests, the two cousins tended to *gravitate* toward each other whenever there was a family reunion.

   Gravitate means <u>Get together</u>.

5. Many people think that cybersecurity bills like SOPA (Stop Online Piracy Act) and PIPA (Protect Intellectual Property Act) are too *intrusive*. Critics argue that if bills like these are allowed to become law, governments and corporations will find it all too easy to snoop into the lives of Web users.

   Intrusive means <u>to do damage to, their Privacy.</u>

⊙⌐ READING KEY

◆ Writers don't restrict themselves to one context clue per passage. There may be two or more in the same paragraph. To define an unfamiliar word as precisely as possible, be sure to use all the clues available.

VOCABULARY EXTRA

The words SOPA and PIPA are acronyms. They are, that is, the end result of combining the first letters of individual words. Other acronyms you may have seen before are WHO for World Health Organization, IQ for intelligence quotient, TMI for too much information, and PS for postscript.

Many organizations with two or more words in their names are known more by their acronyms than by their full names. When you read, pay attention to the acronyms that often accompany the first reference to organizations, such as CIA for Central Intelligence Agency. The organization will usually be referred to by the acronym rather than the full name.

◆ EXERCISE 9   Using Context Clues

DIRECTIONS   Each sentence contains one or more of the four types of context clues. Use the clues to determine the approximate meanings for the italicized words.

EXAMPLE   Unless we ourselves have led *exemplary* lives, it probably doesn't pay to be too critical of others.

Exemplary means perfect, good enough to be an example to others .

EXPLANATION   This is a general knowledge clue. Most of us know that if we are critical of others, we really should be on our best behavior. In other words, "people in glass houses shouldn't throw stones."

1. After the hurricane, the river was once again *tranquil*. [calm+ still] It was hard to believe that only hours before it had been wild and dangerous.

   Tranquil means free from disturbance: calm .

2. President Bill Clinton was famous for being *gregarious*. [social] He couldn't enter a room without shaking hands and hugging people. In short, he was a nightmare for the Secret Service.

   Gregarious means (of a person) fond of company; sociable .

3. Wrongly accused of a crime he did not commit, the young man was overjoyed when the new evidence *exonerated* him. took blame off

Exonerated means _release someone from a duty or obligation_

4. Try as they might, the police were unable to *quell* the riot. Even with the aid of tear gas and fire hoses, the officers couldn't control the demonstrators. stop

Quell means _put an end to (a rebellion or other disorder) typically by the use of a force._

5. I like Uncle Al, but sometimes being around him is annoying. He is always trying to teach my brother and me lessons about life. Every time he tells us about some event or experience, he ends it with the question "Now what's the *moral* of that story?" Then we have to tell him the lesson about life that we have learned. I don't know about my brother, but I'm sick of both the stories and the messages that go with them. lesson learned

Moral means _concerned with the principles of right and wrong behavior._

6. The Russian soldiers were finding it hard to maintain their *morale*. They had not been paid in months, and now they had been ordered to pick mushrooms if they wanted to eat. hope

Morale means _the confidence, enthusiasm, and discipline of a person or group at a particular time_

7. She ripped the letter into tiny pieces and threw them to the ground. The wind quickly *dispersed* them. Within moments, there was no evidence the letter had ever existed. got rid of

Dispersed means _distribute or spread over a wide area._

8. The soldier's exciting *chronicle* of his adventures was an immediate hit. Everyone wanted to read about his battle experiences. written story

Chronicle means _a factual written account of important events_

9. The two owners couldn't have been more different. While Alex was outgoing and talkative, Andrea was *reticent* and quiet. shy

Reticent means _not revealing one's thoughts or feelings readily_.

10. Married couples often quarrel over the same issues again and again, with each person playing the same role in an increasingly familiar *scenario*. *scene*

    Scenario means <u>a setting in partical for a work of Art</u>.

🔑 **READING KEY**

◆ When trying to determine word meaning, be patient. Check the sentences before and after the one containing an unfamiliar word. You may just find the clue you need.

Context Can Change Meaning

You may think you know the meaning of *critical* because people are always telling you that you are too *critical* of others, meaning "having a negative opinion." But does that meaning fit this context: "In the 1992 election, the African-American vote was *critical* to his winning the election"? In this context, *critical* means "central to," or "essential." If you think you know a word but the meaning you know doesn't fit, you are probably dealing with a word that changes its meaning with the context.

"If you can figure out the words in a text message, you can figure out the words in Chaucer."

Breaking Words into Parts

Lots of words, particularly those used in an academic context, include word parts borrowed from Greek or Latin. Knowing the meanings of these word parts provides you with the building blocks for hundreds of words in the English language. Learn some Greek and Latin word parts—mastering, say, ten a week—and you will be amazed at how quickly your textbook vocabulary improves.

To illustrate, let's say you didn't know what the word *vivacious* means in the following sentence: "Thomas Jefferson[†] was drawn to Dolley Madison's *vivacious* personality." The context here is not adequate for even an approximate definition. But if you know that the root *viv* means "life" and *ous* means "full of," you have your definition. What Jefferson liked about Dolley Madison was her "lively" personality. See what you can do with a little Greek or Latin under your belt?

Roots: Roots provide words with their essential or main meanings. The root meaning of a word never changes no matter what prefixes (beginnings of words) or suffixes (endings of words) are added on to it, e.g., farm, farmer, farming; write, writer, writing, prewriting.

Prefixes: Prefixes don't affect a word's core meaning. But they do modify the word's meaning as a whole, e.g., social and antisocial; annual and biannual.

Suffixes: Most suffixes tell you less about word meaning and more about word function, changing adjectives to nouns or nouns to adverbs, e.g., dry and dryness; grace and gracefully.

The following chart lists common roots, prefixes, and suffixes. Some of the word parts listed here appear in the chapter, but many don't. Still, it's worth your while to take a few minutes every day or so to learn both word part and word meaning.

[†]Thomas Jefferson was the third president of the United States and a widower, so Dolley Madison, wife of Jefferson's friend James Madison, became the unofficial first lady.

Common Prefixes and Roots

◆

Prefix and Meaning[†]	Root and Meaning
ab = away, from	anthrop = man, human
am = love	astro = star
anti = against, opposing	bio = life
bene = good	camera = chamber
bi = two	cardio = heart
circum = around	chrom = color
con = with	chron = time
contra = against	clam = cry out
crypt = secret	cogne = knowledge
de = from, away, down	corpo = body
demi = half	cred = believe
di = two	cyto = cell
dis = not, absence, opposite, remove	demo = people
	derma = skin
du = double	dict = speech, speak
en = in, within, into, to go into	duct = lead
inter = between	gam = marriage
intra = within	gen = birth, begetting
ir = not	geo = earth
mal, male = bad, abnormal	gyno = woman
mono = one	hemo = blood
multi = many	hydro = water
neo = new	lat = side
omni = all	lum, luc, lus = light
pan = all	locut, loqu = speech
para = beside, beyond	log = word
poly = many	magni = great, big
post = after	ortho = straight, right
pre = before, prior to	path = feeling
pro = supporting, in favor of	ped = foot
proto = first	phil = love
re = back, again	phot = light
retro = backward	port = carry
sub = under	reg, rect = straighten, rule
super = above	simil = like
syn = together	spec = see
tele = far	strict = tighten
trans = across, beyond	terra = earth

[†]Note how one prefix can have several meanings.

uni = one

theo = god
thermo = heat
ven = come
verb = word
ver, vert = turn
viv, vit = to live, life
viva, viva = life
voc = call
vor = eat

Some Common Suffixes

◆

Suffixes indicating a person, actor, or agent:

an (American)	ist (violinist)
eer (racketeer)	or (actor)
ent (agent)	path (psychopath)

Suffixes indicating a state, quality, act, or condition:

ance (resistance)	ness (happiness)
ancy (hesitancy)	sion, tion (confusion, function)
hood (childhood)	tude (gratitude)
ism (hypnotism)	ty (loyalty)

Suffixes indicating the presence or absence of a particular quality or characteristic:

ful (beautiful)	ly (lively)
ish (childish)	some (lonesome)
less (hopeless)	y (sleepy)

O⟶ READING KEY

◆ Whenever possible, use context *and* word parts to determine word meaning.

Using Word Maps to Learn Word Parts

Consider making word maps to learn some common prefixes and roots. Start your word map by putting the root in the middle of a page. Circle it. Then make spokes come out from the circled root. On each spoke write a word derived from the root.

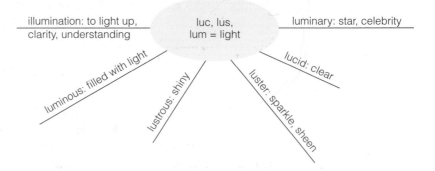

Word maps aid remembering. This is especially true if you recite the words while creating the map. That way your brain will have a three-fold memory of the words that stem from the one word part—visual, verbal, and aural.*

◆ EXERCISE 10 Using Word Parts and Context Clues

DIRECTIONS   Look over the word parts listed below. Use them, along with the context, to define the italicized word.

anthrop = man, human, person	phil = love
path = feeling, emotion, suffering	reg, rec = straighten, rule
	vit, viv = to live, life

EXAMPLE   Because of his contributions to libraries and schools, many people view Andrew Carnegie as a *philanthropist*. Some historians, however, like to remind the public that Carnegie earned much of his money by paying his workers substandard wages. As he grew older, he may well have become a lover of humanity, but he didn't necessarily start out that way.

Philanthropist means a person who helps or loves others   .

EXPLANATION   The restatement clue "lover of humanity" certainly suggests the meaning of *philanthropist*. But so, too, do the roots *phil* and *anthrop*.

―――――――――
*aural: related to hearing.

1. The two boys came from and returned to the same hometown. Yet, having fought on opposite sides during the Civil War, they felt nothing but *antipathy* for one another.

   Antipathy means _Hated or having a Strong Dislike for Something_

2. Even in old age, the actor had a powerful *vitality* that drew people to him. When he was in good spirits, his laughter could be heard booming over the laughter of others. He also told wonderful stories and showed an interest in everyone and everything.

   Vitality means _having a lot of Energy_.

3. After the military *regime* was forced out of power, its members fled for their lives.

   Regime means _Battle or War_ rulers.

4. During the anticommunist scare of the 1950s, the writer had betrayed his friends and given their names to the House Un-American Activities Committee. As a result, some of those friends had gone to jail. Fifty years later he knew, as did they, that there was no way to *rectify* his betrayal. + take it back

   Rectify means _forget about_.

5. Disowned and disinherited, the heiress was forced to live on food stamps. She even had to sleep in homeless shelters. Being rich had not prepared her to earn a living. As one would expect, her experience with being poor gave her more *empathy* for those on welfare. Fortunately, this sense of connection did not completely disappear once her family welcomed her back into the fold, and she funded a work program for women on welfare.

   Empathy means _feelings for others_.

6. Now in her eighties, the actress still had a *regal* bearing. It seemed almost appropriate to bow when she entered the room.

   Regal means _royal or Enchanted_.

7. The soldier's life was very *regimented*. He did everything according to a strict schedule. Every hour of every day was carefully accounted for.

   Regimented means ~~hard working~~ structure .

8. When human bones were discovered at the building site, the city called in a team of *anthropologists* to see how old they were. To everyone's shock, the anthropologists all came to the same conclusion: The bones were not ancient. Rather, they were of recent origin.

   Anthropologists means doctors who discover human Bones

9. Even after living in England for ten years, he was still not an *Anglophile*. Deeply American, he remained highly critical of his adopted country. He might have to work there, but he didn't have to like it.

   Anglophile means a Person from a Different Country

10. She had a *vivid* writing style that made her books extremely popular.

    Vivid means Good writing or Amazing

◆ EXERCISE 11   Using Word Parts

DIRECTIONS   Use the word parts listed below to fill in the blanks.

bene = good	poly = many
bi = two	pre = before, prior to
mono = one	

EXAMPLE   Although their religion allowed men to be _poly_gamists, believers seldom appeared in public with more than one wife.

EXPLANATION   As you know from the charts on pages 68–69, the root *gam* means "marriage" and the suffix *ist* means "person," "actor," or "agent." Thus, the word *polygamists* means "people married to several people."

1. In contrast to polygamy, the word _Mono_gamy means "marriage to one person."

2. A person who marries two people at the same time is a _bi_gamist.

3. If a crime is thought out before it occurs, it is said to be _____Pre_____meditated.

4. The root *lat* means "side." Thus, a _____bi_____lateral agreement would involve two sides.

5. Groups that do good works are often called _____bene_____volent associations.

6. A culture that has not yet begun to rely on machinery is called a _____pre_____industrial society.

7. The root *theo* refers to God. Thus, the word _____Poly_____theism refers to the belief in many gods.

8. The word for belief in one God would be _____Mono_____theism.

9. The root *dict* refers to speech. Thus, the word _____bene_____diction would refer to a blessing.

10. A person who uses one tone of voice is said to speak in a _____mono_____tone.

◆ EXERCISE 12   Using Word Parts

DIRECTIONS   Use the word parts below to fill in the blanks.

Prefixes

anti = against or opposing
bene = good
bi = two
circum = around
uni = one

Suffix

or = indicating a person who
   does the action described in
   the root

Roots

camera = chamber
chron = time

EXAMPLE   If a main character in a play or novel lacks the usual heroic qualities, he or she will often be called an ____anti____hero.

EXPLANATION   In this case, the prefix *anti* cancels the meaning of the root word.

1. Because it has two branches and two chambers, the U.S. legislature is called ___bi___l.

2. In the 1960s, young men and women wore the same clothes—T-shirts and jeans. That trend in fashion was called ___Uni___sex.

3. The problem with Lyme disease is that it's hard to cure. Often it proves ___Chron___ic and keeps coming back over time.

4. Because there is no way to police the high seas, many cruise ships find ways to ___circum___vent laws designed to control pollution of the earth's oceans.

5. If someone came to your aid whenever you needed it, you might call him or her your ___Bene___fact___or___.

6. The ___Uni___fication of East and West Germany in 1991 was celebrated throughout Europe.

7. People who experience mood swings—one minute they are happy, the next depressed—are likely to suffer from a ___bi___polar disorder.

8. When the police interviewed the suspect, he mentioned specific times for the events he described. Unfortunately for him, his ___Chron___ology didn't make sense.

9. Even the president of the United States does not make ___Uni___lateral decisions; for the most part, he must consult with Congress.

10. The explorer Ferdinand Magellan launched the first successful attempt to ___circum___navigate the earth.

WEB QUEST/CLASS ACTION

Anti-heroes are central characters who don't display the characteristics we think of as heroic. Self-sacrifice, for instance, isn't high on their list of character traits. But while they may not be nice people whom you'd want for friends, anti-heroes have been some of the most memorable characters in fiction and film. Use the Web to find at least five famous anti-heroes[†] in either movies or novels. Compile a master list in class and see if you can come up with characteristics that are typical of anti-heroes.

© Warner Bros/Courtesy Everett Collection

◆ EXERCISE 13 Using Context Clues and Word Parts

DIRECTIONS Use context and your knowledge of word parts to select the *best* definition for the italicized words.

1. [1]If we wish to start a conversation with a stranger standing nearby, we are likely to use nonverbal signals. [2]We might, for instance, nod our heads or smile. [3]This is a way of indicating that we are *receptive* to a verbal exchange. [4]However, we also use nonverbal signals to communicate that we are not interested in chatting with a stranger. [5]We use, for instance, something called "civil inattention." [6]Civil inattention consists of brief eye contact quickly followed by gaze *aversion*, to show a withdrawal of interest. [7]In addition to civil inattention, we also use other signals to *acknowledge* a person's presence

---

[†]Like heroes, anti-heroes can also include women.

but still indicate that we don't want to chat. [8]After observing chance meetings in public places, researcher David Givens discovered that we frequently use body language to avoid conversation. [9]For instance, we use *constricted* postures like crossing our arms and holding them at the elbows to indicate we don't want to chat. [10]We also make faces. [11]Facial expressions intended to avoid conversation include pressing or biting our lips and *protruding* the tongue.

1. *Receptive* in sentence 3 probably means
   a. annoyed.
   b. fearful.
   c. welcoming.
   d. rejecting.

2. *Aversion* in sentence 6 probably means
   a. turning away.
   b. returning.
   c. turning inward.
   d. turning toward.

3. *Acknowledge* in sentence 7 probably means
   a. ignore.
   b. recognize.
   c. repeat.
   d. reject.

4. *Constricted* in sentence 9 probably means
   a. wrapped or closed.
   b. wide open.
   c. abnormal.
   d. broken or fractured.

5. *Protruding* in sentence 11 probably means
   a. moving away.
   b. moving backward.
   c. invading.
   d. sticking out.

2. [1]Do you know why you buy the products you do? [2]Like most American consumers, you probably purchase specific products for one or more of five main reasons. [3]You buy some products because you have an immediate use for them. [4]Families, for example, need pots and pans for cooking. [5]Students need books to complete assignments. [6]You purchase other products for convenience. [7]Cordless telephones and electric can openers are *dispensable*. [8]You could live without them. [9]However, they make life so much easier; therefore, you buy them. [10]You also buy products because you believe they *enhance* your wealth. [11]Antiques or gold coins, for instance, are considered good investments. [12]Homeowners buy paint, plants, and decorative (as opposed to *functional*) fences to add to the value of their property. [13]In addition to increasing income, pride of ownership is another reason for making a purchase. [14]Consumers buy items like Rolex watches and designer clothes mainly because they *confer* status, or a sense of importance. [15]Finally, you, like most people, sometimes buy for safety. [16]If we can afford it, we willingly *procure* insurance, smoke detectors, burglar alarms, and sensor lights, all because they make us feel more safe and secure. (William M. Pride, Robert J. Hughes, and Jack R. Kapoor, *Business*, 10th ed., pp. 373–74. © Cengage Learning.)

1. *Dispensable* in sentence 7 probably means

a. inexpensive.

b. essential to our lives.

c. high quality.

d. easy to give up.

2. *Enhance* in sentence 10 probably means

a. increase.

b. decrease.

c. display.

d. announce.

3. *Functional* in sentence 12 probably means

a. useful and necessary.

b. pretty and decorative.

c. wooden.

d. fancy.

4. *Confer* in sentence 14 probably means
   a. undermine.
   b. pretend.
   c. hide.
   d. give.

5. *Procure* in sentence 16 probably means
   a. give away.
   b. lose.
   c. obtain.
   d. eliminate.

◇ Getting Brief Definitions from Your Search Engine

Much of the time when you come across an unfamiliar word in your reading, context will supply you with an approximate meaning. Often that meaning will be close enough to let you continue without checking a dictionary. But for those times when context fails you and the word is not part of a subject's specialized vocabulary, consider using a search engine, such as Google or Bing, to get a brief definition.

Just type the word *define* plus a colon (:) and the word into the Google search box. Up will come a brief definition. For instance, here's what you would see if you typed *define: intermediary* into Google's search box:

> **in·ter·me·di·ar·y**/ˌintərˈmēdēˌerē/◀◦⟩)
>
> *Noun:* A person who acts as a link between people in order to try to bring about an agreement or reconciliation, a mediator.

Print dictionaries are a better choice for double checking the definition of a word you want to use in a writing assignment. Definitions in a print dictionary tend to be more detailed and will include explanations of grammar or usage issues. But for reading assignments, brief online definitions like the ones Google, Bing, and a host of other search engines offer will serve you very well.

ROUNDING UP THE KEYS

Here is a list of all the reading keys introduced in the chapter. Use them to review for the test on page 85. If a particular reading key doesn't make sense on its own, go back to the page where it appeared and review the section preceding it.

READING KEY: Context Clues

◆ Approximate definitions derived from context allow you to keep reading without interruption. (p. 49)

READING KEYS: Restatement Clues *says again, define*

◆ Restatement clues are the most common context clues in textbooks. (p. 50)
◆ In addition to boldface and italics, colons, dashes, parentheses, and the letters *i.e.* can also signal the presence of restatement clues. (p. 50)

READING KEYS: Contrast Clues *opposite.*

◆ Contrast clues tell you what a word doesn't mean. (p. 54)
◆ Look for contrast clues when the author describes differences between two people, things, or ideas. (p. 54)
◆ Transitional words like *however, whereas,* and *yet* also signal the presence of contrast clues. (p. 54)

READING KEY: Example Clues *illustrate*

◆ Example clues usually follow the words they illustrate, but they can also precede them. (p. 59)

READING KEY: General Knowledge Clues *what you already know*

◆ General knowledge clues draw on what you already know about the experience described on the page. (p. 61)

READING KEYS: Tips on Using Context Clues

◆ Writers don't restrict themselves to one context clue per passage. There may be two or more in the same paragraph. To define an unfamiliar word as precisely as possible, be sure to use all the clues available. (p. 64)

◆ When trying to determine word meaning, be patient. Check the sentences before and after the one containing an unfamiliar word. You may just find the clue you need. (p. 66)

READING KEY: Word Parts

◆ Whenever possible, use context *and* word parts to determine word meaning. (p. 69)

Ten More Words for Your Academic Vocabulary

1. **fertile:** capable of producing or giving birth

   When homesteaders went west in 1862, they expected to find lush, *fertile* fields, but instead they found desert and rock.

2. **allocation:** to set apart or distribute for specific purposes

   The purpose of the meeting was to discuss the *allocation* of resources for the new hospital.

3. **symbiotic:** related in a mutually beneficial way

   The two political blogs had a *symbiotic* relationship; people were always reading one to confirm the claims of the other, driving up the readership for both.

4. **entail:** to require, need, or impose

   The people who work on high bridges make a good deal of money, but they also have to accept the risk the work *entails*.

5. **paramount:** main, chief, primary

   The diplomat's *paramount* concern was to see to it that all parties in the negotiations felt responsible for the outcome.

6. **transient:** short-lived, temporary

   Some psychological disorders are mild and *transient*; others are severe and chronic, lasting, in some cases, a lifetime.

7. **contention:** point of an argument, claim

   The *contention* of Susan Brownmiller's 1975 book *Against Our Will* was that rape was more about power than sex, an idea that was new at the time but is now widely accepted.

8. **denigrate:** to speak in a negative or an insulting way

   People who suffer from depression are often inclined to *denigrate* their accomplishments and focus on their shortcomings.

9. **denounce:** to condemn, to declare wrong or evil

   Once the revolution had begun, the king's former friends were quick to *denounce* him.

10. **injunction:** a command or court order stating that something must not be done.

    The court issued an *injunction* against the use of stun guns to subdue a suspect.

DIGGING DEEPER New Words Needed?

Looking Ahead   As our culture changes, we need new words to describe new experiences and responses. But sometimes, even when a word is desperately needed, the right one just doesn't materialize, or turn up.

1   These days everyone knows what a *blogger* is. Fifteen years ago, though, people would have looked dumbfounded if someone at a party had announced, "My wife is a passionate blogger." At that time, no one would have understood what the husband was saying about his wife—that she likes to go online to express and exchange ideas with an unseen audience in cyberspace. That's because *blogger*, like blogging, is a neologism. It's a word created to describe something new to our culture that once didn't exist.

2   In its origin, *blogger* belongs to a category that includes words like *moonlighting* and *hacker*. These words came into being to describe new experiences that hadn't occurred before. The word *moonlighting*, for instance, came into being as more and more people began holding two jobs, with one of the jobs requiring work at night. Similarly, as it became common for people to illegally access computer systems not their own, the word *hacker* came on the scene.

3   Based on examples like these, the English language seems to acquire new words in four steps: (1) Some new activity or behavior emerges; (2) a word is created to describe it; (3) numerous people use and popularize the word; and (4) the word becomes a part of the language. Easy and sensible as those four steps sound, Allan Metcalf, the author of *Predicting New Words*, would probably not agree. In fact, in his book, he lists several of what he calls the "neediest cases," i.e., situations or behaviors desperately in need of a word to describe them. Yet the need goes ignored. Among those words needed are the following:

1. A substitute for *boyfriend* or *girlfriend* when talking about men and women who are no longer in their teens and who have a committed relationship.

2. A word meaning "to state an opinion." The word *opine* exists, but no one uses it because people are likely to laugh when they hear it.

3. A word other than *yes* to indicate that you're listening to someone. *Yes* implies agreement, and you may disagree while still wishing to lend an ear.

4   Metcalf's list is actually based on an earlier list created by a *New York Times Magazine* editor in 1955, which means that these gaps in the language have existed for decades. The question that neither Metcalf nor

anyone else seems able to answer is why these gaps and others remain while some are quickly filled. Did we, for instance, desperately need a word for the illegal accessing of someone's computer—i.e., *hacking*—but never really needed a word to describe a fifty-five-year-old widow's current dating partner? Clearly our language changes all the time to meet the needs of the culture. But sometimes those needs go begging and no one really knows why that happens. In some ways, language has an inexplicable life of its own and may not always do our bidding, much as we would like to believe that it does.

Sharpening Your Skills

DIRECTIONS   Answer the following questions by filling in the blanks or circling the letter(s) of the correct response.

1. What kind of context clues to the meaning of *neologism* appears in the reading?
   a. example
   b. restatement
   c. contrast
   d. general knowledge

2. What word parts are additional clues to the meaning of *neologism*?
   Neo and _Log_ .

3. Which statement best paraphrases the point of this selection?
   a. As American culture changes, so does the language.
   b. Our language does not always supply us with the words we need.
   c. The language we use to describe our culture affects how we conduct our lives.
   d. The English language is constantly changing.

4. Based on the context, what does *inexplicable* in paragraph 4 mean?
   Not Explaining

▶ **SHARE YOUR THOUGHTS**
What people, ideas, or experiences can you think of that don't have words to express what they mean?

What is the word for a not married couple

▶ TEST 1   Reviewing the Key Points

DIRECTIONS   Answer the following questions by circling *T* (true) or *F* (false). *Note*: Read the questions carefully. Part of a question may be true and part may be false, making the whole sentence false.

T *F*   **1.** Although there are several different types of context clues, the following four are the most common: (1) restatement, (2) example, (3) comparison, and (4) contrast.

 gen. knowledge

T *F*   **2.** Context clues will always give you an exact dictionary definition.

T *F*   **3.** When you discover an unfamiliar word, scan both the rest of the sentence and the sentence that follows for a context clue. You may well find a clue that gives you a definition for the word you don't know.

T *F*   **4.** Colons, dashes, and parentheses can signal the presence of restatement clues. So, too, can words such as *unlike*, *but*, *similarly*, and *however*.   *contrast*

T *F*   **5.** Words like *with*, *and*, *for*, and *or* often signal the presence of contrast clues.   *no contrast = opposite*

T *F*   **6.** You should be alert to contrast clues whenever the author describes differences in people, things, times, or ideas.

T *F*   **7.** Particularly in textbooks, example clues are often introduced by phrases such as *for instance* and *for example*.

T *F*   **8.** Example clues never come after the words they illustrate.

T *F*   **9.** If you have a good context clue, you don't need to pay attention to word parts.

T *F*   **10.** One prefix can have several meanings.

To correct your test, turn to page 587. If one or more of your answers is incorrect, re-read the Rounding Up the Keys section of the chapter to find out where your mistake might be.

◆ **TEST 2**   **Using Context Clues**

DIRECTIONS   For each italicized word, use the context to determine an approximate meaning.

1. Although some smokers are *physiologically* addicted to cigarettes, others suffer from a dependence that is more of the mind than of the body.

   a. physically
   b. ridiculously
   c. endlessly
   d. critically

2. During the Eisenhower era (1953–1961), it was widely assumed that poverty had disappeared. In reality, poverty was *rife* in both urban and rural areas.

   a. decreasing
   b. disappearing
   c. widespread
   d. challenging

3. The process by which lawyers and judges examine *prospective* jurors can, sometimes, be lengthy.

   a. trustworthy
   b. untrustworthy
   c. possible
   d. unlikely

4. The two researchers were a study in contrasts when they answered questions: While the younger one liked to talk about his work, the older one showed more *restraint* and didn't reveal much.

   a. attention
   b. silence
   c. self-control
   d. satisfaction

5. In the 1950s, Dr. Benjamin Spock was considered an expert on the care of babies, and only the Bible outsold his book *The Common Sense Book of Baby and Child Care*. At his suggestion, breastfeeding, which had gone out of fashion, came back into *vogue*.

a. fashion

b. disagreement

c. conflict

d. history

6. The birth control pill has not been a universal *panacea*. One woman's medical concern became another woman's medical problem. To date, the Pill has neither significantly limited population growth nor ended unwanted pregnancies in the United States. (Paul Boyer et al., *The Enduring Vision*, 7th ed., p. 881. © Cengage Learning.)

a. mistake

b. solution

c. adoption

d. challenge

7. In 1980, with Democratic President Jimmy Carter's popularity *abysmally* low, Ronald Reagan, who promised a break with the past, won the presidency. (Adapted from Boyer et al., *The Enduring Vision*, p. 932.)

a. climbing

b. cheerfully

c. horribly

d. casually

8. In the nineteenth century, when workers rebelled against the *tempo* of factory production, owners responded by cutting wages or paying only for items produced rather than by the hour.

a. slowness

b. pace

c. length

d. description

9. The prehistoric tylosaurus was not a *terrestrial* animal; it lived mainly in water.
   a. pretty
   b. large
   c. land-based
   d. waterborne

10. Many people do not believe that human beings *evolved* from apes.
    a. developed
    b. divided
    c. ran
    d. changed

▶ **TEST 3**   **Using Context Clues**

DIRECTIONS   Read the sentence. Then for each italicized word, fill in the blanks to identify the kind of context clue and the approximate definition.

1. Union forces expected to win at the Battle of Bull Run, but instead they were *routed*.

   The _____ _Contrast_ _____ context clue suggests that *routed* means _____ _stopped_ _____.

2. Max Wertheimer's research led to new discoveries about the nature of *perception*—the processes by which we organize and understand impressions from the external world.

   The ____ _restatment_ ____ context clue suggests that *perception* means ____ _look at_ ____.

3. In the military, rules are *mandatory*. It's not a matter of soldiers deciding which ones they want to obey and which ones they do not.

   restatement

   The ____ _general knowledge_ ____ context clue suggests that *mandatory* means ____ _must obey_ ____.

4. As the first president, George Washington was keenly aware that his every act created a *precedent* for the future. Once, while on a visit to Boston, Washington was informed that John Hancock, the governor of Massachusetts, was ill and would be unable to call. Believing that governors were less important than presidents, Washington forced Hancock to appear despite the man's obvious illness. (Alan Gitelson et al, *American Government*, 8th ed. © Cengage Learning.)

   example

   The ____ _restatement_ ____ context clue suggests that *precedent* means ____ _Something that went before_ ____.

5. Many members of the music industry believe that the major record companies would be better off *consolidating* rather than trying to go it alone in an increasingly difficult market.

The _____contrast_____ context clue suggests that *consolidating* means _____working together_____.

6. Polls are *ingrained* in the political process; they have, in fact, been firmly established for over thirty years despite coming under constant criticism.

   The _____restatement_____ context clue suggests that *ingrained* means _____put into use_____.

7. The musician felt herself highly *compensated* by the loud applause, which was good because she was being paid very little for the performance.

   The _____contrast_____ context clue suggests that *compensated* means _____to pay someone for work or time_____.

8. When a state trooper stops a car and asks to see a license, he or she expects immediate *compliance*.

   The _____example_____ context clue suggests that *compliance* means _____following the rules_____.

9. William Marcy "Boss" Tweed, the boss of New York City's Democratic machine during the 1860s and 1870s, *detested* political cartoons. Shortly after viewing a cartoon by Thomas Nast, who was critical of New York politicians, Tweed was said to have ordered his lieutenants to "Stop them damned pictures." (Adapted from Gitelson et al., *American Government*, 8th ed., p. 161.)

   The _____example_____ context clue suggests that *detested* means _____Not liking something_____.

10. In contrast to the Great Plains, where people of different nationalities created their own ethnic *enclaves*, western mining camps were ethnic melting pots.

    The _____contrast_____ context clue suggests that *enclaves* means _____just one kind of person_____.

▶ **TEST 4**   **Using Word Parts and Context Clues**

DIRECTIONS   Using your knowledge of context clues and word parts, select the best definition for each italicized word by circling the appropriate letter.[†]

Word Parts	Meanings
cline	lean, bend
clu, clud	shut
de	down, from, away, out
ex	out, from, away
pre	before
re	back, backward
sol, soli	alone, lonely
trac	pull

1. She had once been a wealthy woman, but over the years her fortune had *declined*.

   a. decreased
   b. grown larger
   c. changed
   d. disappeared

2. She had never liked *exclusive* clubs that made a point of leaving people out.

   a. not open to all
   b. open to all
   c. fancy
   d. expensive

3. He had been frightened on the way up the mountain, but it was the *descent* that really scared him.

   a. way up
   b. way down
   c. temperature
   d. challenge

[†]The word parts included here may have additional meanings.

4. Her critics tried to *detract* from the value of her proposal, but they only succeeded in proving her right.

   a. add to

   b. take away from

   c. imitate

   d. draw conclusions

5. That decision is too *premature*. Nothing should be decided before all the facts are in.

   a. silly

   b. early

   c. late

   d. unpopular

6. The owner of the supermarket demanded that the paper *retract* its original statement, but the editor publicly refused to do so.

   a. revise

   b. deny

   c. carry

   d. take back

7. Although he liked to spend time among friends, he still needed some *solitude*.

   a. amusement

   b. extra time

   c. time alone

   d. financial assistance

8. After *reclining* in the hammock for most of the afternoon, he complained of fatigue from too much yard work.

   a. sitting

   b. yawning

   c. lying

   d. chatting

9. Her decision to take the retirement package *precludes* her return-ing even on a part-time basis.

   a. makes easier

   b. eliminates

   c. allows for

   d. encourages

10. The *extraction* of the minerals had left the earth riddled with ugly holes.

    a. refining

    b. taking out

    c. selling

    d. melting

▶ **TEST 5** **Using Word Parts and Context Clues**

DIRECTIONS Using your knowledge of context clues and word parts, write an appropriate definition for each italicized word.

Word Parts	Meanings
am, amor	love, liking, friendliness
dis	not, lack of, apart
equ	equal
inter	between

1. Let the kids settle the argument by themselves. Don't *intervene*.

   Intervene means ___get between___.

2. How can you *equate* her problems with his? He doesn't have enough money for food. She can't afford the insurance on her second car.

   Equate means ___make it the same___.

3. After they had been in business together for several years, their relationship was no longer *amicable*.

   Amicable means ___liking each other___.

4. In her case, a request is *equivalent* to a command. The tone of her voice makes it clear you're not allowed to refuse.

   Equivalent means ___the same___.

5. After he testified against the company, the accountant's *interaction* with his coworkers was strained.

   Interaction means ___being social to___.

6. They may be brothers, but their personalities are remarkably *disparate*. They don't have anything in common.

   Disparate means ___not the same___.

7. She kept on trying to *interject* her opinions into the argument, but no one paid any attention.

   Interject means ___Say excuse me + get their attention___.

8. The profits were not distributed *equitably*. Two of the owners received 70 percent of the profits, while the other two received only 30 percent.

   Equitably means ___the same___.

9. The duck approached its mate with *amorous* intentions, but she quacked in outrage and flew away.

   Amorous means ___to like him___.

10. He wanted to *dissociate* himself from his early career. But the public could not forget what he had done as a young man.

    Dissociate means ___get rid of___.

▶ **TEST 6**   **Enlarging Your Academic Vocabulary**

DIRECTIONS   Circle the letter of the sentence that uses the opening word correctly.

1. **fertile** *able to produce*

   a. All attempts by the defendant's attorney to convince the jury of her innocence were *fertile*.

   b. Isaac Asimov had such a *fertile* mind that he could write several books per year.

   c. Anyone *fertile* in basic arithmetic can see that the numbers in the congressional budget don't add up.

2. **allocation** *portion*

   a. A home in such a bad condition could be sold only because of its prime *allocation*.

   b. Anyone living on a small income is faced with an *allocation* problem: What should I buy and what should I do without?

   c. "To each his own" is an *allocation* that goes back to the ancient Romans.

3. **symbiotic** *relationship good for both sides*

   a. The *symbiotic* relationship between humans and dogs existed in prehistoric times.

   b. The quarterback engineered a last-minute drive that was *symbiotic* for the team's entire season: They always came through when they had to.

   c. Chest pains can be *symbiotic* for a serious illness.

4. **entail** *what's needed*

   a. The candidate left his startling confession to the *entails* of his speech when half the audience had already left.

   b. Sauces that include cream are hard to *entail* for people who cannot tolerate milk and milk products.

   c. Learning a language *entails*, among other things, the often boring task of memorizing words in a new vocabulary.

5. **paramount** *important*

   a. He had been a *paramount* of the community, and his funeral was attended by a great number of people.

   b. Self-reliance is the *paramount* message put forth by many motivational writers.

   c. For a majority of voters, foreign policy is an issue too *paramount* to be taken into consideration.

6. **transient** *short-lived*

   a. Fads are always *transient* and unchanging.

   b. Because she was staying in the country only a few days, the agent marked her passport *Transient.*

   c. My opponent's motives should be *transient* to anyone who cares to listen carefully to what she says.

7. **contention** *main point*

   a. Some claim that power is a greater source of *contention* than sex.

   b. His span of *contention* is very limited; he can't stay focused for more than a few minutes.

   c. The artist left the entire *contention* of her studio to the local museum.

8. **denigrate** *speak badly about*

   a. If you are a *denigrate*, you probably have bad genes.

   b. It's disgraceful to *denigrate* people because of physical handicaps.

   c. The actor has a *denigrating* voice that makes him an ideal choice for playing villains.

9. **denounce** *criticize*

   a. The Congresswoman forcefully *denounced* the latest orders coming from the White House.

   b. As the organ was playing, the pastor *denounced* the couple man and wife.

   c. In a classic mystery, the *denouncement* comes at the end when the murderer's identity is finally revealed.

10. **injunction** *legal order against something*

   a. The *injunction* of Hollywood Boulevard and Vine Street in Los Angeles has been famous since the 1920s.

   b. The attorneys tried to obtain an *injunction* against the publication of an article that contained some very unflattering remarks about their client, all of them true.

   c. To add *injunction* to injury, the reporter misspelled Shakira's name.

Understanding Sentence Relationships

3

"When a text lacks explicit links between sentences, the reader must infer those links."
—Judith W. Irwin, *reading researcher*

"Live in fragments no longer, only connect . . ."
—E. M. Forster, *novelist*

Some textbook passages require a second reading. A few even need a third. When this happens, you need to slow down your normal reading rate so you can do a close reading of the passage sentence by sentence. A major goal of a close reading is to figure out how the previous sentence relates or connects to the sentence that follows it. To help you accomplish that goal, this chapter introduces some common relationships likely to underlie both sentence pairs and groups of sentences.

The Starting Point for Them All: General and Specific

While not all sentences make comparisons or describe cause and effect, all of the sentences in your textbooks can be identified according to how general or how specific they are in relation to one another. For that reason, the relationship between general and specific sentences gets some extra attention in this chapter.

General Sentences Are Summary Statements

With the exception of poets and novelists, writers almost always need **general sentences** to sum up different but in some way related people, events, ideas, or thoughts. Take, for instance, this sentence: "Over the past fifty years, the link between marriage and parenthood has weakened."

Although how general or how specific a sentence is changes with the **context,** or setting, in which it appears, this sentence is most likely a general sentence. It's likely to be general because it sums up several decades of change in a huge number of people. That's what general sentences do. They sum up the experience of individual people, events, or ideas. It's the summarizing ability of general sentences that makes them so essential to both writing and speaking.

Just think about it. Can you imagine asking someone how their day was and having them record it minute by minute? "Well I woke up at eight. I had my breakfast, I got dressed...." You would be beside yourself with boredom and irritation. What you expect and what you usually get with a question like that is a **generalization** *based on* the individual events. "It was great." "It was long." "It was the day from hell."

Why General Sentences Can't Stand Alone

The problem with general sentences is this: They cover a lot of ground and are broad enough to be misunderstood. Consider our sample sentence on marriage and parenthood. With only that sentence to go on, it's hard to tell how the link between the two has weakened. Are we being told that married people don't want to be parents anymore? Or is the author saying that married people aren't good parents? Or perhaps the author is arguing that more people are becoming parents without getting married?

This is a typical problem for general sentences, precisely because they sum up a number of different people, events, or ideas. As a result, they are open to several different interpretations. That's why the general and specific relationship is so central to communication. *While general sentences summarize a number of individual and varied experiences, the specific sentences nail down precisely what specific events, people, or ideas the writer or speaker has in mind.*

Sometimes specific sentences accomplish this by clarifying the meaning of a word or phrase. Sometimes they offer an illustration or proof. Here, for instance, is the more specific sentence that follows the general one shown above. "The share of babies born to unmarried mothers increased eight-fold from 1960 to 2008."[†] Now we know exactly what the author meant by the verb *weakened*. A growing number of people don't think being married is the first step toward having children.

Now that you have a basic understanding of the terms *general* and *specific*, let's look at one of the most common ways these two types of sentences link up in reading.

General Sentences and Specific Illustrations

But writers don't use specific sentences just to clarify key words or phrases. To make their ideas clear to readers, writers often follow a general statement with a specific example or illustration. Take, for example, this sentence: "In 2001, China's Tiananmen Square was the scene of great tragedy."

Now if you have some background knowledge about what happened in Tiananmen Square in 2001, you might not need a specific example to understand the depth of the tragedy. However, unless the author is dealing with experts on the subject, he or she can't assume that readers can supply the necessary information. Thus, that general sentence about the tragedy in Tiananmen Square gets a companion like this one: "During the demonstrations in the square, five people set fire to themselves in order to protest China's lack of a true democracy." For the most part, in prose, as opposed to fiction, general and specific sentences always go hand in hand.

[†]Sentences come from the *Pew Research Newsletter*, April 19, 2002.

Transitions Are Useful Clues

Transitions are words, phrases, and entire sentences that writers use to help readers move smoothly from sentence to sentence. They are verbal bridges that tell readers, "Look out! Here's what's coming up next."

The phrases "for example" and "more precisely" are both transitions. So, too, are the words and phrases listed in the box below. If you spot any one of these transitions at the beginning of a sentence, it's usually there to tell readers, "What's coming up next is a specific example of the general point just made." Here's an illustration:

> *Chimes of Freedom*, a collection of Bob Dylan songs put out in honor of Amnesty International's[†] fiftieth birthday, features an odd mix of musical artists. For instance, folk singer and political activist Pete Seeger is in the lineup along with former teen idol Miley Cyrus.[†]

Transitions to Watch For ◆	for instance	more precisely	in short
	for example	more specifically	in brief
	as an illustration	in other words	typically

General and Specific Within Sentences

In the sentence below, the general and specific ideas are connected in a single sentence. The author is writing about Haiti's battle for independence from Britain and France. Note, in particular, the colon (:) that links the two parts of the sentence.

Colons are common in sentences where the writer wants to follow up a general point with an example or a more specific restatement:

> Ill-armed, barefoot and hungry, the rebels fought against huge odds: Britain dispatched an armada of 218 ships, and its troops battled for five years before withdrawing. (Adam Hochchild, "Tragic Island," *The New York Times*, January 1, 2012, p. 8.)

In this case, the colon introduces a specific example of what the author means when he says Haiti's rebels "fought against huge odds."

[†]Amnesty International is an organization founded to protect the rights of political prisoners around the world.
[†]Miley Cyrus's performance on *Chimes of Freedom* has won critical raves.

Although used less frequently, the semicolon sometimes steps in to tell readers that the author is going to illustrate or explain the previous sentence:

In the eyes of many, Thomas Paine helped launch the American Revolution; Paine's pamphlet *Common Sense* effectively argued that the American colonies would reap huge economic benefits by throwing off British rule.

READING KEYS

◆ General statements can be interpreted or understood in a number of ways. Thus, they need clarification through more specific explanation and examples. The more specific explanation narrows the range of meanings and helps eliminate confusion between reader and writer.

◆ Because communication relies so heavily on general statements, skillful readers are alert to specific explanations and examples offered as clarification. They know that the specific sentences will narrow the range of meanings the more general sentences might suggest.

◆ When you are trying to untangle the ideas in a particularly difficult passage, it helps to determine where the author's general ideas are located. Then check to see if they are further developed by more specific illustrations and explanations.

◆ EXERCISE 1   Matching the Specific to the General

DIRECTIONS One general sentence is followed by two more specific ones. Circle the letter of the sentence that clarifies the opening statement.

1. Some people just will not believe that Elvis is dead.

   a. Decades after his death, websites with names like "Elvis Lives" report sightings of the man once called the "King of Rock and Roll."

   b. Sting, Sheryl Crow, and Justin Timberlake are just a few of the musicians who have said Elvis was a big influence on their music.

2. Stress takes a toll on the body.

   a. Unlike the chronic stress of an illness, the stress of working toward an achievable goal can actually boost one's sense of well-being.

   b. Prolonged stress has been shown to weaken the immune system, leaving the body prone to illness.

3. The Roman Empire was a victim of its own success.

    a. As time went on, the Romans were unable to control the territories they had conquered, and the empire did not have enough soldiers to suppress rebellions.

    b. The Romans were known for being cruel to the inhabitants of the territories they conquered.

4. Many well-known writers are in the habit of re-reading their favorite books.

    a. J. K. Rowling, the author of the Harry Potter books, told Oprah Winfrey that her favorite book was *The Woman Who Walked into Doors*, a novel about a woman in an abusive relationship.

    b. Best-selling writer Stephen King has read *Lord of the Flies* at least three times.

IDIOM ALERT: Backwater

Describing a place as a backwater suggests that it is not very up-to-date or important in relation to the rest of the world. Here, for instance, the writer points out that Islamabad, the capital of Pakistan, is most certainly *not* a backwater: "Islamabad is a lively, bustling city, not some rural *backwater*."

◆ **EXERCISE 2**   **Understanding General and Specific Relationships**

    DIRECTIONS   Circle the letter of the statement that most accurately describes each pair of sentences.

    EXAMPLES

1. [1]Scientology was founded in 1952 by science fiction writer L. Ron Hubbard. [2]Some people call Scientology a cult; others call it a religion.

    a. Sentence 1 makes a general statement about Scientology. Sentence 2 offers a more specific explanation or illustration of that point.

    b. Sentences 1 and 2 are on the same level of generality.

2. [1]Although movie star dog Rin Tin Tin was the focus of ads encouraging dog owners to donate their dogs to fight the Germans on the battlefields of World War II, his canine origins were German, not American. [2]Rin Tin Tin was actually German-born, the offspring of a breed specifically developed to be used as dog soldiers in the German army.[†]

   (a.) Sentence 1 makes a general statement about the role of Rin Tin Tin in World War II. Sentence 2 offers a more specific explanation or illustration of that point.

   b. Sentences 1 and 2 are on the same level of generality.

EXPLANATION For *a* to be the correct answer in the first example the second sentence would have to further explain or illustrate sentence 1. But there is no reference to the founding of Scientology or to L. Ron Hubbard. Instead we hear about different perspectives on Scientology, making *b* the correct answer. In the second example, sentence *b* rephrases, in more specific form, the explanation of Rin Tin Tin's Germanic origins. That's why *a* is the correct answer in this case.

1. [1]Aspirin has been in use for a very long time. [2]In fact, over 2,000 years ago, the physician Hippocrates described how he prescribed willow bark, which contains a natural form of aspirin.

   a. Sentence 1 makes a general statement about the history of aspirin. Sentence 2 offers a more specific explanation or illustration of that point.

   b. Sentences 1 and 2 are on the same level of generality.

2. [1]The term *conformity* means changing one's behavior to match that of a group. [2]For example, you may have showed conformity when everyone around you stood up to applaud a performance you considered awful, but you got to your feet anyway. (Adapted from Douglas Bernstein and Peggy Nash, *Essentials of Psychology*. © Cengage Learning.)

   a. Sentence 1 makes a general statement about the nature of conformity. Sentence 2 offers a more specific explanation or illustration of that point.

   b. Sentences 1 and 2 are on the same level of generality.

[†]See Susan Orlean's *Rin Tin Tin: The Life and the Legend*. It's spellbinding.

3. [1]Reggae singer Bob Marley was born in 1945 in a Jamaican backwater called Saint Ann. [2]When he was twelve, he moved to Kingston, Jamaica, and took up residence in a place called Trench Town.

   a. Sentence 1 makes a general statement about the life of singer Bob Marley. Sentence 2 offers a more specific explanation or illustration of that point.

   b. Sentences 1 and 2 are on the same level of generality.

4. [1]In some Muslim countries, women must cover their heads and part or all of their face out of fear that they will be accused of immorality. [2]In Saudi Arabia, for instance, the Mutawa, or religious police, have been known to arrest a woman found walking on the street without having her head and face covered.

   a. Sentence 1 makes a general statement about women in some Muslim countries. Sentence 2 offers a more specific explanation or illustration of that point.

   b. Sentences 1 and 2 are on the same level of generality.

Not all Muslim countries force women to cover their faces completely.

5. [1]Daniel Ellsberg, the man responsible for leaking the Pentagon Papers[†] to the press, is a controversial figure. [2]While some see Ellsberg as a heroic figure, who did his country a great service, others see him as a traitor, who should have gone to prison.

   a. Sentence 1 makes a general statement about the way people view Daniel Ellsberg. Sentence 2 offers a more specific explanation or illustration of that point.

   b. Sentences 1 and 2 are on the same level of generality.

READING KEYS

◆ Transitions such as *for instance*, *for example*, and *in fact* are good indicators that the relationship binding sentences together is general statement and specific illustration.

◆ The colon is likely to introduce a more specific illustration of a general idea that was just introduced. Semicolons sometimes fulfill the same function.

WEB QUEST/CLASS ACTION

What European leader said that the veiling of women was "not welcome" in his country? _President Nicolas Sarkozy_ In general, how did the Muslim women of that country react to that statement? _They Protested_ A number of Western governments have enacted laws forbidding women to wear veils that cover their faces. The officials who support this position argue that the veils are anti-democratic and encourage discrimination against women. To their surprise, many of the women they say they want to protect insist that the veil grants them freedom of movement.

Should women who want to wear head scarves or veils over their faces because their religion demands it be left alone to do what they want? Or should the government intervene when a religious custom appears to discriminate against women? Be prepared to discuss in class.

[†]Pentagon Papers: A secret report about the Vietnam War ordered by Secretary of Defense Robert McNamara in 1967. The report's negative assessment of the war contradicted the government's public optimism. When Ellsberg, a member of the State Department, found out about it, he brought the report to the *New York Times*.

◆ Making More Connections Between Sentences

Each time you read a new sentence, you need to be able to answer questions like these: "What does this sentence have to do with the one that came before it?" "What do I know now that I didn't know before?" To help you answer those questions, here are several more relationships that sentences can express. Keep in mind that as the writer's ideas change so do the relationships that connect them.

1. Connecting Cause to Effect

No matter what the subject matter, writers frequently link their sentences through **cause and effect**. They explain, that is, how one event (the cause) led to another event (the effect). Here's an example of that relationship within the same sentence:

> To pay back years of war debt, the British Parliament passed the Stamp Act of 1765 on goods such as sugar and tea.

Note that the author could have presented the events in this sentence as unrelated, e.g., "The British had years of war debt to pay. In 1865, the English Parliament passed the Stamp Act on goods such as sugar and tea." But part of what the author wants readers to understand is that one event led to, or caused, the other. That relationship is part of the content.

To make that cause and effect relationship as clear as possible, the author opens with the phrase, "To pay back years of war debt." Like so many sentence openings, this one directs readers to the relationship the author has in mind, in this case cause and effect.

In the next example, a cause and effect relationship connects two different sentences.

> British taxes on tea and sugar made both items extremely expensive for the American colonists. Furious at having their lives made more difficult by foreign interference, the colonists rebelled.

In this case you have what's called a *chain of causes and effects*. In other words, effect turns into a cause that produces another effect. The first sentence explains that British taxes caused tea and sugar to become more expensive. The added expense then fueled the colonists anger at the British and caused rebellion. If you diagram the chain of relationships, it would look like this:

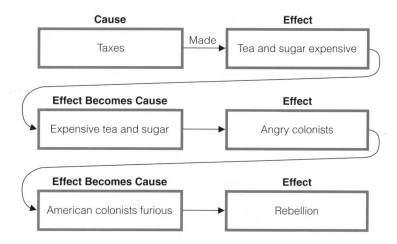

A single cause and effect relationship is more likely to unite the parts of a sentence. However, when two sentences are united by this relationship, they might well contain a chain or cycle of causes and effects, like the one shown above, in which the effect of one event becomes the cause of another.

Transitional Clues to Cause and Effect Relationships

The words listed below usually signal that the sentences you are reading are making a connection between cause and effect.

Transitions Linking Cause to Effect[†] ◆	as a result	in response
	consequently	thanks to
	due to	therefore
	in reaction to	thus

Verbs Are Additional Clues

Like the above transitions, verbs can also signal the presence of a cause and effect relationship.

[†]You'll learn about more transitions and verbs linking cause to effect in Chapter 7, Recognizing Patterns of Organization.

Verbs Linking Cause to Effect ◆	affect	incur	incite
	begin	induce	set off
	bring about	produce	cause
	create	stimulate	trigger

Once you determine that the sentences you are reading are describing how cause led to effect, be sure you know precisely what events or experiences are presented as causes and precisely which ones are described as effects. You should also be clear about which effects also become causes of additional effects. (For more on cause and effect, see Chapter 7.)

○━ READING KEYS

◆ Sentences connecting cause to effect describe how one event produces or produced another.

◆ Like transitions, verbs are also clues to the presence of cause and effect.

◆ Good readers know exactly when an effect becomes the cause of another event or series of events.

◆ EXERCISE 3   Connecting Cause to Effect

DIRECTIONS   Read each sentence or pair of sentences. Then fill in the blanks that follow.

EXAMPLE   Because many of us don't trust our ability to understand or question statistics, we all too willingly accept that every statistic cited as proof of a social problem is a hard fact rather than an educated guess.

In this sentence, the cause is _we don't understand statistics_ .

The effect is _we accept the statistics without question_ .

EXPLANATION   As it so often does, the cause comes at the beginning of the sentence—many of us don't feel comfortable with statistics. That cause is then followed by the effect—we treat statistics as facts that need not be questioned.

1. Disgusted by the policies of President William Howard Taft, former president Theodore Roosevelt decided to form the "Bull Moose" Party in 1912 and run again for president.

   In this sentence, the cause is _disgusted by the politics President Theodore_ .

   The effect is _form the Bull Moose Party in 1912_

2. In addition to putting us [Americans] at a marked disadvantage in the global marketplace, our ignorance of other languages and cultures is downright dangerous to our national security. (Gary Ferraro and Susan Andreatto, *Cultural Anthropology*, p. 129. © Cengage Learning.)

   In this sentence, the cause is _In addition to putting us Americans disadvantage at a marked in the global marketplace_
   The effect is _Other languages are Dangerous_ .

3. Walt Disney, the brilliant creator of famed cartoon figures like Donald Duck, Goofy, and Mickey Mouse, was a harsh and tight-fisted employer, who had a hard time giving credit to others. By 1936, Disney's employees were so fed up, they went out on strike.

   In the first sentence, the cause is _Walt Disney was a harsh and tight fisted employer_
   The effect introduced in the second sentence is _Disney's employees were out on strike_ .

4. The effects of global warming are showing themselves most strikingly in the Arctic, where icebergs are melting and polar bears now swim for miles before finding a place to rest.

   In this sentence, the cause is _global warming is slowing in the Arctic_
   The effects are _icebergs are melting, polar bears are now swimming for miles before finding a place to rest._

Arctic icebergs are melting, leaving polar bears without resting places as they search for food in Arctic waters.

© Ulrich Flemming

2. Describing Contrast or Difference

To evaluate ideas and events, writers often need to **contrast**, or point out differences between, two topics. In the pair of sentences that follow, the authors contrast two different approaches to studying other cultures.

[1]The *emic* approach refers to the insider view, which seeks to describe another culture in terms of the categories, concepts, and perceptions of the people being studied. [2]By contrast, the *etic* approach refers to the outside view, in which anthropologists use their own categories and concepts to describe the culture under analysis. (Gary Ferraro and Susan Andreatta, *Cultural Anthropology*, p. 16. © Cengage Learning.)

Read sentence 1 and you know that the *emic* approach to studying other cultures uses that culture's concepts and categories to describe cultural characteristics. After you read sentence 2, you know that the *etic* approach *differs* from the *emic* approach. It differs because it relies on the concepts and categories that belong to the anthropologists' culture rather than the culture under observation.

And, yes, a relationship that contrasts people, events, or ideas can most certainly connect parts of the same sentence.

During the presidential campaign of 1954, Dwight D. Eisenhower portrayed himself as a man of action and won, while his opponent, Adlai Stevenson, presented himself as a serious intellectual and lost.

Transitional Clues

In the first example above, the second sentence opens with the transition "By contrast." That transition is obviously a tip-off to a relationship based on difference. The transitions listed below are additional clues to this particular relationship.

Transitions Emphasizing Difference		
although	just the opposite
but	on the contrary
however	quite the contrary
in a different way	whereas
in opposition to	while
in or by contrast	

🔑 READING KEYS

- ◆ Sentences related by contrast highlight the difference between two topics.
- ◆ Readers who want to understand this relationship need to clearly determine what two topics are being contrasted. They also need to understand how the two topics differ as well as what the differences prove or illustrate.

◆ EXERCISE 4 Defining Differences

DIRECTIONS   Read the following sentences. Then fill in the blanks.

EXAMPLE   In contrast to *external motivation*, i.e., the promise of rewards or punishment, *internal motivation* is based on personal desires or longings that are not always conscious, like the need for parental approval.

This sentence contrasts what two topics? ___external motivation___ versus ___internal motivation___

What is the difference between the two? External motivation is based on outside punishment or reward; internal motivation comes from within and is not necessarily conscious.

EXPLANATION   Here again the transition "in contrast" introduces the difference between the two topics identified. The difference is the source of motivation, which can be internal or external.

1. "The sympathetic listener makes no judgments about what's said. The critical listener, however, evaluates both the content and tone of the message."

   These sentences contrast what two topics? _The Sympathetic Listener_
   versus _The Critical listener_

   What is the difference between the two? _They Both evaluates_
   The content and tone of message.

2. Facts can be verified or checked for accuracy. Opinions, in contrast, cannot be proven true or false.

   These sentences contrast what two topics? _facts_
   with _Opinions_

   What is the difference between the two? _Cannot be Proven_
   True or false

3. Unlike legislators, state judges are permitted very little outside income. (Ann Bowman and Richard Kearney, *State and Local Government*, p. 270. © Cengage Learning.)

   This sentence contrasts what two topics? _legislators_
   with _State Judges_

   What is the difference between the two? _Permitted very_
   little outside income

4. People from *monochronic cultures*—for example, the United States, Germany, and Switzerland—view time in linear fashion, prefer to do one thing at a time, and place a high value on punctuality. People from some other cultures tend to be *polychronic*, preferring to do many things at the same time and seeing no particular value in punctuality.

   These sentences contrast what two topics? _Monochronic cultures and_
   and _Polychronic_

What's the difference between the two? <u>Preferring</u>
<u>to do many things at the Same time</u>
<u>and Seeing no Particular value in</u>
<u>Punctuality.</u>

3. Making Comparisons

Writers who organize information based on **comparison** point out how two ideas, events, things, or people are, in some way, similar. Here's an example in which the comparison relationship connects different parts of the same sentence.

> Bright, witty, and articulate,* Adlai Stevenson was intellectually head and shoulders above every one of his political contemporaries until the equally bright, witty, and articulate John F. Kennedy came on the scene.

In this case, the author starts off with a statement about the politician Adlai Stevenson. The author then links the second part to the first by making a comparison: John F. Kennedy was Stevenson's peer in wit, eloquence,* and brains.

As you would expect, comparison can also connect two different sentences, for example:

> George Pullman, the inventor of the railroad sleeping car, took a hard line with workers during the Pullman strike of 1894: He refused to negotiate and hired replacement workers. President Grover Cleveland took a similar approach and ordered federal troops to put an end to the strike.

The first sentence describes George Pullman's approach to striking workers. Then in the second sentence, the author uses the phrase "took a similar approach" to tell you that President Grover Cleveland followed the same pattern. In short, the two sentences are linked by a comparison.

Transitional Clues

Here again, transitions can sometimes help you identify the comparison relationship. All of the following signal that the author is about to tell you how two people, things, events, places, or experiences resemble one another.

---

*articulate: good with words.
*eloquence: gift for language.

Transitions Identifying Comparison ♦	Along the same lines
	Based on the same principle
	Following in the footsteps of
	In the same vein
	Likewise, in a like or same manner
	Similar to, similarly

⊶ READING KEY

♦ As with sentences united by contrast, the comparison relationship gives up its message more quickly if you determine what two things are being compared and identify their similarities along with the point they explain or prove.

♦ EXERCISE 5   Seeing the Similarities

DIRECTIONS   Read each pair of sentences. Then fill in the blanks.

EXAMPLE   Mark Twain's *The Adventures of Tom Sawyer* (1876) can be read as a children's book, but it also offers adult readers a rather sophisticated take on American culture. The same is true of Twain's later work, *The Adventures of Huckleberry Finn* (1884), only more so: Huck's story is a critique* of social conformity and race relations in America.

What two topics are compared in these two sentences?

The Adventures of Tom Sawyer   and   The Adventures of Huckleberry Finn

What similarity do the two topics share?

Both can be read as children's books, but the content is also sophisticated enough for adults.

EXPLANATION   In this example, the author starts out by telling readers that Tom Sawyer is more than a children's book. She then uses a transition, "The same is true," at the beginning of the sentence to signal to readers that she is going to say something similar about a second

———————

*critique: analysis.

topic, in this case, *The Adventures of Huckleberry Finn*, which resembles Twain's novel *The Adventures of Tom Sawyer*.

1. Like the French in Vietnam, the Americans got bogged down in a guerilla* war they could not win.

   What two topics are compared in this sentence?

   _____French_____ and _____Americans_____

   What similarity do the two topics share?

   _____Guerilla War could not be won._____

2. Long considered safe from virus attacks, the Mac operating system is secure no more. Like the Windows operating system, it too has been successfully hit by a hard-to-eliminate virus.

   What two topics are compared in these sentences?

   _____Windows_____ and _____Mac_____

   What similarity do the two topics share?

   _____Being hit by Viruses._____

3. Around 1910, a group of artists later known as the "Ashcan School" emerged in America; the goal of the group was to make urban life the focus of their painting. A group with similar intentions emerged in the 1920s, with "American scene" painters concentrating on the plain everyday reality of American life.

   What two topics are compared in these two sentences?

   _____Ashcan School_____ and _____American Scene_____

   What similarity do the two topics share?

   _____Paintings_____

4. Much like the popular game *Angry Birds*, *Ninja Dogs* favors vivid colors and a cartoon style. Also like *Angry Birds*, which is focused on destroying the enemy with a slingshot, *Ninja Dogs* launches big-headed dogs into the air with the goal of destroying enemy cats.

---

*guerilla: person not fighting a war in conventional terms but instead taking a hit-and-run approach.

Which two topics are compared in these two sentences?

Angry Birds and _Ninja Dogs_

What similarities do the two topics share?

Cartoon Style and Colors and Destroying Enemies

🔑 READING KEYS

◆ In response to comparison relationships that connect sentence parts or whole sentences, readers need to identify the two topics along with their similarities.

◆ Writers don't rely on one single relationship throughout a reading. The ideas writers choose to communicate dictate the relationships sentences express.

◆ Aware that relationships in and between sentences change with the writer's thoughts, skillful readers stay alert to the various relationships that link the ideas in a reading.

4. Agreement Followed by Modification

Writers often acknowledge or agree that some state of affairs is either true, long accepted, or widely believed before they challenge, modify, or revise what they've just said.

> Although most people believe that urban riots are a modern problem, they have actually been with us since the 1700s.

In this example, the author first acknowledges what's conventionally believed about urban riots. He then challenges that belief by stating the true state of affairs: Urban riots have been around for a much longer period of time.

Here's the same relationship, only this time it connects two different sentences:

> Descriptions of memory development generally focus on children's use of strategies to enhance* recall. However, many researchers now argue that this emphasis is not adequate to explain the full complexity of cognitive processing in children. (Adapted from Danuta Bukatko and Marvin W. Daehler, *Child Development*, p. 317. © Cengage Learning.)

---

*enhance: improve.

In this case, the first sentence acknowledges the traditional view of memory development. The second sentence then explains how this point of view has been revised.

Transitional Clues

Despite being extremely common, sentences connected by agreement followed by modification are among the most problematic. Readers who aren't paying close attention sometimes fail to notice when the writer goes on to modify or undercut what he or she just said was true. Then, all of a sudden, they discover that the reading has ceased to make sense. This won't happen to you if you (1) remember that writers often agree in order to pave the way for disagreement and (2) remain alert to the presence of the transitions like the ones listed below. All of these transitions can be used right after the author has said, "Yes, this is true." They tell the reader when the writer is getting ready to say "But here is where I disagree."

Transitions Indicating Agreement- Modification ◆	But	Nonetheless
	Despite that fact	Still
	Even though	While this is true
	Having said that	Yet
	However	

Once you know that the agreement-modification relationship links sentence parts or entire sentences, be sure you can identify what point of view has been acknowledged. Then figure out exactly how the author has revised or reversed that initial position.

⚷ READING KEYS

- ◆ Sentences based on the agreement followed by modification relationship describe an existing or assumed state of affairs and then modify it in some way.
- ◆ Stay alert to transitional signals announcing something is about to change in the author's line of thinking.
- ◆ Make sure you understand the traditional or conventional point of view as well as the author's revision of it.

♦ **EXERCISE 6**   **Noticing the Modification**

DIRECTIONS   Read the following sentences. Then fill in the blanks.

EXAMPLE   Yes, freedom of speech is a right that needs to be protected. But that doesn't mean we should let someone cry "fire" in a crowded building.

The author begins by agreeing that _freedom of speech needs protection_.

After that acknowledgment, how does the author revise, challenge, or contradict what's just been said? _He says freedom of speech doesn't mean_

that we should be allowed to yell "fire" in a crowded building.

EXPLANATION   The sentence begins by agreeing that freedom of speech needs to be protected. The transition *but* then signals a change in direction. At this point, the author identifies circumstances in which free speech should not be encouraged.

1. Brainstorming has been repeatedly described as a source of creative thinking. Research, however, has never confirmed its value as a source of creativity.

    The author begins by agreeing that _Brainstorming is a_ _Source of creative thinking_. After that agreement, how does the author revise, modify, or contradict what's just been said? _Research, however, has never confirmed its value as a source of creativity_

2. Educational historian Diane Ravitch is correct: In poll after poll, parents generally think their neighborhood public schools are doing a good to great job. Yet, somehow when those same parents are asked about the quality of public school education nationwide, they say the public school system is in deep trouble.

    The author begins by agreeing that _the Public schools_ _are Doing a good job_. After that agreement, how does the author revise, modify, or contradict what's just been said? _The School System is in Deep Trouble._

3. Although scientists thought until recently that humans were born with a certain number of brain cells and would never generate more, they now know better. In the 1990s...researchers determined during autopsies that adult human brains contained quite a few new neurons. (Gretchen Reynolds, "Jogging Your Brain," *New York Times Magazine*, April 22, 2012, p. 46.)

The author begins by agreeing that _humans were born with a certain number of brain cells_. After that agreement, how does the author revise, modify, or contradict what's just been said? _Adult human brains contained quite a few new Neurons._

4. While everyone agrees that there are cybercriminals on the Web, there is widespread disagreement when it comes to how to combat that threat.

The author begins by agreeing that _there are cybercrimings_. After that agreement, how does the author revise, modify, or contradict what's just been said? _how to combat that threat._

▶ **SHARE YOUR THOUGHTS**
How far would you go in defense of free speech? Do people have the right to express themselves even when what they say is cruel and hateful? _No they would not have to Say those things_

5. Tracing Time Order

Whenever the timing of events or steps in real time is important to the topic or idea under discussion, sentence parts and whole sentences will link up based on chronological, or **time order**. They will, that is, contribute an event or events to the underlying time sequence, which ties the sentences together. Here you see that happening within a single sentence:

Henry the Eighth had his second wife, Anne Boleyn, beheaded in 1536; just days after Anne's death, he married his third wife, Jane Seymour.

Since Henry's beheading of Anne occurred before his marriage to Jane Seymour, it comes first in the sentence. His marriage to Jane comes second so that the sequence, or order, of events is clear.

As you might expect, the time order relationship doesn't provide the foundation just for dates and events. It's also at work when the writer describes the steps in a process. Look, for example, at these two sentences:

> The tire building machine on an assembly line first assures that all the tire components are in the correct location; then it forms the tire into a shape and size that are fairly close to the tire's finished dimensions. The next step is to run the tire into a curing machine, which functions something like a waffle iron, molding in all the markings and traction patterns.
>
> (Adapted from Marshall Brain, *How Stuff Works*, New York: Hungry Minds, 2001, p. 71.)

Here again, time order is the underlying relationship that ties the sentences together. Each sentence recounts a new step, ordered chronologically, or according to time, in the process of building a tire.

Transitional Clues

In addition to numerous dates, transitions like the ones listed below frequently open sentences that rely heavily on the time order relationship.

Transitions Marking Dates and Events ♦	
A few days, months, years later	
After arriving, appearing, founding	
At the end of the decade	
From (specific year) to (specific year)	
In that year	
In the following year	

The following transitions often mark off the steps or stages in a process.

Transitions Identifying Steps in a Process ♦	
First	Next
Second	Afterwards
Third	Finally
At the end	When completed

Whenever sentences are linked by time order, make sure that you understand the specific steps or events in the sentences along with the order in which they occurred. Know exactly how many there are and be able to sum up each one. This focus on the individual events or steps becomes even more important when the time order pattern governs not just pairs of sentences but entire paragraphs and readings.

⌐ READING KEYS

♦ The time order relationship connects dates and events as well as steps or stages in a process.
♦ Use transitions to sort out the individual steps or events. Know what each step or event in the sequence consists of along with the order in which it occurred.

> ### IDIOM ALERT: Follow suit
>
> This idiom originates with card games, where players follow in the same suit, e.g., hearts, diamonds, clubs. But the phrase has taken on a more general meaning. When a person or group follows suit, they follow the example that has already been set by someone else. "After his older and much-admired brother abandoned Facebook as a time waster, Todd reluctantly *followed suit*."

♦ EXERCISE 7   Linking Cause to Effect

DIRECTIONS   Read each sentence or pair of sentences. In the blanks that follow, identify the events introduced in the sentence or sentences.

EXAMPLE   In November of 1989, Germans scaled the Berlin Wall[†] dividing East and West Germany and tore it down; the following October, the two Germanys reunited. By then other eastern European countries dominated by the Soviet Union had also begun to rebel, and the Soviet Union[†] began to fall apart. (Adapted from Mary Beth Norton et al., *A People and a Nation*, p. 866. © Cengage Learning.)

How many different steps or events are described in these two sentences? ___4___

[†]After World War II, Germany was divided up with West Germany ruled by democratic governments, and East Germany by the communist Soviet Union. But so many East Germans wanted to escape to the western half, the Soviet Union, in the course of one single night in 1961, put up a wall in Berlin to stop them.

[†]The Soviet Union was the name used to identify communist Russia and the countries it controlled, e.g., Hungary, Lithuania, Poland, etc.

List and describe those events in chronological order.

1. 1989 Germans tear down Berlin Wall

2. 1990 the two Germanys become one

3. Other eastern European countries rebel

4. The Soviet Union starts to crumble

EXPLANATION The opening date is a clue to the time order pattern. In this case, the author traces a chain of events that led to the fall of the Soviet Union. Your goal as a reader is to pull out the individual events and paraphrase them, first to yourself and then in your notes. Your notes should indicate when the events happened, as the sample notes above do. However, when two or three events happen around the same time, you don't have to keep repeating the date, unless of course you want to.

Note: If you are looking at the two sentences above and thinking, "Isn't there also a cause and effect relationship involved?" you are absolutely correct. The rebellion of the eastern countries led to the collapse of the Soviet Union. If you were taking notes on those two sentences, you would make sure to connect the events in the sequence *and* the cause to effect. But, if you were taking a standardized reading test, you would focus on the use of transitions and label it time order. (*Sequence* is another way this relationship can be labeled on a standardized reading test.) Since standardized tests don't generally allow for subtlety of thought, you probably won't be able to circle two answers.

1. In 1905, educator, writer, and activist W. E. B. Du Bois (1868–1963) helped found the Niagara Movement, which led to the creation of the NAACP* in 1909. From 1910 to 1934, he edited the NAACP magazine, *Crisis*, consistently arguing for a militant* approach to civil rights.

How many different steps or events are described in these two sentences? 4

List and describe those events in chronological order.

1905 Founded Niagara

1905 created Naacp

---

*NAACP: National Association for the Advancement of Colored People.
*militant: openly aggressive.

1910—1934 Edited the Magazine
1910—1934 Militant aProach
forcivil rights

2. On June 25, 1950, North Korea invaded South Korea; two days later, the U.N. Security Council called on members to support South Korea.

   How many different events are described in this sentence? ___*2*___

   List and describe those events in chronological order.

   On June 25, 1950, North Korea
   invaded south Korea; two Days
   later, The U.N. Security Council
   Called on members to support South Korea

3. Although the majority of Confederate[†] soldiers were volunteers, the Confederacy did institute a draft in 1862. In 1863, the Union imposed a draft as well, but draftees with money could buy their way out of the army for $300.

   How many different steps or events are described in these two sentences? ___*3*___

   1862 Confederacy did a Draft
   1863 The union imposed a Draft
   Some Draftees Bought their
   Way out With 300 Dollars

4. Collaboration between management and employees involves several steps. First, managers tell their subordinates what goals and plans top management has established; next, managers meet with their subordinates on a one-on-one basis to arrive at a set of goals and plans. (Adapted from Ricky W. Griffin, *Management*, p. 219. © Cengage Learning.)

   How many different steps or events are described in these two sentences? ___*2*___

[†]Confederate: related to the Southern side of the Civil War. The South was the Confederacy; the North was the Union. The word spelled with a small *c* means "friend" or "ally."

List and describe those events in chronological order.

First mangers tell Subordinates

2nd Mangers meet their Subordinates

◆ **EXERCISE 8** **Recognizing Relationships**

DIRECTIONS Read the following sentences. Then identify the relationship that connects the sentence parts or sentences.

EXAMPLE The Civil War had ravaged the countryside, leaving thousands of farmers desperate with barely enough money to make ends meet. From the farmers' desperation emerged "The Farmers' Alliance," an agricultural organization determined to gain political power and change how the nation was run.

a. cause and effect
b. agreement followed by modification
c. contrast

EXPLANATION The first sentence links cause (the Civil War's destruction) to effect (the farmers' desperation). The second sentence continues the same relationship. The farmers' desperation, formerly an effect, now becomes the cause of a new agricultural organization.

1. A study of Indian-American families found that Indian-American parents had separate dating standards for their sons and daughters. A quarter of all the daughters wanted to date but couldn't (half were dating without their parents' knowledge), whereas a full 80 percent of the boys were dating. (Adapted from Paul S. Kaplan, *Adolescence*, p. 205. © Cengage Learning.)

   a. agreement followed by modification
   b. contrast
   c. comparison

2. Most labor contracts contain a clause that prohibits strikes during the life of the contract. However, a union may strike while the contract is in force if members believe that management has violated

the terms of the contract. (Adapted from William M. Pride, Robert J. Hughes, and Jack R. Kapoor, *Business*, p. 337. © Cengage Learning)

a. agreement followed by modification
b. comparison
c. time order

3. Following in the footsteps of his hero, Mahatma Gandhi, the man who helped break British rule in India, civil rights activist Martin Luther King Jr. believed that mass activism and nonviolent protest were the twin engines of social change.

a. agreement followed by modification
b. general statement and specific example
c. comparison

4. Thanks to their flavorful meat, catfish are normally a popular lake inhabitant. The armored catfish, however, is another matter altogether, and it's generally considered an unwelcome menace that preys on other fish and is hard to get rid of.

a. comparison
b. contrast
c. cause and effect

5. True, many organizational leaders say they do not encourage kissing up and that they prefer honest feedback from subordinates. Yet, without meaning to, these same managers and leaders encourage flattery and servile* praise. (Adapted from Andrew J. Dubrin, *Leadership*, 6th ed., p. 212. © Cengage Learning.)

a. contrast
b. agreement followed by modification
c. comparison

6. Over the years, psychologists have tried with varying degrees of success to define the nature of love. Robert Sternberg, for instance, considered love to be composed of three elements: intimacy, passion, and commitment. (Adapted from Paul S. Kaplan, *Adolescence*, p. 346. © Cengage Learning.)

---

*servile: having an excessive desire to please; anxious to take orders.

a. contrast

b. cause and effect

c. general statement and specific example

7. While it's true that the most notorious gangs are those in the poorest sections of major cities like Los Angeles, New York, and Chicago, gang activity is certainly *not* limited to urban areas. Gangs can also be found in suburbs and rural communities.

a. comparison

b. cause and effect

c. agreement followed by modification

8. Benjamin Franklin published *Poor Richard's Almanack*,[†] a collection of wise sayings and tips on the weather, between 1732 and 1757. After 1757, the publication was taken over by someone else, and Franklin was no longer involved.

a. contrast

b. cause and effect

c. time order

9. Twitter and Facebook aren't encouraged in the courtroom. Judges regularly warn jury members that tweets and posts about an ongoing trial can lead to both legal appeals and lawsuits.

a. general statement and specific example

b. contrast

c. comparison

10. Look at the literature on raising children, and it's clear that mothers are thought to have a huge influence on how daughters develop. The role of the father in a daughter's life, however, gets much less attention.

a. contrast

b. cause and effect

c. time order

[†]"Many complain of their memory, few of their judgment" is one of the sayings in *Poor Richard's Almanack*.

> **WEB QUEST/CLASS ACTION**
>
> Use the Web to find five sayings from *Poor Richard's Almanack* that you like and think are worth remembering. Come to class ready to share at least two of the sayings and explain why you think they express good advice.

Expanding the Relationship Between General and Specific Sentences

This section of Chapter 3 moves away from sentence pairs and into paragraphs, preparing you for the chapters that follow. As you read, you'll notice that the focus on general and specific sentences continues. The reason for this is simple. Particularly in textbooks, writers are always moving back and forth between the two, even when other sentence relationships are binding the sentences together. That's why it pays to understand the different ways general and specific sentences can combine.

What follows are three patterns of general and specific sentences common to writing in general and textbooks in particular. The first one will be familiar from your work with sentence pairs.

Paragraph Pattern 1: From General to Specific

Here the author starts off with a general statement that expresses the **main idea**, or central point, of the paragraph. Then the more specific sentences take over the passage. This is one of the most common ways general and specific sentences connect in paragraphs.

1

> ¹Dog owners have more in common with parents than one might think at first glance. __G__ ²As dog owners, we can't just spontaneously take off for the weekend or on short notice without getting a pet sitter first. __S__ ³We have to be careful around people who don't like animals and make sure Spot doesn't slobber on their clothing or do something even worse. __S__ ⁴A potential romantic interest also has to be thoroughly examined concerning his or her fondness for pets. __S__ ⁵People who love dogs tend to look with suspicion on those who don't feel the same way, much like people who love children look

at those who don't. ___S___ (Source of idea: Gina Spadafori, "But Does He Like Dogs?" www.pets.com.)

Diagram this passage, and you'll come up with something like this:

General statement
Specific example
Specific example
Specific example
Specific example

Your goal when dealing with general and specific relationships is to note exactly when sentences broaden to become more general or narrow to become more specific. Recognizing the difference between the two kinds of sentences will help you stay in touch with the writer's train of thought. When you can identify how sentences broaden or narrow in text, you'll also know exactly when a new point is being introduced or the previous one continues to be developed.

When sentences become more general, ask yourself, What's the point here? What message is the author trying to communicate? When they become more specific, ask, Why is this information here? What does it contribute to the author's point or message?

READING KEYS

◆ Becoming familiar with the larger patterns of general and specific sentences can help you follow the writer's train of thought.

◆ When sentences become more general, you will know that a new point is being introduced. If they stay specific, you will know that the previous point is still under discussion.

◆ When sentences become more general, ask, What's the point here? What message is being conveyed? When they become more specific, ask, Why is this information here? What does it contribute?

Paragraph Pattern 2: Building Up to the General Point

In this next paragraph, the general sentence doesn't start the paragraph. It concludes it *after* the author has provided a number of specific statements on which the general statement is based.

2

[1]When a female elephant is about to give birth, the members of the herd who are close by will call to members who are farther away. __S__ [2]Those in the distance will hurry to the site of the birth, bellowing and waving their trunks as if in anticipation. __S__ [3]Like birth, death also elicits powerful emotions in elephants. __S__ [4]Animal researchers have noticed that elephants remember and stop at those locations where herd members died. __S__ [5]In addition to grief, terror and rage are also part of the elephant's range of emotions. __S__ [6]Baby elephants that have seen family members killed wake up screaming from what might well be nightmares. __S__ [7]From years of observation, researchers believe that elephants have a rich emotional life that resembles our own. __G__

Diagram this paragraph and it would look something like this:

Specific example
Specific example
Specific example
Specific example
Specific example
Specific example

General statement

Those who have observed them closely believe that elephants have an emotional range that is similar to humans.

© Ulrich Flemming

Paragraph Pattern 3: Moving Back and Forth Between General and Specific

This next paragraph doesn't stay for long on any one level of generality or specificity. Instead, the author moves back and forth between a general statement and a specific example. This relationship is repeated three times throughout the paragraph. It can be repeated even more if the subject matter requires it.

3

[1]The mass media is an essential part of modern presidential campaigns. __G__ [2]Candidates use the media to make major policy statements, criticize opponents, and create the up close and personal image they think voters want. __S__ [3]Political consultants are also considered essential to modern campaigning. __G__ [4]Since the 1950s, everyone from Dwight D. Eisenhower to Hillary Clinton has worked hand-in-hand with consultants in order to identify and win over potential voters. __S__ Currently, social media plays a huge role in political campaigning. __G__ This trend started with the 2008 political campaign of Barack Obama, and it shows no sign of slowing down. __S__

If you diagrammed the above paragraph, it would look something like this:

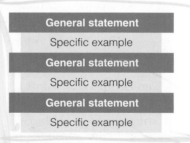

| General statement |
| Specific example |
| General statement |
| Specific example |
| General statement |
| Specific example |

The thing to remember about all three of these paragraphs is this: Writers don't follow a fixed pattern of general and specific sentences. Sometimes they start out general and become more specific. Sometimes they do the opposite, letting the specific sentences build up to a more general point. They can, if the subject matter requires it, move back and forth between general and specific statements. But whatever writers do, your job as the reader is to identify the pattern of general and specific sentences they employ.

READING KEY

◆ Your job as a reader is to stay tuned to the writer's flow of thought. Be aware when the writer lists a series of specific details, one after the other, or moves back and forth between general ideas and specific explanations or examples.

◆ **EXERCISE 9** **Recognizing Three Patterns of General and Specific Sentences**

DIRECTIONS   Read the passage through once to get a sense of how the general and specific sentences are used. Then fill in the blanks following each sentence with a *G* to indicate general statement or an *S* to indicate specific example.

EXAMPLE   [1]The National Association for Shoplifting Prevention counts at least 27 million shoplifters in the United States. __S__ [2]No wonder retailers take costly security measures in order to protect their property. __S__ [3]Shoppers may not realize it but the cost of those security measures and items lost due to shoplifting is passed on to consumers in the form of higher prices. __S__ [4]When prices go up, the community gets hurt because people shop elsewhere and the community loses revenue. __S__ [5]Shoplifting is a more serious crime than many of us like to think. __G__

EXPLANATION   Sentences 1–4 are related by addition. Each one offers a specific piece of information about shoplifting. Taken together the specific pieces of information add up to the general idea expressed in the last sentence.

1. [1]In the nineteenth century, Vaseline had a number of different uses. __G__ [2]Fishermen, for example, used it as bait for their fishhooks. __S__ [3]Some people even smeared Vaseline on their sandwiches if they couldn't afford butter. __S__ [4]Cooks sometimes fried fish in Vaseline. __S__ [5]Vaseline was what women used before mascara was invented; they mixed it with coal dust and brushed the mixture on their eyelashes. __S__

2. [1]Statistical figures used as evidence look like hard facts, but they're not; they are subject to human interference. __S__ [2]Researchers can, for instance, define the problem they are studying so broadly that

the figure they come up with is bound to be large. ___S___ [3]They can also select a sample, or experimental group, that all but guarantees the outcome they are after. ___S___ [4]Then, too, it's possible to frame the questions asked in a way that elicits the desired response. ___G___

3. [1]Through her observations of the chimpanzees of Tanganyika, Jane Goodall altered our ideas about chimp life. ___G___ [2]She made us realize, for instance, that chimpanzees were capable of warfare. ___S___ [3]Dian Fossey, working in Rwanda, brought the public's attention to the plight of the great apes. ___G___ [4]Without Fossey's protection, the apes might have been hunted to extinction. ___S___ [5]But the most well-known woman in the wild has to be Joy Adamson, who in the fifties adopted a lion called Elsa. ___S___ [6]Adamson wrote about her experiences in her book *Born Free*, which became a bestseller and the basis for the 1966 movie *Born Free*. ___S___

ROUNDING UP THE KEYS

Here is a list of all the reading keys introduced in the chapter. Use them to review for the test on page 145. If a particular reading key doesn't make sense on its own, go back to the page where it appeared and review the section preceding it.

READING KEYS: General Statement and Specific Example

◆ General statements can be interpreted or understood in a number of ways. Thus, they need clarification through more specific explanation and examples. The more specific explanation narrows the range of meanings and helps eliminate confusion between reader and writer. (p. 103)

◆ Because communication relies so heavily on general statements, skillful readers are alert to specific explanations and examples offered as clarification. They know that the specific sentences will narrow the range of meanings the more general sentences might suggest. (p. 103)

◆ When you are trying to untangle the ideas in a particularly difficult passage, it helps to determine where the author's general ideas are located. Then check to see if they are further developed by more specific illustrations and explanations. (p. 103)

◆ Transitions such as *for instance, for example,* and *in fact* are good indicators that the relationship binding sentences together is general statement and specific illustration. (p. 107)

◆ The colon is likely to introduce a more specific illustration of a general idea that was just introduced. Semicolons sometimes fulfill the same function. (p. 107)

READING KEYS: Cause and Effect

◆ Sentences connecting cause to effect describe how one event produces or produced another. (p. 110)

◆ Like transitions, verbs are also clues to the presence of cause and effect. (p. 110)

◆ Good readers know exactly when an effect becomes the cause of another event or series of events. (p. 110)

READING KEYS: Contrast

◆ Sentences related by contrast highlight the difference between two topics. (p. 113)

◆ Readers who want to understand this relationship need to clearly determine what two topics are being contrasted. They also need to understand how the two topics differ as well as what the differences prove or illustrate. (p. 113)

READING KEYS: Comparison

◆ As with sentences united by contrast, the comparison relationship gives up its message more quickly if you determine what two things are being compared and identify their similarities along with the point they explain or prove. (p. 116)

◆ In response to comparison relationships that connect sentence parts or whole sentences, readers need to identify the two topics along with their similarities. (p. 118)

◆ Writers don't rely on one single relationship throughout a reading. The ideas writers choose to communicate dictate the relationships sentences express. (p. 118)

◆ Aware that relationships in and between sentences change with the writer's thoughts, skillful readers stay alert to the various relationships that link the ideas in a reading. (p. 118)

READING KEYS: Agreement Followed by Modification

◆ Sentences based on the agreement followed by modification relationship describe an existing or assumed state of affairs and then modify it in some way. (p. 119)

◆ Stay alert to transitional signals announcing something is about to change in the author's line of thinking. (p. 119)

◆ Make sure you understand the traditional or conventional point of view as well as the author's revision of it. (p. 119)

READING KEYS: Time Order

◆ The time order relationship connects dates and events as well as steps or stages in a process. (p. 123)

◆ Use transitions to sort out the individual steps or events. Know what each step or event in the sequence consists of along with the order in which it occurred. (p. 123)

READING KEYS: General and Specific Relationships

◆ Becoming familiar with the larger patterns of general and specific sentences can help you follow the writer's train of thought. (p. 130)

- When sentences become more general, you will know that a new point is being introduced. If they stay specific, you will know that the previous point is still under discussion. (p. 130)
- When sentences become more general, ask, What's the point here? What message is being conveyed? When they become more specific, ask, Why is this information here? What does it contribute? *(p. 130)*
- Your job as a reader is to stay tuned to the writer's flow of thought. Be aware when the writer lists a series of specific details, one after the other, or moves back and forth between general ideas and specific explanations or examples. (p. 133)

Ten More Words for Your Academic Vocabulary

1. **legitimate:** legal, respected, in good standing

   The prince was a *legitimate* successor to the throne; nevertheless, his subjects preferred his stepbrother, who had no legal right to be king.

2. **perseverance:** the ability to stick to a task; refusing to give up easily

   Hard work, long hours, and *perseverance*, the simple refusal to give up, had taken the young woman to the top of her profession.

3. **successive:** one after the other

   Before Lyndon Johnson became president in 1963, four *successive* Democratic administrations had tried, unsuccessfully, to pass legislation guaranteeing medical coverage.

4. **inadvertently:** unintentionally, done without any conscious purpose in mind

   Some critics suggest that IBM, the computer company, *inadvertently* developed a culture that discouraged risk taking.

5. **inclusion:** the act of accepting or including

   Some of the early unions were reluctant to allow the *inclusion* of women and minorities.

6. **comprehensive:** complete, broadly inclusive, wide-ranging

   In the late nineteenth century, city leaders who were impatient with small, piece-by-piece reforms began demanding *comprehensive* solutions to the problem of urban poverty.

7. **fiscal:** relating to government spending

   Founding father Alexander Hamilton believed that the United States needed a central bank if the country were to ever have a sound *fiscal* policy.

8. **entrepreneurial:** willingness to take risks in business

   The British were quick to criticize the American colonies for their refusal of British rule, but even the British had to admire the country's *entrepreneurial* spirit.

9. **allegedly:** supposedly, suspected but lacking in hard evidence

   When President Woodrow Wilson was so ill he had become a shadow of his former self, his wife Edith *allegedly* took over many of his presidential duties.

10. **incentive:** motive or reward for doing something

    Many educators believe that students perform better when their *incentive* for achievement is internal—a sense of accomplishment—rather than external—money.

◆ EXERCISE 10 Making Academic Vocabulary Familiar

DIRECTIONS Each sentence uses a more conversational or simpler version of the words listed below. At the end of the sentence, fill in the blank with the more academic word that could replace the underlined word in the sentence.

> incentives   entrepreneurial   legitimate   inclusion   successive
> perseverance   comprehensive   fiscal   inadvertently   allegedly

1. After a string of <u>continuous</u> victories in the primaries, the success of Barack Obama's candidacy was no longer a long shot. <u>successive</u>

2. J. Edgar Hoover, the former director of the FBI, <u>supposedly</u> kept a secret file on every important public official. <u>allegedly</u>

3. Good managers provide their employees with strong <u>rewards</u> to do good work. <u>incentives</u>

4. It was obvious that a <u>complete</u> overhaul of the tax code would take a year or more. _Comprehensive_

5. The <u>allowing in</u> of reporters at the conference made everyone less willing to speak freely. _Inclusion_

6. If the World Bank lends money to a financially troubled country, it expects to dictate the country's <u>financial</u> policy. _Fiscal_

7. Bill Bowerman and Phil Knight, the co-founders of Nike, are perfect examples of the <u>risk-taking</u> spirit at work. _Entreprenerial_

8. The researcher <u>without meaning to</u> reversed the number of "no" responses and significantly changed the outcome of the interviews. _Inadvertently_

9. In studying those who achieve great success in life, researchers found that <u>not giving up</u> was just as important as talent. _Perseverance_

10. No <u>real</u> lawyer would betray the confidence of his or her client. _legitimate_

DIGGING
DEEPER **Family Ties**

Looking Ahead This reading describes Chang and Eng, the two brothers from whom the term *Siamese twins* was derived. The questions that follow will test your knowledge of sentence relationships and your understanding of the reading.

1 Chang and Eng, the twin boys who gave rise to the term *Siamese twins*, were born in what is now Thailand on May 11, 1811. At birth, their bodies were tightly connected by a band of cartilage that united them at the breastbone. Initially, at least, that unbreakable link seemed to spell their doom. Considered an omen of misfortune, the boys were ordered put to death. But at the last minute, the king of Siam intervened, taking pity on them and sparing their lives.

2 When Chang and Eng turned eighteen, a Scottish trader paid their parents a small sum of money and got permission to take them on tour in a circus act. Billed as the "Siamese Double Boys," Chang and Eng were the prize exhibition in a tour of Britain and the United States. Aware, however, that they were being exploited, the twins left the show to go out on their own.

3 In 1839, they applied for U.S. citizenship and set out to become farmers in North Carolina. In the mid-forties, Chang and Eng married a pair of sisters, Adelaide and Sally Yates. They also took a very American name. They called themselves Bunker. Accepted and even admired by many members of the community, the Bunker brothers developed a special "double-chop" method for felling the trees on their land. Their method, uniquely adapted to their own physical requirement, caught on and is still in use today.

4 Like the "double-chop" method they created, the brothers themselves have not been forgotten. Between them they fathered twenty-one children, and to this day, the descendants of those children meet for regular reunions. Unfortunately, the publication of a book, *Chang and Eng*, by writer Darin Strauss in 2000 brought heated controversy to what were once happy family get-togethers. Told from Eng's point of view, the novel suggests that Eng, at least, dreamed of being free and separate from his brother.

5 Although some of Chang and Eng's descendants thought Strauss's novel a great tribute, others loathed the book. When the author, on a book-signing tour, visited White Plains, North Carolina, home of the Bunkers and scene of the reunions, the controversy heated up. Betty Bunker Blackmon bought nine copies of *Chang and Eng* and asked the author to sign every single one. Tanya Rees, however, a great-great-granddaughter of Eng, was furious. From her perspective, Strauss had "cheapened" her family history.

6   Aware that some family members were not happy with his portrayal of their ancestors, Strauss attended the 2000 Bunker family reunion. He brought with him a peace offering in the form of fried chicken. What Strauss didn't bring were any copies of his book. Yet, to his surprise and delight, a number of family members showed up with their own copies, all of which he graciously autographed.

7   It's generally agreed that Strauss truly healed the family's wounds when he was called on to make a speech. Thanking the Bunker descendants for their hospitality, Strauss explained that he had never meant to cheapen or sensationalize their family history. On the contrary, his intent had been to do Chang and Eng justice. In his words, they were "two of the most heroic people in American history." When the author finished speaking, he received a round of applause. Strauss had apparently won over even those who had initially hated the book and its attendant publicity. At the reunion's end, the Bunker family was once again united, secure in the belief that their famous ancestors had been accorded the respect they justly deserved.

Sharpening Your Skills

DIRECTIONS   Answer the following questions by filling in the blanks or circling the letter of the correct response.

1. Which of the following sentences best sums up the point or message of this reading?

    a. Chang and Eng were remarkable people who let no obstacle stand in their way, and, to this day, there are tributes to them in White Plains, North Carolina, where they settled.

    b. The descendants of Chang and Eng are understandably proud of their ancestors.

    c. A novel portraying the life of conjoined twins Chang and Eng temporarily disrupted what had once been happy family reunions.

    d. The term *Siamese twins* originated with the brothers Chang and Eng, who were born in 1811.

2. Which of the following details in the reading illustrates the brothers' entrepreneurial spirit?

    a. They fathered twenty-one children.

    b. Darin Strauss's book about their lives angered some of their relatives.

    c. They developed a "double-chop" method for cutting wood.

    d. They married sisters.

3. What's a good synonym for *omen* in this sentence: "Considered an omen of misfortune, the boys were ordered put to death." _____

_____

4. The opening sentence of this reading suggests the time order relationship but by the time the paragraph concludes, what relationship connects the sentences?

    a. agreement followed by modification

    b. cause and effect

    c. contrast

    d. comparison

5. The transition opening paragraph 2 suggests what relationship?

    a. contrast

    b. time order

    c. comparison

    d. agreement followed by modification

6. What relationship connects the two parts of this sentence? "Aware, however, that they were being exploited, the twins left the show to go out on their own."

    a. comparison

    b. general statement and specific example

    c. time order

    d. cause and effect

7. In paragraph 5, what relationship connects the opening and closing parts of the first sentence?

    a. agreement followed by modification

    b. contrast

    c. comparison

    d. time order

8. The parts of the first sentence in paragraph 6 express a cause and effect relationship. What's the cause?

   The family wasn't happy with his Book

   What's the effect?

   They forgive him.

9. These two sentences from paragraph 5 express a contrast relationship: "Betty Bunker Blackmon bought nine copies of *Chang and Eng* and asked the author to sign every single one. Tanya Rees, however, a great-great-granddaughter of Eng, was furious."

   What two topics are being contrasted?

   Betty was happy and tanya was Angry

   What differences do the sentences express?

   how They felt about the Book

10. The first sentence of paragraph 7 is based on a cause and effect relationship. What's the cause?

    his speech

    What's the effect?

    healed.

▶ **TEST 1**   **Reviewing the Key Points**

DIRECTIONS   Fill in the blanks or circle the correct response.

1. When the ideas in the passage change, so do the _contexts or the meanings_.

2. General statements can be interpreted _in a number of ways_.

3. To be clear, general statements usually require _clarification_.

4. *True* or *False*. Writers always move back and forth between the general and the specific. _false_

5. Sentences expressing agreement followed by modification will first _described and assumed state_ and then _modify it in some way_.

6. Cause and effect sentences explain how _one thing produces another_.

7. Sentences linked by contrast point out how _two things are different_.

8. Sentences linked by comparison _relationship between two things_.

9. Sometimes the effect of one event becomes the _cause of another event_.

10. Sentences connected by time order will identify _dates_ or describe _steps_.

To correct your test, turn to page 587. If one or more of your answers is incorrect, re-read the Rounding Up the Keys section of the chapter to find out where your mistake might be.

▶ **TEST 2**   **Making Sentence Connections**

DIRECTIONS   Read the following sentences. Identify the connection between sentence parts or sentences.

1. Every year Americans spend millions of dollars celebrating Mother's Day; last year they spent over $4 million on phone calls alone.

   a. general statement and specific example
   b. cause and effect
   c. agreement followed by modification
   d. contrast

2. Showing a firmness of purpose is not the same as moral courage. Moral courage requires doing the right thing despite the threat of painful consequences; however, we can be firm of purpose in situations that threaten no negative consequences.

   a. cause and effect
   b. contrast
   c. general statement and specific example
   d. agreement followed by modification

3. In 2004, Janet Jackson's baring of her breast during the Super Bowl intermission caused a public uproar resulting in demands for more censorship of obscene jokes and behavior on television.

   a. general statement and specific example
   b. addition
   c. cause and effect
   d. comparison

4. It's well-known that around the world, girls generally outnumber boys at birth. In India, however, women account for only 49.4 percent of the total population.

   a. general statement and specific example
   b. comparison
   c. cause and effect
   d. agreement followed by modification

5. In 1854, Barbara Leigh Smith Bodechon fired the first shot in the battle to improve the lives of married women by publishing a pamphlet titled "A Brief Summary, in Plain Language, of the Most Important Laws Concerning Women." In 1856, 26,000 British women signed a petition demanding that Parliament better protect the financial interests of married women.

   a. general statement, specific example
   b. time order
   c. cause and effect
   d. contrast

6. Cecilia Payne-Gaposchkin (1900–1979), one of the great astronomers of the twentieth century, claimed that seeing a meteor when she was only five years old made her decide, at that very moment, to become an astronomer.

   a. cause and effect
   b. agreement followed by modification
   c. contrast
   d. comparison

7. To be a winner in the USA Memory Championships, contestants first must memorize ninety-nine names and faces. Next they have to memorize an unpublished fifty-line poem in only fifteen minutes, then a series of random numbers, random words, and finally a shuffled deck of playing cards.

   a. agreement followed by modification
   b. contrast
   c. comparison
   d. time order

8. There were several reasons why Europe in the fourteenth century was so vulnerable to the Black Death, which killed millions of people. Among them were lack of good health care, poor sanitation, and overcrowding in the cities.

   a. general statement and specific example
   b. time order

c. contrast

d. comparison

9. Researchers once thought that polar bears were the descendants of brown bears. A new study, however, proves that idea incorrect: In fact, polar and brown bears share a common ancestor, making polar bears 600,000 years old.

   a. general statement and specific example

   b. time order

   c. cause and effect

   d. agreement followed by modification

10. "Watch kids of any age at play. Little boys set up wars and play-fights. Little girls fight, but not for fun." (Deborah Tannen, "The Feminine Technique," nytimes.com, March 15, 2005.)

    a. cause and effect

    b. contrast

    c. comparison

    d. time order

▶ **TEST 3**   **Recognizing Sentence Relationships**

DIRECTIONS   Circle the appropriate letter to identify the sentence relationship referred to in the question.

1. Which of the following illustrates the general statement–specific example relationship?

   a. The U.S. Coast Guard is trying to get more control over ships at sea. To do more effective monitoring, it now requires a four-day notice of advance arrival in port.

   b. Cindy Crawford had a long and lucrative career as a supermodel, but she probably won't be able to match the forty-year career of supermodel Lauren Hutton, who is still going strong at sixty plus.

   c. In 1939, while Hitler was casting his dark shadow over Europe, the United States remained neutral. But after 1941 and the attack on Pearl Harbor, there was no longer any question about U.S. involvement in the fight against Hitler and his allies.

   d. Everyone agrees that the containers arriving into U.S. ports need to be thoroughly inspected. Still, because a thorough examination of a container can take hours, only about 2 percent of the 6 million containers that arrive actually get opened. (Source of information: William Langewiesche, *The Outlaw Sea*, p. 68.)

2. Which of the following illustrates a cause and effect relationship between sentences?

   a. As every zookeeper knows, orangutans are master escape artists. In addition to an ability to pick locks, orangutans have escaped through electric fences by covering their hands and feet with "oven mitts" made out of straw.

   b. After two psychologists, R. Allen Gardner and Beatrix Gardner, proved that their chimpanzee subject could use at least 130 signs from American Sign Language, studies of animals and language doubled.

   c. Give a screwdriver to a gorilla, and it will try to eat it. Give one to an orangutan, and it will take its cage apart.

   d. When a young male orangutan was isolated in a Topeka, Kansas, zoo, he carefully studied the mechanisms controlling the door of his cage for several days. He then figured out how to use a piece of cardboard to flip up the pin holding his door closed and

made his escape. (Source of information for all items: Eugene Linden, "Can Animals Think?" *Time*, September 6, 1999, pp. 57–60.)

3. Which of the following illustrates how sentences can contrast two topics?

   a. In the world of fairy tales, gnomes are mythical humans, described as deformed, living underground, and inclined to mean-spirited mischief. Pixies, on the other hand, are fairies famed for their cheerful nature and cute faces.

   b. Ivan Kelly, a widely published and long-time critic of astrology, points out there is no hard evidence to support the idea of the stars affecting our lives. He is correct. Still, astrology is believed by millions of people, and it has survived for thousands of years. That has to mean something.

   c. In 1879, when Henrik Ibsen's play *A Doll's House* premiered, it caused a scandal. The idea of a woman—the play's heroine, Nora—who didn't enjoy being a wife or want to be a mother, outraged many.

   d. Brothers William and Henry James were both drawn to the study of how the human mind orders reality. Henry, like William, insisted that the mind imposed order on what was actually a very disorderly and multi-layered experience.

4. Which of the following illustrates how sentences can compare two topics?

   a. For many famous intellectuals fleeing Hitler's Germany, Los Angeles was their address in exile. Bertolt Brecht, Thomas Mann, and Theodor Adorno all found their way to L.A.

   b. Together, Raymond Chandler (1870–1959) and Dashiell Hammett (1894–1961) created a whole new kind of crime novel. They abandoned the aristocratic British heroes of the past and focused on homegrown, American tough guys.

   c. By the 1890s, professional sports gained a new-found respectability. Highest in public esteem by 1900 was professional baseball, and by 1905 the public showed a particular fondness for the Cincinnati Red Stockings.

   d. In 1900, professional football's popularity in no way matched that of baseball, although it was solidly popular in the Midwest.

5. Which of the following illustrates a time order relationship?

   a. As everyone knows, penguins don't mind the cold. That's not true, however, of baby penguins, who would freeze if they didn't take shelter under their mother's belly.

   b. April can be miserable for allergy sufferers: It's the month when pollen grains start taking to the air.

   c. On March 25, 1585, Sir Walter Raleigh was granted the right to explore and settle in North America. By June 4 of the same year, he had established the first colony in Roanoke, Virginia.

   d. Rising oil prices are decreasing the demand for SUVs.

▶ **TEST 4**　　　　**Recognizing Patterns of General and Specific Relationships**

DIRECTIONS　　Read through each paragraph. Then in the blanks label each of the sentences *G* for general or *S* for specific.

1. To increase crop yields, farmers in developed countries use huge quantities of fertilizer containing artificially produced nitrates. _____ Unfortunately there is an ever-growing mountain of evidence indicating that nitrates are having a damaging effect on nature. _____ Before the nitrates can be broken down and changed into nitrogen, they are often leached out of the soil by rain. _____ The dissolved nitrates then get carried into streams and rivers. _____ They go into our groundwater and from there into what we eat. _____ Animals that have ingested feed high in nitrates have become ill due to nitrate poisoning. _____

2. Think of Moses in the bull rushes being rescued by an Egyptian princess or Rome's founders Romulus and Remus being raised by wolves. _____ Then, too, there's Charles Dickens's famous orphan Oliver Twist and Tolkien's equally famous Frodo Baggins, both left without parents to raise them. _____ By the end of the novel, Mark Twain's Huck Finn is an orphan, and Charlotte Bronte's Jane Eyre is one from the start. _____ Not to be forgotten, there's J. K. Rowling's famous orphan Harry Potter, who must make his way through life with the guidance of wizards instead of parents. _____ Featured in some of the world's oldest and most beloved stories, orphans are everywhere in literature. _____

3. Storms are disturbances of the atmosphere accompanied by strong winds. _____ Blizzards, for instance, have winds with a minimum speed of thirty-five miles per hour. _____ Storms are also accompanied by some form of precipitation. _____ Hurricanes, for example, arrive with extremely high winds *and* heavy thunderstorms. _____ All storms are likely to cause serious damage. _____ However, tornados are among the most destructive, capable of tearing houses from foundations and hurling automobiles into the air. _____

4. For years, the American Central Intelligence Agency (CIA) analyst Aldrich Ames fooled everyone he worked with and destroyed numerous lives in the process. _____ In 1985, Ames was in the

middle of an expensive divorce. _S_ Heavily in debt he decided to make money by spying for the Russians. _G_ Ames volunteered to give the Russian secret service, called the KGB, the names of Russian citizens who were cooperating with the CIA. _S_ The KGB took the names and arrested the people on Ames's list. _G_ Many people on the list were imprisoned. _S_ At least ten were executed. _S_ Although the CIA knew there was a leak, it took years for them to figure out that it was Aldrich Ames. _S_

▶ **TEST 5**   **Enlarging Your Academic Vocabulary**

DIRECTIONS   Circle the letter of the sentence that uses the opening word correctly.

1. **legitimate** *legal*

   ⓐ The plumber next door does not run a *legitimate* business; he has no license and pays no taxes.

   b. Any citizen must be *legitimate* in order to be able to read and understand the Constitution.

   c. A *legitimate* claim is a claim written in plain language.

2. **perseverance** *not give up*

   a. The verdict was a complete *perseverance* of justice.

   ⓑ *Perseverance* led the team to victory—even when they were trailing badly, they did not lose their concentration or their will to win.

   c. After their *perseverance*, the two countries remained on friendly terms and trade flourished between them.

3. **successive** *one after another*

   ⓐ *Successive* prison sentences cannot be served simultaneously; they must follow one another, which is how stockbroker and con man Bernie Madoff ended up with a 150-year prison sentence.

   b. A college degree is not needed if you want to become a *successive* businessman or businesswoman.

   c. In spite of some *successive* dialogue, the movie got a PG-13 rating because it contained no explicit sex scenes.

4. **inadvertently** *not meaning to*

   a. There was a time when teachers might throw a piece of chalk at an *inadvertent* student who had fallen asleep in class.

   b. The reporters waited *inadvertently* for the arrival of the prime minister even though her plane was delayed.

   ⓒ He *inadvertently* revealed his intentions when he sent an e-mail to the wrong person.

5. **inclusion**  _including_

   a. The _inclusion_ of "under God" in the Pledge of Allegiance goes back to an act of Congress passed in 1954.

   b. More than anything else, the patient needs an _inclusion_ of fresh blood.

   c. After deliberating for only four hours, the jury came to the _inclusion_ that the defendant was guilty as charged.

6. **comprehensive**  _complete_

   a. Operating manuals must be written in language that is _comprehensive_ for everybody.

   b. The report starts with a _comprehensive_ review of the challenges facing the town.

   c. One has to be very selective in order to become truly _comprehensive_.

7. **fiscal** _do with money_

   a. Because of _fiscal_ limitations, the budget proposed severe cuts for several popular programs.

   b. It's the _fiscal_ responsibility of the government to stay within the boundaries of the law in every decision it makes.

   c. In the _fiscal_ analysis, the mayor did not say anything new in his address.

8. **entrepreneurial** _new ideas or rist in business_

   a. The keynote address was very _entrepreneurial_—the speaker had the audience in stitches.

   b. The head of the tech startup already had an _entrepreneurial_ spirit as a kid; when she saw how well Girl Scout cookies sold in her neighborhood, she asked her mom to bake cookies. Then she sold them door-to-door.

   c. Huck Finn was more _entrepreneurial_ than Tom Sawyer—he wasn't interested in money; he just wanted to drift down the Mississippi on a raft.

9. **allegedly**  *supposedly*

   a. His wife stood *allegedly* by him and defended him passionately against any criticism.

   b. The talk show host apologized only *allegedly*—it was clear that he wasn't really sorry.

   c. The defendant *allegedly* entered the home through an open back door and walked away with a TV set.

10. **incentive** *reward*

    a. The candidate's speech was so *incentive* that it almost caused a riot.

    b. Many people are easier to motivate by *incentives* than by threats.

    c. Again, the president's address showed that he was very *incentive* to women's issues.

Identifying Topics, Main Ideas, and Topic Sentences

4

IN THIS CHAPTER, YOU WILL LEARN

- how to identify the topic and main idea of a paragraph.

- how to recognize topic sentences expressing the main idea.

- how to determine if your topic sentence and the author's are one and the same.

*"Let's not play down the significance
of the core idea."*

—James W. Sire, author of *How to Read Slowly*

Chapter 1 encouraged you to read for main ideas in paragraphs. Sometimes that's easy. The paragraph opens with a general statement. Then three specific examples of that statement follow. You can tell right off that the main idea of the paragraph is expressed in the first sentence.

However, determining a paragraph's main idea, or core message, is not always that easy. If the subject is unfamiliar or the writing difficult, you may need to read slowly and work at making the author's main point clear in your mind. Chapter 4 prepares you for those times when determining the main idea is a challenge.

What's the Topic?

The **topic** of a paragraph is much like the topic of a conversation. It's the person, place, event, or idea under discussion. It's the subject the author has chosen to discuss, describe, or explain.

The topic of a paragraph or, for that matter, an entire reading does not just pop up once or twice and then disappear. On the contrary, references to the topic are threaded through the paragraph. Those references, however, can vary in the form they take. Let's start with the simplest one.

Repetition

The easiest topics to spot are those that describe physical objects, actions, or events. Often the words referring to these objects, actions, or events are repeated throughout the paragraph. The only thing that changes is the grammatical form the word takes or the occasional use of a pronoun. Here's an example:

Notice how the heading already announces the topic.

Sentence 3 repeats the word in its adjective form, "allergic."

In sentences 5 and 8, the pronoun they refers to allergies.

Allergies [1]Allergies are among the most common types of hypersensitivity problems. [2]Millions of people suffer from some type of allergy. [3]Hay fever, asthma, and contact dermatitis (rashes) are common allergic reactions. [4]These allergies are mainly just bothersome. [5]But they can be a serious health threat. [6]Severe asthma, for example, can be life threatening. [7]Food allergies are also common in some populations. [8]They can, however, be difficult to diagnose. (Adapted from Marianne Neighbors and Ruth Tannehill-Jones, *Human Diseases*, 2nd ed., p. 67. © Cengage Learning.)

In this case, the topic, *allergies*, is hard to miss. Look how often it's repeated. And when the word or a form of the word *allergies* isn't repeated, it's referred to with the pronoun *they*.

Topic Phrases

As you might expect, paragraph topics can be expressed in phrases as well as single words. Actually, particularly in textbook paragraphs, topics are more likely to be phrases rather than single words, for instance:

[1]The birth of conjoined, or Siamese, twins is a rare occurrence. [2]Approximately one set of conjoined twins is born for every 400,000 births. [3]Although precisely what causes the birth of conjoined twins is

still debated, the most widely accepted theory is based on a failure of the fertilized egg to completely divide. [4]According to this theory, the birth of conjoined twins occurs when an ovum, or fertilized egg, begins to divide into two separate fetuses, each with the same sex and physical features. [5]Then, for some reason, genetic or environmental, the fetuses do not completely separate. [6]Instead, they remain joined at some part of the body, with the abdomen and chest being the most common. [7]The majority of conjoined twins do not survive more than twenty-four hours after birth. [8]Of those that do, the majority are female. (Source of statistics: www.pregnancy-info.net/conjoined_twins.html.)

In this case, the author is focused on a "theory about the birth of conjoined twins." But an entire phrase, rather than one word, sums up the topic.

Why Phrasing the Topic Is Important

When you are reading, your goal is to identify the author's main idea, or central message. Determining the topic is usually the starting point for zeroing in on the author's message. Most of the time, making the topic into a phrase will get you to that idea more quickly than a single-word topic will.

In the paragraph about conjoined twins, for instance, you could say twins are the topic and then keep adding information to the topic until you get to the main idea: "There is a widely accepted theory about what causes the birth of conjoined twins." But if you start out with the phrase "theory about the birth of conjoined twins," you are already three-quarters of the way to the main idea.

⚬━ⵀ READING KEYS

◆ The topic is the person, place, event, or idea repeatedly mentioned or referred to throughout the reading.

◆ The topic never pops up and then disappears. It's a constant presence in the passage.

Start General and Keep Getting More Specific

The trick to phrasing the topic is to start out general and let each sentence guide your modification of the topic. Look, for instance, at the way the following paragraph first suggests that the topic is a man named Tommy Jordan. But as the paragraph unfolds, the topic becomes something more specific, i.e., Tommy Jordan's unique form of punishment.

By sentence 2, it makes sense to consider Tommy Jordan the topic.

But notice how the sentences that follow restrict the reader's focus to one aspect of Tommy Jordan's life—his use of video to punish his daughter's behavior.

[1]Depending on your point of view, dad Tommy Jordan is a hero or psychopath. [2]After Jordan's daughter aired some family differences on her Facebook page, Jordan decided to mete out punishment in a similar fashion. [3]Using YouTube to go public with his response to his daughter's complaints about doing chores, Jordan posted a video in which he explains how ridiculous he finds his daughter's complaints. [4]Then he shoots his daughter's computer and dedicates the video to all of his daughter's friends who thought her Facebook post "cute." [5]Jordan also posted his unique form of punishment on Facebook and Reddit to make sure that he could attract a wide audience. [6]He apparently succeeded because his video went viral in a matter of hours.

This is another case where you could certainly call Tommy Jordan the topic and arrive at the main idea. However, the sentences in the paragraph all focus on one aspect of his life, his unique approach to punishment. Thus it makes sense for readers to do the same and make that phrase the topic. With that topic, you are already closing in on the main idea: "Dad Tommy Jordan came up with a unique form of punishment after his daughter criticized her parents on Facebook."

READING KEY

◆ Writers do sometimes identify topics with a single word. But, particularly in academic writing, where more general and abstract theories get discussed, they are likely to express their topic in a phrase.

▶ SHARE YOUR THOUGHTS

What do you think of Mr. Jordan's approach to parenting? If you were or are a parent, would you choose a similar method to punish your son or daughter for publicly criticizing his or her parents in a Facebook post?

◆ EXERCISE 1 Tracking Topic Repetition

DIRECTIONS In the following paragraphs, the topic is expressed in a single word or phrase and repeated throughout the paragraph. For each paragraph, circle the word or phrase that gets repeated the most. Then circle the letter of the topic.

1. The Venus flytrap is one of several carnivorous, or meat-eating, plants that actually eats insects. The plant's leaves, which look like a steel trap with teeth, remain open until an insect lands on them. When the insect brushes against tiny trigger hairs on the leaves, they snap shut. The plant then secretes enzymes to digest its prey. For about a week, the Venus flytrap uses the dead insect as a source of food. Once the insect is completely digested, the Venus flytrap opens its leaves again, ready to catch another meal.

Topic
   a. insects
   b. carnivorous plants
   c. the Venus flytrap
   d. plant digestion

2. Tunisian cave dwellings are a major tourist attraction. Although in some parts of the country, cave dwellings have fallen into ruin, they are carefully maintained in the village of Matmata. Matmata is an especially popular site because its cratered landscape was the setting for the first of the *Star Wars* films. Tourists climb the hills surrounding the village to look down into the cavity-filled landscape. At mealtimes, they can watch the smoke curling up from the holes in the ground. While the Berber tribespeople who live in the cave dwellings haggle over purchases in an above-ground marketplace, it's in the cave dwellings below ground that daily life goes on. Cave dwellings like the one in Matmata were once common sources of housing in parts of Southern Tunisia. They were the perfect home—cool at night, warm during the day—for people too poor to afford anything else. But nowadays, the Tunisian government encourages young people to leave the cave dwellings of their parents and move to nearby villages. The government hopes to maintain Tunisia's remaining cave dwellings as tourist attractions rather than personal homes.

Topic
   a. Tunisia
   b. the Berbers
   c. Tunisian cave dwellings
   d. the tourist attraction in Matmata

In some parts of Tunisia, cave dwellings are still inhabited.

3. Cirrhosis (sir-ROH-sis) of the liver is a chronic, incurable disease, also known as "end-stage liver disease." Cirrhosis is characterized by the replacement of normal liver cells with non-functioning scar tissue known as "hobnail" liver. This change in structure and function of the liver cells due to cirrhosis leads to impaired blood flow and altered function of the liver. (Marianne Neighbors and Ruth Tannehill-Jones, *Human Diseases*, 2nd ed., p. 211. © Cengage Learning.)

Topic

    a. liver disease

    b. cirrhosis of the liver

    c. the hobnail liver

    d. impaired blood flow to the liver

Repetition and Reference

As you already saw in the paragraph on allergies, writers refer to topics through pronouns. But pronouns are not the only way writers keep the topic front and center in the reader's mind. Often they maintain the topic by referring to things, people, or events associated with it.

In the following paragraph, for example, the topic, the siege of Leningrad, appears only once. The remaining sentences then refer to it in a variety of ways.

In sentence 2, the author only uses the word *siege*.

Sentence 4 refers to the siege as a "tragedy."

Sentences 5–8 refer to it by mentioning associated events.

[1]Among the many horrors that made up World War II, the siege of Leningrad stands high on the list of the worst. [2]During the siege, the Nazis surrounded the Russian city of Leningrad. [3]They cut off access to all supplies. [4]Deprived of food, the people of Leningrad suffered a tragedy that few could comprehend. [5]Thousands of people starved to death. [6]Corpses piled up in the streets. [7]Families were forced to eat once-loved pets. [8]Stories about cannibalism were whispered and believed. [9]Those who survived were marked forever by the experience.

This paragraph illustrates how the various details in a paragraph can suggest the topic without ever referring to it **explicitly,** or directly. Sentences 4 through 8 call up or evoke the topic because they are events that occurred during the siege of Leningrad. Sentence 9 uses the more general word *experience* that, within the context of the paragraph, also evokes in the reader's mind the paragraph topic.

Repetition, Reference, and a Little Help from the Reader

Often the author puts all the words to define the topic into the paragraph but leaves it up to readers to put the words together. For an illustration, read this paragraph through. In the blank at the end, write the phrase that best expresses the topic.

> Early in the nineteenth century, the swelling numbers of urban poor had given rise to a new kind of politician, the "boss," who listened to his urban constituents and lobbied to improve their lot. The boss presided over the city's "machine"—an unofficial political organization designed to keep a particular party or faction in office. Whether officially serving as mayor or not, the boss, assisted by local ward or precinct captains, wielded enormous influence in city government. Often a former saloonkeeper or labor leader, the boss knew his constituents well.
> (Adapted from Paul S. Boyer et al., *The Enduring Vision*, 7th ed., p. 578. © Cengage Learning.)

The way the Police Divide the City to Patrol.

The word *boss* is repeated numerous times in the paragraph. But if you track its appearance from sentence to sentence, it becomes clear that the authors are not talking about bosses in general. The authors are talking about "political bosses" and the role they played in nineteenth century city politics. However, it's up to the reader to combine the words *boss* and *political*.

When the Reader Fills in the Gaps

There's something else you need to know about paragraph topics. Sometimes all the words you need to fully express the topic aren't in the paragraph. Take this next example. The topic is riding a bicycle or bike. But guess what, only the words *bicycle* and *bike* appear. It's up to the reader to add the word *riding* to complete the topic.

The start of the topic appears in the first sentence and the last. The rest is up to you.

[1]A bicycle consists of two wheels and a simple steel frame equipped with handles, pedals, cranks, and a saddle. [2]The rider sits on the saddle, grasping the handlebars. [3]The pressure of the rider's foot on the pedals turns the cranks. [4]This action drives a chain over the front and rear sprockets, causing the rear wheel to revolve and setting the bike in motion. have a good ride!

◆ EXERCISE 2   Identifying and Contributing to Topics

DIRECTIONS   Circle the letter of the correct topic. *Note*: Sometimes the topic will need to be pieced together by the reader, sometimes not.

EXAMPLE

The topic here is maintained mainly through reference to the activities that occur during online banking.

[1]Online banking offers great convenience, but it also has some serious drawbacks. [2]It's practically an invitation to poor customer service. [3]Walk into a brick-and-mortar bank where you know everyone and the chances are good that questions and complaints will be dealt with quickly. [4]The same is not true for online banking. [5]Often, you will have at your disposal nothing but an 800 number, where you might or might not find someone knowledgeable about your question. [6]Deposits to your online account can vary in the amount of time they take and you can't rely on quick access. [7]If the website is down, it can stay down for a lengthy amount of time. [8]Meanwhile you have no recourse but to wait for the website to be functioning again. [9]And if you pay your bills via online banking, you may have to put up with bad customer service because switching accounts for bill payments is a time-consuming nuisance.

Topic   a. banks

b. brick-and-mortar banks

c. customer service

d. drawbacks of online banking

EXPLANATION   This paragraph has several references to the drawbacks of online banking. But it's up to the reader to combine the words *drawbacks* and *online banking* in order to express the topic.

1. Sophisticated methods of detecting lying are in the experimental stage. There is hope, for instance, that facial movements may one day reveal deception. Some companies are using the fMRI[†] to look for patterns of brain activation associated with lying. If this technique proves out, it may be especially useful to law enforcement, intelligence agencies, and transportation security officials. There may even come a day when you will need to have your brain scanned when applying for a sensitive position in government or industry. But that day is not here. As of yet, we lack any reliable indicator of lying, let alone anything akin to Pinocchio's nose, which grew each time the puppet told a lie. (Adapted from Jeffrey S. Nevid, *Psychology: Concepts and Applications*, 4th ed. © Cengage Learning.)

Topic   a. lying
b. lie detectors in law enforcement
c. possible methods of lie detection
d. brain scans for lie detection

2. Thomas Edison is rightly famous for his brilliance as a clever inventor. Among other things, he helped bring us electricity, phonographs, and motion pictures. Edison is less known, though, for his role in inventing the electric chair. In 1887, the New York State legislature was searching for a method of execution other than hanging. A member of the legislature had heard rumors about people who were accidentally electrocuted and died. The legislature wrote to Edison, posing a question: Would electrocution be a more humane method of execution? Edison wrote back, saying he thought 1,000 volts of electricity could provide a quick and painless death. Edison then conducted a series of experiments to prove his claim. In the course of those experiments, he put to death numerous dogs and cats, some cattle, and at least one horse. It's not that Edison wanted to take credit for inventing the electric chair. Rather, he wanted the

---

[†]fMRI (functional magnetic resonance imaging): an imaging technique that measures brain activity by means of blood flow.

State of New York to use a generator* made by his archrival,* West-inghouse. Edison hoped the general public would grow fearful of Westinghouse products once it knew that, as he liked to put it, prisoners were being "Westinghoused" to death.

Topic   a. Edison and the electric chair
          b. Edison's rivalry with Westinghouse
          c. the genius of Thomas Edison
          d. Edison's cruelty to animals

3. Even beautiful people sometimes feel unattractive. There are handsome actors who won't let their right side be photographed for fear of looking unattractive. There are gorgeous models who obsess because they are a few pounds overweight. For some people, however, feeling unattractive is not a momentary state. On the contrary, victims of body dysmorphic disorder, or BDD, feel ugly all the time, no matter what their mirror shows. For victims of BDD, even tiny flaws, like a freckle, a small mole, or a pimple, are a source of misery. These minor imperfections are viewed as a catastrophe, so much so that BDD victims frequently refuse to leave their homes or be in the company of other people. Victims of BDD avoid the society of other people because they imagine that their horrifying physical appearance will earn them nothing but ridicule. When the disorder reaches this state, a combination of medication and therapy is needed because victims can become so desperate, they commit suicide rather than expose their "ugliness" to the world. Ironically, victims of BDD are often extremely attractive. They are also likely to be people who have had repeated cosmetic surgeries.

Topic   a. the beautiful people
          b. victims of body dysmorphic disorder
          c. models who obsess about their looks
          d. people with physical imperfections

4. The term *weathering* refers to the change or breakdown of rocks or mineral masses. While weathering sometimes reduces huge boulders

---

*generator: machine that produces electricity.
*archrival: main opponent.

to little more than a pile of rubble, it also can produce shapes and forms of extraordinary beauty. Particularly lovely are *ventifacts*. These are stone sculptures left behind from windblown sand beating against a hard surface. The desert terrain of Death Valley is strewn with ventifacts. Many of them appear to have been shaped by a human hand. Ventifacts, however, are not made by humans. They are Mother Nature's impressive creation.

Topic
   a. weathering
   b. natural sculptures
   c. Death Valley
   d. ventifacts

Death Valley in California is littered with sculptures created by Mother Nature.

© Ulrich Flemming

VOCABULARY EXTRA

The previous paragraph uses the word *terrain*. If you have any trouble remembering the meaning of that word, keep in mind that *terra* means "earth" in Latin. From that Latin root come words like *territory*, *territorial*, *terrain*, and *terrestrial*. You may not be familiar with the last of those words. But you are probably familiar with the word *extraterrestrial*, which means "out of or beyond earth." *Extraterrestrials* is the word we use to describe beings believed by some to live in places outside of earth.

⊶ READING KEYS

◆ If the author seems to start out with one topic and end with another, it's usually the topic at the end that's the most important.

◆ Although one word can sometimes sum up the topic, you'll often need several words to express it.

◆ Frequently readers have to come up with some or even all the words for the topic.

◆ The topic should be general enough to include everything discussed in the paragraph but specific enough to exclude what isn't.

◆ Often the first general clue to the topic is in the first couple of sentences. Then the additional sentences make the topic more specific. When you read, keep thinking about what each sentence adds to your understanding of the topic.

◆ EXERCISE 3   Identifying Topics Repeated, Referred to, and Implied

DIRECTIONS   Select the topic of each paragraph by circling the appropriate letter.

1. In an attempt to control cable charges to consumers, Congress passed the 1992 Cable Act to regulate cable rates. The cable companies, facing competition from the local telephone companies, argued that Congress should remove rate regulation to allow them to compete and to help raise cable income. Congress must have been listening. The Telecommunications Act of 1996 removed most rate regulation for all companies. All that remains is regulation to monitor the "basic tier" of cable service, often called "basic cable." (Adapted from Shirley Biagi, *Media/Impact*, 10th ed. © Cengage Learning.)

   Topic   a. the rise of the cable companies in the United States

   b. congressional mistakes

   c. cable rate regulation

   d. the Telecommunications Act of 1996

2. The Amish are a branch of the Mennonites, a religious group originally from Switzerland. Although Amish settlements exist in Ohio, Indiana, and Pennsylvania, the people in those settlements try to avoid all contact with the outside world. Travel, except for visits to neighbors, is discouraged. In any case, traveling is far from easy because owning bicycles, motorcycles, and automobiles is strictly

forbidden. Horse and buggy is the preferred mode of transportation. The Amish also refuse to use electricity from power lines. They, however, use batteries, wind, and water sources of energy.

Topic (a.) alternative sources of energy for the Amish

b. Amish religious restrictions

c. religious groups

d. the Mennonites

3. Amnesty International was formed in 1961 to protect human rights throughout the world. Created by British lawyer Peter Benenson, it now has more than a million members. Members work to help people who face unjust imprisonment, unfair trials, torture, or execution. The main goal of Amnesty International is to assist those who have been punished for their political beliefs. For example, in 2005 the organization successfully engineered the release of Rebiya Kadeer, a Chinese businesswoman wrongfully imprisoned for over five years. She had been convicted of leaking secret information because she sent newspaper clippings to her husband in the United States. Amnesty International helps people like Kadeer by publicizing their cases, appealing to authorities, and arranging for legal defense. It also exposes human rights violations, encourages governments to change laws, and conducts campaigns to educate the public about human rights.

Topic a. Rebiya Kadeer's tragic story

b. human rights

(c.) goals of Amnesty International

d. political prisoners around the world

4. A famous twelfth-century couple, Heloise and Abelard, is often mentioned when romantic love becomes the subject of scholarly discussion. Yet, in truth, there wasn't much romance in either the couple's courtship or their marriage. When they met, Heloise was the niece of a wealthy scholar. Abelard was the most famous teacher in France. Older and vastly more educated, Abelard became the girl's tutor. The two fell in love. When Heloise bore Abelard's son, they married in secret because the couple did not want the scholar's career hurt by scandal. However, when Heloise's uncle found out what had happened, he forced his niece to become a nun and had

Abelard castrated.[†] Separated for the rest of their lives, Heloise and Abelard wrote passionate love letters so emotionally powerful that they were eventually published. Those letters have assured the lovers their place in the history of romantic love.

Topic   a. the subject of love

       (b.) the story of Heloise and Abelard

       c. the love letters of Heloise and Abelard

       d. love in the Middle Ages

5. Medical reformer Dr. Benjamin Rush (1745–1813) was one of the first to argue that mentally ill people should not be punished for the crime of being sick. Rush also insisted that doctors listen closely to their patients and take careful notes on their complaints. Without question, he was a force for good in medical treatment. That does not mean, however, that Benjamin Rush never did any harm; in fact, even some of Dr. Rush's colleagues considered his prescriptions for health rather dangerous. In an era that believed bloodletting was good therapy, Dr. Rush was overly enthusiastic. He often drew large amounts of blood from patients already weakened by disease. It was suspected, in fact, that some of his patients died from his treatment rather than their illness. Dr. Rush also came up with the idea of the "Tranquilizer Chair." Patients were strapped into a chair with their head packed in a box. Unable to move or speak, they had no choice but to calm down. In addition, Dr. Rush believed that patients suffering from mental disturbances should spend more time swinging in the air. On his recommendation, patients were strapped into chairs. The chairs would then be suspended from the ceiling. Attendants kept them swinging or spinning until the patients showed signs of improvement. Fortunately, vomiting was considered an improvement. Once they got sick enough, the patients were let down from the ceiling.

Topic   a. the tranquilizer chair

       b. eighteenth-century treatments for mental illness

       c. Benjamin Rush's medical reforms

       d. Benjamin Rush's harmful medical treatments

[†]In the twelfth century, castration, or the cutting off of a man's testicles, was not an unusual punishment for a sexual crime.

WEB QUEST/CLASS ACTION

How does the Amish community punish those who commit crimes? _They Leave it UP to God to Punish them They Repent in Church_

Once you think you understand how crime is handled among the Amish, come to class prepared to discuss why you think the Amish version of justice is effective or ineffective.

and are forgiven

Keep an Eye Open for Clues to the Main Idea

While you are trying to determine the topic of a paragraph, you also need to think about what main idea is emerging as you process each sentence. The **main idea** is the central thought, meaning, or point that the author wants to express *about* the topic.

The Difference Between Topic and Main Idea

The difference between a topic and a main idea will become clearer to you if you imagine the following: You happen to overhear a conversation in which your name is repeatedly mentioned. When you ask your friends what they were discussing, they say that they were talking about you. At that moment, you have the topic, but you don't know the main idea.

You don't know, that is, what your friends were saying *about* you. Undoubtedly you would pester them until you knew exactly what they had said about your personality, appearance, or behavior. Who wouldn't?

The same approach should apply to reading because the topic is only a stepping-stone to the main idea. The moment you first get a sense of the topic, ask yourself, What does the author seem to be saying *about* this topic? Even if you decide that the topic you had in mind is not the exact topic, you are still a step closer to determining the main idea.

For instance, the topic of the following paragraph is "name brands" or "branding products." The question now is, What's the main idea? Read the paragraph and see what you think.

Note how the heading offers a clue to the topic.

Sentences 2 and 3 confirm that branding is the topic.

Since the rest of the paragraph describes the benefits of branding, we can say that "branding helps both buyers and sellers" is the main idea.

Branding   ¹Both buyers and sellers benefit from branding. ²Because brands are easily recognizable, they reduce the amount of time buyers must spend shopping; buyers can quickly identify the brands they prefer. ³Choosing particular brands such as Tommy Hilfiger, Polo, Nautica, and Nike can be a way of expressing oneself. ⁴When buyers are unable to evaluate a product's characteristics, brands can help them judge the quality of the product. ⁵For example, most buyers aren't able to judge the quality of stereo components but may be guided by a well-respected brand name. ⁶Brands can symbolize a certain quality level to a customer. . . . ⁷Brands thus help reduce a buyer's perceived risk of purchase. ⁸Finally, customers may receive a psychological reward that comes from owning a brand that symbolizes status. ⁹The Lexus brand is an example. (William M. Pride , Robert J. Hughes, and Jack R. Kapoor, *Business*, 10th ed. © Cengage Learning.)

In this case, the main idea appears in the first sentence, which tells readers that branding has benefits for both buyers and sellers. The remainder of the paragraph then offers some specific examples, all of which point back to the opening statement about the benefits of branding.

In other words, threading its way through the entire paragraph is the idea introduced in the opening sentence: "Branding is a good thing for both consumers and sellers." That's what the author wants to say about the topic, and that's the main idea.

Introducing Topic Sentences

That first sentence is also what's called a **topic sentence.** Topic sentences are one of the major ways textbook authors communicate the main idea or central point to the reader. This is particularly true, by the way, of business texts. Anytime you read through a paragraph and see a sentence that seems to sum up the main idea you have been formulating as you read, it's probably the topic sentence. But more about topic sentences in the next section.

READING KEYS

◆ The main idea is the central point or thought the writer wants to communicate to readers. It's what ties all the sentences in the paragraph together.

◆ Topic sentences are general sentences that sum up the point of the paragraph. They are one of the main ways textbook writers communicate key points to readers.

◆ **EXERCISE 4**   **Recognizing the Main Idea**

DIRECTIONS   Read each paragraph and circle the letter of the topic and the main idea expressed in the paragraph.

1. [1]By the end of the nineteenth century, the bison in this country were almost extinct. [2]Yet, miraculously, the American bison survived— largely because of human laziness. [3]As the animals grew rarer, hunting them became much harder. [4]Only very experienced hunters were willing to risk the bitter winters in the valleys where the bison took shelter. [5]In these areas, the snow was waist-deep. [6]Temperatures were often 25° below zero. [7]Few were fearless enough to follow the bison into such bone-chilling cold, As a result, the hardy bison survived.

Topic
   a. nineteenth-century hunting

   b. hunting bison in the snow

   c. survival of the American bison

Main Idea
   a. By the end of the nineteenth century, America's bison were extinct, and hunters turned their sights on other prey.

   b. Against all odds, America's bison survived, mainly because few hunters were determined enough to follow their tracks.

   c. The bison are yet another example of how early Americans failed to preserve the country's natural resources.

2. [1]The story of King Solomon and the Queen of Sheba appears in both the Bible and the Koran; it also belongs to the legends of Syria and Egypt. [2]Although there are several versions of what happened between King Solomon and the Queen of Sheba, the stories agree on several basic points. [3]According to all accounts, the beautiful young queen journeyed to Solomon, the king of Israel, to test his wisdom. [4]Solomon is said to have fallen in love with the young queen and she with him. [5]After bearing Solomon a son, the Queen of Sheba returned to her own country. [6]Many people believe that the biblical book *Song of Songs*, a collection of love poems attributed* to King Solomon, is a record of his love for the Queen of Sheba.

---

*attributed: credited to or said to be the work of.

Topic   a. legends from the Middle East

               b. the story of Solomon and Sheba

               c. the wisdom of Solomon

Main Idea   a. The story of Solomon and Sheba has become part of almost every culture, perhaps because it so beautifully illustrates the nature of true love.

               b. Several versions of the story of Solomon and Sheba exist, but there are similarities among the various versions.

               c. The *Song of Songs* from the Bible is believed to have been inspired by King Solomon's love for the Queen of Sheba.

3. [1]At one time, home schooling was dismissed as a rare educational alternative practiced only by a very few oddballs. [2]But the long-term successes of home-schooled children have caused parents and educators to reconsider the practice. [3]About 25 percent of home-schooled students are one grade level ahead of their peers. [4]Home-schooled kids consistently score in the top third on achievement tests. [5]Also, their SAT scores are higher than those of kids enrolled in public or private schools. [6]In the 2001 National Spelling Bee, an event that attracts some of the best students in the country, 27 of the 248 participants were homeschoolers. [7]In 2000, homeschoolers placed first, second, and third in that contest. [8]Furthermore, the majority of homeschoolers go on to college. [9]In fact, quite a few of them are winning admission to elite schools such as Harvard University. [10]In 1998, more than seventy National Merit Scholarship semifinalists were home-schooled high school seniors. [11]By 2003, that number had doubled.[†] [12]In 2009 home-schooled students earned an average score of 22.5 on the ACT (American College Test) entrance exam while the national average was 21.1.

Topic   a. home schooling and National Merit Scholarships

               b. success of home schooling

               c. criticism of home schooling

Main Idea   a. At one time, home schooling children was considered odd, but that time is long gone, and home schooling's success has made it a legitimate alternative for many parents.

[†]For this figure to be meaningful, you need to know that over 10,000 scholarships get awarded every year.

b. As it turns out, home-schooled children do better in college than do those who attended public schools.

c. Home schooling is now being practiced by the majority of parents who have children of school age.

4. [1]Although thirty-one states have officially banned corporal, or physical, punishment each year, about 200,000 students across the country are disciplined using that method. [2]Corporal punishment is still used even though those who oppose it cite several reasons why it is not only ineffective but harmful. [3]First of all, paddling a child is no more effective than other forms of discipline. [4]In fact, spanking usually just delays the next incident of misbehavior. [5]Even worse, many children who are spanked react with increased aggression and rebelliousness. [6]It's also just too easy to use corporal punishment inappropriately. [7]Some teachers may simply consider it the easiest method for subduing students. [8]Those who are free to paddle may then not make the effort to try more positive discipline strategies. [9]In the most extreme cases, teachers who use corporal punishment could easily cross the line into child abuse.

Topic

a. pros and cons of corporal punishment

b. teacher abuse of corporal punishment

c. harmful effects of corporal punishment

Main Idea

a. Punishing children through the use of corporal punishment is the main reason why children are engaging in criminal behavior at an increasingly early age.

b. All too often, corporal punishment in the classroom crosses the line into child abuse.

c. Corporal punishment in school persists despite claims that it has no positive effect and causes harm.

Topic Sentences and Textbooks

Topic sentences are an effective tool for writers who want to communicate, as quickly as possible, a large body of unfamiliar information to their readers. It makes sense, then, that textbooks, which have precisely that **purpose**, or intention, make more use of topic sentences than any other kind of writing.

Particularly in subjects like business and communications, textbook authors frequently—make that *very frequently*—start their paragraphs with topic sentences, Here's an example from a communications text:

The topic sentence is the most general sentence.

The rest of the sentences work to make the opening sentence more specific.

[1]In 1998 . . . Congress passed the Child Online Protection Act (COPA). [2]The goal of COPA was to prevent minors from getting access to sexually explicit online material. [3]Congress based the legislation on the idea that the government has a responsibility to protect children from content that is legal for adults but could be considered harmful to minors. (Adapted from Shirley Biagi, *Media Impact*, 10th ed. © Cengage Learning.)

Here's another example, this one from a business text.

Again the topic sentence is the most general sentence. It's further explained by the sentences that follow.

[1]**Planning**, in its simplest form, is establishing organizational goals and deciding how to accomplish them. [2]It's often referred to as the "first" management function because all other management functions depend on planning. [3]Organizations such as Nissan, Houston Community Colleges, and the U.S. Secret Service begin the planning process by developing a mission statement that defines company goals in detail. (Adapted from William M. Pride et al., *Business*, 10th ed. © Cengage Learning.)

Frequently Does Not Mean Always

Even business texts, however, which are very likely to introduce a string of paragraphs opening with topic sentences, don't always follow that exact template, or pattern. Look, for example, at this next paragraph:

Although the paragraph starts out with what seems to be a general topic, "maintaining positive relationships," it quickly narrows to "relationship marketing."

The second sentence is the topic sentence that gets more specific development from the details that follow.

[1]Maintaining positive relationships with customers is an important goal for marketers. [2]The term *relationship marketing* refers to "marketing decisions and activities focused on achieving long-term, satisfying relationships with customers." [3]Relationship marketing continually deepens the buyer's trust in the company, which, as the customer's loyalty grows, increases the company's understanding of the customer's needs and desires. [4]Relationship marketing encourages cooperation and mutual trust. [5]For example, Chico's, a specialty women's retailer, offers a Passport Program that gives members such benefits as monthly coupons, free shipping, and 5 percent off all future purchases. [6]Such initiatives* are a common part of relationship marketing and build consumer loyalty. (Adapted from William M. Pride et al., *Business*, 10th ed. © Cengage Learning.)

*initiatives: new plans for realizing goals.

In this case, the first sentence is an **introductory sentence**. Introductory sentences are general sentences that provide context or background for the topic sentence that follows. Notice how sentences 3 through 6, all make more specific the "decisions and activities" mentioned in the second sentence. The fact that the second sentence is developed by the more specific sentences that follow is what makes the second sentence a topic sentence.

⊶⫟ READING KEYS

- ◆ Topic sentences have three characteristics: (1) they are among the most general sentences in a paragraph, (2) they introduce an idea that is developed in more specific detail by other sentences in the paragraph, and (3) they answer questions, like What's the point of the paragraph? Why did the author write it?
- ◆ Topic sentences can and do appear anywhere in a paragraph. However, particularly in textbooks, they are quite likely to be the first or second sentence in the paragraph.
- ◆ If the second sentence adds more specific information to the first, then the first sentence is probably the topic sentence. You can be certain that the first sentence is the topic sentence if the third sentence also continues developing the idea introduced in the opening sentence.
- ◆ Introductory sentences are general sentences that provide context or background for the topic sentence that appears later in the paragraph.

◆ EXERCISE 5　　Recognizing Topic Sentences

DIRECTIONS　In each group of three sentences, one is more general than the other two and could function as the topic sentence. Circle the letter of that sentence.

EXAMPLE

a. Jupiter's four largest moons are Io, Europa, Ganymede, and Callisto.

b. Io and Europa are closer to Jupiter than Ganymede and Callisto.

c. Jupiter is surrounded by numerous moons.

EXPLANATION　Answer *c* is correct because the other two sentences continue the discussion of Jupiter's numerous moons. This information is covered in topic sentence *c*, only in a more general way.

1. a. With a few exceptions, most states tax personal income.
   b. Wisconsin was the first state to enact a personal income tax.
   c. Only Alaska, South Dakota, Florida, Texas, Nevada, Washington, and Wyoming leave all personal income untaxed.

2. a. Dog owners have been known to go overboard in their love for their pets, treating them with all the privileges of spoiled children.
   b. In the seventeenth century, some dog owners let their favorite hunting dogs roam freely throughout the house, terrorizing strangers and guests alike.
   c. When the eighteenth-century general Napoleon Bonaparte married the widow Josephine de Beauharnais in 1796, he discovered that his new wife wouldn't spend the night with him unless her beloved dog was in the bed.

3. a. During the chariot races, a featured part of ancient circuses, it was an unusual event when either a horse or a charioteer did not die.
   b. During the reign of Augustus, more than 3,500 lions, tigers, and other jungle cats died in the circus arena, taking with them hundreds of gladiators.
   c. The two biggest draws of ancient circuses were bloodshed and death.

4. a. If a modern fictional heroine can't meet her sweetheart at the train station, she can always text message him the reason, but in novels past, her inability to reach him was the cause of tragedy.
   b. Cell phone technology has had a profound effect on fictional storytelling, making plots of the past no longer seem possible.
   c. If they want to make their victims helpless and unable to call for help, writers of thrillers now need a setting like a subway station, where the person being stalked can't always whip out a cell phone and call 911.

◆ **EXERCISE 6**   **Topic Sentences in First and Second Position**

DIRECTIONS   Circle the correct letter to indicate if the topic sentence opens the paragraph or follows an introductory sentence.

Sentence 1 raises questions, like, What remarkable ability?

Sentence 2 provides an example of sentence 1. What does that tell the reader?

The word *brain* is the most repeated word in the paragraph so it's the topic.

EXAMPLE [1]Scientists now believe that the brain, if it stays active, has a remarkable ability to develop even in old age. [2]Research on rats, for example, shows that intellectual exercise causes their brain cells to branch like trees. [3]These new branches then function as additional connections between individual brain cells. [4]Scientists think that these newly formed connections, produced by strenuous intellectual exertion, serve to enhance both memory and mental sharpness, despite the passage of time. [5]That theory certainly seems to be confirmed by the Sisters of Notre Dame in Mankato, Minnesota. [6]Although advanced in age, the sisters show little, if any, loss of memory or mental quickness, and one reason for that may be their lifestyle. [7]The nuns are engaged in a variety of intellectual activities from morning until night. [8]They cook, write, sing, pray and study from almost dawn until dusk. [9]Their constant mental activity may be why their brains stay sharp even into advanced old age.

a. Sentence 1 is the topic sentence.
b. Sentence 2 is the topic sentence.

EXPLANATION The first sentence is the most general in the paragraph. The remaining sentences offer specific evidence for the claim that the brain continues to develop even into old age. The sentences following the first one further explain what it means to stay active.

1. [1]Michael Faraday was the son of a poor blacksmith and had very little formal education. [2]Yet despite his lack of formal education, Faraday's accomplishments reveal a brilliant and imaginative mind. [3]Faraday invented the first electric motor. [4]He also showed that magnetism could be transformed into electricity and constructed a dynamo.* [5]The first electrical transformer* is another one of Faraday's inventions. [6]He also showed how magnetism could affect polarized light—light that vibrates in only one direction. [7]His discoveries won him fame in several different fields.

   a. Sentence 1 is the topic sentence.
   b. Sentence 2 is the topic sentence

---

*dynamo: a machine that produces electric current.
*transformer: a device used to increase electrical current.

2. [1]For years now, parents of children with attention deficit disorder (ADD)—the inability to concentrate—have relied on medication to improve their children's attention span. [2]Currently, however, many parents of children with ADD are singing the praises of a new and promising therapy—the practice of martial* arts. [3]And the parents are not alone. [4]A number of doctors, along with organizations like the National Attention Deficit Disorder Association, argue that training in self-defense systems like karate, jujitsu, and tai chi can ease the symptoms of ADD. [5]These symptoms include impulsiveness, inability to concentrate, and hyperactivity. [6]According to Dr. John J. Ratey, an associate professor of clinical psychology at Harvard Medical School, the martial arts require the kind of concentration that forces the attention centers in the brain to work together. [7]Therein lies the special benefit of the martial arts for children and adults who find it difficult to concentrate.

   a. Sentence 1 is the topic sentence.

   b. Sentence 2 is the topic sentence.

3. [1]Americans use the word *love* as a catchall term that refers to very different emotions: We love the music of Bruno Mars, jelly doughnuts, Cocoa Puffs, our parents, spouses, and pets. [2]The ancient Greeks, in contrast, were far more precise when talking of love. [3]They used different words to identify different kinds of love. [4]When they talked about romance or sexual passion, the Greeks used the word *eros*. [5]But if the conversation turned to love between friends, they used the word *phila*. [6]To talk about spiritual love, the Greeks used *agape*, which emphasized the need to love without expecting anything in return.

   a. Sentence 1 is the topic sentence.

   b. Sentence 2 is the topic sentence.

4. [1]Interest groups frequently use a host of media, from television, radio, and traditional print media to blogs and the Internet, to lobby for public policies that support their well-being. [2]But in doing so, interest groups often use secret tactics to influence both public opinion and our elected representatives. [3]Industries, companies, and trade associations will hide behind neutral named not-for-profits and other institutions to represent them in media campaigns dealing with political issues and public policy. [4]For example, Americans

---

*martial: having to do with battle or war.

Against Food Taxes is a self-described "coalition of concerned citizens . . . opposed to the government's proposed tax hike on food and beverages." [5]While it sounds like a consumer advocacy group, in reality the members of this organization are dominated by industries that sell food and beverage products, including 7-Eleven convenience stores, the Pepsi Cola Company, Burger King, McDonald's, Dairy Queen, and the Dr. Pepper Snapple Group. (Adapted from Alan R. Gitelson et al., *American Government*, 10th ed. © Cengage Learning.)

   a. Sentence 1 is the topic sentence.
   b. Sentence 2 is the topic sentence.

5. [1]Unlike Mercury and Venus, which have no moons, Mars has two small moons. [2]Named *Phobos* (Fear) and *Deimos* (Panic) for the horses that drew the war god Mars's chariot, they are, on a cosmic scale, little more than large rocks. [3]Both moons are irregularly shaped and heavily cratered. [4]They both also have dark surfaces, which make them difficult to observe from Earth. [5]Both moons can be seen with a small telescope, however. (Adapted from James Shipman et al., *An Introduction to Physical Science*, 11th ed. © Cengage Learning.)

   a. Sentence 1 is the topic sentence.
   b. Sentence 2 is the topic sentence.

WEB QUEST/CLASS ACTION

For decades we were told that there were nine planets. Now we are hearing that there are only eight. What planet got bumped from the list of nine? Be prepared to explain as well why it was eliminated.

Pluto is not a planet Because of it's size and location in space.

Reversal Transitions and Topic Sentences

Reversal transitions already turned up in Chapter 2, where they signaled the presence of contrast context clues. Reversal transitions, however, can also help you identify topic sentences. Note, for instance, how they set the stage for the topic sentences in these two paragraphs from a previous exercise:

> [1]Michael Faraday was the son of a poor blacksmith and had very little formal education. [2]*Yet despite his lack of formal education,* Faraday's accomplishments reveal a brilliant and imaginative mind. [3]Faraday invented the first electric motor. [4]He also showed that magnetism could be converted into electricity and constructed a dynamo. [5]The first electrical transformer is another one of Faraday's inventions. [6]He also showed how magnetism could affect polarized light—light that vibrates in only one direction. [7]His discoveries won him fame in several different fields.

> [1]For years now, parents of children with attention deficit disorder (ADD)—the inability to concentrate—have relied on medication to improve their children's attention span. [2]*Currently, however,* many parents of children with ADD are singing the praises of a new and promising therapy—the practice of martial arts. [3]And the parents are not alone. [4]A number of doctors, along with organizations like the National Attention Deficit Disorder Association, argue that training in self-defense systems like karate, jujitsu, and tai chi can ease the symptoms of ADD. [5]These symptoms include impulsiveness, inability to concentrate, and hyperactivity.

In the first paragraph, the writer uses the introductory sentence to tell readers about Faraday's lack of education. Knowing that they will perceive this lack as a drawback, the author prepares them for good news by saying, "Yet despite his lack of formal education."

Similarly, in the second paragraph, the author starts out by telling readers what parents used to do when their children suffered from ADD. But since the author really wants to say, "That was then, this is now," the topic sentence starts off with a reversal transition, which paves the way for that shift in thought.

Pushing the Topic Sentence Deeper into the Paragraph

As you saw above, writers often like to give readers some background or context before getting to the real point. They tell readers "this is the way things used to be done" or "this was the obstacle to be overcome."

Sometimes, though, that background or context requires more than one sentence. When that happens, the topic sentence can take up residence closer to the middle of the paragraph, as it does here. And once again, the reversal transition plays a key role.

Notice how sentences 1–4 remain fairly specific. They aren't especially open to different interpretations.

By sentence 5, the sentences are becoming more general. By sentence 6, we know that the forests are disappearing, but we don't know why.

Sentence 7 tells us why they are dwindling.

The remaining sentences tell us what's being done about the dwindling forests.

[1]In 1975, an American salesman was on a hiking vacation in Central Mexico. [2]Roaming through a darkened forest, he came upon a spectacular sight—millions of monarch butterflies nesting in trees. [3]The butterflies were so densely clustered it was hard to catch a glimpse of the underlying trunks. [4]A mystery for years, the winter home of the monarch butterfly had finally been found. [5]Scientists were ecstatic. [6]*Yet* sadly, much of that original ecstasy has vanished because the forests inhabited by monarch butterflies are rapidly dwindling. [7]Local farmers have been cutting the trees for both fuel and income. [8]Because logging is a matter of survival, the farmers have not responded to government efforts to protect the areas where monarchs rest in midwinter. [9]In the hopes of saving the forests and thereby the butterflies, the Mexican government has established a $5 million fund to compensate those farmers who relinquish logging rights. [10]In addition, nonprofit groups are working with local communities to help them develop alternative sources of income.

In business, communication, and government texts, you won't see the above pattern too often. The topic sentence won't, that is, show up in the middle of the paragraph.

History is another matter. History texts do often feature long paragraphs in which the topic sentence splits the specific details in half. Thus you need to be aware of the possibility and on the lookout for a paragraph pattern that has this shape:

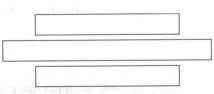

And, yes, when topic sentences appear in the middle of paragraphs, they are frequently introduced by reversal transitions. But that's not always the case. Rather than relying on the presence of a reversal transition, you are better off visualizing the shape of paragraphs with a midpoint topic sentence. They bulge in the middle and get narrow at the beginning and end. They bulge in the middle because specific sentences introduce the general point. Then that general point is followed by more specific sentences that explain it.

Transitions Signaling Contrast, Reversal, or Change ◆	but	nonetheless
	conversely	on the other hand
	despite	still
	however	unfortunately
	in contrast	whereas
	nevertheless	yet

O━ READING KEYS

◆ If a transition like *however*, *unfortunately*, or *yet* opens the second sentence in a paragraph, the second sentence is likely to be the topic sentence.

◆ Much of the time, topic sentences starting in the middle of a paragraph will begin with a reversal transition. But that's not always the case.

◆ Paragraphs with a topic sentence in the middle bulge at midpoint when the general sentence takes center stage. After that midpoint, the paragraph slims down again as it gets more specific.

IDIOM ALERT: To lay claim

When people lay claim to something, they say that it belongs to them. "When the orphans arrived on the train,[†] residents of the western towns would line up and lay claim to the healthiest and the strongest, not to adopt them but to use them as servants."

◆ **EXERCISE 7** **Recognizing Topic Sentences and Reversal Transitions**

DIRECTIONS After reading each paragraph, write the number of the topic sentence in the blank. Circle any reversal transitions that appear before the topic sentence.

[†]In the nineteenth century, orphans from the East were routinely put on trains and shipped out West for "adoption."

Look at the way sentences 1 and 2 are just about equally specific in their description of Stanley's activities.

Sentence 3 gets a little broader, but it's not the one that gets developed.

Sentence 4 is the general sentence that gets developed in the remainder of the paragraph, making it the topic sentence.

EXAMPLE   ¹In the 1870s, Welsh explorer Henry Morton Stanley sailed the length of the Congo River under the sponsorship of King Leopold of Belgium. ²All along the length of the river, Stanley made treaties with the African tribes he encountered. ³Thanks to those treaties, Leopold was able to lay claim to territory that was eighty times the size of Belgium. ⁴Calling his newly acquired land the "Belgian Congo," Leopold began extracting its rich store of natural resources, torturing and killing its inhabitants in the process. ⁵Agents of the Belgian government would give each Congolese family a basket to be filled with rubber. ⁶If family members did not return with their baskets filled to the top, their homes would be burned to the ground. ⁷Anyone who rebelled was imprisoned. ⁸Thanks to this system, Leopold grew rich and squandered his blood money on yachts, mansions, and mistresses. ⁹Eventually, when word of Leopold's brutality in the Congo made the newspapers, King Leopold was forced to give up control of the Congo because of public outrage.

Sentence ___4___ is the topic sentence.

EXPLANATION   Here again, the topic sentence is edging toward the middle as the author first describes how King Leopold got his hands on the Belgian Congo. None of the first three sentences, however, gets more specific support. That means that sentence 4 is the topic sentence because it does get further developed.

1. ¹Occasionally audience members are invited to join in theater productions. ²Usually, the people involved in such productions— writers, directors, and even the theatergoers—think that audience participation is a modern invention. ³But, in fact, audience participation in theater is at least 400 years old and dates back to the Japanese theater known as *kabuki*. ⁴Originating in the sixteenth century, kabuki theater blended music, song, and dance. ⁵Its purpose was to spread Buddhist thinking. ⁶In early kabuki productions, actors would often directly address members of the audience. ⁷The audience would respond and even clap in time to the music. ⁸Some theatergoers would also call out the names of favorite actors or request popular songs or dances. ⁹It's not clear, however, that this practice was encouraged by members of the acting troupe.

Sentence ___3___ is the topic sentence.

2. [1]Most people know that snake venom can be deadly. [2]However, few people are aware that snake venom can, on occasion, save lives and ease pain. [3]The venom of a snake called Russell's viper, for example, has clotting properties. [4]In the past, it has been used to stop uncontrolled bleeding in hemophiliacs.* [5]Researchers have also discovered that the venom of the deadly Malayan pit viper can dissolve blood clots. [6]Thus, the venom has been used to treat patients who have undergone surgery and are in danger of developing blood clots. [7]Some venoms also have properties that make them useful as painkillers in the treatment of arthritis and cancer.

Sentence ___2___ is the topic sentence.

3. [1]Childhood is supposed to be a carefree and happy time. [2]And perhaps it is for some children. [3]But for children who are seriously overweight, childhood can be pure hell. [4]Overweight children as young as three can find themselves targeted for aggression by their peers. [5]Heavy kids are teased and laughed at. [6]Sometimes they are even beaten up, all because they have committed the sin of being overweight. [7]And it's not just their peers who are cruel. [8]A study done by researchers at Yale University and the University of Hawaii suggests that parents and educators also tend to be critical of children who are overweight. [9]Surprisingly, parents, in particular, seem embarrassed by having produced an obese child. [10]They express their embarrassment by publicly humiliating the child about his or her eating habits and excess weight.

Sentence ___3___ is the topic sentence.

4. [1]How does U.S. family leave policy compare with that in other countries? [2]Most industrialized countries have much more generous policies than those in the United States, providing not only more extended leaves of absence so that working parents can take care of their young children but also financial support for part or all of the leave period. [3]In Sweden, Germany, and France, one parent can take a paid infant-care leave supported by the employer or a social insurance fund. [4]If both parents choose to continue to work, they are guaranteed access to high-quality day care for their child. [5]In

---

*hemophiliacs: people suffering from a rare blood disease that inhibits the blood's ability to clot.

Sweden, either the mother or father is entitled to a twelve-month paid leave to stay home with a new infant. [6]The parent on leave is reimbursed 90 percent of her or his salary for the first nine months following the child's birth, receives $150 per month for the next three months, and then is allowed to continue with an unpaid leave and a job guarantee for six additional months until the child is eighteen months old. (Kelvin L. Seifert and Robert Hoffnung, *Child and Adolescent Development*. Boston: Houghton Mifflin, 1999, p. 222.)

Sentence _____ is the topic sentence.

5. [1]When you pick up a handful of newly fallen snow to make a snowball, it seems to weigh very little. [2]But snow is frozen water. [3]You must know from your own experience that it can get heavy very quickly. [4]You do not feel water's weight in a glass of water. [5]But you do when you carry a gallon of it. [6]A five-gallon bottle of water weighs about forty pounds and is already too heavy for many to carry. [7]A cubic foot of water weighs about sixty-two pounds—too heavy for many to lift, let alone carry around. [8]Therefore, it should come as no surprise to learn that heavy winter snows are a menace to roofs, which can collapse under the weight of piled up snow. [9]It follows, then, that roofs have to be engineered to withstand the heaviest expected snowfall for the particular area where they are located. [10]But things can go wrong even when engineers, architects, and contractors consciously design and put up roofs capable of

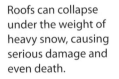

Roofs can collapse under the weight of heavy snow, causing serious damage and even death.

maintaining heavy snow loads. [11]If a region experiences much heavier than average snow loads, roofs can and do collapse under the weight.

Sentence _____ is the topic sentence.

When Topic Sentences Come Last

Topic sentences appearing at the end of paragraphs are not as common as topic sentences appearing at the beginning. But that's not to say they are unimportant. The contrary is true. Particularly in longer readings, paragraphs that end with the topic sentence play a very big role.

But for now, let's focus on single paragraphs that hold off on the topic sentence until the very end, for instance:

Sentences 1–4 are equally specific. They all characterize how fathers are portrayed.

Sentence 5 is general enough to sum up and include all the sentences that came before.

[1]Fathers of children born outside marriage are sometimes pictured as lacking a sense of responsibility for their actions. [2]At other times, they are portrayed as people who would like to be responsible for their children if only they were given a chance. [3]Yet in reality, some fathers do take responsibility for their children and others would do so if they could. [4]Then there are those who flatly refuse all responsibility. [5]The truth is that no one pattern or picture fits all fathers of children born outside of marriage. (Adapted from William M. Kephart and Davor Jedlicka, *The Family, Society, and the Individual*. Boston: Addison-Wesley, 1990, p. 227.)

Like this example, paragraphs ending in the topic sentence often use specific illustrations to build up to the main point. But that's not always the case. The main characteristic of paragraphs concluding with the topic sentence is this: The sentences that precede the last one are much more specific, for example:

[1]Discussion boards in online courses sometimes bring out the worst in people, which is one reason why some participants post as Anonymous. [2]For one thing, they don't want anyone tracking them down and harassing them. [3]Others, though, have a different reason. [4]They worry about the reaction of their peers and don't want to see their comments criticized under their own name. [5]Unfortunately, trolls, people who post nasty, often off-topic comments on an online forum, also like to use Anonymous because they don't want their comments attached to their name, not even a pseudonym, or false name. [6]Then, too, there are those who argue that attaching a name

to a comment tends to make people focus more on the person than the comment. ⁷Thus, they prefer to use Anonymous. ⁸Clearly there are any number of reasons why people post as Anonymous in online discussion boards.

In this case, the paragraph uses examples and bits of explanation to lead up to the main idea at the end. If it were diagrammed, it would look something like this:

Specifc examples, reasons, illustrations, events, facts, etc., build up to the topic sentence.
Topic sentence comes at the very end of the paragraph and is general enough to include or refer to all the statements that came before.

⊶ READING KEY

◆ If the paragraph's concluding sentence is more general than all the rest, then that last sentence is probably the topic sentence.

◆ EXERCISE 8   **Recognizing Concluding General Sentences**

DIRECTIONS   Read through each list of sentences. If the last sentence is more general than the others, write a *G* in the blank. If the last sentence is equally specific, put an *S* in the blank.

EXAMPLE

a. Physicians have easy access to the drugs that can be used to end a life.
b. Fearful of hurting their practice, physicians find it hard to admit to problems with depression and often suffer in silence.
c. Every year, 300 to 400 doctors commit suicide.
d. Although the problem is rarely talked about, physicians have an extremely high rate of depression and suicide.

   _____G_____

EXPLANATION   The last sentence could be used to sum up the other sentences. That's what makes it the most general sentence of the four.

1. a. A star undergoing a dramatic increase in brightness is called a *nova*.
    b. A nova is the result of a nuclear explosion on the surface of a *white dwarf*, or cooling star.

c. A nova is not a new star but a faint, white dwarf that temporarily increases in brightness.

d. Some stars appear dim and insignificant but suddenly, in a matter of hours, become a million times brighter.

2. a. An eyewitness's testimony about an event can be affected by how questions posed by the police are worded.

b. Police instructions can affect an eyewitness's willingness to make an identification.

c. Eyewitnesses are more accurate when identifying members of their own race than members of other races.

d. The presence of a weapon impairs an eyewitness's ability to accurately identify the perpetrator's face.

3. a. Women are harsher trial jurors than men are.

b. No one who is innocent would ever confess to a crime he or she did not commit.

c. The more confident an eyewitness is about an identification, the more likely it is that the testimony is accurate.

d. Many of the things people believe about jury trials are completely untrue.

4. a. In the 1950s, millions of television viewers watched Senator Estes Kefauver grill mobsters about their ties to city governments.

b. In 1952, Dwight Eisenhower's pioneering use of brief "spot advertisements" won him the presidency.

c. In 1960, John F. Kennedy's glamorous image played a major role in his winning the presidency.

d. The arrival of television had a powerful effect on America's political life.

◆ **EXERCISE 9**   **Recognizing When Topic Sentences Move Around**

DIRECTIONS   Read each paragraph and identify the topic sentence by filling in the blank. The topic sentence might be anywhere in the paragraph.

1. ¹In general, when men talk to one another, they like to trade sports opinions or discuss hobbies. ²Men say things like, "No one can take the Giants this year" or "My circular saw is already rusty, can you believe it?" ³Overall, they tend to talk more about political than personal relationships. ⁴Professional problems or challenges are also hot topics—a proposal that may not get through a committee, a union vote that did not go well. ⁵If men do mention their wives or families; they are likely to be brief. ⁶They don't go into depth or detail. ⁷The wife is fine; the children are good. ⁸In other words, men don't usually talk about their personal lives, at least not to one another.

    Sentence ___3___ is the topic sentence.

2. ¹There are four general categories of sleep disorders. ²The first and largest category includes sleep disturbances caused by psychological conditions. ³Prolonged stress or depression, for example, can cause insomnia. ⁴The second group includes disorders that result from unusual physical activity that takes place during sleep. ⁵Some people, for example, are repeatedly awakened by the jerking or twitching of their muscles. ⁶The third group is composed of disorders created by the disruption of the body's normal rhythm. ⁷A person who is constantly switching work shifts, from day to night and back again, is likely to have difficulty sleeping. ⁸The final group is made up of disorders caused by personal behavior that disrupts sleep. ⁹For example, a person who eats a heavy meal late at night may be uncomfortable from a full stomach and, as a result, may toss and turn.

    Sentence ___1___ is the topic sentence.

3. ¹For years now English teachers have introduced high school students to the classics, and kids were required to read books like Harper Lee's *To Kill a Mockingbird*, Shakespeare's *Julius Caesar*, and Mark Twain's *Huckleberry Finn*. ²That tradition, though, is changing, and it's changing rather dramatically. ³In some schools teachers no longer choose what novels their class *should* read; instead, they let

students decide what novels they *want* to read. [4]Take, for instance, Lorrie McNeill of Jonesboro Middle School in Atlanta, Georgia. [5]In the past, her students read *To Kill a Mockingbird*, among other novels that McNeill considered "good fiction." [6]But in 2009, she dropped her favorite novel from the curriculum. [7]In fact, she dropped all her favorite novels and let her eighth-grade students pick the books they wanted to read. [8]If students chose James Patterson's crime novel *Maximum Ride* or even the *Captain Underpants* comic-book novels, McNeill didn't bat an eye. [9]She, like many other high school and middle school teachers across the country from Seattle, Washington, to Chappaqua, New York, are experimenting with what's called the "reading workshop" approach. [10]With this method, kids get to read books of their own choosing, and teachers mainly make suggestions for what might be good follow-up books to the students' original choices. [11]Only a few books almost always get automatically vetoed by teachers. [12]The *Gossip Girl* series, for instance, generally does not make the cut. [13]Anything from the *Fifty Shades of Grey* series is similarly frowned upon. (Source of information about this trend: Motoko Rich, "A New Assignment: Pick Books You Like," *New York Times*, August 30, 2009, p. 1.)

Sentence ___3___ is the topic sentence.

4. [1]In 1963, the Warren Commission was formed to investigate John F. Kennedy's death. [2]A year later, after more than 27,000 interviews and 3,000 investigative reports, the commission completed its investigation. [3]The conclusion of the report was clear. [4]Lee Harvey Oswald had acted alone in murdering the president. [5]Yet no sooner was the Warren Commission's report released, than conspiracy theorists began to challenge its conclusions. [6]According to one theory, the Mafia ordered the assassination of Kennedy as payback for his brother Robert's investigation of organized crime. [7]Another scenario proposed that the Central Intelligence Agency had had Kennedy murdered because he was too "soft" on communism. [8]Yet another insisted that Fidel Castro had ordered the president's assassination because of the Bay of Pigs invasion. [9]Although these were the most popular theories, there were others as well. [10]One theory argued that Kennedy had been accidentally shot by a Secret Service agent. [11]Still another theory was that the real target had been Texas governor John Connally, but Kennedy got in the way.

Sentence ___5___ is the topic sentence.

5. [1]The psychologist Abraham H. Maslow (1908–1970) coined the term *peak experience* to describe feelings of great wonder, happiness, and sensory awareness. [2]According to Maslow, "the peak experience" makes a person feel at one with the world. [3]At the same time, it fosters a sense of physical control. [4]Many who came after Maslow have likened his "peak experience" to the athlete's sense of being "in the zone." [5]Others have compared it to the feeling of intense concentration that researchers call "being in the flow."

Sentence _____ is the topic sentence.

Concluding Topic Sentences in Chapter Sections

Often entire chapter sections start off with paragraphs that end in a topic sentence. When that happens, the topic sentence usually serves double duty. It sums up the main idea for the opening paragraph to be sure. But it also sums up the main idea for the paragraph or paragraphs that follow as well. Here's an example:

Gender Differences

The title gives you a hint about the topic, which is?

Sentence 3 is the topic sentence that sums up the more specific pieces of description.

Notice how the first sentence of paragraph 2 picks up on the nonverbal reference in the previous sentence.

Sentence 5 picks up on the reference to verbal differences.

1 [1]The idea that women and men communicate differently has been the subject of much research and writing. [2]It has been the basis of best sellers bemoaning our lack of understanding and inability to communicate with each other. [3]The truth is gender differences surface whenever we examine nonverbal or verbal communication.

2 [1]Compared with men's nonverbal communication patterns, women smile more. [2]They express a wider range of emotions through their facial expressions. [3]They occupy, claim and control less space. [4]They also maintain more eye contact. [5]In their use of language and their styles of speaking, further differences emerge. [6]Women use more modifiers (for example, "It's sort of cold out"). [7]They also use more tag questions ("It's sort of cold out, *don't you think*?"). . . . [8]Male speech contains fewer words for such things as color, texture, food, relationships, and feelings. [9]But men use more and harsher profanity. (Adapted from Bryan Strong et al., *The Marriage and Family Experience*, 10th ed. © Cengage Learning.)

The two paragraphs above show a common textbook template, or pattern. The first paragraph ends with a topic sentence. The idea expressed in that topic sentence is then further developed in the paragraph that follows.

This is actually a very common explanatory pattern in textbook writing. Whenever you start a chapter section and discover that the first paragraph ends with the topic sentence, there's a good chance that the topic sentence expresses the main idea not just for the first paragraph but for all of the paragraphs that follow.

▶ **SHARE YOUR THOUGHTS**
Do you think there are noticeable differences in the way males and females communicate? *yes*

◆ **EXERCISE 10 Connecting Paragraphs**

DIRECTIONS For each paragraph pair, circle the appropriate letter to indicate if the order of the paragraphs is correct or if it needs to be changed for the paragraphs to make sense together. *Note*: As in the example about gender differences, the paragraph with the topic sentence at the end should go first.

EXAMPLE

The focus here is on a specific individual whose charisma led him and his company astray.

The previous paragraph discusses the negative side of charisma. That means the connection between the two lies elsewhere in the paragraph.

Here's the connection. This is a general topic sentence that is further developed by paragraph a.

Concerns About Charismatic Leadership

a. Gary Winnick, the former chairman of Global Crossing Ltd., is a modern-day symbol of how destructive a charismatic leader can be. Winnick, a former junk bond broker, charmed thousands with his affable* personality, all the while leading Global Crossing into bankruptcy. While thousands of the company's workers were being laid off, Winnick was building the most expensive private residence in the world for himself and his family.

b. For the most part, an optimistic picture has been painted of charisma and charismatic leaders. For the sake of fairness and scientific integrity, contrary points of view must also be presented. The topic of charismatic leadership has been challenged from a number of perspectives, or sides. But one argument, in particular, comes up again and again. Charismatic leaders can do serious harm. (Adapted from Andrew J. Dubrin, *Leadership: Research Findings, Practice, and Skills,* 6th ed. © Cengage Learning.)

---

*affable: sociable.

a. The order of the paragraphs is correct as is.

b. The paragraphs need to be reversed to make sense.

EXPLANATION   If we kept the paragraphs ordered as they are now, the author opens with an anecdote, or story, about Gary Winnick, a man whose charisma led his company astray. But then the next paragraph starts out by describing how we tend to focus on the positive side of charisma. The connection to Winnick's story doesn't come until the end of the second paragraph. That would be like starting a story, interrupting it with another completely different story, and then coming back to resume the one you started. It makes no sense.

Reverse the order of the paragraphs and the first paragraph ends with a general statement about the danger of too much charisma. Winnick's story then follows as a specific illustration of that general point. That reversed order makes sense.

1. When the Labels Are Rejected

a. It has been nearly four decades since the United States government mandated the use by federal agencies of the terms *Hispanic* or *Latino* to categorize Americans who trace their roots to Spanish-speaking countries. However, the labels still haven't been fully embraced by the group to which they have been affixed.

b. Only about one-quarter (24%) of Hispanic adults say they most often identify themselves by "Hispanic" or "Latino," according to a new nationwide survey of Hispanic adults by the Pew Hispanic Center, a project of the Pew Research Center. About half (51%) say they identify themselves most often by their family's country or place of origin—using such terms as Mexican, Cuban, Puerto Rican, Salvadoran, or Dominican. And 21% say they use the term "American" most often to describe themselves. The share rises to 40% among those who were born in the United States. (http://pewresearch.org/pubs/2235/hispanics-latinos-identity-racial-identification?src= prc=newsletter.)

a. The order of the paragraphs is correct as is.

b. The paragraphs need to be reversed to make sense.

2. Think Twice About Ordering Hamburger?

a. Samples of the processed trimmings have been tested. And guess what? They came back loaded with pathogens.* Of course, that didn't stop the makers of what has been nicknamed "pink slime." Acknowledging the pathogen problem, BPI started disinfecting the "meat product" with ammonia. They even convinced the Food and Drug Administration to let them label the ammonia a "processing ingredient." With that label, no one would be the wiser about what they were eating.

b. A decade ago, slaughterhouses sold a substance called "trimmings" to pet food makers. Trimmings were considered a cheap waste product. While they might end up in Fido's bowl, they weren't about to end up on your table. Consisting of fat, muscle, blood, the remains of undigested food, and bits of actual meat, the trimmings were generally loaded with bacteria, another reason why they were considered unfit for human consumption. But that was a decade ago. Now, a South Dakota company called Beef Products Inc. (BPI) processes the trimmings to separate the muscle from the meat and sells what's left of the meat frozen as an additive to hamburger. BPI insists that the processed trimmings are perfectly safe for human consumption. Still, you might be happier not knowing what's in them.

a. The order of the paragraphs is correct as is.

b. The paragraphs need to be reversed to make sense.

IDIOM ALERT: To hit pay dirt

Miners were the first to use this expression. In the context of mining, hitting pay dirt meant that a miner had found a layer of precious metals that could be sold and earn a profit. In a more general context, it means that someone has made a valuable or useful discovery. "The researcher was looking for proof that the painting was a real Jackson Pollock† and she had studied the painting for days on end. Then suddenly, when she was just ready to give up, she hit pay dirt."

---

*pathogens: disease-producing substances.
†Jackson Pollock (1911–1956): Pollock is one of the most famous American painters of all time. He made dripping paint onto canvas an art form. In 2006, one of his paintings sold for $140 million.

◈ Testing Your Topic Sentence

If you think you have found the topic sentence and want to test it, try turning the topic sentence into a question. Then see if some or all of the remaining sentences in the paragraph answer the question. If they do, you know you have understood the main idea of the paragraph. See how this technique works with the following paragraph:

> [1]For a while now, invasive species of plants and animals have been causing problems. [2]Kudzu, gypsy moth caterpillars, and zebra mussels are famous for the amount of damage they can do. [3]Nationwide, invasive species cause billions of dollars in damage. [4]And the cost of environmental damage is likely to go up now that snakehead fish have been found in a lake in Maryland. [5]Snakehead fish have no known predators. [6]In other words, no one hunts or eats them. [7]Thus they can thrive and multiply. [8]The more they increase the more endangered other species will become because snakeheads eat other fish. [9]As if that weren't enough bad news, snakeheads are extremely hardy. [10]They can survive in extremely cold temperatures. [11]Like something out of a horror movie, some snakeheads can wriggle their way across land from stream to stream. [12]Fortunately, northern snakeheads, the ones found in Maryland, can't wriggle all that far.

Let's say someone who wasn't paying much attention finished the paragraph and thought, "I'll bet the first sentence is the topic sentence. That's a typical location for it."

To test that idea, we can turn the first sentence into a question. "What invasive species have been causing problems?" Well, sentence 2 does provide an answer to that question. Unfortunately, none of the other sentences do. That means the first sentence is not the topic sentence. It doesn't matter that the first sentence is a popular location for a topic sentence.

We can apply the same test to the second sentence. "How much damage can kudzu, gypsy caterpillars, and gypsy mussels do?" This is another dead end. The remaining sentences don't answer that question either.

Now let's skip to sentence 4 and ask, "Why is environmental damage likely to go up now that snakehead fish have been found in Maryland?" Here we hit pay dirt. Several of the remaining sentences answer that question.

The snakeheads are trouble because they are not hunted by anything else in their surroundings. Therefore, they can easily multiply, particularly since they are hardy creatures. The more they multiply the more other fish populations get reduced.

Anytime you think you have found the topic sentence but you aren't quite sure that you are correct, try turning the topic sentence into a question. Most of the time, it will tell you whether you are on the right or the wrong track.

READING KEY

◆ Test your topic sentence by (1) asking yourself if it could sum up the other sentences in the paragraph, and (2) turning the topic sentence into a question and checking to see if the remaining more specific sentences answer that question.

ROUNDING UP THE KEYS

Here is a list of all the reading keys introduced in the chapter. Use them to review for the test on page 207. If a particular reading key doesn't make sense on its own, go back to the page where it appeared and review the section preceding it.

READING KEYS: Topics

- ◆ The topic is the person, place, event, or idea repeatedly mentioned or referred to throughout the reading. (p. 159)
- ◆ The topic never pops up and then disappears. It's a constant presence in the passage. (p. 159)
- ◆ Writers do sometimes identify topics with a single word. But, particularly in academic writing, where more general and abstract theories get discussed, they are likely to express their topic in a phrase. (p. 160)
- ◆ If the author seems to start out with one topic and end with another, it's usually the topic at the end that's the most important. (p. 168)
- ◆ Although one word can sometimes sum up the topic, you'll often need several words to express it. (p. 168)
- ◆ Frequently readers have to come up with some or even all the words for the topic. (p. 168)
- ◆ The topic should be general enough to include everything discussed in the paragraph but specific enough to exclude what isn't. (p. 168)
- ◆ Often the first general clue to the topic is in the first couple of sentences. Then the additional sentences make the topic more specific. When you read, keep thinking about what each sentence adds to your understanding of the topic. (p. 168)

READING KEY: Main Ideas

- ◆ The main idea is the central point or thought the writer wants to communicate to readers. It's what ties all the sentences in the paragraph together. (p. 172)

READING KEYS: Topic Sentences

- ◆ Topic sentences are general sentences that sum up the point of the paragraph. They are one of the main ways textbook writers communicate key points to readers. (p. 172)

◆ Topic sentences have three characteristics: (1) they are among the most general sentences in a paragraph, (2) they introduce an idea that is developed in more specific detail by other sentences in the paragraph, and (3) they answer questions, like "What's the point of the paragraph? Why did the author write it? (p. 177)

◆ Topic sentences can and do appear anywhere in a paragraph. However, particularly in textbooks, they are quite likely to be the first or second sentence in the paragraph. (p. 177)

◆ If the second sentence adds more specific information to the first, then the first sentence is probably the topic sentence. You can be certain that the first sentence is the topic sentence if the third sentence also continues developing the idea introduced in the opening sentence. (p. 177)

◆ Introductory sentences are general sentences that provide context or background for the topic sentence that appears later in the paragraph. (p. 177)

READING KEYS: Reversal Transitions and Topic Sentences

◆ If a transition like *however*, *unfortunately*, or *yet* opens the second sentence in a paragraph, the second sentence is likely to be the topic sentence. (p. 184)

◆ Much of the time, topic sentences starting in the middle of a paragraph will begin with a reversal transition. But that's not always the case. (p. 184)

◆ Paragraphs with a topic sentence in the middle bulge at midpoint when the general sentence takes center stage. After that midpoint, the paragraph slims down again as it gets more specific. (p. 184)

READING KEY: Topic Sentences at the End

◆ If the paragraph's concluding sentence is more general than all the rest, then that last sentence is probably the topic sentence. (p. 189)

READING KEY: Testing Your Topic Sentence

◆ Test your topic sentence by (1) asking yourself if it could sum up the other sentences in the paragraph, and (2) turning the topic sentence into a question and checking to see if the remaining more specific sentences answer that question. (p. 198)

Ten More Words for Your Academic Vocabulary

1. **correlation:** relationship, connection

   Fortunately for most of us, there is no *correlation* between spelling ability and intelligence.

2. **orbit:** circle, move in a circular motion

   In the fifteenth century, people believed that the sun *orbited* the earth.

3. **obligated:** pledged, bound morally or legally

   Far Eastern cultures believe that relationships ought to be long lasting and that individuals should show loyalty to others simply because we are all *obligated* to each other. (Gamble and Gamble, *Contacts*, p. 382.)

4. **disclosure:** making known, revealing

   The *disclosure* of negative information early in a relationship can be positive because we tend to be attracted to those who are willing to be honest and take responsibility for their actions. (Gamble and Gamble, *Contacts*, p. 398.)

5. **plight:** unfortunate situation or state; misery, sad condition

   John Steinbeck's novel *The Grapes of Wrath* movingly portrayed the *plight* of migrant workers.

6. **monopoly:** single party control over a product or service

   In 1807, Robert L. Livingston and Robert Fulton introduced the steamboat *Clermont* on the Hudson River, and they soon gained a *monopoly* from the New York legislature to run a New York–New Jersey service. (Adapted from Paul S. Boyer et al., *The Enduring Vision*, 7th ed., p. 258. © Cengage Learning.)

7. **repertoire:** range

   As we grow older, our *repertoire* of relationships increases and we realize that we can have different kinds of friends.

8. **factor:** element, part, piece

   More than one *factor* accounts for the success or failure of new technology.

9. **derivative:** developed or received from another source

In the nineteenth century, physicians, medicine peddlers, and legitimate drug companies freely prescribed or sold opium along with its *derivatives*, morphine and heroin. (Adapted from Paul S. Boyer et al., *The Enduring Vision*, 7th ed., p. 640.)

10. **antithetical:** opposite, contrasted

Alexander Hamilton's attitude toward the federal government was *antithetical* to Jefferson's: Hamilton wanted the nation's government to hold more power; Jefferson did not.

◆ EXERCISE 11   Making Academic Vocabulary Familiar

DIRECTIONS   Each sentence uses a more conversational or simpler version of one of the words listed below. At the end of the sentence, fill in the blank with the more academic word that could replace the underlined word or words in the sentence.

derivatives	antithetical	repertoire	monopolies	orbit
factors	plight	disclosure	correlation	obligated

1. John Stuart Mill was a nineteenth-century philosopher who was extremely sympathetic to the underlined unhappy state of women. _plight_

2. Several things contributed to the mortgage crisis of 2008, among them a lack of banking regulations. _factors_

3. In the marketplace, single companies with too much control can discourage competition, and that's not good for the consumer. _monopolies_

4. Some useful drugs are actually effects of deadly poisons. _derivatives_

5. The artistic temperament is often the exact opposite to the spirit of the marketplace, and artists don't always make good businesspeople. _antithetical_

6. Recent research has found a <u>connection</u> between heavy alcohol use and memory loss. *correlation*

7. In some cultures, acceptance of a gift means the recipient is <u>forced</u> to offer an even bigger gift in return. *obligated*

8. Like most powerful people, the queen insisted that everyone within her <u>circle</u> be loyal unto death. *orbit*

9. Pressed about the <u>publicizing</u> of her personal wealth, the candidate's wife said that her money was her business. *disclosure*

10. The disease is accompanied by a wide <u>collection</u> of odd behaviors. *repertoire*

VOCABULARY EXTRA

The reading that follows will use the word *narcissistic*, which derives, or comes from, the myth of Narcissus. According to the myth, a handsome young boy named Narcissus went to drink water from a stream. The stream was so clear it was like a mirror, in which Narcissus saw himself for the first time. The boy was so taken by his own appearance, he could not pull himself away from the stream. He ended up starving to death while hopelessly longing to find the boy he saw in the water. Now when we talk about someone being narcissistic, it means the person is so overcome by love of self, he or she can't think about anyone or anything else. Good synonyms for the word would be *self-absorbed* or *egotistical*.

DIGGING DEEPER

Life's Lessons from the Family Dog

Looking Ahead   The following reading by *New York Times* writer Dana Jennings suggests that there may be a very good reason why dog owners are so devoted to their pets.

1   Our family dog started failing a couple of months ago. Her serious health problems began at about the same time I was coping with my own— finishing my radiation and hormone therapy for prostate cancer. Since last summer, I've learned that my cancer is shockingly aggressive, and the surgery, radiation and hormone treatments have left me exhausted, incontinent* and with an AWOL libido.* These days I'm waiting for the first tests that will tell me the status of my health.

2   Even so, as I face my own profound health issues, it is my dog's poor health that is piercing me to the heart. I'm dreading that morning when I walk downstairs and . . . well, those of us who love dogs understand that all dog stories end the same way. Her full name is Bijou de Minuit (Jewel of Midnight)—my wife teaches French. She is a 12-year-old black miniature poodle, and she is, literally, on her last legs. Her hindquarters fly out from beneath her, her back creaks and cracks as she walks, she limps, she's speckled with bright red warts the size of nickels, her snore is loud and labored (like a freight train chugging up some steep grade), and she spends most of the day drowsing on her pillow-bed next to the kitchen radiator. Bijou's medicine chest is impressive for a 23-pound dog: a baby dose of amoxicillin for chronic urinary tract infections; prednisone and Tramadol for pain; phenobarbital for seizures; Proin for incontinence—all of it wrapped in mini-slices of pepperoni.

3   She is, I realize, "just" a dog. But she has, nonetheless, taught me a few lessons about life, living, and illness. Despite all her troubles, Bijou is still game. She still groans to her feet to go outside, still barks at and with the neighborhood dogs, is willing to hobble around the kitchen to carouse with a rubber ball—her shrub of a tail quivering in joy. I know now that Bijou was an important part of my therapy as I recovered from having my prostate removed. I learned that dogs, besides being pets, can also be our teachers.

4   Human beings constantly struggle to live in the moment. We're either obsessing over the past ("Gee, life would've been different if I'd only

---

*incontinent: unable to control urination or defecation.
*libido: sexual desire.

joined the Peace Corps"), or obsessing over the future ("Gee, I hope my 401K holds up"). We forget that life, real life, is lived right now, in this very moment.

5   But living in the moment is something that dogs (and cancer patients) do by their very nature. Bijou eats when she's hungry, drinks when she's thirsty, sleeps when she's tired, and will still gratefully curl up in whatever swatch of sunlight steals through the windows. She'd jump up onto my sickbed last summer, nuzzle me, and ask for her ears and pointy snout to be scratched. It made both of us happy as she sighed in satisfaction. And she was the subject of one of our favorite family jokes as I recuperated: "You take the dog out. I have cancer."

6   In spending so much time with Bijou, I began to realize that our dogs, in their carefree dogginess, make us more human, force us to shed our narcissistic skins. Even when you have cancer, you can't be utterly self-involved when you have a floppy-eared mutt who needs to be fed, walked, and belly-scratched. And you can't help but ponder the mysteries of creation as you gaze into the eyes of your dog, or wonder why and how we chose dogs and they chose us.

7   Dogs also tell us—especially when we're sick—of our own finitude. And, partly, that's why we cry when they die, because we also know that all human-being stories end the same way, too. Good dogs—and most dogs are good dogs—are canine candles that briefly blaze and shine, illuminating our lives. Bijou has been here with us for the past 12 years, reminding us that simple pleasures are the ones to be treasured: a treat, a game of fetch, a nose-to-the-ground stroll in the park.

8   Simple pleasures. As I lazed and dozed at home last summer after surgery, there was nothing sweeter to me in this world than to hear Bijou drinking from her water dish outside my door. It was as if her gentle lap-lapping ferried me to waters of healing. I'll miss her. ("Life Lessons from the Family Dog" by Dana Jennings from *The New York Times*, March 31, 2009. Copyright © 2009 the New York Times Co. Reprinted by permission.)

Sharpening Your Skills

DIRECTIONS   Answer the following questions.

1. Like single paragraphs, multi-paragraph readings usually express one overall main idea that ties everything in the reading together. In your own words, what's the overall main idea of this reading?

_____ how dogs teach humans about life. _____

2. In paragraph 1, the author uses the word *AWOL*, which is an acronym for Absent Without Official Leave. How would you define an acronym?

    it is a Shorter way to say Something,

    What does the author mean when he says his libido was AWOL?

    missing.

3. What does the author mean when he says dogs "make us more human" (paragraph 6)?

    They remind us whats important.

4. Based on the context, how would you define the word *finitude* in paragraph 7?

    Something that Ends,

5. Why does the author refer to dogs as "canine candles" in paragraph 7? What does that phrase mean?

    They make us happy, They light our lives,

    Is that language literal or figurative?

    figure of speech,

▶ TEST 1 **Reviewing the Key Points**

DIRECTIONS Answer the questions in the blank lines. Make sure to use complete sentences.

1. How would you define the topic?

   The Person, Place, event, or idea Repeatdely Mentioned

2. How would you define the main idea?

   The Main Idea is the Central Point.

3. What's a topic sentence?

   Genreal Sentences that Sum uP the Point.

4. What are the three characteristics of a topic sentence?

   1 among the most general sentences.
   2. introduce an Idea develoed later in specific detail.
   3. They Aswear questions like "what is this about."

5. Where in a paragraph do topic sentences appear?

   Anywhere.

6. If the paragraph's second sentence adds more information to the point of the first, what is very likely the case?

   The first sentence is Probably the topic sentence.

7. If a reversal transition starts off the second sentence, what is likely to be true?

   The Second Sentence is likey to be the topic sentence.

8. What is the shape of paragraphs with topic sentences in the middle?

   Bulge at the midPoint.

9. What dual function do topic sentences serve when they appear at the end of the first paragraph in a chapter section?

the last sentence is Probably the topic sentence.

10. If you think you have found the topic sentence, how do you confirm it?

1. Ask if it sums up.

2. Make it a question and see if the other sentences answer it.

To correct your test, turn to page 587. If one or more of your answers is incorrect, re-read the Rounding Up the Keys section of the chapter to find out where your mistake might be.

▶ **TEST 2**   **Identifying Topics and Topic Sentences**

DIRECTIONS   Circle the appropriate letter to identify the topic. Then fill in the blank with a *1* or a *2* to identify the topic sentence.

1. ¹Powwows are Native-American social gatherings that serve an important cultural purpose: They keep Native-American traditions alive. ²That's why each year thousands of Native-Americans travel long distances to be part of a powwow where drums and dances tell the story of their lives. ³As blogger Rose Kern explains, "A powwow helps to drive home the fact that we are not a vanishing race; we are here because we have always been here." ⁴In addition to the dancing and drumming, which is usually done competitively, powwows generally offer displays of other Native-American arts and crafts such as beading, quilting, and leatherwork. ⁵Most powwows are usually open to non-Indians. ⁶That's because the goal of the powwow is not just to keep Native-American traditions alive but to enlarge the audience that knows of and admires their existence.

Topic   a. Native-American culture
           b. powwows
           c. Native-American social gatherings

Sentence ____1____ is the topic sentence.

2. ¹Mining sapphires* is a difficult and dangerous process. ²First, the miner digs a square pit about forty feet deep in sandy earth. ³When he reaches a layer of gravel, he begins digging sideways into the wall of the pit, removing rocks as he goes. ⁴This is treacherous work because the dirt can cave in, burying the miner. ⁵Loads of gravel are then hauled to a river and washed. ⁶Finally, the miner removes the sapphires from the gravel and sells them to gem buyers who must travel with weapons because of the frequent robberies and murders in their business.

Topic   a. the dangers miners face
           b. mining for sapphires
           c. sapphires

Sentence ____1____ is the topic sentence.

*sapphires: a type of gemstone, usually blue in color.

3. [1]Most successful job interviews that are conducted in person follow three basic steps. [2]If you know the steps, you increase your chances of getting the job. [3]Step 1 lasts about three minutes and occurs when you first introduce yourself. [4]In these three minutes, you need to demonstrate that you are friendly and at ease with others. [5]This is the time to shake hands firmly, make eye contact, and smile. [6]During step 2, you need to explain your skills and abilities. [7]This is your chance to show an employer just how capable you are. [8]Step 3 comes at the end of the interview. [9]Although it lasts only a minute or two, this step is still important. [10]When the employer says, "We'll be in touch," you need to say something like, "I'll check back with you in a few days, if you don't mind." [11]A comment like this indicates your commitment to getting the job.

Topic   a. jobs

b. smiles during job interviews

c. the three steps in job interviews

Sentence _____ is the topic sentence.

4. [1]Spanish-language television has long been dominated by two major broadcast networks, Univision and Telemundo. [2]But now there is a new kid on the block, MundoFox, the newest Spanish-language network in the United States. [3]The network's motto is "Americano Como Tú" or "American Like You." [4]Like Univision, MundoFox will broadcast telenovelas, the dramatic limited-run stories popular in Portuguese and Spanish-speaking countries. [5]However, the network promises to also include new American-style action and comedy programming, with the main difference being that the actors speak Spanish. [6]The network's senior vice president for news is Jorge Mettey, who was formerly with Univision. [7]Mr. Mettey says the network has a "moral obligation" to encourage Latinos in the United States to take an active role in the politics of their country. [8]In addition to extensive news programming, MundoFox will also feature "Minuto Para Ganar," a Spanish-language version of an NBC game show called "Minute to Win It."

Topic   a. MundoFox

b. Univision

c. telenovelas

Sentence _____ is the topic sentence.

▶ TEST 3   Identifying Topics and Topic Sentences

DIRECTIONS   Circle the appropriate letter to identify the topic. Then fill in the blank with a *1* or a *2* to identify the topic sentence.

1. ¹The island of Puerto Rico is rather small; it is only about 111 miles from east to west and just 40 miles from north to south. ²Yet despite its small size, Puerto Rico's landscape shows marvelous variety. ³On the north side of the island, it rains a lot. ⁴The average yearly rainfall is around 180 inches. ⁵With all that rain, it's not surprising that northern Puerto Rico is home to a tropical rain forest. ⁶In the southern portion of the island, there is less rain—only around 60 inches on the average. ⁷As a result, the southern half of Puerto Rico has fewer trees and more thorny shrubs. ⁸Although agriculture has removed much of the original vegetation, the island's hilly landscape is alive with gorgeous splashes of color. ⁹Brilliant orange and red flowers hang from trees like the royal Poinciana and the African tulip. ¹⁰Puerto Rico is also home to several species of rare orchids and some very rare birds. ¹¹The endangered Puerto Rican green parrot is found nowhere else in the world.

    Topic   a. the climate of Puerto Rico

                  b. the rain forest of Puerto Rico

                  c. Puerto Rico's landscape

    Sentence _____ 2 _____ is the topic sentence.

2. ¹When she was only twenty-one years old, architecture student Maya Lin had her design for the Vietnam Veterans Memorial officially accepted. ²Wise beyond her years, Lin knew there would be controversy over the decision because the design was so plain, but even she was not prepared for the controversy that exploded over her memorial to the soldiers fallen in Vietnam.† ³Although the actual number of veterans offended by the memorial's appearance was small, the protesters were extremely vocal. ⁴The veterans were aided by Congressman Henry Hyde, who pushed their cause with all the power at his disposal. ⁵Hyde went so far as to take the petition to the secretary of the interior, James Watt. ⁶Watt, in turn, insisted

---

†Vietnam War (1961–1975): In the civil war between North and South Vietnam, the United States went to war to avoid a takeover of the south by the North Vietnamese.

that the plain black granite wall Lin had designed must be modified. [7]At Watt's command, it was. [8]The entry walk to the memorial now includes an American flag and a statue of three combat soldiers. [9]Yet even that compromise didn't appease some of the young architect's most vicious critics. [10]These were the people who could not forget that Lin was an Asian American. [11]They sent letters to the memorial committee protesting her ancestry. [12]Some of the letter-writers even stooped to calling her a "gook." [13]Throughout this explosive time, Maya Lin, at least publicly, remained calm and composed. [14]But years later, after the memorial had safely been established, she described how difficult that earlier time had been.

Topic   a. additions to the Vietnam Veterans Memorial

b. the controversy over the Vietnam Veterans Memorial

c. Henry Hyde's support of the protest against Maya Lin's design

Sentence ___2___ is the topic sentence.

3. [1]Several types of tissue are found in the human body. [2]*Connective tissue* binds together and supports the body's internal structures. [3]Connective tissue also forms cartilage, bones, and the walls of various organs. [4]For its part, *muscle tissue* is essential to movement. [5]The heart, for example, is made of muscle. [6]It has to pump blood throughout the body. [7]*Nervous tissue* is important for communication between our inner and outer worlds. [8]For example, the tissues in our nervous system keep us aware of our environment. [9]*Epithelial tissue* covers the surface of our body in the form of skin. [10]It also helps the body absorb materials. (Adapted from James H. Otto and Albert Towle, *Modern Biology*, p. 586. © Cengage Learning.)

Topic   a. the human body

b. connective tissue in the heart

c. four kinds of body tissue

Sentence ___1___ is the topic sentence.

4. [1]In 1999, the Nobel Peace Prize was given to an organization called *Médecins Sans Frontières* (MSF) or Doctors Without Borders. [2]Founded in 1971 by a small group of young French doctors, Doctors Without Borders was meant to be an alternative to the International Red Cross based in Geneva. [3]Like members of the

Red Cross, the French organization would go anyplace in the world where people needed medical attention. [4]But in contrast to the Red Cross, Doctors Without Borders insisted on speaking out against injustice. [5]When earthquakes tumbled buildings in Turkey, the organization was among the first to complain about the government's failure to enforce building codes. [6]When Rwanda's civil war resulted in mass murder, members of Doctors Without Borders argued that more could have been done to stop the killing. [7]The organization complained that international leaders dragged their feet instead of taking action. [8]As journalist David Rieff wrote after the winner of the Nobel Peace Prize was announced, Doctors Without Borders has saved many lives, but it has also told some "harsh truths." (Source of information: David Rieff, *The New Republic*, November 8, 1999, p. 8.)

Topic   a. David Rieff's opinion of Doctors Without Borders
         b. the difference between the Red Cross and Doctors Without Borders
         c. civil war in Rwanda

Sentence _____ is the topic sentence.

▶**TEST 4** **Identifying Topics and Topic Sentences**

DIRECTIONS Circle the appropriate letter to identify the topic. Then fill in the blank with a *1*, a *2*, or a *3* to identify the topic sentence.

1. [1]Even diehard meat eaters are uncomfortable with factory farming in the United States. [2]Much as they love their slab of beef or breast of chicken, they don't particularly like to hear the details of how it got to their table. [3]That's because the details of factory farming— raising large numbers of animals in very confined circumstances where movement is difficult if not impossible—are gruesome. [4]Chickens raised this way are squeezed so tightly together they will peck each other's eyes out. [5]For that reason owners of factory farms routinely de-beak the chickens, removing two-thirds of the upper beak. [6]Cattle fare no better, especially those meant to become veal. [7]Veal comes tender to the table only because calves have been kept in tiny pens, which don't allow them to move around. [8]Letting the animals move naturally would make the meat too tough.

Topic
   a. meat eaters
   b. factory farming
   c. de-beaking chickens

Sentence ___2___ is the topic sentence.

2. [1]In 1996, the beverage maker Odwalla Inc, faced a huge crisis when it was discovered that the bacteria E. coli had turned up in fruit juices the company produced. [2]Odwalla, however, survived the crisis by launching a strikingly effective public relations campaign that both saved the company's reputation and limited the spread of the infected juices. [3]As soon as the company discovered the problem, it announced an immediate recall of thirteen different products. [4]It also worked closely with the Food and Drug Administration to thoroughly inspect all the Odwalla processing facilities. [5]As it turned out, the facilities were all free of the bacteria. [6]But Odwalla didn't stop there. [7]It also inspected all the companies that supplied them with fruit. [8]The executive officer of Odwalla also publicly declared the company was searching for even better ways to eliminate the chance of contamination in the future. [9]A month after the first signs of the outbreak, Odwalla took out a full-page ad in several newspapers across the country. [10]In the ad, they thanked their customers for

their continued support and offered sympathy to those suffering the ill effects of drinking the infected juice.

Topic   a. E. coli infections

b. public relations in a crisis

(c.) Odwalla's public relations campaign

Sentence _____2_____ is the topic sentence.

3. ¹Today, spectators of the Olympic Games enjoy the events in comfort and style. ²But ancient Greek sports fans had a much tougher time attending the earliest versions of the Olympic Games. ³Most had to travel to Olympia on foot or by mule across rugged mountains in the blistering summer heat. ⁴The 150-mile hike from Athens usually took two weeks. ⁵When the exhausted travelers finally trudged into the arena, they found almost no facilities. ⁶Athletes bunked in Spartan barracks. ⁷The only inn was reserved for aristocrats. ⁸The 80,000 other spectators had no choice but to turn the surrounding fields into an unsanitary campground, using riverbeds for bathrooms and heaping their garbage in stinking piles. ⁹The ancient Olympic Stadium had no seats and no shade, so the sweaty throng had to stand in the blazing sun to watch the events. ¹⁰ Water was scarce, and fans would regularly pass out from dehydration* and heatstroke. ¹¹At the end of the five-day festival, spectators who couldn't bear the idea of walking home faced yet another indignity. ¹²They were forced to linger for days at the smelly site while trying to arrange a ride home with greedy mule drivers.

Topic   a. the ancient Olympic Stadium

b. Olympia

(c.) attending the first Olympic Games

Sentence _____2_____ is the topic sentence.

4. ¹Despite the racism that prevailed in the early part of the twentieth century, African Americans made important cultural contributions. ²Written in 1914, W.C. Handy's "St. Louis Blues" set the pattern for

---

*dehydration: loss of fluids.

hundreds of blues songs, and Handy was widely acknowledged as the father of the blues. [3]Playing his trumpet in Chicago, New York, and New Orleans during the twenties, Louis Armstrong made a name for himself as the king of jazz. [4]Around the same time, the Harlem Renaissance[†] spilled out beyond Harlem's borders. [5]Writers like Zora Neale Hurston, Langston Hughes, and Jean Toomer wrote poems, novels, and short stories that explored and celebrated black culture. [6]But black writers' focus on race didn't stop white writers like Sherwood Anderson and Allen Tate from reading and being influenced by African-American literature.

Topic

a. Jean Toomer

b. inventions by African Americans

c. cultural contributions of African Americans

Sentence _____ is the topic sentence.

[†]Harlem Renaissance (c. 1918–1930s): With 175,000 African-American residents, Harlem in the early twentieth century was a place where black-owned newspapers and magazines flourished, making it possible for black writers to become famous both in and out of Harlem.

▶ **TEST 5**   **Enlarging Your Academic Vocabulary**

DIRECTIONS   Circle the letter of the sentence that uses the opening word correctly.

1. **correlation**

    a. The *correlation* of cattle is still mainly done on horseback.

    b. In the nineteenth century, unmarried women were usually considered the poor *correlations* in the family.

    (c.) Educational researchers have found a strong *correlation* between reading and vocabulary knowledge.

2. **orbit**

    (a.) Gravity is the force that makes the planets *orbit* the sun rather than spin off into the vastness of space.

    b. When *orbiting* for a job, experience is important, but appearance and personality also play a role.

    c. The cat's *orbit* had been badly broken in two different places.

3. **obligation**

    (a.) As part of their marketing campaign, the store lets customers sample their food without any *obligation* to buy something.

    b. The new employee got a standing *obligation* from his co-workers when he stood up at the meeting.

    c. The *obligation* was performed under the head surgeon's watchful eye.

4. **disclosure**

    a. The *disclosure* of the landmark diner was mourned by many in the community.

    (b.) Reviewers need to make a full *disclosure*: They need to indicate if they have a personal relationship with any of the authors involved in the contest.

    c. Horse *disclosures* often consist of white fences that contrast nicely with the green pastures.

5. **plight**

   a. Mildew is a *plight* that may affect any number of plants.

   b. When new troops arrived at the battle site, they saw that the enemy was already in full *plight*.

   c. The first transport of food and medication arrived to ease the *plight* of the refugees.

6. **monopoly**

   a. In most American towns, people cannot chose between competing cable companies; that is, cable service is a *monopoly*.

   b. Greater *monopolies* lead to greater competition.

   c. I'm sick of taking care of my house—I want to join a *monopoly*.

7. **repertoire**

   a. The grandest room in their new house is the *repertoire*.

   b. The candidate was a great debater; he always had a quick *repertoire* when someone contradicted him.

   c. Along with her confidence, the singer's *repertoire* of songs has steadily grown.

8. **factor**

   a. A *factor* is the owner of a factory.

   b. Fuel economy is a *factor* I will consider when I buy a new car.

   c. The team is strong on defense, but their offense could do with two or three experienced new *factors*.

9. **derivative**

   a. The entire article is *derivative*—it does not contain a single new idea; every idea has been "borrowed" from someone else.

   b. The speaker bored the audience to tears with her *derivatives*.

   c. Diplomats work under the *derivative* not to accept any favors that could be considered bribes.

10. antithetical

   a. In some societies, lending money to collect interest is considered an *antithetical*.

   b. Slaughtering animals for food is *antithetical* to the beliefs of many vegetarians.

   c. Will Rogers could get along with everybody and therefore could not be accused of being *antithetical*.

Working Together: Topic Sentences and Supporting Details

5

IN THIS CHAPTER, YOU WILL LEARN

● how supporting details make the main idea expressed in the topic sentence clear and convincing.

● how to tell the difference between major and minor details.

● how to outline, summarize, or diagram what you read.

> *"General terms and specific terms are not opposites. . . . Instead, they are the different ends of a range of terms."*[1]

You already know that to communicate effectively, a writer needs to pair general sentences with specific ones. There's no clearer illustration of this principle than the relationship between general and specific sentences in paragraphs. Topic sentences are general and that makes them open to interpretation. The reader can, as a result, sometimes get off track and follow a train of thought the author never intended. It's the job of supporting details to eliminate meanings the writer never intended.

---

[1]There is no author for this quotation. It can be found on this website, which offers a great discussion of the relationship between general and specific ideas: http://grammar .ccc.commnet.edu/grammar/composition/abstract.htm.

The Function of Supporting Details

> JOHN: Honestly, raising a child is difficult.
>
> DAVID: I know exactly what you mean. You can't do what you want anymore; you're tied down all the time. Once you have a child, your life is over.
>
> JOHN: I didn't mean that at all. I just meant it's difficult to make decisions for another human being. I'm always nervous about making the wrong one.

Note the communication problem between these two people. John makes a general statement about raising children. In response, David assumes he understands what John has in mind. But, in fact, he hasn't understood John's message at all. To make David see what he means, John provides specific details.

This kind of confusion is not restricted to conversation. It can also occur between writer and reader. The writer has an idea in mind and communicates it in writing. But readers may take away a completely different message, one the writer never intended.

Fortunately, most writers—particularly writers of textbooks—are aware of this potential problem and try to prevent it. Because they know that most general statements are open to misinterpretation, or misunderstanding, they are careful to include supporting details.

Supporting Details Clarify, Explain, and Convince

By means of **supporting details**, writers anticipate and answer questions readers might have about a main idea. By means of supporting details, writers supply the reasons, dates, examples, statistics, facts, studies, and so on that make main ideas both clear and convincing. For an illustration of what supporting details contribute to a paragraph, take a good look at this topic sentence, which sums up the main idea of a paragraph.

> In the eighteenth century, few American poets achieved any lasting fame; Phillis Wheatley, however, was an astonishing exception.

After reading this topic sentence, you certainly know the author's point. However, you might not know who Phillis Wheatley was or what she wrote. For that information, you need some supporting details like the ones shown below:

Topic sentence sums up the main idea.

Sentences 2–6 focus on the phrase "astonishing exception." They answer readers' most likely question, "What made her an astonishing exception?"

[1]In the eighteenth century, few American poets achieved any lasting fame; Phillis Wheatley, however, was an astonishing exception. [2]A slave in a Massachusetts household, Wheatley was taught to read and write by her owners, whose name she also took. [3]By the age of thirteen, she was writing religious poems. [4]When the Wheatley family traveled to England, the Wheatleys took Phillis with them. [5]While they were there, they arranged for her to read her poems at public gatherings. [6]The response was so enthusiastic, word of the girl's talent got back to the colonies. [7]By the time she returned home, Phillis Wheatley was internationally famous.

Supplied with the appropriate supporting details, you are now more likely to understand and accept the main idea of the paragraph: Against all odds, Phillis Wheatley did not suffer the fate of most eighteenth-century American poets. She became famous.

READING KEYS

◆ Supporting details supply the reasons, illustrations, facts, figures, and studies that make the main idea clear and convincing to readers.

◆ Supporting details are the author's way of guiding readers to the appropriate meaning. They are the author's way of saying to readers, "I mean this and not that."

◆ The form of supporting details varies. Details can range in form from reasons to statistics. The main idea is what causes supporting details to vary. When the main idea changes, so do the details that develop it.

IDIOM ALERT: Unsung hero

An *unsung hero* is a person who has done great or important work but has never been recognized for his or her contributions. Here's an example: "Although his wife, Lucille Ball, got most of the credit for their successful show, *I Love Lucy*, Desi Arnaz, Ball's Cuban-born husband, was the unsung hero behind the show's phenomenal success."

Sadness
She didn't want to change
her Beliefs
yes

> **WEB QUEST/CLASS ACTION**
> Find a copy of Wheatley's poem "On Being Brought from Africa to America" on the Web. Read it carefully and come to class prepared to discuss what the poem suggests about being made a slave and brought to America meant to her. What emotion is she expressing? Why does she feel that way? And most important of all, do you believe what she says?

◆ **EXERCISE 1** **Matching Topic Sentences to Supporting Details**

DIRECTIONS Read each topic sentence. Then circle the letters of the two sentences that qualify as supporting details.

EXAMPLE

Topic Sentence Talking to a therapist online has some definite advantages.

Supporting Details (a.) If you can't see the therapist, you are likely to be less self-conscious.

b. Online therapy is becoming increasingly popular.

c. Online the therapist can't read the patient's body language.

(d.) Patients are more willing to speak freely when they talk to a therapist online.

EXPLANATION The key word in the above topic sentence is *advantages*. A reader is bound to ask, "What are those advantages?" Sentences *a* and *d* provide answers to that question.

Topic Sentence 1. Mammals are warm-blooded animals classified according to a number of different characteristics.

Supporting Details a. There are more than 4,000 species of mammals.

(b.) Mammals always have hair and a middle ear formed by three small bones.

c. A number of mammals are on the Red List of endangered species.

(d.) In mammals, the lower jaw consists of only two bones.

Topic Sentence 2. A growing number of men are having cosmetic surgery to hold on to their youth.

Supporting Details
    a. In an even more disturbing trend, teenage girls as young as thirteen are begging their parents for cosmetic surgery.

    b. In the past, cosmetic surgery has been considered the province* of women.

    c. Disturbed by fat accumulating on their chests in middle age, men are resorting to surgery to get rid of it.

    d. Many men, nervous about being seen as too old on the job market, are having the bags under their eyes removed.

Topic Sentence
    3. To this day, Fred Shuttlesworth remains an unsung hero of the civil rights movement.

Supporting Details
    a. No matter what happened, Fred Shuttlesworth was always convinced that he was doing God's work.

    b. The Ku Klux Klan tried to stop Shuttlesworth's organizing activities by bombing his house, but he refused to give in.

    c. Although the intrepid Shuttlesworth was active in every aspect of the civil rights movement, the media preferred to focus on the bravery of Martin Luther King Jr., whose speaking talent made him so quotable.

    d. Diane McWhorter's book *Carry Me Home*, an account of both her Alabama childhood and the civil rights movement, won a Pulitzer Prize.

Topic Sentence
    4. Every year, thousands of Tibetan children flee their homeland in a desperate attempt to escape Chinese rule.[†]

Supporting Details
    a. Very often, the children are sent on their journey by parents who want their sons and daughters to be Tibetan rather than Chinese.

    b. For fifteen years, photographer Nancy Jo Johnson has used photographs to publicize the plight of the Tibetans.

    c. Today, Tibet has been completely transformed and little remains of the pre-1950 Tibetan culture.

    d. The fleeing children cross the Himalaya Mountains hoping to reach India or Nepal, where they can stay in special villages established just for them.

---

*province: territory, area.
[†]Chinese rule: The Chinese invaded Tibet in 1950, drove out the Dalai Lama (Tibet's religious leader), and took control of the country.

◆ **EXERCISE 2**   **Matching Topic Sentences to Supporting Details**

DIRECTIONS   Read each set of three supporting details. Then look over the two topic sentences that follow. Circle the number of the topic sentence that the details support.

EXAMPLE

Supporting Details
a. At one time, many therapists believed that anorexia nervosa, also called the starvation disease, was a form of rebellion.

b. However, other therapists argued that anorexia was a way of avoiding adulthood.

c. Researchers are now finding evidence that the disease may be caused by a chemical imbalance in the brain.

Topic Sentence

1. Some victims of anorexia nervosa—unnecessary or irrational dieting—seek out psychiatric treatment; however, they more often try to hide their disease.

2. Although no one really knows what causes anorexia nervosa—unnecessary or irrational dieting—several theories have been put forward.

EXPLANATION   Each supporting detail introduces a theory about what causes anorexia nervosa. Because the second topic sentence tells us there are several different theories about what causes the disease, it's the better choice.

Supporting Details
1. a. Some people worry that friends will envy them if they become successful.

b. Others are afraid that success will make them stand out in a crowd.

c. Then there are those who simply fear the hard work necessary to maintain a high level of achievement.

Topic Sentence

> 1. In our society, far too many people are successful but unhappy workaholics.
>
> 2. A surprising number of men and women are afraid of being successful.

Supporting Details 2. a. People with claustrophobia, or fear of enclosed spaces, get anxious on elevators.

b. People suffering from agoraphobia, the fear of open spaces, are unlikely to leave home.

c. People with zoophobia, or fear of animals, are unlikely to own pets.

Topic Sentence

> 1. Phobias are irrational fears that persist even when there is no real danger.
>
> 2. Social phobia is the fear of situations in which one might be observed, judged, or embarrassed.

Supporting Details 3. a. About 95 percent of all adults use the left side of the brain for speaking and writing.

b. The left side of the brain is also superior at doing math.

c. The right side, however, excels at recognizing patterns, faces, and melodies.

Topic Sentence

> 1. The left side of the brain controls the right side of the body.
>
> 2. The two sides of the brain perform different activities.

Supporting Details 4. a. People interested in dating often ask their friends if they know anyone who is available.

b. Some people look for dates in online newspapers and magazines.

c. Others prefer to use dating services that, for a fee, guarantee a perfect match.

Topic Sentence

> 1. Nowadays, there are a number of ways for people to get a date.
>
> 2. American-style dating is all but unknown in Europe.

🔑 READING KEY

- ◆ If the supporting details don't fit what you think is the topic sentence, you probably need to look for another topic sentence.

VOCABULARY EXTRA

From the context and your knowledge of word parts (*ir* means "not"), you probably figured out that *irrational* (p. 226) means "not based on reason." If you are adding that word to your list of words to study, make sure you also add the antonym, *rational*, meaning "reasonable." You should also add the word *rationalize*, which frequently refers to a type of behavior that falls between the two poles of reason and unreason. Here's an example: "She tried to *rationalize* her rudeness by telling her friends she was under stress." Used in this context, *rationalize* means to offer a reason that appears logical but is really self-serving. To remember all three words, learn them together and create sample sentences that reflect their meanings. Consider as well making a word map like the one shown on page 70.

rationalize ← rational → irrational

◆ Major and Minor Details

Until now, we've talked only about supporting details in general. However, there are actually two kinds of supporting details: major and minor.

Major Details

Major supporting details pin down general words or phrases introduced in the topic sentence. In the absence of supporting details, it's the most general words that typically lead readers astray. Supporting details prevent that from happening.

To illustrate, here's a topic sentence set free from the larger context of a paragraph: "Unwanted noise, especially if it persists over time, can cause problems."

Spotting the general word *problems*, readers are free to interpret the word in different ways. They could assume the *problems* have to do with anything from angry neighbors to hearing loss.

To be sure, however, that readers get the intended meaning, the author of this topic sentence was careful. He supplied three more specific major details. Notice how the details pinpoint precisely the "problems" the author had in mind:

The underlined topic sentence raises the question, What problems does it cause?

Note how the supporting details itemize three separate problems.

[1]Unwanted noise, especially if it persists over time, can cause problems. [2]Research suggests, for example, that continued exposure to noise in the workplace can contribute to heart disease and ulcers. [3]In addition, people who live in noisy areas have been found to have higher blood pressure than those who live in quieter surroundings. [4]Moreover, people continually exposed to high noise levels, whether at home or in the workplace, report a high degree of conflict in their lives. (Adapted from Zick Rubin, *Psychology*. Boston: Houghton Mifflin, 1990, p. 105.)

In this paragraph, sentences 2, 3, and 4 are major supporting details. Each detail identifies one of the "problems" mentioned in the topic sentence. In this way, the reader knows precisely what problems the writer is talking about.

Minor Details

Minor supporting details are even more specific than major ones. They appear in the paragraph for three reasons: (1) Minor details flesh out, or further explain, major ones; (2) they repeat key points for emphasis; and (3) they add colorful tidbits of information to stimulate reader interest.

Fleshing out major details is the most important function of minor details. Look, for example, at the following paragraph. Note the italicized minor details. Each adds to the major detail that precedes it.

[1]Unwanted noise, especially if it persists over time, can cause problems. [2]Research suggests, for example, that continued exposure to noise in the workplace can contribute to heart disease and ulcers. [3]*It's not surprising, then, that factory workers who spend eight hours a day surrounded by noisy machinery are likely to have heart and stomach problems.* [4]In addition, people who live in noisy areas have been found to have higher blood pressure than those who live in quieter surroundings. [5]*It's been shown, for example, that among those living near airports, train tracks, or interstate highways, high blood pressure is*

a common problem. [6]Moreover, people continually exposed to high noise levels, whether at home or in the workplace, report a high degree of conflict in their lives. [7]*They tend to argue more readily with family members and coworkers.* (Adapted from Zick Rubin, *Psychology*. Boston: Houghton Mifflin, 1990, p. 105.)

⊙━┰ READING KEYS

◆ Major details pin down general words and phrases introduced in the topic sentence.

◆ Minor details have three functions: (1) They make major details more specific, (2) they provide emphasis, and (3) they add color. The first function is the most important.

Evaluating Minor Details

Although major details are essential for clarifying topic sentences, don't assume that minor details have no importance. In fact, when you take notes on a paragraph, you should always *evaluate the minor details.* That is, you should decide how necessary minor details are to your understanding of the paragraph.

For example, in the paragraph about noise, you might want to remember that people who live and work in noisy areas tend to argue with family members and coworkers. True, this is a minor detail. But without it, the major detail—that persistent noise seems to cause conflict—remains unclear. That's because the word *conflict* is extremely general. Over time, you might forget what kind of conflict the author had in mind unless you mentally connected the major detail to the more specific minor one.

Minor details are slippery. Sometimes they just repeat what came before. Sometimes they provide information essential to understanding what's just been said. Thus you always need to evaluate minor details within the context of the paragraph they inhabit.

⊙━┰ READING KEYS

◆ Minor details that make major ones more specific are worthy of your attention.

◆ Minor details need to be evaluated. Sometimes they simply restate a major detail. But sometimes they add information essential to understanding the major detail.

◆ EXERCISE 3   Identifying Major and Minor Details

DIRECTIONS   Each paragraph is followed by a partially completed diagram. Complete the diagrams by filling in the remaining boxes with the appropriate sentence numbers.

Notice that the topic sentence tells you how many major details to look for.

The transition "First" announces the arrival of the first fact.

The transition "A second interesting fact" tells you here is the second of the "two interesting facts" mentioned in the topic sentence.

EXAMPLE   ¹Most people are unaware of two interesting facts about the Declaration of Independence. ²First, although the document is dated July 4, 1776, the day of our current annual celebration, the actual document was not created or signed on that day. ³The final draft was approved and sent to the printer on July 4, but most of the men who signed it did not do so until August 2. ⁴A second interesting fact is that the document's author, Thomas Jefferson, may have meant for the Declaration to be recited aloud. ⁵His handwritten draft included marks to indicate pauses and stresses that an orator would need as he read the document aloud to an audience.

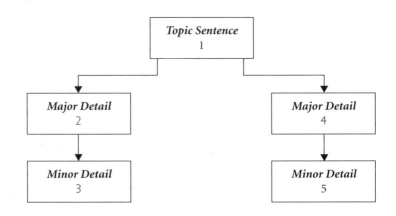

EXPLANATION   The topic sentence introduces the general phrase "two interesting facts about the Declaration of Independence." As you would expect, the major details identify those facts. The minor details provide more information about each of the two facts. In this case, both minor details have significance. Sentence 3 tells readers when the Declaration of Independence was really signed. Sentence 5 says *why* it's believed that Jefferson wanted it read aloud.

Tupac Shakur was one of the first rappers to die a violent death, but many more followed.

1. [1]Few would deny the energy and originality of rap music, but even diehard fans admit that the world of rappers has been plagued by violence. [2]Some of rap music's biggest superstars have been gunned down in their prime. [3]Tupac Shakur was shot to death in 1996 at age twenty-five; the Notorious B.I.G. was murdered in 1997 at age twenty-four; and Jam Master Jay, DJ for the popular group Run-DMC, was shot to death in his recording studio in 2002. [4]Many less well-known rappers—including Mr. Cee, Malcolm Howard, MC Big L, MC Ant, Q-Don, Yusef Afloat Muhammad, and Bruce Mayfield—have also been murdered since 1990. [5]In 2001, rapper Lloyd "Mooseman" Roberts was killed in a drive-by shooting, and upcoming rapper Tonnie Sheppard was stabbed to death. [6]In 2009, Ortega Henderson, a rapper on the rise, died of gunshot wounds he sustained in a shoot-out. [7]Henderson's death occurred just a few weeks after the twenty-one-year-old rapper Dolla was gunned down in a Beverly Hills shopping mall.

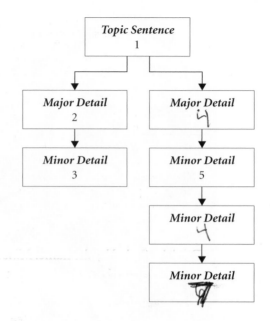

2. [1]The Soap and Detergent Association describes women in terms of five different attitudes toward cleaning. [2]One group is the *Mop Passers*. [3]These women—11 percent—like their homes to be clean, but they don't spend much time cleaning, and a dirty house does not embarrass them. [4]The next group is the *Strugglers*. [5]Twenty-one percent of women don't view housework as an important part of their lives and find it difficult to keep their homes neat. [6]*Dirt Dodgers* are a third group. [7]These women, 18 percent of all females, usually avoid cleaning and are generally dissatisfied with their homes' level of cleanliness. [8]Twenty-four percent of women, however, are *Mess Busters*. [9]They take pride in keeping their homes clean, and a neat environment gives them a sense of personal satisfaction. [10]The final category is called the *Clean Extremes*. [11]This group, 26 percent of women, cannot relax unless their houses are spotless, and many would rather clean house than do anything else.

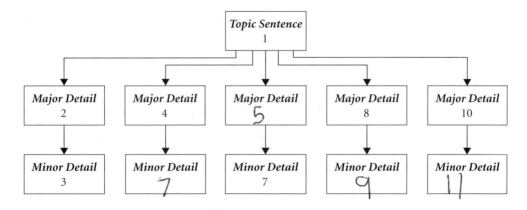

⊙━ **READING KEY**

◆ Don't be fooled by the name. *Minor* details may or may not be important. It depends on what they contribute to the major details.

IDIOM ALERT: Take the initiative

When someone *takes the initiative*, he or she is the first one to begin a task or plan of action—for example, to quote tennis champion Chris Evert, "You've got to *take the initiative* and play 'your' game. In a decisive set, confidence is the difference."

◆ EXERCISE 4   Recognizing Major and Minor Details

DIRECTIONS   Read each paragraph. Then fill in the diagrams with the appropriate numbers.

1. [1]The invention of air conditioning had a big impact on the southern way of life. [2]First, the availability of cool, dehumidified air altered southern architecture. [3]Before air conditioning, Southerners built homes with wide, shady porches; afterward, porches became far less common. [4]Second, air conditioning decreased the amount of social interaction among people. [5]Once air conditioning arrived, people stayed inside their houses, where they were cooler but more isolated from their neighbors. [6]Third, air conditioning changed summer leisure-time activities. [7]Prior to the arrival of air conditioning, people flocked to beaches and pools and avoided hot, enclosed spaces; however, with air conditioning in place, people could go to concerts, films, and plays without fear of sweltering.

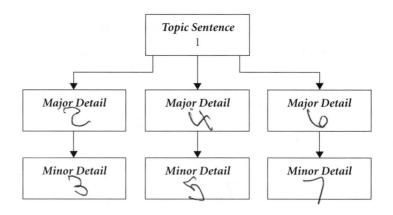

2. [1]For more than a decade, several state governments have been taking the initiative in an attempt to combat rising divorce rates. [2]In 1998, Florida, for instance, decided to make marriage a course of study for teenagers. [3]Thus, marriage education and relationship training officially became part of the curriculum in Florida's public schools, where teenagers learned, for instance, how to resolve disagreements with a partner. [4]Similarly, Arkansas has tried using education to reduce divorce rates. [5]Under the state's "community marriage" policy, clergy members voluntarily agree to marry only those couples who have completed a premarital education course. [6]Louisiana, like Arkansas, has made "covenant marriage" a legal alternative to traditional marriage agreements. [7]Couples who agree to a covenant marriage have a more difficult time finding grounds for divorce. [8]Accepted grounds for divorce in a covenant marriage are usually restricted to circumstances where one of the partners has been abusive, committed a felony, or engaged in adultery. [9]Oklahoma is yet another state trying to combat divorce. [10]The state spent millions of dollars on its Marriage Initiative program, which provides support for secular* and religious premarital education.

---

*secular: nonreligious.

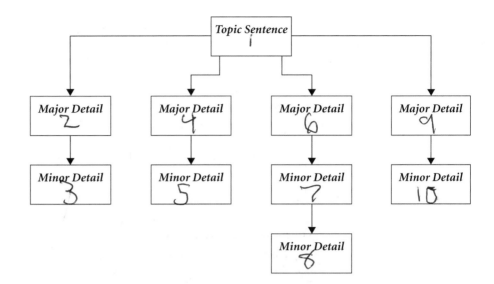

Clues to Major Details in Topic Sentences

When you are trying to distinguish between major and minor details, it helps if the topic sentence includes a category word. **Category words** refer to groups that can be divided or broken down into a number of component parts. Luckily for you, category words are particularly common in academic writing. The box below contains some of the most frequently used category words.

advantages	factors	reasons
attitudes	forms	roles
categories	functions	similarities
causes	goals	stages
characteristics	groups	steps
classes	kinds	symptoms
clues	methods	types
decisions	patterns	varieties
differences	points	ways

Category Words Help Identify Major Details

Words like those shown above, for instance, *forms*, *factors*, and *advantages* announce to readers that the major details will introduce examples of those *forms*, *factors*, or *advantages*. Look, for example, at the following paragraph. Note how each major detail hones in on an individual example of the *forms of communication* introduced in the topic sentence.

> ¹Although animals can't speak, they have other *forms of communication*. ²Some animals communicate with sounds. ³They use high-pitched cries to signal "move closer," or they growl to say "go away." ⁴Animals also use smells to communicate. ⁵Some beetles, for example, give off an odor when they want to greet a potential mate. ⁶Body language is another way animals communicate. ⁷To keep intruders away, geese puff up their feathers, making themselves look larger. ⁸Similarly, cats make themselves look more imposing by arching their backs and rapidly swinging their tails back and forth.

In this passage, the major details—sentences 2, 4, and 6—all identify the forms of communication the author had in mind.

Number Clues

Identifying major details through the use of category words becomes even easier when the topic sentence supplies a number. Take, for example, the following paragraph:

Topic Sentence

> ¹A group can be defined as two or more people who work together to achieve a goal. ²However, for a group to function effectively, *three elements need to be present*. ³Although there is no fixed limit on the size of a group, it shouldn't get too large. ⁴A group that gets too large stops working as a unit. ⁵Then, too, members must have the chance to meet regularly, so they can learn to know one another as individuals. ⁶Group members must share a common purpose. ⁷For example, individual workers might become a group in an effort to change company policy. ⁸Similarly, managers might unite to develop a new product. (Adapted from David Van Fleet, *Contemporary Management*, p. 383. © Cengage Learning.)

In this case, the category word *elements* in the topic sentence is modified by the number *three*. That number sends a signal to the alert reader: "If you don't end up with *three* major details, you are missing something."

⊙━┓ READING KEYS

- ◆ Check the topic sentence for broad, general words like *forms*, *groups*, *causes*, and *advantages*. These words are clues to major details.
- ◆ Be alert as well to numbers in the topic sentence that tell you how many major details are present.

◆ EXERCISE 5 **Recognizing Clues to Major Details**

DIRECTIONS Read each paragraph. Identify the category word or phrase that guides your selection of major details. Then, on the blank lines that follow, number and paraphrase all the major details in the paragraph.

Notice how the major details introduce symptoms that define each of the three categories mentioned in the topic sentence.

Note how transitions like *first* and *second* tell readers, "This is a new category coming up."

Sentence 5 shows that some major details require more than one minor detail of explanation.

EXAMPLE [1]Post-traumatic stress disorder (PTSD) symptoms usually start occurring within three months of the traumatic event. [2]For the most part, the symptoms of post-traumatic stress disorder can be grouped into three categories. [3]In the first and most common category of symptoms are intrusive, or haunting, memories that won't go away. [4]The person suffering from PTSD may have regular nightmares and flashbacks of the traumatic event. [5]The second category of symptoms involves avoidance of past experiences and emotional numbness. [6]Victims of PTSD often have difficulty developing or maintaining a close relationship. [7]Although clearly suffering, they can't talk about painful past events. [8]The third category is marked by extreme anxiety and a tendency to easily startle. [9]People suffering from post-traumatic stress disorder are often quick to anger, easily startled, and have trouble sleeping.

Category Word or Phrase   three categories

Major Details   1.   Haunting memories characterize the first group of symptoms.

2.   The second group includes symptoms marked by unwillingness to feel and the refusal to discuss the past.

3.   The third group of symptoms involves a high level of anxiety and a readiness to startle.

EXPLANATION The topic is post-traumatic stress disorder, and the topic sentence tells us that the disease has three kinds or "categories of symptoms." That phrase is a tip-off to the major details, telling us that each new category of symptoms is a major detail.

1. [1]No one knows exactly what causes insomnia. [2]It seems, in fact, that people suffer from insomnia for different reasons. [3]Some people can't sleep because they take their daytime worries to bed with them. [4]Consequently, they toss and turn. [5]Depression is another common reason. [6]Those suffering from the disease usually find it hard to sleep. [7]Then, too, people with irregular schedules are frequently plagued by insomnia. [8]Pilots and nurses, for instance, often suffer from bouts of sleeplessness.

Category Word or Phrase

insomnia is the topic sentence

Major Details

1. Daytime worries
2. Depression
3. irregular Schedules

2. [1]Researcher Ernest Hilgard has described several changes that frequently take place in people under hypnosis. [2]When hypnotized, the subject's attention becomes totally focused. [3]Instructed, for instance, to listen only to a particular voice, the hypnotized subject seems not to hear other voices in the room. [4]Hypnotized subjects also tend to believe whatever the hypnotist says. [5]If told, for instance, that a puppy is sitting on the table in front of her, the hypnotized subject may begin playing with an imaginary dog. [6]A good hypnotist can also change someone's behavior. [7]Under hypnosis, a shy young man can become lively and outgoing. [8]Or an outgoing young woman can become withdrawn under the influence of hypnosis.

Category Word or Phrase

Changes under hypnosis = topic

Major Details

1. Totally focused
2. Believe what the hypnotist says
3. Change Behavior

3. ¹Across the country, enthusiasm for the death penalty seems to be fading. ²Actually, many people now believe that a life sentence without parole has three definite advantages over the death penalty. ³First, a life sentence without parole protects society without taking human life. ⁴Second, it eliminates the lengthy court appeals that result from a death sentence. ⁵Finally, it ensures that criminals really pay for their crimes by staying in jail. ⁶With parole allowed, a life sentence can be as short as fifteen years. ⁷However, a life sentence without parole means just that. ⁸It lasts a lifetime.

Category Word or Phrase

Less Support for the Death Penalty = topic

Major Details

1. it Doesn't take a life.
2. eliminates court appeals
3. they serve all thier time.

4. ¹Power and leadership go hand in hand. ²There are, however, different types or categories of power. ³Probably the most commonly cited categories of power were identified by John Raven and Bertram French in the 1960s, and by their count, there are five. ⁴*Legitimate power* is the product of a role assignment in an organizational structure. ⁵A manager, for example, can tell employees what to do and expect to be obeyed. ⁶The second type of power is *reward power*—the power to give and deny rewards. ⁷People with reward power don't have to be in an organization, but they do have to have access to money or some other form of reward. ⁸*Coercive* power* uses force and threats to make people obey. ⁹In military and prison settings, coercion is the main source of power. ¹⁰*Expert power* is based on knowledge and experience. ¹¹The scientist who knows his subject matter thoroughly has expert power. ¹²The fifth type of power is *referent power*, and it's based on gaining admiration for personality and style. ¹³If, for example, a teenager dresses like his or her favorite singer, that singer has referent power over the teenager.

---

*coercive: applying force or punishment to control behavior.

Category Word
or Phrase

Major Details

Catagories of Power = topic

1. legetimate Power
2. Reward Power
3. Coercive Power
4. expert Power
5. referent Power

5. [1]Each year, thousands of Americans, mostly men,[†] use a marriage service to find a foreign-born spouse. [2]Why do they look overseas for a mate? [3]Actually, there are several reasons why men are drawn to the idea of looking abroad for a wife. [4]Almost half of those looking for foreign-born wives have already failed with an American spouse and hope to do better with a foreign one. [5]Then, too, some believe that the screening process provided by the matchmaking service will effectively weed out bad choices. [6]These mate seekers believe they increase their odds of finding the right wife if somebody else eliminates all the potentially wrong choices. [7]While the men themselves might be taken in by a pretty face, they assume the professional matchmaker will not be so easily won over. [8]At least a quarter of the men seeking wives overseas also claim that American women are not willing to play the appropriate wifely role. [9]In the eyes of these men, American women are too independent and not obedient enough.[10]Thus, some men seek wives abroad in the hope that women from other countries where feminism is not an issue will be more likely to let men rule the roost. [11]It's also true that a number of men are looking both at home and overseas simply to enlarge their pool of choices.

Category Word
or Phrase

Major Details

Overseas Mate

1. They failed with U.S. Wife
2. Screening for Good Choices
3. US. Women too independent

[†]Yes, some women do use a service to find a foreign-born spouse. But in general, it is mainly American men who look overseas for a wife.

4. Larger number of Choices

Topic Sentences, Transitions, and Major Details

In addition to numbers and plural words in topic sentences, writers in general—and textbook authors in particular—often use transitions to introduce major details. (Some of these transitions will be familiar from Chapter 3 on sentence relationships.)

For an illustration, see how the topic sentence in the following paragraph announces that there are concrete steps a person can take to remain positive. To make sure that readers recognize each new step, the author prefaces each one with an **addition** or **continuation transition**. Addition transitions are words or phrases that say, "Here's another idea that continues the train of thought begun previously." These transitions, italicized in the following paragraph, tell readers that the author has finished describing one step and is moving on to another.

Topic Sentence

¹Positive thinking—the belief in our own self-worth and the worth of others—is essential. ²But, as we all know, it's sometimes hard to think positive thoughts and easy to think negative ones. ³There are, however, concrete* steps we can all take to develop a positive frame of mind. ⁴*First*, actively seek out good news: ⁵If you're talking to friends or chatting with strangers, encourage them to talk about situations in which they emerge as heroes or winners. ⁶The conversation will make them feel great and probably raise your spirits as well. ⁷*Second*, always keep in mind that very few important goals can be achieved overnight. ⁸If you're still far away from achieving an objective, remind yourself that this is normal, and keep taking things one step at a time. ⁹*Third and last*, make a list of positive statements that you can recite whenever negative thoughts come to mind. ¹⁰Anytime you feel that you're not capable of achieving the goals you've set for yourself, it helps to say something like "I know I can do this; all I need is time."

---

*concrete: real, physically doable or observable.

The authors use three different examples to illustrate the underlined topic sentence: To make sure that readers know where one step leaves off and another begins, the authors separate the major details with transitional phrases that signal addition.

Transitions Signaling Addition and Continuation ♦	above all	for instance	moreover
	adding to that	for one thing	plus
	another	it's also true that . . .	similarly
	besides	like	then, too
	finally	likewise	yet another
	first, second, third		

⚷ **READING KEY**

♦ Transitions signaling addition and continuation frequently introduce major details, but they are more common in business and government texts than they are in history textbooks.

♦ **EXERCISE 6**   **Recognizing Transitions That Identify Major Details**

DIRECTIONS   Underline the topic sentence and circle any addition transitions introducing major details. Then on the lines below, paraphrase the major details according to the order in which they appear. *Note*: Because you cannot rely on addition transitions to be in every single paragraph, one of the paragraphs in this exercise won't have any. However, the topic sentence should still direct your attention to the major details.

EXAMPLE   [1]Psychologist Bruce Tuckman's theory of group development has become very influential. [2]According to Tuckman, groups develop in a series of four stages. [3]The (first) stage is called *forming*. [4]During this stage, members come together to discuss a common goal or purpose. [5](In the second) or *storming*, stage, conflicts start to emerge and members begin to argue. [6]Some members may even talk about leaving the group. [7](During the third) or *norming*, stage, people either bond with other group members or abandon the group altogether. [8](In the fourth), or *performing*, stage, members actively start to work toward common goals. [9]Conflict decreases and while disagreement may exist, there are procedures in place to address them without destroying the group.

Major Detail 1 "Forming" is the first stage.

Major Detail 2 In the "storming" stage, there are arguments and conflict.

Major Detail 3 During the "norming" stage, people accept or leave the group.

Major Detail 4 In the "performing" stage, members work together to achieve common goals.

EXPLANATION In the context of the paragraph, *first, in the second, during the third,* and *in the fourth* are all transitions indicating addition. With the help of these transitions, it's easy to identify the four major details in the paragraph.

1. [1]Although animals signal danger in a variety of ways, many rely primarily on their tails to communicate the presence of a threat. [2]The white-tailed deer, for instance, raises its highly visible white tail as a warning. [3]If deer are contentedly grazing, and one of them lifts its white tail, they will all disappear in a flash. [4]Like deer, beavers also use their tails to signal danger. [5]They will slap the water with a loud smack if a threat approaches. [6]Similarly, geese and pigeons ruffle or fan out their tails when angry or fearful.

Major Detail 1 The white tailed deer raises its tail

Major Detail 2 Beavers slap thier tails on the water

Major Detail 3 Geese and Pigeons Fan thier tails

2. [1]According to the *Oxford Dictionary of Literary Terms*, there are three types of biography. [2]The most well-known is the autobiography. [3]The autobiography recounts the life of the person writing it. [4]Tina Fey's *Bossypants* is a popular autobiography. [5]Anne Frank's *The Diary of a Young Girl* is perhaps the best-known autobiography of all time.

[6]Autobiographies are by necessity incomplete. [7]For obvious reasons, the person writing one cannot record his or her own death. [8]A *biography*, in contrast, tells the story of someone else's life, usually the life of someone famous. [9]Some biographies describe the life of a group or of an animal. [10]*The Presidents Club*, for instance, describes how presidents and ex-presidents have both cooperated and clashed during the changing of the guard. [11]Susan Orlean's *Rin Tin Tin* tells the story of America's most famous, and in his own way, influential dog. [12]A *memoir* describes some aspect of the writer's life and often involves the lives of friends and family. [13]Readers tend to think that memoirs are nonfiction, but some memoir writers, like journalist Vivian Gornick,[†] have argued that memoirs can be partially fictionalized if the account is true to the spirit of events. [14]Gornick's memoir of the relationship with her mother is titled *Fierce Attachments*, and she acknowledges having combined events to *communicate* a particular feeling or attitude. [15]*Love in Condition Yellow* by Sophia Raday tells the story of a peace activist married to a military man during the Iraq War.

Major Detail 1 ___Autobiography___

Major Detail 2 ___a biography___

Major Detail 3 ___A memoir___

3. [1]In 1936, Arthur Kallet and Colston Warne founded the Consumers Union (CU). [2]The goal of the organization was to protect the interests of consumers and respond to unfair market practices and false advertising. [3]From its inception, Consumers Union was designed to help buyers in several key ways. [4]Most importantly, Consumers Union sorts out low-quality and unsafe products from those that will give you the best value for your money. [5]They do this primarily through product testing, the results of which are published in the organization's magazine *Consumer Reports*, which millions consult before making a purchase. [6]Consumers Union also employs lobbyists and organizers who focus on introducing and improving

---

[†]In her book *The Situation and the Story: The Art of Personal Narrative*, Gornick makes this argument, which was, at one time, the source of much controversy.

legislation protecting consumers.[7] In addition, Consumers Union buys automobiles in order to evaluate the vehicles' reliability and pass on tips about how to bargain for the best prices.

Major Detail 1   Sort out Bad Quality or unsafe Pro ducts.

Major Detail 2   Legislation Protecting Consumers,

Major Detail 3   Vehicle reliability and Best prices,

Paraphrasing for Note-Taking

This section goes into more detail about a topic already introduced in Chapter 1—paraphrasing. The emphasis here is on the difference between paraphrasing for reading notes and paraphrasing for term papers.

Keep in mind, however, that you can always adapt what you learn here to your particular purpose. If you are taking marginal notes in your text, feel free to write brief sentence fragments designed to trigger the right memory. If you are taking more detailed reading notes, separate from the text itself, decide how complete your sentences or phrases need to be so that you can easily review your notes when it's time to prepare for exams. It's only when you paraphrase for term papers that your paraphrase needs to be expressed in a complete sentence.

Accurate Paraphrasing

You can't paraphrase without a piece of text written by someone else. So let's start there. Here's an excerpt you have seen before:

The psychologist Abraham H. Maslow (1908–1970) coined the term "peak experience" to describe feelings of great wonder, happiness, and sensory awareness. According to Maslow, the "peak experience" makes a person feel at one with the world while at the same time fostering a sense of physical control. Many who came after Maslow have likened his "peak experience" to the athlete's sense of being "in the zone" or to the feeling of being "in the flow" that some people get in moments of intense concentration.

The excerpt has three sentences; however, that does not mean the paraphrase has to have three sentences. It does have to express the key components, or parts, of the original text. The paraphrase has to (1) mention Maslow's name and profession, (2) define the peak experience, and (3) indicate that some people have likened the peak experience to other, similar states of mind. Thus we might paraphrase the original like this:

Paraphrase   According to the man who invented the term, psychologist Abraham Maslow, the "peak experience" induces a feeling of physical mastery combined with a sense of wonder at being so perfectly in tune with the rest of the world. People who have studied similar experiences compare Maslow's peak experience to an athlete's sense of being "in the zone" or "in the flow," which some people get when they are deeply engrossed in a mental activity.

This paraphrase has all of the elements in the original, but most of the language is different. In other words, it fulfills the central rule of accurate paraphrasing: Change the wording, not the meaning.

The above paraphrase, though, is the kind that you might create for a term paper. If you are paraphrasing for reading notes, you certainly don't need to use only complete sentences. What's important is the recording of all the essential points included in the original. The reading notes below meet that standard:

Abraham Maslow coined term "peak experience" to express a sense of

1. physical self-control
2. oneness with the world
3. feeling of awe

Others who came after compared Maslow's peak experience to

1. athlete's sense of being "in the zone."
2. feeling of being "in the flow" that focused concentration produces.

Inaccurate Paraphrasing

How you paraphrase depends on the context in which you are working. For reading notes, fragments and abbreviations will do just fine as long as you can remember the original meaning based on what you've written. For term papers, you need to make your paraphrases complete, grammatically correct sentences.

What you can't do in either context, though, is change the meaning. That's precisely the problem with the following paraphrase:

Inaccurate Paraphrase

According to the man who coined the term, the psychologist Abraham Maslow, a "peak experience" makes a person feel a sense of awe at being closely connected to someone else. Thus the "peak experience" would be typical for someone newly married. Those, however, who came after Maslow have criticized his use of the term and substituted phrases like "in the zone" or "in the flow."

There are several major distortions of the original in this paraphrase. First, the original doesn't talk about being connected to other people. It talks about feeling in unity with the *world*, a word that includes nature and humans. The narrowing of the word *world* leads to the second distortion, when it's suggested that newlyweds illustrate the "peak experience." They might, but nothing in the original really suggests that they do. That's the writer's point of view, not Maslow's, and paraphrases shouldn't alter the meaning of the original.

Finally, those who came after Maslow did not criticize his definition. They simply pointed out that Maslow's peak experience resembled feelings that others had described in a different way.

⌐ READING KEY

- ◆ To remember more of what you read *and* to test your understanding, make paraphrasing a regular habit.

Paraphrasing Pointers
◆

1. Use questions to get the author's meaning clear in your mind.

Anytime the words for a paraphrase don't come to you immediately, ask questions, such as What's the author's topic? How can I rephrase that topic? What's being said about the topic? How can I rephrase that claim or comment?

2. Change the words but never the meaning.

You defeat the purpose of paraphrasing if your choice of words distorts the original point.

Original Text: After the humiliation of writing ridiculous dialogue for a film titled *Way Down South*, African-American poet Langston Hughes publicly attacked Hollywood racism.

Accurate Paraphrase: African-American poet Langston Hughes spoke out against Hollywood racism after he was forced to write silly dialogue for a movie called *Way Down South*.

Inaccurate Paraphrase: When African-American poet Langston Hughes couldn't find work as a writer in Hollywood, he spoke out against the discrimination he had experienced.

3. Make the end the beginning.

When asked to paraphrase, many students say, "I don't know where to start." I always pass on to them a tip from a former student: Start at the end. *Usually*, you can create a new version of the original text by opening with content that the author put at the end. This works for the original and paraphrase given above. It also works for the original and paraphrase below.

Original Text: Of all the organizations [in the nineteenth century] working to bring religion and sports closer together, none was more influential than the Young Men's Christian Association. (Clifford Putney, *Muscular Christianity*. Harvard University Press, 2003, p. 62.)

Accurate Paraphrase: The Young Men's Christian Association (YMCA) was crucial to the nineteenth-century effort to unite religion and athletics.

4. Paraphrase in chunks.

When you paraphrase, don't think of exchanging each original word for a new word. Instead, look closely at the phrases the author uses to describe both content and relationships. Then try to come up with different phrases that have similar meanings and make similar connections. Once you have the major thoughts and relationships in place, it's easier to fill in single words.

Original: Those who claim to have had near-death experiences don't always agree on what the experience was like. Many have described "a white light at the end of a tunnel"; others report torture by demons.

Accurate Paraphrase: Some reports of near-death experiences have described pain inflicted by demons; others describe a long tunnel with a white light at the end. In short, reports of near-death experiences are likely to differ.

5. Don't be afraid to combine sentences.

If the author uses two sentences to express an idea, you don't have to do the same. If you can combine sentences and make the paraphrase shorter than the original, good for you. Just make sure you don't leave out any key information in the process.

Original: Massage therapists who are certified by the National Certification Board for Therapeutic Massage & Bodywork must take 500 hours of education classes and pass an examination. They must know some basic anatomy and physiology, as well as some first aid. (Robert Todd Carroll, *The Skeptic's Dictionary*, Wiley, 2003, p. 46.)

Accurate Paraphrase: People seeking to be certified by the National Certification Board for Therapeutic Massage & Bodywork are required to take 500 hours of classes and pass an exam testing their knowledge of basic anatomy, physiology, and first aid.

Inaccurate Paraphrase: All massage therapists are certified by the National Certification Board for Therapeutic Massage & Bodywork. In order to get licensed, they have to know as much about the body as doctors do.

6. Keep in mind that some words have no substitutes.

Many students incorrectly believe that a paraphrase has to change every single word in the original text. But sometimes that's impossible to do. There really is no substitute for, say, the "Young Men's Christian Association," "near-death experiences," or "demons" in the previous examples. If you can change the order and three-quarters of the words in the original text, you are doing just fine.

7. Make paraphrasing a habit.

Paraphrasing requires thought. It's not as easy as it might seem at first glance. Thus, readers sometimes start out paraphrasing while reading and then give up because it seems like too much effort. But if you are dealing with fairly complicated text that's important to your understanding of the subject matter, paraphrasing is worth the effort. Paraphrasing won't just improve your comprehension. It will help you remember what you read.

◆ EXERCISE 7   **Writing Accurate Paraphrases**

DIRECTIONS   Underline the topic sentence. Then paraphrase it in the blanks that follow. For the sake of practice, make these paraphrases resemble the ones you would write for papers.

EXAMPLE   [1]Internet users seem to love cats, and cat videos on sites like YouTube outweigh dog videos by two to one. [2]What's also clear, though, is that Internet cat lovers have a preference for Japanese cats. [3]To name just a few of Japan's cat celebrities, there's Maru, Mao, Shironeko aka Zen cat, Papi-chan, and Winstonsan. [4]<u>Perhaps even more interesting than Japan's dominance of the cat video market is the anonymity of the cats' owners.</u> [5]Unlike Americans who, by and large, post pet videos on YouTube with their own names prominently displayed, Japanese posters usually offer only their cats to public view. [6]They themselves stay in the background and do not identify themselves by name. [7]If there is any glory to be had, it goes to the cat, not the owner.

Paraphrase   Although Japanese cat videos are enormously popular, the cats' owners keep their

identity to themselves.

EXPLANATION   As it should, the paraphrase alters the author's words without changing the meaning.

1. [1]It's been more than one hundred years since Mary Surratt was hanged for her role in the assassination of Abraham Lincoln. [2]Yet, even today, there are those who doubt Surratt's involvement in Lincoln's death. [3]<u>There is, after all, no hard evidence linking her to the assassination.</u> [4]Then, too, one of the three men executed with Surratt insisted on her innocence until his death. [5]Some people also believe the place of her execution, Fort McNair, is haunted by a ghost proclaiming her innocence. [6]Children report playing with a woman in black, and the lights mysteriously flicker. [7]One man even claims to have heard a woman crying "I am innocent" on Lincoln's birthday.

Paraphrase   People doubt Surratt's involvement in Lincoln's death.

2. [1]The financial and human costs of the Civil War were enormous. [2]Estimates for the total cost of the war exceed $20 billion. [3]This

amount is five times the amount spent by the federal government from its creation to 1861. [4]The South, which bore the brunt,* borrowed over $2 billion and lost much more than that in damages and destruction. [5]In southern war zones, houses, crops, barns, and bridges were destroyed. [6]Factories were looted by Union troops, who also put two-thirds of the South's railroad system out of service. [7]The human toll, too, was huge. [8]In a nation of only 31 million people, the total number of military casualties on both sides was over 1 million. [9]About 360,000 Union soldiers died from battle wounds or disease, and another 275,175 were wounded. [10]An estimated 260,000 Confederate soldiers were killed, and almost as many were wounded.

(Adapted from Mary Beth Norton et al., *A People and a Nation*, 7th ed. © Cengage Learning.)

Paraphrase

The People and Money costs were enourmous.

Note-Taking with Outlines and Summaries

Now that you know the basic elements of the paragraph and have some experience with paraphrasing under your belt, you are ready to think more about a topic already discussed in Chapter 1, **note-taking**. There are several different ways to take notes, depending on (1) the type of text you are reading and (2) your personal preference. This chapter section explains two of the most effective and widely used methods: outlining and summarizing.

Outlines

When you take notes on paragraphs using the outline format, the outline you create for your notes is somewhat different from the formal outlines you may have learned about in composition courses. When you outline a chapter section for later reviews, you can use all numbers instead of letters. You can also combine sentences with phrases, if you wish. You don't have to use one *or* the other. The kinds of symbols you use are strictly up to you. Note-taking outlines are informal versions of the formal ones you may have learned about in other classes.

---

*brunt: burden.

Outlining for note-taking has only three requirements: (1) the items in your outline need to use a system of indention, or spacing, so that relationships between ideas are obvious at a glance; (2) the sentences and phrases in the outline need to be paraphrased, not copied from the text; and (3) the sentences or phrases in your outline need to be detailed enough to make sense over time. There's no point using a shorthand code that even you can't understand after three weeks have passed.

For an example of a good outline, read the following paragraph. Then study the accompanying outline:

> Gossip actually serves three important purposes: networking, enhancing one's image, and forming social alliances. Networking is a way of gathering information about other people in a social hierarchy.* Knowing about the other people within a social structure gives individuals a better understanding of their own position within it and helps them attain a higher ranking. The second function of gossip is to suggest that the person in possession of the gossip is someone of importance. Those in possession of up-to-date gossip appear to be closely connected to people who are professionally or socially powerful. Forming useful alliances is the third purpose of gossip. People sometimes offer up gossip in order to be looked upon favorably by those higher on the social or professional ladder.

Main Idea

Supporting Details

The minor details identify the benefits of each purpose.

Gossip fulfills three goals.

1. Networking: gathering info about others in social hierarchy
   Benefit: people understand their function or role in group
2. Bestows importance: person who knows the gossip is considered important to the group
   Benefit: those with gossip to tell seem well connected
3. Creates alliances
   Benefit: people exchange gossip as way of connecting professionally and advancing up the professional ladder.

You can see from even a quick glance at the outline how the major details fill out the category word *purposes* introduced in the topic sentence. This is precisely what an outline should do. Outlines should bring into immediate focus the relationships between the main idea and supporting details.

It's important to point out that in this paragraph the minor details are significant because they add crucial information to the major details. Thus, they appear in the outline.

*hierarchy: order from higher to lower.

Outline Pointers ◆	1. Indent and label to show relationships between the main idea and details.
	2. Paraphrase rather than copying verbatim, or word for word.
	3. Abbreviate carefully so that the meaning does not disappear with the words eliminated.
	4. Be selective about which major and minor details you need to include and which you don't.

◆ EXERCISE 8 Making Outlines

DIRECTIONS Outline the paragraphs in the blanks that follow.

EXAMPLE Abraham Maslow, an American psychologist whose best-known works were published in the 1960s and 1970s, developed a theory of motivation based on what he called a "hierarchy of needs." At the most basic level of the hierarchy, are physiological needs, the things we require to survive, like food, water, clothing, shelter, and sleep. At the next level are safety needs, the things we require for physical and emotional safety. Modern safety needs may be satisfied through job security, health insurance, pension plans, and safe working and living conditions. Next are social needs, the human requirements for love, affection, and a sense of belonging. At the next-to-last level are esteem needs, the desire for respect and recognition from others. At the top of the hierarchy are our self-actualization needs, the longing to grow and develop and become all we are capable of being. (Adapted from William M. Pride, Robert J. Hughes, and Jack R. Kapoor, *Business*, 10th ed. © Cengage Learning.)

Need Level 5
Self-actualization needs — Feeling of personal growth and fulfillment in ethical and creative terms

Need Level 4
Esteem needs — Having a sense of achievement, confidence, status, and importance

Need Level 3
Belongingness and love needs — Desire for family, friends, colleagues, and sexual intimacy with a partner

Need Level 2
Safety needs — Longing for protection and security—physically, legally, and financially

Need Level 1
Biological and physiological needs — Fulfillment of basic physical requirements: air, food, drink, housing, sex, sleep, etc.

Main Idea   Psychologist Abraham Maslow came up with a theory of motivation that focused on what he called, a "hierarchy of needs."

Supporting Details

1. At the bottom of the hierarchy are physical needs that keep us alive: need for food, sleep, shelter, etc.

2. Next come safety needs, which can be satisfied through things like job security, laws, and health insurance.

3. Social needs are the next step up in the hierarchy, and they refer to the desire for warmth, community, and love.

4. Next to last comes the longing for the respect of others.

5. At the highest level are spiritual needs and what Maslow called self-actualization, the need to feel we are fulfilling our potential.

EXPLANATION   As is typical for a business text, the first sentence is the topic sentence. The topic sentence tells us about Maslow's theory, which ranked human needs from the lowest to the highest. Each description of a level is a major supporting detail. Note how the outline combines major and minor details into single sentences.

1. [1]The full moon has long been linked to any number of events. [2]Crime, suicide, mental illness, the birthrate, and even werewolves have all been linked to the presence of a full moon. [3]Yet for decades, studies of the full-moon effect have never supported such claims without making a dent in what amounts to superstition. [4]In 1996, for instance, Ivan Kelly, James Rotton, and Roger Culver examined more than 100 studies of the full-moon effect and concluded that the studies failed to show a connection between the full moon and any of the other irrational events normally connected to it. [5]The lack of hard evidence for the full-moon effect naturally raises the question, "Why then do so many people believe that a full moon has powerful effects on everything from the homicide rate to psychiatric admissions?" [6]Kelly and his colleagues suspect that tradition plays a role in passing on the superstition. [7]And once the false belief becomes ingrained through unscientific sources and casual comments, people find it hard to give it up even if they are confronted with evidence to the contrary.

Main Idea

The full moon has long been linked
to a number of events

Supporting Details

1. crime
2. suicide
3. mental illness
4. the Birthrate
5. Werewolves

2. [1]Travelers who go to exotic foreign countries should prepare themselves by becoming aware of differences among cultures. [2]If you dine in an Indian home, for instance, you should always leave food on the plate to show the host that the portions were generous and that you had enough to eat. [3]Yet as a dinner guest in Bolivia, you need to show your appreciation by cleaning your plate. [4]If you shop in an outdoor market in the Middle East, expect to negotiate the price of everything you buy. [5]Nothing personal. [6]Even the way we space ourselves from each other is culturally determined. [7]Americans, Canadians, British, and Northern Europeans keep a polite distance between themselves and others. [8]They feel crowded by the touchier, nose-to-nose style of the French, Greeks, Arabs, Mexicans, and South Americans. (Adapted from Sharon S. Brehm, Saul Kassim, and Steven Fein, *Social Psychology*, 6th ed. © Cengage Learning.)

Main Idea

the customs right; ~~India Leave~~
~~food on your plate~~
India: Leave food on your plate
Supporting Details
Bolivia: clean your plate
Middle East: haggle prices
In some cultures keep a distance
but others like being close

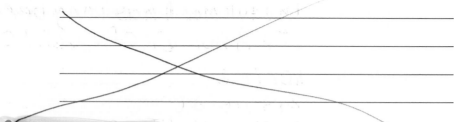

READING KEYS

◆ At a quick glance, informal outlines reveal not just the main idea and the major and minor details needed to explain it but also the relationships those ideas share.

◆ Informal outlines need not rigidly adhere to one format. You can mix sentences with phrases and letters with numbers, and use dashes and abbreviations.

◆ Never make the items in your outline so abbreviated that you don't understand what they refer to after time has passed.

VOCABULARY EXTRA

The Latin word for moon is *luna*. Because it was believed that a full moon could cause madness, the word *lunatic* came into being sometime in the sixteenth century. It referred to someone who had been driven mad by exposure to a full moon.

Summaries

Outlines are good for detailed textbooks that have a lot of specifics. Summaries, however, work well with texts that are less detailed. Summaries are particularly good for more general writing, especially when the author gives an **opinion**, or personal point of view, and then follows it with reasons or examples designed to convince, as in the following example:

[1]The name giraffe comes from the Arab word *Zirapha*, which means "one who walks very fast." [2]Yet while it's true that giraffes can run very fast, it's not clear why they need to except when fleeing hunters. [3]The world's tallest living animal, giraffes don't hunt. [4]They survive on tree leaves, which they can easily reach thanks to their long, muscular necks. [5]However, the giraffe's love of greenery may be what

Main Idea

causes the animals to become extinct. [6]An adult giraffe can weigh as much as 4,200 pounds and consume around 140 pounds of foliage per day.[7]As the leafy trees where they seek dinner are destroyed by the invasion of humans who build houses where giraffes like to graze, the giraffe has fewer and fewer trees from which to grab a meal. [8]Although listed as "low risk" on the World Conservation Union's list, giraffes have already become extinct in the African countries of Mauritania and Senegal. [9]They are also threatened with extinction in Mozambique.

If you decide to summarize a reading, your goal should be to reduce the text to around one-quarter to one-half of its original length. That means you need to think hard about what's absolutely essential to your understanding of the material.

Identifying What's Essential

Whatever form of note-taking you choose, *the main idea is always essential.* Summaries are no exception, so this one would have to begin with a paraphrase of the fifth sentence, which also happens to be the topic sentence: "The giraffe's leafy diet may lead to its extinction."

The next sentence in the summary should answer any question raised by that statement of the main idea. The most likely question would be something like this: "Why would the giraffe's diet of leaves cause it to become extinct?" The answer comes in sentence 7. This is where the reader learns that trees are being destroyed so humans can build houses. The content of that sentence, therefore, has to become part of the summary.

So, too, does the answer to the third likely question, "How serious is the situation?" One indication appears in sentences 8 and 9, where the reader learns that giraffes are already extinct in two African countries. Thus a paraphrase of that sentence, too, has to make it into our summary. The result looks like this:

Sample Summary
The giraffe's leafy diet may lead to its extinction. Leafy trees are being destroyed by human settlement, leaving the giraffe with less access to food. Despite being listed as "low risk" by the World Conservation Union, giraffes are already extinct in Mauritania and Senegal.

Giraffes are uniquely suited to gathering their dinner from even the tallest of trees.

© Ulrich Flemming

A summary always has to identify the main idea. But the number of major and minor details can vary. The number of details you include depends on the main idea being explained and the questions it might raise for the reader.

Your Summary Should Also Reflect the Author's Purpose

Much of the material you will be summarizing from your reading assignments will have an **informative purpose**. The author wants, that is, to inform readers about a particular topic or issue without trying to convince them to share a particular point of view or take a specific action.

However, if you are assigned to write a summary of an outside reading, say an article from *Time* magazine, you need to ask yourself if the author's purpose is still strictly informative. If, in fact, it isn't and the author writes with a **persuasive purpose**, i.e., with the clear intent to convince you that his or her opinion, or point of view, is more thoughtful and more informed than any other points of view on the subject, then that purpose should make its way into your summary.

To get a sense of how purpose makes a difference, compare these opening lines. The ones on the left are based on informative writing. Those on the right are based on persuasive writing.

1. Mary Shelley, the author of *Frankenstein*, was a teenager when she wrote the classic horror story.

2. Social media currently play a significant role in marketing.

3. All but banished in the fifties through the seventies, breast feeding has made a comeback and new mothers are encouraged to breast feed.

1. Mary Shelley's *Frankenstein* may have been written by a teenager, but it should not be forgotten that Shelley, the child of philosopher William Godwin and writer Mary Wollstonecraft, was an extraordinarily gifted teenager.

2. In her book *Quiet*, Susan Cain insists that we need to spend less time being connected and more time alone.

3. As Anna White correctly points out in her editorial, when three-year-olds are still nursing, it's safe to say that breast feeding is being taken to extremes.

Pointers on Summary Writing
◆

1. Open with the main idea expressed in your own words.

2. If there is introductory material in the paragraph, add only the pieces of it that are essential to understanding the main idea.

3. Consider what questions the main idea might raise in the reader's mind.

4. Determine what major or minor details answer those questions. Include those in your summary as well.

5. Use addition and reversal transitions to clarify relationships. Because you are pulling sentences out of their original context and paraphrasing them, the result might sound choppy. Use transitions to smooth out the style.

6. Make your summary reflect the author's purpose. When the purpose is persuasive, you should include the author's name and clearly link it to the point of view being expressed, e.g., "In an effort to demonstrate just how brilliant Mary Shelley was, scholar Ann Mellor shows readers how many different philosophers her supposedly simple horror story cites."

○━╥ **READING KEYS**

◆ Summaries reduce the original text to the bare bones of the original content. They should include the main idea and any major or minor details essential to answering questions raised by the main idea.

◆ Your summary should reflect the purpose of the original text.

◆ Summaries usually benefit from the presence of transitions that clarify relationships.

◆ EXERCISE 9   Writing Summaries

DIRECTIONS   Summarize each of the following paragraphs.

Notice how the transition *however* sets the reader up for the topic sentence.

The statement "things can go terribly wrong" sets the stage for the reader to ask, "What went wrong?"

The description of the side effects answers the question and therefore needs to be in the summary.

The last sentence pretty much repeats the point of the fourth sentence, so eliminate it from your summary.

EXAMPLE   ¹Under pressure from both consumers and drug makers, the Food and Drug Administration (FDA) has fast tracked certain drugs. ²*Fast tracking is a* **process** designed to make it easier for drugs treating serious diseases or filling an unmet medical need to come to market. ³The goals of fast tracking sound worthy. ⁴However, when speed plays a role in evaluating drug side effects, things can go terribly wrong, as was the case with GlaxoSmithKline's drug Avandia. ⁵Fast tracked by the FDA, Avandia, a drug used to treat diabetes, was once one of the biggest-selling drugs on the market. ⁶Thanks in large degree to a massive marketing campaign by GlaxoSmithKline, Avandia had $3.2 billion in sales in 2006. ⁷But it was only a year later that reports began to surface about the drug's serious side effects, heart attack and heart failure. ⁸Although GlaxoSmithKline maintained that evidence about the drug's side effects were contradictory, internal memos show that doubts about the drug surfaced before it went on the market. ⁹GlaxoSmithKline is currently conducting post-market trials of the drug. ¹⁰But the results won't be available until 2014. ¹¹Meanwhile, sales of Avandia have dropped dramatically. ¹²The case of Avandia has raised new doubts about the benefits of fast tracking drugs that can, if not properly tested, kill those they are supposed to heal.

Summary   Fast tracking, the FDA's speeded up process of bringing new drugs to market, may not be a good idea. Avandia is an example of a drug that was fast tracked and ended up causing two serious side effects, heart attack and heart failure. When a drug can kill some of the people it's supposed to help, slowing down the process of approval might be better than speeding it up.

EXPLANATION   The topic sentence raises a key question, What can go wrong when a fast tracked drug is too quickly approved? The rest of the paragraph answers that question by describing what happened with the drug Avandia. In addition to the main idea, the summary has to describe the side effects associated with Avandia and link them to fast tracking of potentially dangerous drugs.

1. [1]Leaders in groups usually fall into one of two categories. [2]**Instrumental leaders** focus on achieving goals. [3]They try to keep the group on track and are likely to say things like, "We might be getting sidetracked here" or "Isn't it time we got back to work?" [4]**Expressive leaders** are less goal-oriented. [5]They are more concerned with how the members of the group are functioning. [6]Their goal is to make sure that the individual members are satisfied with their work in the group. [7]Instead of goals, these leaders are more likely to focus on members' feelings, such as, "Is everybody satisfied with how things are going?"

Summary

Leaders in groups usually fall into one of two Catagories, instrumental leaders focus on goals, expressive leaders focus on how the people are doing.

2. [1]All over the country, police departments use sophisticated computer technology to fight crime. [2]But some police departments have found that a more ancient means, the horse, offers several advantages even in today's modern times. [3]First, police officers on horseback have a height advantage. [4]They can see more of what's going on around them than an officer on foot. [5]Second, horses are effective for crowd control. [6]The physical presence of a horse is intimidating. [7]As a result, agitated* crowds, such as those engaging in protest demonstrations, are less likely to try to injure a mounted officer. [8]Furthermore, people often develop affection for a police horse they encounter regularly. [9]This fondness for the animal can lead to greater respect and admiration for the officer who rides it.

Summary

The horse offers Advantages, first there is an advantage of Height, horses help with crowd control. also when they get to know the horse they respect the officer who rides it.

*agitated: stirred up, excited and angry.

ROUNDING UP THE KEYS

Here is a list of all the reading keys introduced in the chapter. Use them to review for the test on page 271. If a particular reading key doesn't make sense on its own, go back to the page where it appeared and review the section preceding it.

READING KEYS: The Function of Supporting Details

◆ Supporting details supply the reasons, illustrations, facts, figures, and studies that make the main idea clear and convincing to readers. (p. 222)

◆ Supporting details are the author's way of guiding readers to the appropriate meaning. They are the author's way of saying to readers, "I mean this and not that." (p. 222)

◆ The form of supporting details varies. Details can range in form from reasons to statistics. The main idea is what causes supporting details to vary. When the main idea changes, so do the details that develop it. (p. 222)

◆ If the supporting details don't fit what you think is the topic sentence, you probably need to look for another topic sentence. (p. 227)

READING KEYS: Major and Minor Details

◆ Major details pin down general words and phrases introduced in the topic sentence. (p. 229)

◆ Minor details have three functions: (1) They make major details more specific, (2) they provide emphasis, and (3) they add color. The first function is the most important. (p. 229)

READING KEYS: Evaluating Minor Details

◆ Minor details that make major ones more specific are worthy of your attention. (p. 229)

◆ Minor details need to be evaluated. Sometimes they simply restate a major detail. But sometimes they add information essential to understanding the major detail. (p. 229)

◆ Don't be fooled by the name. *Minor* details may or may not be important. It depends on what they contribute to the major details. (p. 233)

READING KEYS: Clues to Major Details in Topic Sentences

◆ Check the topic sentence for broad, general words like *forms*, *groups*, *causes*, and *advantages*. These words are clues to major details. (p. 237)

◆ Be alert as well to numbers in the topic sentence that tell you how many major details are present. (p. 237)

READING KEY: Topic Sentences, Transitions, and Major Details

◆ Transitions signaling addition and continuation frequently introduce major details, but they are more common in business and government texts than they are in history textbooks. (p. 242)

READING KEY: Paraphrasing

◆ To remember more of what you read *and* to test your understanding, make paraphrasing a regular habit. (p. 247)

READING KEYS: Creating Outlines and Summaries

◆ At a quick glance, informal outlines reveal not just the main idea and the major and minor details needed to explain it but also the relationships those ideas share. (p. 256)

◆ Informal outlines need not rigidly adhere to one format. You can mix sentences with phrases and letters with numbers, and use dashes and abbreviations. (p. 256)

◆ Never make the items in your outline so abbreviated that you don't understand what they refer to after time has passed. (p. 256)

◆ Summaries reduce the original text to the bare bones of the original content. They should include the main idea and any major or minor details essential to answering questions raised by the main idea. (p. 260)

◆ Your summary should reflect the purpose of the original text. (p. 260)

◆ Summaries usually benefit from the presence of transitions that clarify relationships. (p. 260)

Ten More Words for Your Academic Vocabulary

1. **momentum:** strength or force gained as events unfold

   Any presidential candidate who wins a string of primaries has *momentum* on his or her side.

2. **sustain:** maintain; keep going; experience

   After his successful speech in Chicago, presidential candidate William Jennings Bryan tried to *sustain* the momentum inspired by the convention. (Adapted from Paul S. Boyer et al., *The Enduring Vision*, 7th ed., p. 615.)

3. **divergent:** different, various

   Trade associations, which represent entire industries, have widely *divergent* interests, ranging from government regulation of food and drugs to the regulation of the import of beef from Argentina. (Alan Gitelson, Robert Dudley, and Melvin Dubnick, *American Government*, 8th ed., p. 213. © Cengage Learning.)

4. **subordinates:** those subject to the control of a higher authority; secondary in rank

   The former secretary of defense was famous for treating his *subordinates* with contempt.

5. **delegate:** (*v.*) to assign work or roles to others; (*n.*) person representing some group

   (1) The primary reason managers *delegate* is to get more work done. (2) Twelve of the original thirteen states sent *delegates* to the Constitutional Convention in 1787.

6. **inception:** beginning, start

   One reason for the company's success since its *inception* was the presence of truly top-rate management.

7. **deprive:** to take away; to keep from possessing

   The war lasted for six long, bloody years and *deprived* them of their childhood.

8. **extensive**: widespread

   Damage from the oil spill was much more *extensive* than anyone had initially realized.

9. **foster:** stimulate, encourage

   A leader can strengthen a group by his or her ability to *foster* responsibility among group members.

10. **coherent**: connected, unified

    Before taking the drug, the patient's speech had been clear and *coherent,* but after only thirty minutes, his speech was slurred, and he stopped making sense.

◆ **EXERCISE 10**   **Making Academic Vocabulary Familiar**

DIRECTIONS   Each sentence uses a more conversational or simpler version of one of the words listed below. At the end of the sentence, fill in the blank with the more academic word that could replace the underlined word in the sentence.

foster	delegate	coherent	momentum	sustaining
inception	deprived[†]	extensive	divergent	subordinates

1. After scoring three goals in a row, the underdog team had the <u>energy</u> to win. _momentum_

2. From its <u>start</u>, the National Organization for Women focused on discrimination against women in the workplace. _inception_

3. In the United Nations, members are inclined to differ because they come from <u>so many different</u> countries. _divergent_

4. The president's ability to <u>assign responsibility to others</u> is said to be one of his strengths. _delegate_

[†]You will need to add the preposition *of* when you use this word as a replacement for a more familiar one.

5. The commissioner's <u>employees</u> resented the rude tone he used when he thought he needed to interrupt. _subordinate_

6. In the hopes of <u>maintaining</u> the rebellion, the chief called on neigh-boring tribes to join in the uprising. _sustaining_

7. The discussion, meant to calm troubled waters, only served to <u>encourage</u> anger on both sides. _foster_

8. If the opposition offers a clear and <u>unified</u> plan, agreement is possible. _coherent_

9. The early colonists believed they were <u>denied</u> their rights and decided to throw off British rule. _deprived_

10. The damage from the fire was more <u>widespread</u> than was originally thought. _extensive_

DIGGING DEEPER Maslow's Hierarchy of Needs: Ordering Needs from the Basement to the Attic of Human Experience

Looking Ahead What follows is a reading from a psychology text. The author of the text, Jeffrey Nevid, describes Maslow's hierarchy of needs in more detail. Nevid also outlines some of the problems associated with the theory.

1 Biological and psychological needs play important roles in human motivation. But how do these needs relate to each other? Let's consider a model that bridges both sources of motivation—the hierarchy of needs developed by humanistic psychologist Abraham Maslow.

2 Maslow's hierarchy of needs consists of five levels: (1) physiological needs, such as hunger and thirst; (2) safety needs, such as the need for secure housing; (3) love and belongingness needs, and (4) esteem needs, such as the need for the respect of one's peers; and (5) the need for self-actualization, which motivates people to fulfill their unique potential and become all they are capable of being. In Maslow's view, our needs are ordered in such a way that we are motivated to meet basic needs before moving upward in the hierarchy. In other words, once we fill our bellies, we strive to meet higher order needs, such as our needs for security, love, achievement, and self-actualization.

3 Since no two people are perfectly alike, the drive for self-actualization leads people in different directions. For some, self-actualization may mean creating works of art; for others, striving on the playing field, in the classroom, or in the corporate setting. Not all of us climb to the top of the hierarchy; we don't all achieve self-actualization.

4 Maslow's hierarchical model of needs has intuitive* appeal. We generally seek satisfaction of basic needs for food, drink, and shelter before concerning ourselves with psychologically based needs like belongingness. However our needs may not be ordered in as fixed a manner as Maslow's hierarchy suggests. An artist might go for days with little if any nourishment in order to complete a new work. People may forget seeking satisfaction of their need for intimate relationships to focus their energies on seeking status or prestige in their careers. Maslow might counter that eventually the emptiness of their emotional lives would motivate them to fill the gap.

5 Another problem with Maslow's model is that the same behavior may reflect multiple needs. Perhaps you are attending college to satisfy

*intuitive: natural.

physiological and safety needs (to prepare for a career so that you can earn money to live comfortably and securely), love and belongingness needs (to form friendships and social ties), esteem needs (to achieve status or approval), and self-actualization needs (to fulfill your intellectual or creative potential). Despite its limitations, Maslow's model leads us to recognize that human behavior is motivated by higher pursuits as well as satisfaction of basic needs.

6   Maslow did not believe the need hierarchy captures all of human striving. Later in his career, he proposed other needs that motivate human behavior, including cognitive needs (need to know, understand, and explore), aesthetic needs (needs for beauty, symmetry, and order), and self-transcendence (need to connect to something beyond the self and help others realize their own potential). Whereas self-actualization is directed toward fulfilling one's own potential, self-transcendence represents a higher level need expressed through commitment to ideals, purposes, or causes that go beyond the self. Although Maslow believed there is an interrelationship between his original needs and these additional needs, he did not specify how both sets of needs should be combined. (Jeffrey S. Nevid, *Psychology*: *Concepts and Applications,* 4th ed. © Cengage Learning.)

Sharpening Your Skills

DIRECTIONS   Answer the following questions by circling the letter of the correct response or filling in the blanks.

1. Already in the first paragraph, the author tells readers what is significant about the topic under discussion, in this case "Maslow's hierarchy of needs." What does the first paragraph tell readers about the focus of the reading?

    a. The reading will describe Maslow as a humanistic psychologist, who favored spiritual needs over instincts.

    b. The reading will describe how psychological and biological needs interact to motivate human beings into action.

    c. The reading will show how Maslow's theory connects biological and psychological needs.

2. In paragraph 2, what category word helps direct the reader's attention to the major details? _consists_

3. Paragraph 3 only has three sentences. Which one is the topic sentence?

   (a.) sentence 1

   b. sentence 2

   c. sentence 3

4. In paragraph 4, the topic sentence is the

   a. first sentence.

   (b.) second sentence.

   c. third sentence.

5. What kind of transition links paragraphs 4 and 5?

   a. addition

   (b.) reversal

   c. time order

6. In what paragraph does the author identify the first problem with Maslow's hierarchy? _Paragraph 4_

   In your own words, what problem with the hierarchy does the author identify?

   Same Behavior Will have Different needs

7. Is this sentence in paragraph 4 a major or a minor detail? "An artist might go for days with little if any nourishment in order to complete a new work." _Minor Detail_

8. Where does the author identify the second problem?

   Paragraph

   In your own words, what problem with the hierarchy does the author identify?

   he added new But he didn't tell the reader how to combine it.

9. Is this sentence in paragraph 6 a major or a minor detail? "Later in his career, he proposed other needs that motivate human behavior, including cognitive needs (need to know, understand, and explore), aesthetic needs (needs for beauty, symmetry, and order) and self-transcendence (need to connect to something beyond the self and help others realize their own potential)." Major Detail

10. Which statement best expresses the author's purpose in writing this excerpt?

   a. The author wants to tell you about Maslow's hierarchy and the criticisms that have been leveled against it.

   b. The author wants to convince you that, despite some criticism, no one has explained behavior better than Maslow.

▶ **TEST 1**   **Reviewing the Key Points**

DIRECTIONS   Answer the following questions by filling in the blanks or circling the correct response.

1. Topic sentences are open to _interpretation_.

   For that reason, writers and speakers are careful to include _____ _Supporting Details_.

2. *True or* (*False*) Supporting detail sentences are more general than introductory or topic sentences. ~~True~~ _false_

3. Major supporting details supply the reasons, examples, dates, and so on that _Make the main Idea Clear._

4. The content of the supporting details depends on _the main Idea._

5. *True or* (*False*). Major details are more specific than minor ones. _false_

6. The one thing you cannot do with a paraphrase is _Change The meaning_.

7. Minor supporting details have three functions. Those functions are

   1. _They make maJor Detalls more Specific_
   2. _They Provide emphasis_
   3. _they Add color_

8. The most important function of a minor detail is to _Make The maJor Detail more Specific_.

9. (*True*) *or False*. Minor details may or may not be important enough to be included in your notes.

10. Two examples of words that offer clues to major details are _____ _Reasons, advantages, goals, studies, Programs, Catagories, groups._

11. Supporting details are the author's way of saying to readers __I__ _Mean this And not that_.

12. Outlines make heavy use of _indentions_ in order to show _Relationships_.

13. *True* or *False* When you make an outline, you need to be consistent about using all sentences or all phrases.

14. *True* or *False*. In general, introductory material doesn't have to make its way into your summary unless it's essential to an understanding of the main idea.

15. Summaries reduce the original text to its _Barebones_, which are the main idea and any _major or Minor_ _Details essential to understanding it_.

To correct your test, turn to page 587. If one or more of your answers is incorrect, re-read the Rounding Up the Keys section of the chapter to find out where your mistake might be.

▶ **TEST 2**   **Recognizing Supporting Details**

DIRECTIONS   Read each topic sentence. Then circle the letters of the two sentences that qualify as supporting details.

Topic Sentence 1. Newborns have definite preferences.

Supporting Details   a. Newborns prefer moving objects to still ones.

b. Some research suggests that infants may actually remember sounds heard in the womb.

c. As they get older, infants sleep less during the day.

d. Babies only a day or two old appear to like high-pitched "baby" talk more than a normal adult voice.

Topic Sentence 2. In Brazil, family ties are extremely important.

Supporting Details   a. In Brazil, children often choose to live at home until they are married.

b. When Brazilian children grow up and leave home to marry, they often establish their new home close by.

c. For Brazilians, personal relations are an important part of doing business.

d. Brazilians are more likely than Americans to greet one another with a kiss on the cheek.

Topic Sentence 3. For ancient Greek and Roman males, the presence or absence of a beard was highly significant.

Supporting Details   a. The Roman male prized his beard as a symbol of masculinity.

b. Throughout history, hair has been considered a sexual symbol.

c. In the story of Samson and Delilah, Samson loses his physical strength when Delilah cuts his hair.

d. The Greeks shaved daily because being beardless was considered a sign of beauty.

Topic Sentence 4. Although there hasn't been a case of smallpox in years, the virus still exists.

Supporting Details a. A test tube containing the virus is in a Moscow laboratory.

b. Like the flu virus of 1918, the smallpox virus could do unimaginable harm if it were let loose on the world.

c. A second dose of the virus is in Atlanta at the Centers for Disease Control and Prevention.

d. Some people believe the smallpox virus should be destroyed.

▶ TEST 3   **Recognizing Supporting Details**

DIRECTIONS   Circle the letters of the three details that could support the topic sentence.

Topic Sentence   1. Frogs are disappearing from the face of the earth.

Supporting Details
- a. Many frogs are dying from a waterborne fungus called chytrid.
- b. Frogs and toads belong to the class of animals called amphibians.
- c. One researcher, desperate to save Panama's frogs from being attacked by the chytrid fungus, housed those that were still healthy in a luxury hotel.
- d. Frogs are one of Panama's national symbols.
- e. In some locations, frogs multiply in great numbers and are considered a major nuisance.
- f. Frogs are also disappearing because their habitats are being destroyed by humans.

Topic Sentence   2. President Lyndon Baines Johnson didn't just talk about the Great Society; he tried to build it through legislation.

Supporting Details
- a. Johnson was an insecure man who was worried about how he would be viewed compared to his predecessor, the glamorous John F. Kennedy.
- b. Johnson used all of his mastery of congressional rules to get Congress to pass important civil rights legislation.
- c. Thanks to Lyndon Baines Johnson, legislation giving people over the age of 65 medical insurance got passed.
- d. Johnson proposed legislation increasing funding for both education and the arts.
- e. The Vietnam War eventually drove Lyndon Baines Johnson from office.
- f. Lyndon Baines Johnson began his professional life as an elementary school teacher, who was adored by his mostly Mexican-American pupils.

Topic Sentence   **3.** Unions have tried, unsuccessfully, to organize Walmart employees.

Supporting Details

   a. Walmart was founded by Sam Walton and is a family-owned business.

   b. At one point, the Teamsters tried to organize Walmart but failed after the company launched a publicity campaign focusing on allegedly illegal Teamster activities.

   c. A number of women have filed lawsuits against Walmart, claiming that the company's hiring practices discriminate against females.

   d. The United Food and Commercial Workers union tried to organize Walmart employees after the chain started selling groceries.

   e. In 2005, Walmart agreed to pay $11 million to settle allegations that it had failed to pay overtime to janitors, many of whom worked seven nights a week.

   f. When the United Food and Commercial Workers union won the right to organize Walmart butchers, Walmart defeated union efforts by ordering cut meat from suppliers outside the company.

Topic Sentence   **4.** Eleanor Roosevelt, wife of President Franklin Delano Roosevelt, played an active role in her husband's administration.

Supporting Details

   a. Eleanor Roosevelt was a personal hero of former New York senator and former first lady Hillary Clinton.

   b. Eleanor Roosevelt, in an attempt to shape presidential policy, made it a point to introduce her husband to reformers and social activists.

   c. Eleanor Roosevelt traveled so much during her husband's administration that a newspaper headline once announced, "Mrs. Roosevelt Spent Night at White House."

   d. A passionate supporter of women's rights, Eleanor Roosevelt ensured that women were appointed to public office in her husband's administration.

   e. Eleanor Roosevelt played a key role in launching the Public Works Administration, which provided jobs for the unemployed.

   f. Eleanor Roosevelt had many admirers, but there were just as many who detested her and complained about her unelected role in the administration.

Topic Sentence 5. Good leaders seem to have several traits in common.

Supporting Details

a. One of the key characteristics researchers have noted is that good leaders have a high level of self-confidence.

b. Good leaders are also able to inspire faith in their ability to take charge and lead effectively.

c. Good leaders are able to balance their sense of confidence with a healthy dose of humility.

d. Personality traits are observable both within and outside the work situation.

e. There is a difference between being in a position of power and being a leader.

f. The traits of a good leader can vary depending on the culture.

▶ **TEST 4**   **Outlining Paragraphs**

   DIRECTIONS   Complete the notes following each paragraph.

1. The A.C. Nielsen Company dominates the television rating business. Based on the Nielsen ratings, advertisers pay for commercial time in the hopes of reaching the audiences they want. Nielsen ratings provide two kinds of numbers, rating and share. The **rating** is a percentage of the total number of households with television sets. If there are 95 million homes with TV sets, for example, the rating shows the percentage of those sets that were tuned to a specific program. The **share** (an abbreviation for share of audience) compares the audience for one show with the audience of another. Share means the percentage of the audience with TV sets turned on that is watching each program.

Main Idea   Nielson Ratings lead tv Rating Business

Supporting Details   Decide how much ads cost
Rating of the total number of tv sets
The Share is a Share of Audience
Watching the Show.

2. While humor has the potential to make us feel good, it can also be used as a form of attack. Men who make fun of feminists, for example, are typically voicing some measure of hostility. Similarly, jokes at the expense of gay people express the tensions and anxiety surrounding rigid notions of sexual roles. Around the world, conflict and hostility among ethnic groups is expressed by means of jokes. In this kind of negative humor, an ethnic group is portrayed as too stupid to master even the most basic skills, such as screwing in a light bulb. Minorities also like to use humor to attack those in power. Women, for instance, frequently make jokes about the inability of men to understand even the most obvious emotions. Similarly, African Americans joke about white people in ways that make them look awkward and uptight.

Main Idea

Using humor as an attack

Supporting Details

Men make fun of females
Jokes about gay people
People bullying Racism
People who don't have
power make fun of those
who do.

▶ **TEST 5** **Writing Summaries**

DIRECTIONS Circle the letter of the better summary.

1. At one time, kids in public schools memorized poems. Yes, that's right—memorized. Although memorizing has somehow become a dirty word in many educational circles, it used to be an essential part of elementary and high school training, and for good reason. Children committed poems and entire speeches to memory, and, without realizing it, they expanded their vocabulary to include the words they had learned by heart. They also developed a sophisticated sense of how words can produce different rhythms and emotional effects. Memorizing great poems and speeches also gave children some very sophisticated examples of sentence syntax, or word order. This may be one reason why letters written during the Civil War, even by lowly foot soldiers, reveal such writerly sophistication. The letter writers had memorized, already as children, some of the finest examples of English prose.

Summary a. Children lost out when schools stopped asking them to memorize great speeches and poems. Memorizing famous examples of poetry and prose boosted children's vocabulary. It also made them familiar with the kinds of music and feelings words can produce. The practice of asking children to memorize poems and speeches in elementary and high school may be one reason why the letters of Civil War soldiers were sophisticated in style and syntax.

b. Civil War soldiers generally wrote very sophisticated letters to their families and friends back home. The style was so sophisticated that those who came after have wondered how soldiers, with relatively little education, could write with such skill. The reason has now been identified. In the nineteenth century, memorizing poems was part of the school curriculum, and children in all grades were exposed to good writing. Having been exposed to good writing, Civil War soldiers took pains to make their own writing imitate what they had memorized. Memorization in schools was abandoned in the twentieth century, making the teaching of writing much harder.

2. In 1997, the Food and Drug Administration (FDA) softened its rules on the advertising of prescription drugs. For the first time, the FDA

allowed pharmaceutical companies to advertise their drugs in magazines and on television and market directly to consumers. Up until this time, the industry's ads focused solely on physicians. That single change in FDA policy had numerous consequences. One of the biggest was the increase in patients who asked their doctors for specific drugs that they had read about or seen on television. Often at the request of their insistent patients, doctors wrote more prescriptions, and as a result, spending on drugs increased. The increases in prescription spending put pressure on insurance companies to raise consumer premiums. Yet the truth is patients might be misled by the ads about new and better drugs that bombard them. One study by the non-profit National Institute for Health Care Management suggested that the "advertisements might be persuading consumers to push for newer, costlier medicines when less expensive drugs would work just as well." For instance, despite the pricey ads, the drug Celebrex, used to treat arthritis pain, may be no better than Tylenol or ibuprofen.

Summary

a. Since 1997, the FDA has allowed drug companies to market drugs directly to the consumer. This has been a disaster for all parties concerned. Patients march into their doctors' offices and ask for drugs they have seen on television. They are upset if they don't get them. And if they do get what they ask for, they might not really need the drug prescribed. Celebrex, for instance, is believed to be no more effective than Tylenol. It just costs a lot more, and people believe if it's more expensive, it's better. In addition, pharmaceutical companies feel free to overcharge for these drugs because they know people want them. The FDA should reverse this ruling before it does more damage.

b. Since 1997, the FDA has allowed drug companies to market drugs directly to consumers through magazine and television advertising. That change in FDA policy has caused some problems. There has been, for instance, an increase in the amount of money spent on prescription drugs and insurance companies have passed the increases on to consumers in the form of higher insurance premiums. Also, a study by the National Institute of Health Care Management suggests that heavily advertised and pricey drugs might not be any more beneficial than much cheaper medications.

▶ **TEST 6**   **Enlarging Your Academic Vocabulary**

DIRECTIONS   Circle the letter of the sentence that uses the opening word correctly.

1. **momentum**

   a. The decisive *momentum* in the debate came when the incumbent refused to answer a question about her health.

   b. On his first day in office, the new chief executive sent a *momentum* to all employees asking for their support during the difficult times that lay ahead.

   c. The match was so entertaining to watch because *momentum* shifted several times—one could never be sure who would be on top in the end.

2. **sustain**

   a. Throughout the trial, the defense council had *sustained* his client's innocence.

   b. In order to *sustain* growth, the company had to open branches overseas.

   c. Although his argument was perfectly *sustainable*, the speaker was heckled during her talk and booed when she left the podium.

3. **divergent**

   a. After a long and sometimes heated debate, the committee finally *diverged* on a single report.

   b. She thought that in order to have a lively debate in class, students must be encouraged to express *divergent* points of view.

   c. Exercise is still the best *divergent* for weight loss.

4. **subordinate**

   a. Given his busy schedule, the chairman had to *subordinate* a great many tasks to his staff.

   b. Many great inventors already were *subordinate* as children and refused to follow the rules.

   c. A great leader knows that when *subordinates* are treated with respect, their motivation improves.

5. delegate

a. Since she found it impossible to *delegate* work, she got bogged down in day-to-day operations and failed to see the overall picture.

b. Many authors *delegate* their first book to their spouses and children.

c. They were close *delegates* in high school, but started to drift apart when each went to a different college.

6. inception

a. The play is based on a promising *inception*, but fails in the execution.

b. Being called "oriental" is considered an *inception* by many Asian-Americans.

c. At the *inception* of World War II, many Americans believed the United States should stay out of it.

7. deprive

a. The ex-wife claimed that the divorce settlement *deprived* her children of the comfort they were entitled to.

b. Only a severely *deprived* mind could subject a helpless animal to torture.

c. Being able to collect art and antiques is one of the *deprivations* great wealth affords.

8. extensive

a. For all *extensive* purposes, the war was over before it had gotten under way in earnest.

b. The actor has such an *extensive* face—you know what he thinks even if he doesn't say a word.

c. The damage done by Hurricane Sandy was *extensive* and went far beyond the cities lying directly in her path.

9. **foster**

   a. A disease that is allowed to *foster* untreated will only get worse over time.

   b. In order to *foster* self-confidence in children, parents should praise them when they deserve it.

   c. Try as they might, they were unable to *foster* the vote.

10. **coherent**

   a. Peter Singer has advanced a *coherent* argument for the ethical treatment of animals. *disagree*

   b. Being pursued by paparazzi is a *coherent* part of being a celebrity.

   c. In the debate, the challenger tried to insult her opponent by calling him *coherent*.

Drawing Inferences About Implied Main Ideas

IN THIS CHAPTER, YOU WILL LEARN

- how inferences are part of everyday life.
- how to infer implied main ideas in paragraphs lacking topic sentences.
- how to evaluate the inferences you draw.

"An inference . . . is a statement about the unknown made on the basis of the known."
—S. I. Hayakawa, *Language in Thought and Action*

Drawing inferences is not restricted to reading. We do it all the time. We take what we know and draw inferences about things left unsaid. Imagine, for example, that your best friend came in from a blind date looking utterly miserable. Without a word spoken, you knew that the date didn't go well. In other words, you drew an inference using the evidence at hand—in this case, the unhappy expression, the slumping shoulders, and the heavy silence. As this chapter shows, when you read you sometimes do much the same thing. Based on the clues supplied by the author, you fill in the gaps left in the text.

◇ Inferences Are Everywhere

If you were to consciously count all the inferences you draw during a day, you would probably be astonished at the huge number. Just think about it. You go to the grocery store and someone bagging your groceries says, "Paper or plastic?" In response, you answer, "paper," correctly inferring the question asked, "Should I put your groceries into paper or plastic bags?" Similarly, if a friend says to you, "What's up?" you don't look toward the ceiling. Instead you tell him or her what your plans are for the moment.

Or imagine that you are storming around the house because you are angry at a good friend and your mother says, "Think twice, say once." You know she is *not* telling you to think the same thought twice. She is telling you to think before you speak.

It's also true that almost anytime you read the comics or look at a cartoon, the artist expects you to supply inferences in order to understand it. Look, for example, at the cartoon shown here. What inferences does the creator of the cartoon expect readers to draw in order to get the joke?

How many times do I need to say this? "Thinking outside the box" is a FIGURATIVE expression!

To understand just this one cartoon, these are some of the inferences the reader has to draw almost automatically:

1. The woman is annoyed at the cat for failing to use the litter box.

2. The cat doesn't care that she's annoyed.

3. The woman talks to the cat as if it spoke English.

Those inferences are based on all the elements that go into making the cartoon—for instance, the woman's expression and the line of the cat's tail. They are also based on the use of capitalization and the presence of an exclamation point. Note, too, that the cartoon also relies on the reader to know the difference between literal and figurative language. Without that information and help from the reader, the cartoon doesn't make sense.

The point is that drawing inferences is something you already know a good deal about. You just may not realize it yet.

◆ EXERCISE 1   **Making Everyday Inferences**

DIRECTIONS   For each headline, motto, statement, or series of events, identify the inference you need to draw to make it make sense.

1. "Limiting the freedom of news 'just a little bit' is in the same category with the classic example 'a little bit pregnant.'"[†] What is Heinlein suggesting about "limiting the news 'just a little bit'"?

   It's True news if it's not limited.

2. The headline reads, "Barking Guards Stay on the Job," and you don't need to read the article to know what about the guards?

   They're Dogs

3. The ad says, "When your skin needs moisture, think Revlon's 'Inner Light.'" The makers of the ad expect you to infer what?

   it's going to make your skin look Better

4. The local high school sends a letter to parents telling them that panic buttons have been added to every classroom so that, if necessary,

---

[†]Robert Heinlein, American science fiction writer.

teachers can call for a security guard. From the letter, you can infer what about the school?

it could be an unsafe Neighborhood

5. In his famous letter from a Birmingham jail, Martin Luther King Jr. wrote, "Injustice anywhere is a threat to justice everywhere." What did he imply about injustice?

it's not fair to have injustice

Inferring Main Ideas

When paragraphs don't contain a general sentence that sums up the main idea, it's up to readers to infer one. Fortunately, inferring main ideas in reading relies on the same kind of thinking you would use to interpret a friend's mood or get a chuckle from a cartoon. First you look at the evidence, then you figure out what it suggests or implies.

When that general thinking process is applied to reading, the sequence goes something like this: (1) Look for chains of repetition and reference. What people, events, ideas, or experiences are consistently repeated or, just as important, referred to? These words will give you an idea about the topic and the implied main idea. (2) Consider the point of each individual statement. (3) Think about how those statements combine to suggest an idea larger, or more general, than what each one says individually. That more general statement is the implied main idea.

For an illustration, read the following paragraph. There's no stated topic sentence. However, you can infer a main idea based on what's actually said in the paragraph.

Writers often describe an existing set of conditions and pose a question about those conditions without providing an answer. That's a strong signal that you need to infer the answer, which is also the main idea.

Over the last ten years, speed limits on America's roads and highways have increased by as much as a third. Yet many motorists are still speeding. The question is, Why? For some people, the right to speed is practically a civil rights issue. Because they believe that speed limits exist so that city and state governments can collect money, they consider them an unnecessary interference with their right to drive as fast as they please. A second group of speeders acknowledges that speeding is dangerous. However, these drivers feel that at certain times they have a justifiable reason to speed. They might be late for work or for a doctor's appointment. A small minority

Notice the repeated references to speed limits and how different groups respond to them.

of speeders seem to do it simply for the excitement. Young males make up the majority of this group. In addition to the thrill seekers, there are the speeders who think they don't run a serious risk of punishment, so why not ignore speed limits. The odds are in their favor.

In this example, there's no sentence general enough to cover all the specific points made in the passage. However, the consistent references to speeders and the reasons why they speed provide the basis for an inference like this: "People speed for different reasons" or "There are several reasons why drivers exceed the speed limit." This implied main idea does what a stated topic sentence would do: It generally sums up the specific statements in the paragraph.

Inferring Main Ideas

◆

To infer the implied main idea, you need to do the following:

1. Read each sentence in the paragraph.
2. Pay close attention to the way one sentence refers or connects to the other.
3. Try to determine what the sentences have in common.
4. Think of a general statement that could sum up the specifics as effectively as any stated topic sentence.
5. Check to see that none of the sentences in the passage contradicts your general statement.
6. Ask yourself which specific statements support the main idea you inferred. If none do, you need to draw another inference.

READING KEYS

◆ No matter what the context—everyday life or textbook assignment— drawing inferences requires you to look at the existing evidence and figure out what it suggests about the person, situation, or passage.

◆ Your implied main idea should never be contradicted by the author's actual statements.

◆ The main idea inferred by readers should sum up a paragraph as effectively as a topic sentence.

VOCABULARY EXTRA

Many people confuse the words *infer* and *imply*. But, in fact, they have different meanings. They are *not* interchangeable. Authors or speakers *imply* by setting forth the evidence for a suggested but unstated conclusion. Readers and listeners then *infer* the author's or speaker's implied conclusion. In other words, only **readers** and listeners infer, whereas only **authors** or speakers imply.

IDIOM ALERT: Small world

The idiom *small world* is used to suggest that people are more connected and more likely to know one another than is commonly expected or assumed. "When David found out that his new girlfriend had just met his previous one at the gym, he muttered 'small world' and tried to change the subject."

◆ EXERCISE 2   Identifying the Implied Main Idea

DIRECTIONS   Circle the appropriate letter to identify the implied main idea.

Note that most of the sentences are on the same level of specificity. No general sentence sums them up.

Note, too, the many references to dinosaurs and dinosaur-like creatures living in lakes.

Add to that the author's statement that no hard evidence of the dinosaur-like creatures exists.

EXAMPLE   "Nessie" is the mysterious aquatic, dinosaur-like creature who reportedly lives in Scotland's cold Ness *loch*, or lake. On the other side of the Atlantic, in the United States, both Lake Erie and Lake Champlain are said to be the home of at least one large creature who, like the Loch Ness monster, has a small head, long neck, and humped back, similar to the ancient dinosaurs. Witnesses also claim to have spotted huge serpent-like creatures in Sweden's Lake Storsjön and Norway's Lake Seljordsvatnet. Canada's Lake Memphremagog and Turkey's Lake Van, too, are believed to house creatures that resemble dinosaurs. Actual sightings, however, are rare, and several scientific expeditions have failed to produce proof of such creatures' existence. Nonetheless, camera-toting tourists flock to all of these lakes. The visitors hope to catch a glimpse of what some believe could be the last living dinosaurs.

Implied Main Idea (a.) While there are isolated sightings of dinosaur-like creatures like the Loch Ness monster, there is no hard evidence that dinosaurs still exist.

b. It's generally believed that, in time, proof of the Loch Ness monster's existence will surface.

c. People are skeptical about the existence of the Loch Ness monster, but there have been numerous sightings of the dinosaur-like creature in Scotland's Ness Lake.

EXPLANATION   Answer *a* is correct because it weaves together the various threads of the paragraph. It combines the references to dinosaurs and dinosaur-like creatures along with the statement about the lack of hard evidence. Answer *b* makes no sense because nothing in the paragraph describes what might happen in the future. Answer *c* can't be right. The Loch Ness monster is not even the topic of the paragraph, let alone the main idea. Only answer *a* effectively summarizes the paragraph's point.

1. Was England's Stonehenge, the 5,000-year-old ring of massive stones, constructed by prehistoric people to serve as a giant calendar? Well, if you stand in the center of the circle on the evenings of the summer or winter solstice (the longest and shortest days of the year), you can watch the sun set directly in line with the large stone that marks the entrance to Stonehenge. This arrangement seems intentional, as if Stonehenge's builders wanted to determine the solstices.[†] Identifying these events would have allowed them to predict and note changes in the seasons. The positions of other stones within Stonehenge's inner circle mark the lunar[*] cycle (29.5 days) and allow for the measurement of months and years.

Implied Main Idea

a. The mystery of Stonehenge is unlikely to be solved anytime soon.

b. Stonehenge is a massive ring of stones in England that was built thousands of years ago.

c. The position of the massive stones that make up Stonehenge suggests it might have been used as a calendar.

2. In 1937, Amelia Earhart was trying to make history by flying around the world in a small plane. However, she and Fred Noonan, her navigator, suddenly disappeared over the Pacific Ocean in July of that year. They were never heard from again. One theory is that their plane ran out of fuel and crashed into the ocean. Another claims

---

[†]solstices: longest and shortest days of the year due to the location of the sun in relation to the equator.
[*]lunar: having to do with the moon.

that the Japanese captured and executed the two aviators, believing them to be spies. Still another theory suggests that their plane crashed on a remote island, where cannibals killed and ate them. Some people have even speculated that Earhart and Noonan disappeared because they were lovers and wanted to live together.

In 1928 Amelia Earhart was the first woman to fly back and forth across the United States.

Implied Main Idea

a. Despite still keen interest, the mystery of Amelia Earhart's disappearance will never be solved.

b. Several different theories have been offered to explain Amelia Earhart's disappearance.

c. Most people believe that Amelia Earhart's plane crashed over the ocean.

3. In the 1960s and 1970s, mothers believed that their babies could sleep well only in complete silence. Today, however, pediatricians advise parents to help their babies learn to sleep with background noise. Thirty to forty years ago, doctors told mothers to lay babies face down to sleep, so they would not choke on vomit or mucus. Nowadays, doctors say babies should sleep on their backs to lower the risk of suffocating. Decades ago, mothers gave their babies cereal beginning at six weeks. These days, pediatricians counsel parents to withhold solid food until the child is four to six months old. Moms of the 1960s and 1970s also believed that wheeled baby

walkers helped their children learn to walk. Now, though, doctors say that walkers actually hinder babies' walking. Decades ago, mothers bathed their infants daily. Today's doctors say babies need baths only about twice a week.

Implied Main Idea
a. Today's baby-care advice contradicts most of the baby-care advice of thirty to forty years ago.

b. Even with advice from experienced pediatricians, raising a child is undoubtedly the toughest job there is.

c. Everything doctors told mothers about baby care thirty years ago has been proven wrong.

4. In 1967, Yale psychologist Stanley Milgram gave a group of midwesterners the name and address of a person they didn't know. Then he instructed them to try to send a letter to that person by passing it only through friends. The group members gave their letters to their friends, who, in turn, passed them on to their friends. On average, Milgram discovered, a letter passed through only five people before it reached its destination. This led him to conclude that everyone in the world is connected by just "six degrees of separation." Milgram's result was also described as the "small world phenomenon." However, in the years since, Milgram's experiment has not been successfully repeated despite several attempts. Also, another psychologist, Judith Kleinfeld of the University of Alaska Fairbanks, found flaws in Milgram's methods. Her study of the original research revealed that Milgram recruited especially sociable people rather than a random sampling of individuals. Kleinfeld also discovered that fewer than a third of Milgram's letters ever arrived at their destination.

Implied Main Idea
a. The notion that everyone is connected by "six degrees of separation" may be more myth than reality.

b. Although Milgram's experiments have not been successfully repeated, many people still believe that his results were correct.

c. We are all much closer than we realize.

[handwritten: Perils of Obidience]

WEB SEARCH/CLASS ACTION

Stanley Milgram is at least partially responsible for adding the phrase "six degrees of separation" to the language. But he is even more famous for his research on obedience. In the wake of World War II, Milgram wanted to find out if Americans would do what many Germans had done during the war: follow orders even if it meant harming their fellow human beings. Use the Web to find out what kind of experiments Milgram performed and what conclusions he came to. Be prepared to answer and discuss those two questions in class.

[handwritten: more people obeyed than they would. They were still doing what they were told. They were still doing]

Logical and Illogical Inferences

The word *logical* derives from the Greek word *logos*, meaning "word" or "thought." Thus a **logical inference** should be based on the author's actual words. It should, that is, fit naturally into the author's existing train of thought. Logical inferences smooth the way for communication between reader and writer. They don't interfere with it. Above all, they don't cause a communication breakdown.

Illogical inferences, in contrast, would be inclined to ignore what the author says and concentrate instead on the reader's ideas about the world. Thus they would develop an idea that the author's statements don't suggest. Not surprisingly illogical inferences stir up confusion between reader and writer.

To illustrate the difference between logical and illogical inferences, read the following paragraph. Then look over the inferences, or implied main ideas, that follow. Put a checkmark next to the logical inference that matches the author's train of thought. Put an *X* next to the illogical inference that would send the reader in the wrong direction.

> In the nineteenth century, African-American Henry Blair helped revolutionize the practice of farming. Blair invented a corn planter in 1834 and a cotton planter in 1836. Later that century, another African American, Sarah Boone, aided housewives all over the country by inventing the ironing board. She patented* her design in 1892.

*patented: gained legal ownership or right to distribute; received official document conferring to an inventor, for a term of years, the exclusive right to make, use, or sell his or her invention.

Writers past and present can thank African-American W. B. Purvis, who patented the fountain pen in 1890. They also should be grateful to J. L. Love, who invented the pencil sharpener in 1897. Another nineteenth-century African American who made life easier and safer was Virgie Ammons, who invented the fireplace damper. Among other nineteenth-century inventions credited to African Americans were the lawn mower, the folding bed, and the golf tee.

Inference 1 In the nineteenth century, African Americans were responsible for a number of inventions essential to both work and play. ____✓____

Inference 2 Although African Americans were responsible for many inventions that improved daily work and leisure, they have seldom been given credit for their contributions. ____✗____

Did you put a check in the first blank and an *X* in the second? Then you already know how logical and illogical inferences differ. The first inference follows the thread of the author's words. Those words focus on inventions by African Americans. Nothing is said about credit for the inventions being given or not given.

The second inference, however, relies far too heavily on the reader's personal opinion. Read the paragraph for specific references to how the contributions of African Americans were ignored, and you won't find any. As soon as you can't find an example, reason, study, story, or fact that supports the main idea you infer, you need to rethink it.

Logical Inferences

- are solidly based on the author's actual words.
- never let the reader's ideas about a topic overshadow the author's.
- are never contradicted by the author's statements.
- keep readers and writers following the same thread of thought.

Illogical Inferences

- aren't fully supported, or backed up, by the author's actual statements.
- rely more heavily on the reader's ideas than on the author's.
- are likely to be contradicted by what the author says in the reading.

READING KEYS

- ◆ Logical inferences keep writers and readers on the same track. Illogical inferences send writers and readers in different directions.
- ◆ To be considered a logical inference, the main ideas you infer should be based on the author's words rather than on your personal opinions.
- ◆ If you rely too much on your own experience for an inference, you are likely to draw an inference the author never intended.
- ◆ The inference you draw should function like a topic sentence and sum up the paragraph.
- ◆ You should be able to look at the paragraph and locate sentences that support the main idea you inferred. If you can't, you need to come up with another inference.

◆ EXERCISE 3   Identifying the Logical Inference

DIRECTIONS   Circle the appropriate letter to identify the most logical inference about the author's implied main idea.

EXAMPLE   For $14.99, a busy or an unimaginative man can buy a list of romantic marriage proposal ideas from an Internet company called WillYouMarryMe.com. He can also surf the Internet for sites that offer free romance tips. Surfing the net will also help him find any number of books describing unique and creative scenarios for a proposal. If he needs more help planning a memorable setting for a proposal, he can hire a romance "specialist." The specialist will help him dream up and then engineer the special event. For example, Will You Marry Me offers personalized services for $180 and up. Other Web companies that put together events such as weddings and parties can also be hired to create a romantic environment for popping the question. And for the man who would like to write his sweetheart a love letter but doesn't know how to get started? Well, he can type www.loveletterhelp.com into a search engine and find some free sample letters for every occasion. There's a birthday love letter and a sweetheart love letter, and, if the need arises, there's even a breakup love letter.

Implied Main Idea   (a.) Romantically challenged men who want to propose marriage can get lots of help from the Internet.

     b. Women are better at proposing marriage than men; they don't need a romance "specialist."

     c. Men are unimaginative when it comes to romance.

     d. Men rely a good deal more on the Internet for finding romance than women do.

EXPLANATION   The focus here is on resources available on the Web for men who don't have a gift for courtship. Nothing is said about women, making *b* incorrect. Statement *c* may or may not be true, but there's no evidence that the author shares this opinion. Because nothing in the passage contrasts men with women, *d* is clearly not the right answer, making *a* the best implied main idea.

1. Most people know that lack of sleep causes irritability and increases the risk of accidents while driving. However, researchers are finding evidence that long-term lack of sleep also weakens the body's immune system. Inadequate sleep may also be contributing to America's rising rates of diabetes and obesity. There is even new evidence that too little sleep may increase the risk of breast cancer and, perhaps, of other cancers, too. Furthermore, chronic lack of sleep affects metabolism and the secretion of hormones, producing striking changes that resemble advanced aging. Cheating on sleep for even just a few nights apparently harms brain cells, too.

    Implied Main Idea

    a. People who don't get enough sleep are likely to develop breast cancer.

    b. Chronic insomnia is a symptom of many different illnesses, including diabetes.

    c. New research suggests that not getting enough sleep can harm your health.

    d. Inadequate amounts of sleep can speed the process of aging.

2. Some readers have accused author J. K. Rowling, author of the Harry Potter novels, of relying too heavily on worn-out stereotypes. And it's true that Harry, like many heroes before him, is an abused but lovable underdog who triumphs because he is a good person. It's also true that evil villains, like Harry's archenemy Voldemort, turn up in lots of adventure tales. So, too, do figures like Professor Dumbledore, Harry's wise and fatherly mentor. Yet, however similar Rowling's characters are to standard characters in other stories, there is a difference. Rowling is a talented writer with the gift of imagination. She supplies all of her characters, even the most traditional, with the kind of original details that make them so memorable.

    Implied Main Idea

    a. The Harry Potter novels are based on stock characters that appear in many other adventure stories.

   b. Critics who claim J. K. Rowling relies on stereotypes are wrong and don't understand that she transforms the stereotypes into something new.

   c. J. K. Rowling knows that kids generally root for an underdog.

   d. J. K. Rowling shot to fame with the Harry Potter novels.

3. If you feel that your phone bill is outrageously high, just be thankful that you are not in a state prison. Inmates who make calls home can run up a seventeen-dollar bill in just fifteen minutes. That's because some phone companies have to pay a commission to win prison phone service contracts. The phone companies then pass on the cost of the commission to inmates and their families. Before you say, "So what, those people are in prison. They shouldn't be chatting on the phone," consider that many inmates come from poor families for whom the phone bill can become a heavy burden. Then, too, the goal of prison is for inmates to regret their crimes and resolve to change. The more cut off inmates are from their families, the less likely that is to happen. No wonder reformers are calling on the Federal Communications Commission to stop overcharging inmates. For prison inmates, the phone is a lifeline.

Implied Main Idea
   a. Phone companies in some states are overcharging inmates.

   b. Prison reform needs to focus on making sure that inmates stay connected to their families.

   c. Given how important it is for prisoners to stay connected to their families, they should not have to pay excessive fees for phone use.

   d. People with very different political viewpoints are generally united on the subject of prison reform.

▶ **SHARE YOUR THOUGHTS**

The paragraph on page 296 suggests that, when it comes to marriage, men are the ones who do the proposing. Do you think this idea is obsolete, or out-of-date? Do you think it is just as natural for a woman to propose to a man? To take that idea a step further, what about marriage? Do you think marriage still plays a big role in people's lives or are more people choosing to stay single or live together without benefit of marriage? And in your opinion, is that a good or a bad idea?

◆ EXERCISE 4   Identifying the Logical Inference

DIRECTIONS   Circle the appropriate letter to identify the most logical inference about the author's implied main idea.

EXAMPLE   Although chocolate does contain sugar, caffeine, and saturated fat—none of which is particularly good for you—studies show that it's also rich in *antioxidants*. Antioxidants are chemical compounds that protect cells in the body. They also appear to raise the good cholesterol that breaks down artery-blocking substances. In addition, antioxidants block the bad cholesterol that clogs arteries. They also can prevent blood clots that cause heart attacks and strokes. Antioxidants release chemicals that relax blood vessels. This helps prevent high blood pressure. The good news about chocolate is sure to cause rejoicing among devoted chocolate lovers. Chocolate fans have long wanted an excuse to consume their favorite sweet. And now, as long as they do it in moderation, they've got it.

Implied Main Idea   a. There's really nothing wrong with eating large amounts of chocolate on a regular basis.

b. Eating chocolate may have its drawbacks, but it also has some health benefits.

c. Foods rich in antioxidants are essential to a healthy diet.

d. Everyone with high blood pressure should eat more chocolate.

EXPLANATION   Because the first sentence of the paragraph points out that chocolate contains some ingredients that are not good for us, answer *a* can't qualify as a good inference. Answer *c* won't work because the paragraph is not about foods, it's about *one* food—chocolate. Answer *d* focuses just on blood pressure whereas the paragraph is more general than that. That leaves *b* as the implied main idea that best fits the author's words. It not only acknowledges chocolate's drawbacks but also recognizes its benefits.

1. Is stuttering purely psychological, or is it caused by physical factors? Scientists know that the left hemisphere, or half, of the brain is responsible for speech. Yet studies show that a stutterer's right hemisphere is quite active during speech. What this suggests is that the right side of the brain may be interfering with the left side's ability to produce words. One study also revealed that the area of the brain

responsible for hearing is inactive in stutterers. This inability to hear his or her own speech may either cause or contribute to the stutterer's problem. Other researchers believe that the cause of stuttering can be found in the genes. Based on an analysis of human DNA,[†] these scientists claim that stuttering is an inherited disorder.

Implied Main Idea

a. Scientists have identified some physical factors that could explain the causes of stuttering.

b. It's clear that psychological factors play a key role in causing stuttering.

c. Stuttering appears to be an inherited disorder passed on from parent to child.

d. The inability to hear one's own speech plays a key role in stuttering.

2. Can background music affect our attitudes toward a product? To answer that question, researchers at Carlsbad Marketing organized a study. Subjects in the study were shown slides of light blue or beige pens. At the same time that they looked at the pens, they heard either pleasant or unpleasant music. Later the subjects were told to choose one of the pens as a gift. The majority of the subjects chose the pen they had looked at while they were listening to pleasant background music. Oddly enough, most of the subjects weren't aware of how the music had affected their choice. Most said they did not know why they chose one pen over the other.

Implied Main Idea

a. There's no real proof that consumers are affected by background music.

b. People buy more when they are listening to pleasant background music.

c. Background music in stores interferes with one's ability to make rational choices.

d. There is some evidence that background music affects what consumers buy.

3. To many of us, the public schools' adoption of zero-tolerance policies for weapons, drugs, and violence is a source of jokes. What else can you do but laugh when, for example, a grown-up claims lemon drops bought in a health food store are a dangerous drug or that a

---

[†]DNA: the genetic information carried in cells.

key chain in the form of a gun can be a deadly weapon? It's kind of funny, right? Well, maybe. But, before laughing too hard, you might also want to consider some of the consequences of the zero-tolerance policy. Since public schools have adopted zero-tolerance policies, a first-grader in Youngstown, Ohio, got suspended from school for ten days. From his perspective, he was taking a plastic knife home from the school cafeteria to show his mother he knew how to butter his own bread. To the authorities, however, he was brandishing a weapon. At Dry Creek Elementary School in Centennial, Colorado, seven fourth-grade boys were pointing "finger guns" at one another as kids have done for decades in the name of play. But the principal thought otherwise and required them to serve one week's detention. At LaSalle Middle School in Greeley, Colorado, one boy ended up enrolled in an anger management program with kids who had actually been convicted of crimes. According to school authorities, he belonged there because he had brought a "firearm facsimile" to school. The facsimile was a two-and-one-half-inch laser pointer, which has been popular with the younger set for over a decade.

Implied Main Idea

a. In schools in the West, the policy of zero tolerance has been taken much too far.

b. Girls are never punished under zero-tolerance guidelines.

c. Examples of school authorities rigidly enforcing zero-tolerance policies may seem funny, but the consequences are not amusing.

d. If parents spoke up more, school authorities would be fearful of rigidly enforcing zero-tolerance policies in ways that defy all common sense.

4. Joseph Merrick, also known as "The Elephant Man," was born August 5, 1862. He died in 1890 at the age of twenty-seven when he went to sleep lying down. During sleep, the weight of his head broke his neck. For most of his life, Merrick had suffered from a mysterious disease that has still not been conclusively* identified. Whatever the ailment was, it twisted Merrick's body into a mass of crooked bones and huge tumors. Although Merrick spent much of his life being displayed in circuses as a freak of nature, he was ultimately rescued from that world by a surgeon named Frederick Treves. Treves wanted

---

*conclusively: without doubt, absolutely

to study Merrick's case. It's largely through Treves's writing about Merrick that the man's personality emerges from under the hood he normally wore to avoid scaring people. The man Treves described was not bitter about the hand life had dealt him. When he finally got the chance, he tried to enjoy himself, despite his grotesque appearance. According to Treves's account, Merrick loved the theater, reading, and long walks. He enjoyed making models and baskets, which he gave to those he thought were his friends. In a book called *The Elephant Man and Other Reminiscences*, Treves said that as a specimen of humanity, Merrick was "ignoble and repulsive." But his spirit, according to the man who knew him best, was "smooth browed and clean of limb, and with eyes that flashed undaunted courage." (Source of quotations from Treves's book: http://www.weird-encyclopedia.com/elephant-man.php.)

Merrick looked normal when he was first born, but in a short time his body became encrusted with tumors.

New York Public Library

a. The Joseph Merrick that Frederick Treves describes seems too good to be true.

b. He may have praised him, but Frederick Treves was using Merrick just as everyone else did.

c. On the outside, Joseph Merrick may have looked like a monster, but from Treves's account, he seems to have been an impressive human being.

d. Joseph Merrick's life was filled with unending misery until he met Frederick Treves, and Merrick was extraordinarily grateful to Treves for all he did.

◆ EXERCISE 5   Identifying the Logical Inference

DIRECTIONS   Circle the appropriate letter to identify the most logical inference about the author's implied main idea

1. Although they are always pictured in the same dreary colors, the Pilgrims who settled Plymouth Colony in 1620 did not wear only black and white. Women, for instance, wore red, green, blue, and violet. In fact, records from that period indicate that even the men wore colorful capes. Although the Pilgrims are always shown wearing buckles on their shoes, hats, and belts, buckles were not popular until later in the seventeenth century. Also, there's no indication that the Pilgrims ever landed at Plymouth Rock in Massachusetts, despite the stone marker there indicating that they did. And they certainly did not graciously lay out a big feast and invite their Native American friends. Whatever food was shared in the Pilgrims' early version of Thanksgiving—probably turkey, pumpkin, and squash—was provided by or supplied with the aid of the local Native Americans. From the beginning, they were the ones who generously kept the Pilgrims from starving.

Implied Main Idea

a. The Pilgrims did not wear the clothing popularly associated with them.

b. Many popular beliefs about the early Pilgrims are inaccurate.

c. The Pilgrims actually loved colorful clothing.

d. The local Native Americans did a good deal more for the Pilgrims than the Pilgrims did in return.

2. What is the most effective cure for a *phobia*—an intense, unreasonable fear not grounded in any experience? Exposure therapy has certainly had some success. With this form of therapy, a person with, say, a fear of cats would start treatment by looking at pictures of cats. Then he would be exposed to a toy cat. Next he might watch a cat video. Step by step, he would work toward being near a cat without feeling any fear. Other people suffering from phobias have overcome them with what's called *virtual reality therapy*. Computer software programs simulate, or imitate, actual exposure to the feared thing or experience. Through repeated computerized experiences, the phobic patient learns not to be afraid. For example, a person who fears flying might take several simulated flights. Through this process, she would conquer her terror. Phobias are also treated with a variety of medications. Some sufferers have found, for example, that the drug Paxil helps them control their fear of social situations.

Implied Main Idea

a. Phobias can be treated in at least three different ways.

b. Exposure therapy is the best way to treat a phobia.

c. Fear of cats is the most common phobia.

d. Virtual reality therapy is the clear winner when it comes to curing phobias.

3. Chimpanzee and human DNA differ by only 1 percent. A chimpanzee's blood composition and immune system are also strikingly similar to those of humans. Similarly, the anatomy of a chimpanzee's brain and central nervous system is also much like a human's. It's also true that chimpanzees have demonstrated the capacity to reason, in ways similar to humans. Chimps can make decisions, show cooperative behavior, and use tools. Furthermore, some chimpanzees have been taught to communicate through American Sign Language (ASL). They also exhibit many nonverbal human behaviors, including hugging, kissing, back patting, and tickling. Like people, chimpanzees feel and express emotions such as happiness, sadness, and fear. They form relationships with one another, too, just as humans do. Special emotional bonds between chimpanzee mothers and their babies, and between siblings, last the animals' whole lives.

Implied Main Idea

a. Although many similarities exist between chimpanzees and humans, this does not mean that chimps deserve human rights.

b. Chimpanzees and human beings share a striking number of mental and physical traits.

c. The chimpanzee's immune system is similar to that of humans.

d. Chimpanzees have the same range of emotions as humans do; they also express their emotions in ways similar to humans.

4. Psychics are people who supposedly have supernatural powers the rest of us do not possess. Thus, psychics claim to contact the dead, read minds, tell the future, even make inanimate objects move. But before you pay hard-earned money to have your fortune told by a psychic, you might want to ask yourself a few pointed questions. For example, why don't psychics display their powers nationwide by performing truly amazing feats? If they can foretell the future, why don't they predict who is going to win a multimillion-dollar lottery prize? If they know what will happen years from now, what about coming up with at least a few hints about how to cure cancer? James Randi, who has made a career of testing the powers of psychics, may have the answer to these and similar questions. Randi claims that when psychics have their powers tested under controlled conditions, such as a laboratory setting where they are under observation, they constantly fail. They can't make spirits appear or read anyone else's mind except their own. What's the reason for the failure? The psychics say that laboratories don't offer the right atmosphere for their work. The failure rate of psychics tested by Randi may be one of the reasons why famed psychic Sylvia Browne hasn't yet fulfilled her promise to let him test her psychic abilities. (Source of information: www.randi.org; Carroll, *The Skeptic's Dictionary*, p. 307.)

Implied Main Idea

a. Psychics have supernatural powers.

b. James Randi has spent years exposing the tricks of psychics.

c. Sylvia Browne will probably be the psychic who proves Randi wrong.

d. Psychics don't really possess supernatural powers; they are frauds.

◆ **EXERCISE 6** **Identifying the Logical Inference**

DIRECTIONS Circle the appropriate letter to identify the best inference about the author's implied main idea.

1. In 2001 only the boys of Afghanistan went to school. The girls, if they went to school at all, went in secret. They knew that if they

were found out, they and their teachers would be severely punished. But after the American invasion of Afghanistan that drove out the Taliban,[†] girls didn't go to school in secret anymore. They didn't have to. However, as time passed and Taliban supporters returned to Afghanistan, they were infuriated by the idea of girls getting an education. There were several cases of girls and teachers having acid thrown in their faces, just for supporting education for girls. After the Taliban's return, hundreds of schools were destroyed or badly damaged. The majority of them were schools for girls. Some of the schools left standing were subjected to gas attacks. Yet the girls of Afghanistan have refused to stop going to school.

Implied Main Idea

    a. Although a few girls in Afghanistan are brave enough to go to school openly, most do so secretly.

    b. Although the Taliban have used brutal methods to discourage the education of girls in Afghanistan, the girls have refused to be intimidated.

    c. Despite American attempts to eliminate the Taliban from Afghanistan, members of this extremist group have made their way back into the country.

    d. Because its efforts have been unsuccessful, the Taliban has now given up on trying to prevent girls from going to school in Afghanistan.

2. Leadership brings with it enormous responsibility. It also exposes one to blame when things go wrong. Given those twin burdens, the question is, Why would anyone want to be a leader? First, some people like to be leaders because the role offers them access to special information. Organizational and institutional leaders know what's going to happen before anyone else. Second, when things go well, the leader usually gets the credit, and praise is always an appealing reward. But people who aspire to be leaders are also inclined to think they can do a better job than anyone else. An instructor, for instance, may want to become department chair to bring about what he or she considers necessary reforms. Acceptance is yet another

---

[†]Taliban: A very conservative Muslim group, which severely restricts the freedom of women. The Taliban controlled Afghanistan from 1996 until the United States forcibly removed it from power in late 2001.

motive for leadership. People who don't feel personally successful sometimes convince themselves that becoming a leader in their profession will win them the approval of others. Finally, some people want to become leaders because they like the idea of gaining public recognition. Becoming the president of a company or, for that matter, of the PTA all but guarantees public notice.

Implied Main Idea

a. Leadership carries with it so many burdens that it's a wonder anyone wants to be a leader.

b. The desire for public recognition is the primary reason people aspire to leadership positions.

c. People in leadership positions are often professional successes but personal failures.

d. People wish to become leaders for a number of different reasons.

3. Students taking the SAT get twenty-five minutes to write an essay on an assigned theme, such as "Is creativity needed more than ever in the world today?" Understandably what most want to know is what counts toward a good score? Well, one answer is vocabulary. Writers who use at least a few sophisticated words tend to get higher scores. Coherence also gets high grades, and essays in which the ideas seem connected and flow gracefully from one to the next do well. Original thinking counts for a lot. One student wrote a three-paragraph essay that was slightly illegible. Yet scorers considered it worth the eyestrain. Rich in original insight and packed with unexpected allusions,* the essay earned a top score. (Source of information: Ramin Setoodeh, "What's Your Score?" *Newsweek*, April 4, 2005, p. 9.)

Implied Main Idea

a. Students taking the SAT are nervous about the writing section.

b. Grading the writing section of the SAT is an almost impossible job.

c. Getting a high score on the writing section of the SAT depends on several factors.

d. Students who want to do well on the writing section of the SAT should work on coherence, an important factor that scorers look for in the essays.

---

*allusions: references to real or fictional people, places, and events, used to make a point—e.g., When it came to housekeeping, no one was ever going to confuse my mother with Martha Stewart.

4. General Douglas MacArthur concluded his farewell speech to Congress by quoting a line from an old barracks song. "Old soldiers never die, they just fade away." But he had no intention of fading away. Establishing his residence and a kind of command center at New York's Waldorf Astoria, MacArthur issued a series of political proclamations aimed at winning him the Republican presidential nomination in 1952. MacArthur, however, was no politician. He believed he was a man of destiny, in the hands of fate. He assumed the people would come to him. They did not. As the savvy politician President Harry S. Truman calculated, the enthusiasm for MacArthur dissipated within a few months. (Adapted from Joseph R. Conlin, *The American Past*, 9th ed. © Cengage Learning.)

Implied Main Idea

a. Harry Truman was a much better politician than General MacArthur, who knew more about military tactics than he did about politics.

b. When General MacArthur resigned, he expected the public to demand that he run for president, but he was wrong in his expectation.

c. General MacArthur had a legendary ego and he often assumed an importance he did not have in anyone else's mind.

d. Many people thought that General MacArthur would be a presidential candidate in 1952, but their expectations were not met.

◆ EXERCISE 7   Inferring the Implied Main Idea

DIRECTIONS   Read each paragraph. Then write the implied main idea in the blanks.

It's impossible to avoid references to coffins, so definitely make that word part of the main idea you infer.

Another theme running through the passage is safeguards to avoid being buried alive.

EXAMPLE   In 1792, Duke Ferdinand of Brunswick had his coffin built with a window. He also included an air hole and a lid that could be opened from the inside. In 1868, New Jersey inventor Franz Vester patented a coffin that included a hollow passageway to the ground's surface. The passageway contained a ladder so that a person buried prematurely could climb out of the grave. Dozens of other coffins invented around this time included signaling devices such as flags and bells. A person who awoke from a coma to find himself buried alive could pull a cord to operate these devices and attract the attention of passersby. Another coffin, invented by a German named Herr Gutsmuth, included a speaking tube. A person mistakenly declared dead could use the tube to yell for help.

Implied Main Idea <u>In times past, people rigged their coffins with safety devices because they were afraid</u>

<u>of being buried alive.</u>

EXPLANATION Because the paragraph offers several examples of people in earlier times who tried to make sure they were not buried alive, we can safely draw this inference.

1. Chemistry has played an important role in the processing of foods. Foods are chemically treated so that they remain fresh and free of harmful toxins for a longer period of time. Industrial chemists are hard at work researching ways to alleviate the world's food shortage. Thousands of drugs to treat disease have been discovered by applying medical knowledge in the chemical and pharmaceutical industries. Just a few of the chemically based products we use are plastics, cleansing agents, paper products, textiles, hardware, machinery, building materials, dyes and inks, fertilizers, and paints. (Adapted from Alan Sherman et al., *Basic Concepts of Chemistry*, 6th ed. Boston: Houghton Mifflin, 1996, p. 8.)

Implied Main Idea <u>Keeping food safe from toxins and</u>
<u>Keeping them fresh from Chemicals.</u>

2. If you want to avoid the flu without getting a shot, stay away from crowds during flu season. Flu viruses are easily carried by coughs and sneezes as well as by hand-to-hand contact, so washing your hands frequently is important. And if you smoke, stop. Smokers are more likely than nonsmokers to get serious viral infections. Taking vitamin and mineral supplements during flu season can also help fight off the flu, so plan on increasing your intake of vitamin C, vitamin A, and zinc. In addition to taking vitamin supplements, eat a lot of garlic, broccoli, and cauliflower. Those vegetables contain natural antibiotics that can protect you against disease.

Implied Main Idea <u>Protecting People from the flu without</u>
<u>Getting Shots.</u>

3. Describing his adventures in America, Captain John Smith, the founder of the Jamestown colony, claimed that Pocahontas, a Native American girl, saved him from execution at the hands of her people. However, John Smith didn't tell anyone this tale until

after Pocahontas and her father, the two primary witnesses, were dead. Captain Smith published three different volumes describing his experiences in the Virginia colony. However, he did not publish his account of Pocahontas's rescue until fifteen years after it supposedly happened. In the meantime, Smith had undoubtedly heard other similar stories. For instance, a Spanish soldier named Juan Ortiz claimed to have been saved in 1529 by an Indian girl in Florida. When Captain Smith finally did start telling his own tale, he changed the details with every telling. In addition, he told other stories of being rescued from danger by foreign maidens. For example, he claimed to have been captured by the Turks, who took him to their capital of Constantinople.[†] There, Smith said, the ruler's wife fell in love with him and helped him escape to freedom.

Implied Main Idea　　*John Smith telling Different Stories of his rescues*

[†]Constantinople is now called Istanbul.

ROUNDING UP THE KEYS

Here is a list of all the reading keys introduced in the chapter. Use them to review for the test on page 317. If a particular reading key doesn't make sense on its own, go back to the page where it appeared and review the section preceding it.

READING KEYS: Inferring Main Ideas

◆ No matter what the context—everyday life or textbook assignment—drawing inferences requires you to look at the existing evidence and figure out what it suggests about the person, situation, or passage. (p. 289)

◆ Your implied main idea should **never be contradicted** by the author's actual statements. (p. 289)

◆ The main idea inferred by readers should sum up a paragraph as effectively as a topic sentence. (p. 289)

READING KEYS: Logical and Illogical Inferences

◆ Logical inferences keep writers and readers on the same track. Illogical inferences send writers and readers in different directions. (p. 296)

◆ To be considered a logical inference, the main ideas you infer should be based on the author's words rather than on your personal opinions. (p. 296)

◆ If you rely too much on your own experience for an inference, you are likely to draw an inference the author never intended. (p. 296)

◆ The inference you draw should function like a topic sentence and sum up the paragraph. (p. 296)

◆ You should be able to look at the paragraph and locate sentences that support the main idea you inferred. If you can't, you need to come up with another inference. (p. 296)

Ten More Words for Your Academic Vocabulary

1. **commerce:** an exchange of goods, especially on a large scale

   The war had interrupted *commerce* between the two countries, and on both sides of the conflict people felt the lack of ordinary necessities.

2. **commodities:** products that are traded or sold

   On the stock market, *commodities* like oil and gas were reaching new highs, and only the very wealthy were unconcerned.

3. **patriarch:** the male head or leader of a family, group, or tribe

   In her grandmother's day, men were more like proud *patriarchs* than husbands, but thankfully her grandmother's way of life was gone; she and her husband were equals.

4. **idealize:** to think of as perfection

   As small children, we often *idealize* our parents; as teenagers, we do exactly the opposite.

5. **deplete:** to destroy or empty out

   Historians suspect that the city's residents were forced to *deplete* the nearby forests in order to get firewood. (Adapted from Bulliet et al., *The Earth and Its Peoples*, p. 383.)

6. **convert:** to change or transform from one thing into another; also a person who changes from one cause or belief to another

   (1) In the fifteenth century, the cathedral was *converted* into a mosque. (2) The newly baptized *converts* waited in the chapel.

7. **ritual:** an established procedure or ceremony

   In some cultures, boys entering puberty endure painful *rituals* before they are allowed to be called men.

8. **garb:** clothing or dress

   Although European travelers commented on the veiling of women in sixteenth-century Iran, paintings indicate that ordinary female *garb* consisted of a long dress and a head scarf.

9. **receptive:** responsive or open to

   American psychology was not always *receptive* to the study of thinking or cognition. (Jeffrey S. Nevid, *Psychology: Concepts and Applications*, 3rd ed. p. 424.)

10. **saturate:** to soak through; to completely fill or cover

    (1) The electrician's gloves were completely *saturated* with oil. (2) The directions from the campaign office were to *saturate* the area with materials promoting and explaining the candidate's position.

◆ EXERCISE 8   Making Academic Vocabulary Familiar

DIRECTIONS   Each sentence uses a more conversational or simpler version of the words listed above. At the end of the sentence, fill in the blank with the textbook word that could replace the underlined word in the sentence.

> receptive   ritual   saturate   garb   commerce
> idealize   patriarch   commodities   deplete   convert

1. The ancient <u>father</u> of the tribe looked as if his face had been carved out of stone. _patriarch_

2. The two young boys <u>worshipped</u> the mysterious man who surfed the waves as if he were dancing on them. _idealize_

3. All of the <u>agricultural products</u> for sale were expected to soar in price. _commodities_

4. The oil reserves are slowly being <u>emptied out.</u> _depleted_

5. After the tanker exploded, the beaches in the area were <u>soaked through</u> with oil. _saturated_

6. The government may make laws governing <u>buying and selling</u>, but making those laws effective is another matter. _commerce_

7. The new land laws forced the Ik to <u>change</u> from a hunting culture to one that relied on farming for survival. _convert_

8. Many cultures have elaborate <u>ceremonies</u> that mark change from child to adult. _rituals_

9. The British prime minister was not <u>open</u> to the idea of a compromise. _receptive_

10. Instead of the traditional motorcycle <u>clothing</u>, all consisting of black leather, he wore a Scottish kilt. _garb_

DIGGING DEEPER **What It Meant to Be Gay Once Upon a Time**

Looking Ahead We are accustomed to hearing discussions about gay rights. Yet there was a time when some Americans thought gay people didn't have any rights. The question this reading tries to answer is, How and when did that attitude change?

1 Prior to the 1970s, gay men and women had little or no way to fight back against discrimination. Sexual intercourse between same-sex consenting adults was illegal in almost every state. In fact, until 1973, the American Psychiatric Association labeled homosexuality a mental disorder. Homosexual couples did not receive partnership benefits, such as health insurance. They also could not adopt children. Even organizations famous for championing the civil rights of minorities did not stand up for gay people. In 1970, the New York City chapter of NOW, the National Organization for Women, expelled its lesbian officers. Of course gay men and women could avoid harassment and discrimination by hiding their sexual identity. However, that also made it difficult to organize politically.

2 At the time, there were small homophile organizations, such as the Mattachine Society and the Daughters of Bilitis. These organizations had started working for gay rights already in the 1950s. But, important as these organizations were, the real breakthrough for gay rights came on a hot night in June of 1969.

3 On June 28, 1969, New York City police raided the Stonewall Inn, a gay bar in Greenwich Village. At that time, it was against the law for more than three homosexual patrons to occupy a bar at the same time. Normally if a police raid took place, everyone in the bar went quietly. But that night was not like any other. The patrons fought the arrest and the photos made the news. The next morning, New Yorkers found a new slogan spray-painted on neighborhood walls, *Gay Power*.

4 Inspired by what came to be known as the Stonewall Riot, some gay men and women began working openly for gay rights. They focused on legal equality and Gay Pride. Others rejected the notion of fitting into straight culture. Instead they argued for separate gay communities. By 1973, there were around 800 gay organizations in the United States. . . . By decade's end, gay men and women were a political force in several cities including New York, Miami, and San Francisco. (Adapted from Mary Beth Norton et al., *A People and a Nation*, 9th ed. © Cengage Learning.)

Sharpening Your Skills

DIRECTIONS Answer the following questions by circling the letter of the correct response or writing one in the blank lines.

1. What's the implied main idea of this reading?

   how Gay People fight for Gay rights.

2. What is the purpose of paragraph 1? What does it contribute to the reading?

   Gay People couldn't fight back against the Bullying.

3. What message did gay men and women infer from the Stonewall Riot?

   Gay Power

4. The last sentence of paragraph 3 is meant to imply what?

   a. People were so mad about the police raid, they defaced property.
   (b.) The gay rights movement had arrived as a political movement.
   c. Gay people had become power hungry.

5. Today, if you walk through Greenwich Village, you'll occasionally see the slogan "Remember Stonewall!" What do you think the slogan is meant to imply?

   It means how Gay People At Stonewall were treated unfairly.

▶ TEST 1   **Reviewing the Key Points**

DIRECTIONS Answer the following questions. Make sure to use complete sentences.

1. When you infer the main idea implied by a paragraph, what should never happen?

    Nothing in the Paragraph Should contradict the main Idea you inferred.

2. In every instance of drawing an inference, what is the first thing you should do?

    Look at the evidence that's given And decide What it suggests.

3. What should the main idea you infer and a topic sentence always have in common?

    They Should both Sum UP the Paragraph.

4. What's the difference between logical and illogical inferences?

    Logical inferrences keep readers and Writers On the same track, While Illogical inferrences draw the reader away from the Writers train of thought.

5. What do the main ideas readers infer have to rely on most heavily?

    the Main Ideas readers infer have to rely most heavily on the Authors Words.

To correct your test, turn to page 588. If one or more of your answers is incorrect, re-read the Rounding Up the Keys section of the chapter to find out where your mistake might be.

▶ **TEST 2**   **Identifying the Implied Main Idea**

DIRECTIONS   Circle the appropriate letter to identify the implied main idea.

1. According to a study in the journal *Pediatrics*, 91 percent of parents believe that a fever is harmful to their children. About 89 percent of them give their kids fever reducers like acetaminophen and ibuprofen before their temperature reaches 102 degrees. However, the American Academy of Pediatrics says that many illness-causing microbes cannot reproduce in the higher temperatures caused by a fever. A fever also stimulates a child's immune system, causing it to increase production of disease-fighting white blood cells. Therefore, fever helps the child's body battle the infection and may actually reduce the length and severity of a cold or flu. Furthermore, a study published in the *Journal of Allergy and Clinical Immunology* found that infants who have a fever during their first year of life are less likely than children who don't have a fever to develop allergies later in childhood.

Implied Main Idea

   a. Most parents believe that fevers are harmful to children.

   b. Fevers help prevent allergies in children.

   c. Contrary to popular belief, fevers can be beneficial.

   d. When children are sick, parents should try to induce a fever.

2. Over a decade ago, scientists at Auburn University created a healthier, low-fat hamburger. This burger contained only 5 percent fat, but it tasted as good as, if not better than, a burger with 20 percent fat. When the researchers conducted blind taste-test studies, they discovered that people actually liked the taste of the leaner burger more than that of the higher-fat version. Not long after, McDonald's created the McLean Deluxe, a lower-fat burger. Four years after introducing it, however, the company removed it from the menu. Customers didn't want the burger because it was billed as the healthy choice. People just assumed it would not taste as good as a regular hamburger and didn't select it.

Implied Main Idea

   a. It's impossible to create low-fat food that tastes good, and fast-food companies should abandon the effort.

b. McDonald's almost went into bankruptcy after adding low-fat foods to its menu.

c. Low-fat foods taste better than foods high in fat.

d. People incorrectly assume that foods labeled "low fat" will not taste as good as higher-fat foods.

3. Every year, the number of deaths due to motor vehicle fatalities ranges somewhere between 40,000 and 45,000 people. In comparison, the number of aircraft fatalities averages 169 per year over a five-year period, making the death rate about 0.3 per 100,000 people. Only about 1 in almost 1.6 million passengers dies in an airplane crash, even though every day more than 3 million people fly in a commercial aircraft. Thirty years ago, fatal air crashes occurred once for every 140 million miles flown. Today, however, a fatal accident occurs only once every 1.4 *billion* miles flown, reflecting a tenfold increase in safety. In contrast, the number of motor vehicle accidents tends to remain steady year after year. In fact, traffic accidents are the number one cause of death for people from six to twenty-seven years old. Yet fear of flying is much more common than fear of driving.

Implied Main Idea

a. Traffic accidents may well double in the next few years.

b. Fear of flying is a good example of how most of our fears are not based on an actual threat.

c. Although air travel is safer than driving, people still fear flying and aren't afraid of driving.

d. Airplane crashes are a thing of the past.

4. For centuries, Chinese families longed for a son who would grow up to be a source of protection and financial support, things it was assumed a girl could not provide. Thus, the Chinese *Book of Songs* (1000–700 BC) advised parents to dress a son "in fine clothes and give him jade to play." If a daughter was born, however, that same *Book of Songs* told parents to "let her sleep on the ground . . . and give broken tiles to play." More recently, after the Chinese government tried to limit population growth by enforcing a one-child-per-family law, girls were sometimes aborted or abandoned in the hope that the next child would be a much-desired boy. Now, however, the Chinese government has launched a "Girl Care Project," a

program of slogans and bonuses designed to promote the importance of females and discourage families from aborting, neglecting, abandoning, or killing female babies. Currently, there are around 120 boys for every 100 girls, and the government is worried that as adults many men won't be able to find a woman to marry if that gender imbalance is not corrected. There is also the worry that men who are unable to settle into a family life and have children will be more likely to engage in antisocial behavior. Already there are "bachelor villages" in China. The fear is that such villages will multiply if more isn't done to make girls a desirable addition to the family.

(Source of quotations: www.msnbc.msn.com/id/5953508.)

Implied Main Idea

a. When the Communists took over the government in China, they brought with them a prejudice against females.

b. The Chinese believe that men are naturally more aggressive, and it is, therefore, dangerous to let too many men live together in one location as many are now doing in "bachelor villages."

c. Because a prejudice against females has produced a gender imbalance in China, the government has launched a program designed to eliminate that prejudice and encourage the birth of more girls.

d. Although the Chinese government has launched the "Girl Care Project" to correct the gender imbalance between males and females, there is little hope for the project's success because prejudice against girls is too strong.

▶ **TEST 3**   **Identifying the Implied Main Idea**

DIRECTIONS   Circle the appropriate letter to identify the implied main idea.

1. The guillotine is named for Joseph-Ignace Guillotin, a French physician who urged his government to adopt a humane method of execution. The sandwich is named after John Montagu, the fourth Earl of Sandwich, who became famous in the eighteenth century for dining while he gambled. The word *mesmerize* comes from Friedrich Anton Mesmer, a German physician who treated disease with animal magnetism, an early form of hypnotism. The leotard is named after Jules Leotard, a nineteenth-century French aerialist who wore a stretchy, one-piece garment. The volt was named in honor of Count Alessandro Volta, an Italian scientist who experimented with batteries and electric current. William Lynch was a vigilante from Virginia. He is responsible for the word *lynch*, which describes mob execution of a person by hanging.

Implied Main Idea
   a. The French have made numerous contributions to the English language.
   b. Many common words are *eponyms*, or words named after people.
   c. The Italians have contributed many words to the vocabulary of science.
   d. Most words in the English language are derived from people's names.

2. When the flu hits a household, the last one left standing is likely to be Mom rather than Dad. The female immune system responds more vigorously to common infections, offering extra protection against viruses, bacteria, and parasites. The genders also differ in their vulnerability to allergies and autoimmune disorders. Although both men and women frequently develop allergies, allergic women are twice as likely to experience potentially fatal anaphylactic shock. A woman's robust immune system also is more likely to overreact and turn on her own organs and tissues. On average, three or four people with autoimmune disorders, such as multiple sclerosis, Hashimoto's thyroiditis, and scleroderma are women. (Dianne Hales, *An Invitation to Health*, 7th ed., p. 322. © Cengage Learning.)

Implied Main Idea

a. Men like to fool themselves into thinking women are the weaker sex, but the opposite is true.

b. Women are less likely to get the flu than men are.

c. Men and women differ in their vulnerability to disease.

d. Women are more subject to diseases that start when the person's immune system turns and attacks the body.

3. No one can say for sure when the first pro-ana (pro-mia for bulimia) appeared on the Web. Although some claim that the first one surfaced around 1998, others insist that 2001 saw the first appearance of a pro-anorexia site. And no, your eyes haven't deceived you. That is the prefix *pro*, meaning "in favor of," appearing right before the word *anorexia*. But not every site interprets the prefix in the same way. While some pro-ana sites do offer scary advice like put soap on your food so you won't eat it or drink two tablespoons of vinegar before every meal to suck the fat out, not all of them suggest an eating disorder is something people should aspire to. Sites like PrettyThin focus more on how to live with an eating disorder, given that diseases like bulimia and anorexia are notoriously hard to cure. Such distinctions, though, have not impressed social media sites like Pinterest and Tumblr, both of which have banned all "self-harm" sites, which means any that seem to accept and, even worse, celebrate the eating disorders that afflict some millions of Americans.

Implied Main Idea

a. The first appearance of a pro-ana site is still a matter of debate.

b. Although not all pro-ana sites are the same, some social media sites will not accept them anymore.

c. Pro-ana sites make it clear that anorexia is a matter of personal choice and individual freedom.

d. Pro-ana sites arose in reaction to the media criticism of anorexia victims.

4. Female roller derbies were popular in the 1970s. In those days, though, all-female roller derby teams were owned and promoted largely by men, who considered the women's roller derby to be a spectator sport. Males showed up at roller derbies to watch women in short skirts and tight-fitting tops knock each other around as the lead skater, the jammer, made her way toward the finish line. Currently, however, roller derbies are witnessing another spike in

popularity. One source of that popularity spurt seems to have been the 2009 movie about female roller derbies, called *Whip It*. Directed by Drew Barrymore, the movie emphasized bonding among the team members as well as the sheer nerve it takes to play a full-contact sport, where injuries are common. Many women currently competing in roller derbies say that the movie inspired them to dig out the roller skates they had shoved in a closet after getting out of middle school. And unlike the largely male audiences of thirty years ago, today's audiences are an enthusiastic and varied mix. Moms, dads, husbands, and kids sit in the stands cheering on their daughters, wives, sisters, and mothers. Although some women skating in roller derbies still wear form-fitting outfits, many don't. They just skate in the team colors even if that means baggy tee shirts and shorts. The emphasis today is on the athleticism, stamina, and the sheer toughness of the women who get onto the track.

Implied Main Idea

a. Drew Barrymore's movie *Whip It* inspired many young women to skate in roller derbies.

b. Today's women's roller derbies are very different from the ones promoted in the seventies.

c. In the past women's roller derbies were only about sex, now they focus on girl power.

d. If it weren't for Drew Barrymore's movie *Whip It*, roller derbies would never have made a comeback.

▶ **TEST 4**　　　　**Identifying the Implied Main Idea**

> **DIRECTIONS**　　Circle the appropriate letter to identify the implied main idea.

1. Women who wear high-heeled shoes can end up with deformed feet. High heels compress the toes and prevent them from functioning as shock absorbers during walking. A condition called hammer toes, or permanently claw-shaped toes, is often the end result. Wearing high heels can also cause neuroma, a painful pinching of the nerves of the feet. Women who wear high heels are also more likely to suffer from ingrown toenails, corns, and bunions. High-heeled shoes also force the knees to rotate more than normal because the toes are locked into place. This additional stress can lead to serious knee problems and even low back pain. Women in high heels are at greater risk of tripping or literally falling off their shoes. They can sprain an ankle or suffer other harm when they fall.

Implied Main Idea　　a. Wearing high-heeled shoes is a bad idea for a number of reasons.

　　　　b. Women who wear high heels are at a disadvantage in situations where they might have to run.

　　　　c. Women know that high-heeled shoes are bad for them but for some reason, they wear heels anyway.

　　　　d. Women are often victims of their vanity.

2. The Robomower was created to mow your lawn while you sit in a lawn chair and watch. Similarly the Roomba vacuum by iRobot allows for automated vacuuming, so that you are free to do other things. iRobot also builds robots that perform minesweeping and information gathering for the military and reconnaissance* for the police. The same company produces robots that can patrol your house while you're out of town. The machine, which can even climb stairs, allows you to view the rooms of your home through the Internet. Another company, called RedZone Robotics, has developed machines that will investigate a contaminated nuclear reactor or clean an oil tank. The Nursebot, a rolling robot that helps busy health care professionals keep an eye on patients, became available in 2010. Robots also help scientists gather information in places like volcanoes and outer space.

---

*reconnaissance: inspection of an area to gather military information.

Implied Main Idea

    a. If people get any lazier, they will need robots to help them stay awake.

    b. Researchers keep building new robots, but the public mistrusts the notion of robots replacing human workers.

    c. Robots can now perform a wide range of tasks that were once done by humans.

    d. Women are the ones most likely to benefit from the newly designed robots.

3. Mohandas Gandhi, influential leader and political reformer of India, said that his school days were the most miserable of his life. Nobel Prize–winning novelist Thomas Mann considered school dull. Albert Einstein, acknowledged as one of the greatest scientific thinkers of all time, was a dreamy child who struggled in school. His parents even feared that he might be brain damaged. As a boy, Winston Churchill, prime minister of Britain during World War II, was placed in classes for slow children. Famed inventor Thomas Edison went to public school for only three months. He didn't seem very bright, so his teacher told his parents not to waste time trying to educate him.

Implied Main Idea

    a. The really brilliant never do well in school.

    b. People who achieve great things in life are not necessarily high achievers in school.

    c. Most schools don't do enough to encourage creativity in students.

    d. Brilliant men often have a hard time in school; the opposite is true for brilliant women.

4. Parents worried that their kids don't get enough sleep because they are up a good part of the night texting won't feel better if they talk to Mike Howell, a sleep doctor at the University of Minnesota Sleep Clinic. Howell says many young people actually text while they sleep. Often they send embarrassing messages that they have forgotten by morning. But the more serious problem is that sleep texting is linked to sleep deprivation. When kids don't get enough sleep at night, they can develop heart and weight problems. They also have trouble paying attention. Dr. Peter G. Polos from the JFK Medical Center in Edison, New Jersey, hasn't studied sleep texting. However, he has studied groups of children and young people who text heavily at night, on average thirty texts at bedtime. What he found was that heavy bedtime texters suffered from anxiety, depression, and learning difficulties. Parents who would like to give up playing the sleep police might have to reconsider going on patrol when nighttime rolls around. (Source of texting statistic: www.medicalnewstoday.com/articles/206546.php.)

Implied Main Idea

a. Young people who sleep text are likely to develop emotional disorders.

b. Parents who worry about their kids texting at night only make things worse when they nag their children about it.

c. Too much texting at night can disrupt sleep and have negative side effects.

d. Texting can lead to being overweight; it can also cause depression.

▶ TEST 5   Inferring the Implied Main Idea

DIRECTIONS   Read each paragraph. Then write the implied main idea in the blanks.

1. In the year 1 AD, Roman citizens did not consider children to be fully human until they walked or talked. If five other people agreed that an infant was sickly, parents could legally abandon the child to die. Lawbreakers in Roman society could be fed to hungry beasts such as lions or tigers. Crowds at these gory "spectacles" would cheer while ferocious animals tore condemned criminals into pieces. For their entertainment, Romans enjoyed watching gladiators fight one another to the death. They also flocked to violent chariot races, delighting in wrecks that produced a tangle of screaming horses and bloodied drivers.

Implied Main Idea   *Roman citizens fighting each other to the Death.*

2. In 1864, a thousand immigrants traveled the Bozeman Trail, a route from the Oregon Trail through Wyoming to Montana. Throughout that year, angry Native American warriors harassed the white settlers building on their land. In 1865, after the Civil War ended, the U.S. Army turned its attention to what was thought to be a pesky little problem with the Indians out West. The government closed the Bozeman Trail to civilians. General Patrick E. Connor and a thousand soldiers were sent to settle the Indian troubles once and for all. Despite Connor's proud boasts of what the troops would accomplish, the expedition was a disaster. His men alternately froze and starved. The single Arapaho village Connor did manage to find and destroy had been, prior to his attack, friendly. It turned hostile only after being attacked.

Implied Main Idea   *the Bozeman trail and angry Native Americans*

3. Many American kids participate in a lot of extracurricular activities. They play sports and musical instruments, join clubs and organizations, and take lessons and extra classes. Some children thrive in a nonstop whirlwind of after-school activities. These kids like the

opportunities to explore their interests, discover their talents, and develop their abilities. They find a constant schedule of activities essential preparation for the competitive world of college admissions. Their involvement and accomplishments give them an edge over other students. Other children, however, cannot handle the stress of juggling so many obligations. This stress can cause burnout, anxiety, or even physical illness. Sometimes these kids turn to drugs or alcohol to cope with their anxiety and feelings of failure. Years of rushing from one event to the next can overwhelm some kids. In response, they quit everything. Refusing to keep up a hectic pace, they may not engage in any activities at all.

Implied Main Idea _____ extra school Activeties for Children _____

4. Want to avoid coming home one night and discovering your apartment has been burgled? Then don't leave money or jewelry lying out in view from a window. If you have a daily routine, never tell strangers about it. The same is true for any vacation time you might plan on taking. Don't mention it in front of people you don't know. It's expensive but worth it to have your locks changed when you move into a new apartment or home. And never, ever leave notes on your door indicating that you will be away for any period of time. Are there tall trees next to your home that someone could climb in order to get into the second floor of your home? Consider asking your landlord to cut any branches that might ease entry through an open window. If you own your own home, call a tree service and get rid of any branches that could help an intruder make it to the second story of your home.

Implied Main Idea _____ Protecting your home from Roberies _____

▶ TEST 6   Enlarging Your Academic Vocabulary

DIRECTIONS   Circle the letter of the sentence that uses the opening word correctly.

1. **commerce**

    a. If you want to get out of the mess you are in, you have to *commerce* a new chapter in your life.

    b. Even though it is rarely talked about, *commerce* in weapons is a major source of income for several developed countries.

    c. The *commerce* in the basement alarmed the dog's owner, who was convinced that the cat and dog had met up in one narrow space.

2. **commodities**

    a. Van Gogh's paintings became hot *commodities* only after the painter's death.

    b. After the president retired, he started to enjoy the *commodities* of life.

    c. There are *commodities* in the mountains that cannot be reached by car.

3. **patriarch**

    a. The ancient tribes of Greece were *patriarchal* until the men took over.

    b. Joseph P. Kennedy was the unchallenged *patriarch* of his large family.

    c. The whole *patriarch* flocked to the cathedral to hear what the bishop had to say.

4. **idealize**

    a. I cannot possibly *idealize* what my boss meant when he talked about the "combining of opposites."

    b. The biography presents a rather *idealized* portrait of the senator, who was known to have her rough edges.

    c. Trench warfare is said to be the great *idealizer* of men.

5. **deplete**

   a. His wealth *depleted*, he spent the last decade of his life in near poverty.

   b. I managed to *deplete* all my files with one mouse click.

   c. The *depletion* of rain made the flowers blossom and the crops thrive.

6. **convert**

   a. The Swiss learn in elementary school to *convert* in more than one language.

   b. Recent *converts* to a cause are often more enthusiastic than those who have supported it for a long time.

   c. Firewood left out in the open should be *converted* by a tarp.

7. **ritual**

   a. Saying grace before a meal is a *ritual* one can observe in restaurants only rarely.

   b. Nobody can tell me that the *ritual* that came with my new table saw was well-written—I could not make heads or tails of it.

   c. It's more *ritual* than realistic to expect that all children will become more successful than their parents.

8. **garb**

   a. Oprah Winfrey certainly has the gift of *garb*.

   b. *Garb* obviously derives from garbage.

   c. The standard *garb* for early rock bands was a suit and tie.

9. **receptive**

   a. In Catholic churches, you typically find a *receptive* for holy water near the entrance.

   b. He was completely *receptive* to my ideas—he practically threw me out of the room.

   c. Speaking in public is much easier when you have a *receptive* audience.

10. **saturate**

   a. After days of heavy rains, the earth was so *saturated* that water collected in pools.

   b. *Saturday Night Live* is a show that loves to *saturate* public figures and celebrities.

   c. When I visit my grandmother, she puts food in front of me until I'm completely *saturated*.

Recognizing Patterns of Organization

IN THIS CHAPTER, YOU WILL LEARN

● how organizational patterns provide clues to underlying relationships.

● how to recognize the clues to each pattern.

● how to match your notes to the pattern.

"Patterns build on one another to convey the logical structure of a text."
—Bonnie Meyer, professor and researcher

This chapter focuses on six common organizational patterns that appear in paragraphs. Although not all paragraphs rely on one **primary**, or central, pattern, many do. Readers who recognize the organizational pattern used automatically know what thought relationships underlie the writer's thinking. That means they also know what information is really critical to understanding the author's message. In addition, they have a built-in mental structure or framework for remembering what they read and for taking notes.

Make it a point to learn what these patterns look like. Most importantly, get a good grip on what their presence in a paragraph tells you about the content and the relationships that structure it.

Time Order

Two different organizational patterns rely heavily on **time order**, or the actual order of events as they happen or happened in real time. One pattern is called *process*. The other is *sequence of dates and events*.

Process

Writers use a **process** pattern of organization to explain step by step how something functions, develops, or occurs. In the process pattern, the order of information is extremely important. The author *must* put the event that happened first in real time at the beginning of the paragraph. The event that happened last *must* go at the end.

You are most likely to find the process pattern in science, business, or psychology textbooks. Look for it whenever you see topic sentences such as "There are three different steps in jury selection" or "People who survive a tragic accident usually go through four stages of emotional recovery."

For an illustration of the process pattern, read the following paragraph. Note how the author explains, step by step, the process introduced in the topic sentence—how a tree decays.

> Note how the phrase "four general stages" tells you how many major details to look for.
>
> The italicized transitions signal the introduction of each new step.

[1]Researchers have identified four general stages in the decay of a tree. [2]*In the first stage*, the wood is firm and solid, but the tree is beginning to show signs of decay. [3]Few new leaves or shoots are present, and the branches may sag. [4]*In the second stage*, the bark begins to soften, and the branches continue to sag. [5]*By the third stage*, the tree loses bark, and branches fall to the ground. [6]*Finally*, the tree becomes a soft, powdery mound.

Clues to the Pattern

This combination of an opening topic sentence that includes a category word like *steps* or *stages* along with a series of transitions that structure the order of events is typical for the process pattern of

Decayed trees may look bad, but they are a great source of both food and shelter for birds and insects.

© Ulrich Flemming

organization. As soon as you spot this pattern, you need to think about the following:

1. What's the larger process described?

2. How many steps or stages does it include?

3. Are there any other terms which are part of the process that I also need to know?

More Transitions That Order Events in Time

Like the transitions in the sample paragraph above, the words and phrases in the following box also suggest that the pattern of organization is process, and the order of events in time is the key relationship to grasp. If several such words or phrases appear in a paragraph, you are probably dealing with a paragraph describing a process.

Transitions to Watch For ♦	after	finally	next
	after a while	first	now
	afterward	following this step	once
	as a result	in a few days	second
	at the end	in the end	then
	at this point	in the final stage	third
	at this stage	(step, phase)	throughout
	during this	in the first stage	within days
	stage (phase)	(step, phase)	within minutes

O—⊓ READING KEYS

- ◆ Writers use the process pattern to explain how something functions, develops, or occurs in real time.
- ◆ If the topic itself is a process and most of the sentences in the passage describe individual stages or steps, you are most likely dealing with the process pattern.
- ◆ Words like *steps*, *stages*, or *phases* in the topic sentence are typical of the process pattern.
- ◆ In the process pattern, the topic sentence often announces the type and number of major details.

What You Should Take Away from the Pattern

What do you absolutely have to learn from a piece of writing based on the process pattern? To begin, you need a solid grasp of the process being described. You also need to know exactly how many steps or stages are involved. You need to know as well what each step or stage entails, or requires. Above all, you need to know the order in which the steps occur.

O—⊓ READING KEY

- ◆ When dealing with the process pattern, make sure you can identify the process described and list each step in the right order.

Using Flow Charts for Note-Taking

Passages that outline a process lend themselves particularly well to **flow charts**. These are diagrams that use boxes or circles to set off the individual steps. They also use arrows to indicate the order of the steps within the larger sequence.

Flow charts are excellent devices for recording information in process paragraphs. They provide a visual image of the sequence described, giving your brain two different ways to store the information. Here's a flow chart for the passage on tree decay:

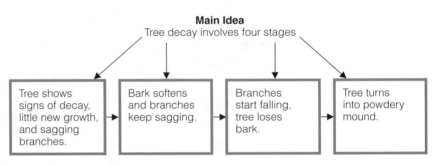

Main Idea
Tree decay involves four stages

| Tree shows signs of decay, little new growth, and sagging branches. | Bark softens and branches keep sagging. | Branches start falling, tree loses bark. | Tree turns into powdery mound. |

Outlining the Steps

Of course, if you prefer, you could also make an informal outline of the process described in the paragraph. That would look something like this:

Main Idea   Tree decay involves four general stages.

Supporting Details   *Step 1*: Signs of decay and sagging branches with few new leaves or shoots
Step 2: Softening bark
Step 3: Falling branches
Step 4: Tree becomes a powdery mound

To determine which note-taking method works best for this organizational pattern, try them both. You'll know soon enough which method makes the material clearer and easier for you to remember.

◆ EXERCISE 1   Understanding the Process Pattern

DIRECTIONS   Read each paragraph. Then fill in the blanks and circle the transitional clues to the process pattern of organization.

EXAMPLE   Rain and warm weather stimulate the growth of seeds. When water enters a seed, the seed leaves get wet and start to swell.

(Then) the seed cover splits, allowing the root to grow out of the seed. (Next,) the root grows downward and absorbs water. (Finally,) the plant grows up out of the ground, where it is exposed to sunshine.

Process   the growth of seeds
_____

How many transitional clues introduce major details? ___3___

EXPLANATION   In this paragraph, the steps all describe the growth of seeds. That's the process under discussion. As the transitions suggest, the process includes three steps.

1. Fireflies do not give off electric light. Rather, fireflies produce light by means of a chemical reaction. That reaction is stimulated by the firefly's need to attract a mate. To create the tiny flashes of light that will draw potential mates, the firefly first sucks in air through tiny breathing tubes. The oxygen in the air then reacts with chemicals in the firefly's abdomen. The chemicals produce a glow, making light shine through the insect's skin.

Process   _how fireflies give off light_

How many transitional clues introduce major details? _2_

2. How does an airplane rise into the air? An airplane's lift into the air occurs when the plane's wings create differences in the pressure of moving air. First, air flows over the top of the wings. It sticks to the curved surface and is pulled downward. Next, the air that is bent downward pulls on the air above it, creating a low-pressure zone. Newton's[†] third law of motion says every action causes an opposite reaction. That's why the low-pressure zone on top of the wings then creates a high-pressure zone underneath the wings. In the end, this upward force on the wings causes them to lift into the air. In other words, the wings push the air down, so the air pushes the wings up.

Process   _lifting un Airplane up i the air_

How many transitional clues introduce major details? _4_

_____

[†]Isaac Newton (1642–1727): English mathematician, scientist, and philosopher who developed, among other things, the theory of gravitation.

◆ EXERCISE 2   Understanding the Process Pattern

DIRECTIONS   Identify the process. Then list the stages or steps involved according to their order in time.

EXAMPLE   The first step in growing bean sprouts is to purchase some tiny green mung beans from a health food store. Next, line the bottom of a pot with pebbles and place a layer of beans over the pebbles. Then put enough water over the beans to wet them thoroughly. Cover them with a damp cloth and place the pot in a warm spot. Once the beans are in a warm spot, they must be rinsed daily with fresh water. In seven or eight days, they should sprout. The sprouts can be used in salads or on cooked vegetables.

Process growing bean sprouts

Steps 1. Purchase tiny mung beans.

2. Line bottom of pan with pebbles.

3. Place layer of beans over pebbles.

4. Wet beans thoroughly with water.

5. Cover beans with damp cloth.

6. Put in warm spot.

7. Rinse daily with fresh water.

8. In seven or eight days, beans will sprout.

EXPLANATION   There is no topic sentence in this paragraph. However, we can infer a main idea that sums up the paragraph: "Growing bean sprouts involves several simple steps." The process then is "growing bean sprouts," and the main idea is less important than the individual steps involved in that process. Those steps are the essential elements in the paragraph and must appear in the correct order.

1. Moths pass through four distinct stages of development: egg, larva, pupa, and adult. The process begins when the female lays her eggs. Within a few days, the eggs hatch and the larvae appear. During this stage, the eggs and larvae are often eaten by birds and other insects. In the pupa stage, wings begin to form and reproductive organs begin to develop. At this point many larvae spin cocoons for

protection. In the final stage, the insects leave the cocoons. Within minutes, they expand their wings and are ready to fly. (Adapted from Will Curtis, *The Second Nature of Things*, Ecco Press, 1991, p. 156.)

Process · · · · · · Development of moths

Stages · · · · · · eggs

larva

Pupa

Adult

Not all moths are the bad kind that eat your wool clothes. Some are very beneficial and perform useful functions in nature.

2. States generally use a three-step procedure to choose juries in court trials. First, a state or county compiles a list of people eligible for jury duty. Usually, they search voter registration or driver's license records for prospects who are at least eighteen and who have no felony* convictions. Second, local officials randomly select a group of potential jurors. Each of these prospects receives a summons to appear at court for jury duty on a certain date. Third, lawyers interview people in the jury pool and decide whether to choose them for a particular trial.

Process · · · · · · Choosing people for Jury Trial

Steps · · · · · · make a list

Select a Group

interview

———————

*felony: a serious crime, such as murder, rape, or burglary.

VOCABULARY EXTRA

Felony is the word for a serious crime. A person who commits a serious crime is a *felon*. The opposite of a *felony* is a *misdemeanor*. Although few people know it, there is a word for someone who commits a misdemeanor. That word is *misdemeanant*. But the word is used so infrequently that the only time you'll use it might well be in a game of Scrabble.

Sequence of Dates and Events

The **sequence of dates and events** version of the time order pattern isn't used to explain how something functions or works. Instead, the pattern is used when a writer wants to (1) trace a series of dates and events considered remarkable or unusual; (2) make some general point about an event, a career, or a life; or (3) describe the events leading up to or following a significant historical happening.

Here are two examples. The first one traces a series of horrific events. The second one describes the career of a famous Cuban musician.

Example 1

Topic sentences in this pattern—if they appear—are likely to be the first or last sentence.

The defining feature of this pattern, though, is the sequence of dates and events that is ordered according to real time.

Sentences 2–9 are all major details that introduce new acts of terrorism. Their goal is to clarify for readers the meaning of the phrase "intimately acquainted with the horrors of terrorism."

[1]Between 1993 and 2001, the United States became intimately acquainted with the horrors of terrorism. [2]On February 26, 1993, the first terrorist attack on U.S. soil took place when a truck bomb exploded at the World Trade Center in New York City. [3]On April 19, 1995, a homemade bomb exploded outside the Murrah Federal Building in Oklahoma City, killing 168 people. [4]On November 13, 1995, a bomb left in a van parked at U.S. military headquarters in Riyadh, Saudi Arabia, exploded and killed 7 people. [5]On June 25, 1996, a truck bomb exploded at U.S. military headquarters in Dhahran, Saudi Arabia, killing 19 Americans. [6]On August 7, 1998, two more truck bombs exploded at U.S. embassies in East Africa, killing 258 and injuring over 5,000. [7]On October 12, 2000, a small boat laden with explosives blew up alongside the navy ship USS *Cole*, killing 17 U.S. sailors. [8]And finally, on September 11, 2001, the World Trade Center was destroyed and the Pentagon damaged when terrorists hijacked four airliners and succeeded in using three of the planes as weapons. [9]The death toll in this attack rose into the thousands.

Here again, the paragraph opens with the topic sentence. Only in this case, the focus is on a sequence of dates and events that comprises a career.

In this case, both major and minor details build the sequence of dates and events that defines Sandoval's career.

To understand this paragraph, you need to remember much of the material from the minor details. Sentence 9 is a good example of a minor detail that contributes important information.

Example 2

[1]Grammy Award–winning trumpet player Arturo Sandoval gave up his native country, Cuba, for his family and his music. [2]In the 1960s, Sandoval studied classical trumpet at the Cuban National School of Arts. [3]It was there that he discovered both a talent and a passion for jazz. [4]Throughout the 1970s and 1980s, Sandoval toured the world, recording albums and performing in jazz ensembles. [5]From 1982 to 1990, he was voted Cuba's best instrumentalist. [6]The Cuban government even allowed him to leave the country. [7]However, it also forced him to pledge his loyalty to the Communist Party and would not allow Sandoval's wife and children to travel with him. [8]In 1990, during a tour with the United Nations Orchestra, the musician finally persuaded the Cuban government to let his family join him in Rome. [9]While in Rome, he appealed to the American government for political asylum,* and then Vice President Dan Quayle helped Sandoval and his family resettle in Miami, Florida. [10]Between 1994 and 1997, Sandoval struggled to become a U.S. citizen. [11]But his attempts were denied because of his previous membership in Cuba's Communist Party. [12]Sandoval persisted, and in 1998 he was finally granted U.S. citizenship.

Clues to the Pattern

Several dates and events all presented in the order in which they occurred are obvious clues to this pattern. But so, too, is a topic sentence like the one in the paragraph on terrorism. When the topic sentence announces that a particular era, or period of time, was significant in some way, a sequence of dates and events is likely to follow.

It's also true that the sequence of dates and events pattern is likely to include transitions like those listed in the following box, where the blanks represent specific dates.

Words and Phrases That Signal the Sequence of Dates and Events Pattern ♦	After the _____ century At a later date Before the _____ century Between _____ and _____ By the _____ century By the year _____	From _____ to _____ In the days (weeks, months) following _____ In the years since On _____ Then in _____ Until _____

*asylum: a place offering legal protection from harm.

O━┓ READING KEYS

◆ Dates and events introduced in the order in which they occurred in real time are a surefire clue to the sequence of dates and events pattern.

◆ Passages or readings using this pattern are likely to focus on three kinds of topics: (1) a particular segment of time, considered unusual or extraordinary; (2) a person's life or career; or (3) the events leading up to or following a significant historical event.

What You Should Take Away from the Pattern

The dates and events are obviously an important element of this pattern. But so is the *order* in which they occurred. Thus, you shouldn't neglect dates that are implied rather than stated. For example, if the passage contains a phrase like "Twenty years after the end of World War II," you need to figure out that the author is talking about 1965. Jot down that date in the margin or make it a point to remember it because, implied or not, the date is likely to be important.

Ask yourself if any statements lacking in dates contribute to the author's main idea. Any that do deserve your attention.

Make Timelines

Flow charts can help you visualize the steps in a process. Timelines can do the same for dates and events. Like flow charts, timelines are easy to create. They also offer you a visual image of the dates and events you are trying to anchor in memory.

To make a timeline, draw a straight vertical line. Then create ruler-like breaks in the line so you can separate each date and event. Here is a timeline based on the paragraph from page 340.

Main Idea   In the years between 1993 and 2001, the United States learned the meaning of terrorism.

2/26/93	Truck bomb explodes at World Trade Center.
4/19/95	Bomb explodes outside Oklahoma's Murrah Federal Building and kills 168.
11/13/95	Bomb explodes at Riyadh military headquarters and kills 7.
6/25/96	Truck bomb explodes at military headquarters in Dhahran, Saudi Arabia, killing 19.
8/7/98	Two more truck bombs kill 258 and injure over 5,000 at U.S. embassies in East Africa.
10/12/00	Explosive-filled boat blows up alongside USS *Cole* and kills 17.
9/11/01	World Trade Center is destroyed and Pentagon damaged by terrorists.

When you are reading chapter sections that deal with a series of dates and events, try using timelines to chart the dates and events mentioned.

○┰ READING KEY

♦ The dates and events that give this pattern its name are always significant. However, don't automatically ignore the supporting details that lack dates. Evaluate them to see if they contribute anything to the main idea.

VOCABULARY EXTRA

The word *asylum* (p. 341) has an important synonym you should also learn. That synonym is *sanctuary*. Although both *asylum* and *sanctuary* offer a place of safety, *asylum* suggests legal safety. Thus, people who seek political asylum hope to gain the legal right to stay in a place where they are safe from harm. The word *sanctuary* suggests a place that is sacred and, therefore, protected. For example, "The political refugees sought *sanctuary* in the church because they knew the soldiers would respect its sacred ground."

IDIOM ALERT: Heyday

Heyday refers to a period in the past when someone was at the height of his or her powers. It can also describe the best years of some institution, theory, or group. Here's an example: "In his *heyday*, Brazilian soccer player Pele had no peer; he was unquestionably the single best soccer player in the world."

◆ EXERCISE 3   Understanding a Sequence of Dates and Events

DIRECTIONS   Read each paragraph. Then create timelines for the supporting details that flesh out the main idea.

EXAMPLE   Rumors that Coney Island was dying have been around for years, but supporters of the Brooklyn amusement park are worried that the park may really be breathing its last breath. In its heyday in the late 1800s, Coney Island was the playground of the rich. By 1910, however, the racetrack and the expensive hotels had closed down. The wealthy had found other, more fashionable playgrounds to visit. Coney Island only got its second wind in the 1920s after a new subway line connected New York City to Coney Island. For more than twenty years, until the end of World War II, a visit to Coney Island became an exciting event for hordes of people. By the 1960s, though, attendance was so low that fifty acres of the resort were demolished and replaced by high-rise apartments. In 2001, it looked like Coney Island might be saved again when New York's mayor promised $30 million worth of improvements designed to lure fun-seekers back to the island. There was even hope that Coney Island might be the site of the Olympics. But when that plan did not materialize, in 2006 the owner of the park sold it to real estate developers, who quickly began evicting the original tenants. While the name Coney Island might survive, the new park probably will be a very different place from the old.

Main Idea   The Coney Island of old may well be disappearing.

Timeline

1800s	playground for the wealthy
1910	wealthy leave; hotels shut down
1920–1945	new subway lines bring crowds
1960s	fifty acres of Coney Island demolished; high rises built
2001	mayor of New York promises $30 million for improvements that might bring fun-seekers back
2006	Coney Island sold to developers who start evictions

EXPLANATION   As it should, the timeline for this passage records dates and events. These dates and events support the idea that Coney Island may not survive the latest threat to its existence.

1. Since their introduction in the late nineteenth century, skyscrapers have been climbing higher and higher. In 1885, the first skyscraper,

the 10-story Home Insurance Building, was erected in Chicago. New York's first skyscraper, the 11-story Tower Building, was built in 1888. New York's 50-story Metropolitan Life Insurance Tower was completed in 1909. It held the title of the world's tallest building until 1913, when the Woolworth Building bested it by 10 stories. In the 1920s and 1930s, a building boom resulted in the construction of many famous skyscrapers, including New York's 77-story Chrysler Building and the 102-story Empire State Building. For forty-two years, from 1931 until 1973, the Empire State Building held the record as the world's tallest building until the dedication of the World Trade Center in 1973. By 1998 the record was broken by the Petronas Towers in Kuala Lumpur, Malaysia, and then came the 1,670-foot, 101-story Taipei 101 Tower in Taiwan in 2004. Currently, the tallest building in the world scrapes the sky at 2,717 feet. It's the Burj Dubai, located in the United Arab Emirates.

Main Idea Skyscrapers seem to get taller and taller with the passage of time.

Timeline[†]

1885	Home Insurance Building
1888	11-Story Tower Building
1909	Metropolitan Life Insurance Tower
1913	Woolworth Building
1920s – 1930s	Chrysler Building and Empire State Building
1931–1973	World Trade Center
1998	Petronas Towers
2004	101-Story Taipei 101 Tower
Today/Present	Burj Dubai

2. The eighteenth-century Danish explorer Vitus Bering (1681–1741) is credited with proving that Asia and North America are separate continents. In the early 1700s, when much of the world was still unknown, the Russians decided to find out if Siberia was connected to the North American continent. Because Bering had served in the

---

[†]The ranking shown here is based on http://architecture.about.com/library/bltall.htm. Rankings differ depending on what's counted; for instance, flagpoles may or may not be factored in.

Russian navy, he was selected to lead an expedition* that set out in 1725 to answer precisely that question. Three years later, in 1728, he sailed through what was later named the Bering Strait, proving that Asia and North America were two separate continents. Its goal accomplished, the expedition returned to Russia in 1730. Bering, however, set out again in 1733 on a quest to map the northern Siberian coast. In 1741, his ship wrecked on the shore of a deserted island. Bering died on the island in December of that same year.

Main Idea The Danish explorer Vitus Bering proved that Asia and North America were two different continents.

Timeline

1700s	Russians examined Siberia
1723	Bering led an expedition
1728	he sailed through the Bering Strait
1730	Returned to russia
1733	Went on a quest
1741	Shipwreck and DEATH

WEB QUEST/CLASS ACTION

Bering Strait and *Bering Sea* are both examples of *eponyms*. Eponyms are words derived, or taken from, the names of people. Here is a list of twenty-two eponyms. Pick one and search out its origin. Be ready to share both definition and origin at the next class session.

bedlam	luddite	spoonerism	Mae West
bloomers	maudlin	tawdry	herculean
boycott	Ponzi scheme	valentine	dunce
cardigan	quisling	tantalize	graham
chauvinism	Heimlich	mackintosh	crackers
galvanize	maneuver	maverick	sadism

American library of medicine named after Heimlich
When someone is choking you push in and up and the air forces out the object.

*expedition: a journey undertaken by a group for a specific purpose

Simple Listing

How the supporting details were ordered was important in the first two patterns introduced in this chapter. However, order is not always a significant element in patterns of organization. In the **simple listing** pattern, supporting details can be switched around without disturbing paragraph meaning. Compare, for instance, the order in these two paragraphs, both of which make the same point: The symptoms accompanying migraine headaches are extremely varied.

Paragraph 1

The underlined topic sentence introduces the category word *symptoms*. The fact that sufferers don't "share the same experience" says order of symptoms overall can't play a key role.

[1]Migraine headaches are accompanied by a number of different symptoms, and sufferers don't necessarily share the same experience. [2]For some migraine victims, the first sign is something called an "aura." [3]This occurs when the actual headache is preceded by flashing lights, spots, wavy lines, or a pins-and-needles sensation in the hands, arms, or face. [4]Many migraine sufferers, however, don't experience an aura. [5]Instead, they experience nausea or vomiting at the same time that their heads start to throb. [6]Then again, some victims don't get an upset stomach. [7]Instead, they get a sudden sensitivity to light or noise. [8]For some, becoming abruptly sensitive to smells is a sign that a migraine is on the way.

Paragraph 2

Notice how just modifying the sentence openings allows the writer to introduce the symptoms in a completely different order. That's because the order in which the symptoms occur is not critical to explaining the topic sentence.

[1]Migraine headaches are accompanied by a number of different symptoms, and sufferers don't necessarily share the same experience. [2]Some migraine sufferers get an upset stomach, and their pounding headache is accompanied by nausea or vomiting. [3]Others, however, have no sign of stomach discomfort. [4]Instead, their migraines are accompanied by a sudden sensitivity to light, noise, even smell. [5]Some migraine sufferers also experience a warning called an "aura" right before the headache hits. [6]The aura can take the form of flashing lights, spots, wavy lines, or a pins-and-needles feeling in the hands, arms, or face.

Both paragraphs make the same point. But they don't order the material in the same way because the content doesn't require it. Within the simple listing pattern, the order of the details is created by the writer. It's not enforced by the content.

⊙━ **READING KEY**

◆ In the simple listing pattern, the author chooses the order of details. The order is not part of the content as it is with process or sequence of dates and events patterns.

Clues to the Pattern

Topic sentences that tell readers about a number of *characteristics*, *studies*, *symptoms*, or *problems* associated with the topic are a strong clue that you could be dealing with the simple listing pattern.

Probably the biggest clue is the ease with which the reader can switch the supporting details around, even if that means turning the first supporting detail into the last. If you can change the order of the details, and the paragraph still seems to make sense, then the paragraph is very likely to be simple listing.

⊙━ **READING KEYS**

◆ The biggest clue to the simple listing pattern is the ease with which the supporting details can be moved around without creating confusion.

◆ A topic sentence that includes a category word like *characteristics*, *symptoms*, *studies*, etc., is also a common element of this pattern.

What You Should Take Away from the Pattern

With the simple listing pattern, a category word in the topic sentence usually tells readers what they need to know. Imagine, for instance, that this was a topic sentence: "Sleep serves several functions." The key word here is *functions*. It tells you that after reading the paragraph, you should be able to explain the different functions of sleep.

⊙━ **READING KEY**

◆ In the simple listing pattern, a category word in the topic sentence often tells readers what they need to know.

Making Concept Maps and Outlines

If the paragraph offers a relatively simple list without much detail, a concept map can be a very effective note-taking device. Concept maps are just like the word maps from Chapter 2. Only the items in the map have a broader meaning because they represent entire ideas, not just single words. For an illustration, read this paragraph and then look at the concept map that follows:

In the English language, money, like sex, is often associated with the presence or absence of dirt. Not surprisingly, several common idioms link the two together. "Money laundering," for example, refers to making illegally earned money look as if it had been gotten by legal means—for example, "Convicted for being involved in a money-laundering scheme, the immigration officer got a long jail sentence." "To grub" is to dig for roots and bugs in the dirt as pigs are known to do. However, when humans are called "moneygrubbers," it means they think of nothing else except money and getting more of it—for example, "He was getting old and he was not proud of the money-grubbing existence he had led." If some person or group takes all of a person's money, that person is said to be "cleaned out," as in "This year my tax bill really cleaned me out." Not surprisingly, when people have a huge amount of money, we say that they are "filthy rich." Donald Trump and Oprah Winfrey, for example, would, currently at least, be considered filthy rich.

To learn these idioms, you could make a concept map like the following:

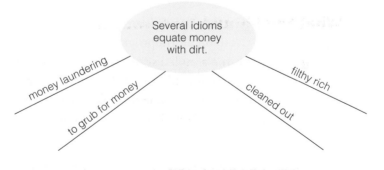

Outlines

If the paragraph based on the simple listing pattern has a lot of detail, you might want to consider making an outline. Outlines give you additional leeway to include more details without inhibiting legibility. Look, for example, at the following paragraph and outline:

During World War I, when the United States was at war with Germany, German Americans became the subject of numerous attacks and insults. One Iowa politician claimed that "90 percent of all the men and women who teach the German language are traitors." German books vanished from libraries. Some towns with German names changed them to sound more American. On menus, names of foods with a German origin or sound were changed so that "sauerkraut" and "hamburger" became "liberty cabbage" and "liberty sandwich." Some orchestras banned the playing of all German music. But if these incidents sound pretty silly, what happened to the German-American Robert Prager was not. Prager, a coal miner, was wrapped in a flag and hanged for the crime of being German-born. When the men who hanged him were brought to trial, they were acquitted and praised for their patriotic loyalty.

In this case, the category words that should focus your notes are *attacks* and *insults*. But because not all of the attacks and insults can be described in a brief phrase or sentence, an outline might be the better choice than a concept map.

Main Idea While America was at war with Germany during World War I, everything German came under attack.

Supporting Details

1. German language teachers accused of being traitors and German books banished from libraries.

2. German food names taken off menus and German music removed from orchestra programs.

3. German-American Robert Prager was lynched.

   a. men who hanged Prager acquitted

   b. Prager's "crime" was being German-born

◆ EXERCISE 4   Recognizing the Simple Listing Pattern

DIRECTIONS   Read each paragraph. Although the paragraphs are similar, not all of them are simple listing. In the blank at the end, write an *S* if the pattern is simple listing and a *T* if the timing of events or steps is a crucial part of the content.

EXAMPLE   Managers are important to most business ventures. There are, however, a number of different management functions.

Marketing managers, for instance, are responsible for pricing, promoting, and distributing a company's products and services. *Operations managers* are responsible for seeing to it that the goods and services produced by the organization are created. *Finance managers* are responsible for managing the financial assets of the organization. They oversee accounting systems and investments, while providing information about the company's financial health. *Human resource managers* are in charge of hiring the right kind of people for the company. They also design compensation and evaluation programs. *Administrative managers* are the most general among the group. They oversee a number of different activities that can include some functions from all areas of the company. (Adapted from William M. Pride , Robert J. Hughes, and Jack R. Kapoor, *Business*, 10th ed. © Cengage Learning.) ___S___

EXPLANATION   *S* is correct because the various areas in management could be put in any order the writer chose. Nothing in the paragraph suggests that order in time plays any role in the organization of the supporting details.

1. Polar bears are amazing creatures with a number of striking features. Although they are most often pictured with white fur, a polar bear's coat can vary from pure white to creamy yellow, even light brown, depending on the season. Polar bears are the largest land carnivores, or meat-eaters, and the biggest polar bear on record weighed over 2,000 pounds, with a length of twelve feet. Polar bears have huge paws, which are large even in comparison to their large body size. The paws of a polar bear have to be big because the bear's paws function like snowshoes, spreading out the bear's weight as it moves over icy snow. Although polar bears are often used in commercials for soft drinks, ski wear, and toilet paper, they are not cuddly and playful as they appear to be in the ads. For polar bears, humans are on the menu. Humans with any brains would do well to keep a distance between themselves and polar bears no matter how cuddly they might appear. ___S___

Due to global warming, the worry is that polar bears may not survive into the next century.

2. Frederick W. Taylor was an industrial engineer interested in something called "scientific management." The goal of scientific management was to find a system that would maximize employee output. Taylor believed, as many did who came after him, that scientific management depended on a sequence of three steps. First, the manager had to study different jobs and identify the skills and talents each one required. Next, the manager had to select and train the workers who appeared to have these particular abilities. Third, the manager had to monitor those he had picked to make sure they were performing their tasks in the most efficient manner. Throughout this process, it was the job of the manager, rather than the workers, to make all planning and organizing decisions. _____

3. Many Americans suffer from sleep apnea, a condition in which the sleeper suddenly has difficulty breathing and wakes up throughout the night. Not all sleep apnea, however, is the same; there are three different kinds. Obstructive sleep apnea (OSA), the most common form of apnea, is typically caused by a breathing obstruction that prevents the flow of air into the nose and mouth. No one knows what causes the obstruction, which occurs in the region of the throat's soft palate. One theory is that the muscles around the soft palate collapse during sleep and close off the air passage. Typically afflicted by this form of apnea are those who are extremely overweight. Central

sleep apnea (CSA) is more rare. It happens when there is a delay in the brain signal that orders the body to breathe. Such delays can be brought about by disease, but they can also be caused by an injury involving the brainstem—for instance, a stroke, brain tumor, chronic respiratory disease, or even a brain infection. Complex sleep apnea refers to the combination of the two other forms of sleep apnea, namely obstructive sleep apnea and central sleep apnea.

4. Old wives' tales are unverified, or unproven, claims that have somehow survived for generations. The notion, for instance, that a mother bird will reject her children if they have been touched by a human is completely false. Birds don't have a strong enough sense of smell to tell if the birds in their nest have been touched by human hands. Also misguided is the idea that the full moon causes mad or criminal behavior. There is absolutely no evidence to justify this claim. Downright dangerous is the idea that eating the leaves of poison ivy will render your skin immune to the rash caused by its leaves. What will happen is that the lining of your throat will develop the rash you would have gotten from touching the leaves with your hands. And don't be afraid to bring flowers to a sick person. Cut flowers in the room do not suck the oxygen out of the air. That's another old wives' tale.

◆ Definition

Paragraphs based on the **definition** pattern almost always start off with the word or phrase being defined. In subjects like business, biology, and psychology, authors usually use boldface type or italics to make the word or phrase stand out. Then they give the definition and follow it with an example or two.

Sometimes authors also explain how the term being defined differs from a similar or a related term. Depending on the object or experience being defined, the author might also define some elements that are essential to the workings of the larger whole. Look, for example, at the following paragraph:

Typically for this pattern, the word defined comes at the very beginning and is highlighted in boldface.

Dams are structures that create barriers to the movement of water. Made of solid material like concrete or carved out of rock, dams block a river's flow to create a reservoir of water. Creating a reservoir is the main purpose of dams, which provide a permanent body of water for use at a later time. The key element of a dam is its *impermeable membrane*, which keeps the

In this case, additional definitions clarify the main definition.

stored water from leaking. An *outlet valve* is another key component, because there has to be some way to let the water out when needed. Dams are used to supply cities with water, irrigate crops, or provide water power to generate electricity. One of the most famous dams in the world is the Hoover Dam, which stands 725 feet over the Colorado River and provides 4 billion kilowatts of electricity per year. The Hoover Dam is a major tourist attraction.

The Hoover Dam, begun in 1930 and finished in 1935, is considered one of the top ten construction achievements of the twentieth century.

© Ulrich Flemming

Clues to the Pattern

Paragraphs using this pattern contain two essential elements: the opening definition of a key term and at least one example of the definition. Often, there's also a sentence or two explaining how the term differs from other similar terms, how it's been misunderstood, or when it was first used.

READING KEYS

◆ Textbook writers using the definition pattern often put the key term in boldface and follow it with a brief definition. Frequently, there's also an example or two illustrating the term being defined.

◆ The definition pattern may also explain how a word came into being, how it differs from related terms, or how the word has been misapplied or misused.

What You Should Take Away from the Pattern

The three essential elements of this pattern that need to go into your notes are (1) the term being defined, (2) the definition along with any additional definitions used to explain the one in the topic sentence, and (3) at least one example used for illustration. However, if an author gives you the history of the word, contrasts it with another term, or explains how it's been misused, you should include that information. It might turn up as a test question like "How do bonuses differ from regular wages?"

Concept Maps and Definitions

To pull out and highlight key elements in a definition passage, consider using a concept map. Look, for example, at the following passage and the accompanying concept map.

> **Litigation** is a legal proceeding used to decide a dispute in which the parties are adversaries, who strongly disagree. Both sides, however, are willing to let a judge decide who has the stronger position. Litigation requires the presence of lawyers, who call witnesses to support each side. Those who participate in litigation must follow a prescribed set of legal rules. A judge is usually in charge of both the application and interpretation of those rules.

What your concept map for a definition paragraph looks like depends a lot on the content of the passage. The only thing typical of concept maps in general is that the term and its meaning appear in the middle because they are the most important thing in the pattern.

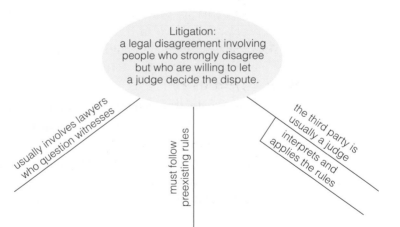

◆ EXERCISE 5   **Understanding the Definition Pattern**

DIRECTIONS   Read each paragraph. Then answer the questions that follow.

EXAMPLE   **Agoraphobia** is a strong fear of being separated from a safe place or person and left without means of escape from a difficult or dangerous situation. People who suffer from agoraphobia are often terrified of leaving their homes. In Western cultures, agoraphobia occurs more often among women. In fact, many women who suffer from agoraphobia are completely homebound by the time they seek help. However, in India, where homebound women are not considered unusual, agoraphobics are more likely to be men. Among all phobias, agoraphobia is the one most likely to be treated. People are more willing to seek help for agoraphobia because it so thoroughly disrupts their everyday life. (Adapted from Douglas Bernstein et al., *Psychology*, 7th ed. © Cengage Learning.)

1. What term is defined in the paragraph?

   agoraphobia

2. In your own words, what's the definition of that term?

   Agoraphobia is a strong fear of being cut off from safety and left alone to face

   a dangerous situation.

3. If the author uses an example to illustrate the definition, describe that example in your own words.

   People with agoraphobia can be afraid to leave the safety of their homes.

4. Does the author do any of the following?
   a. Explain how the term defined differs from or resembles a related term? ___no___
   b. Describe the origin of the word defined? ___no___
   c. Explain how the word has been misused? ___no___

EXPLANATION   The use of boldface type to highlight *agoraphobia* is a strong clue to the definition pattern. And, as usual, the definition follows right after the first mention of the term.

1. **Psychonomics** is a branch of psychology concerned with the relationship between the human mind and objects. Manufacturers have found that understanding how people think about and interact with a product can help designers incorporate features that will make the product easier and more enjoyable to use. Research in psychonomics focuses on matching a product's design to the way consumers

use it. For example, designers created a wireless Web TV keyboard because they knew people wanted to be able to use it while relaxing on the couch. Products such as office equipment, furniture, electronics, and housewares are all being designed with features suggested by psychonomic research.

1. What term is defined in the paragraph?

   Psychonomics

2. In your own words, what's the definition of that term?

   how the Brain and objects interact with each other.

3. If the author uses an example to illustrate the definition, describe that example in your own words.

   The TV keyboard is an example for Psychonomics.

4. Does the author do any of the following?

   a. Explain how the term defined differs from or resembles a related term? _NO_

   b. Describe the origin of the word defined? _yes_

   c. Explain how it's been misused? _No_

2. **Rip currents** are a familiar but misunderstood beach hazard. Also known as riptides and undertows, a rip current is actually a narrow stream of water created by the return of waves thrown onto the beach. As the water retreats from the shore, it forms channels that extend into the ocean for hundreds of yards. Within these channels, which are about ten to thirty feet wide, water can move at up to five miles per hour. The bigger the wave, the stronger the current. Contrary to popular belief, these powerful currents don't pull people underwater. However, they often do drag swimmers into deep water, where they can drown. Rip currents kill 100–200 Americans each year and require lifeguards to rescue 20,000 more.

1. What term is defined in the paragraph?

   Rip currents.

2. In your own words, what's the definition of that term?

<u>a Strong Wave</u>

3. If the author uses an example to illustrate the definition, describe that example in your own words.

<u>Some people that are Swimming</u>
<u>Could Drown and over 200 people would</u>
<u>Die.</u>

4. Does the author do any of the following?

a. Explain how the term defined differs from or resembles a related term? <u>yes</u>

b. Describe the origin of the word defined? <u>No</u>

c. Explain how the word has been misused? <u>NO</u>

◆ **EXERCISE 6** **Taking Notes on the Definition Pattern**

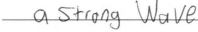 **DIRECTIONS** Read each paragraph and complete the accompanying maps. *Note*: Add new lines, or spokes, if you need to.

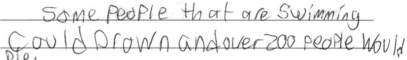 **EXAMPLE** The term **arbitration** refers to a way of formally resolving disputes. When arbitration is required or requested, a third party is brought in to resolve a disagreement. That third party acts like a judge. He or she hears evidence from both sides and then makes a decision on how the conflict should be resolved. The decision is considered binding on both parties because both have previously agreed that they will abide by it. Arbitration is commonly used when prolonged negotiations have failed.

1. The **communication channel** is the medium, or mode, through which messages pass. It's a kind of bridge connecting source and receiver. Communication rarely takes place over one channel. Two, three, or four channels are often used simultaneously. For example, in face-to-face interaction, you not only speak but you also gesture. At times, one or more channels may be damaged. For example, in the case of the blind, the visual channel is impaired, so adjustments have to be made. (Adapted from Joseph D. DeVito, *The Interpersonal Communication Book*, 10th ed., Boston: Pearson Education, 2004, p. 16.)

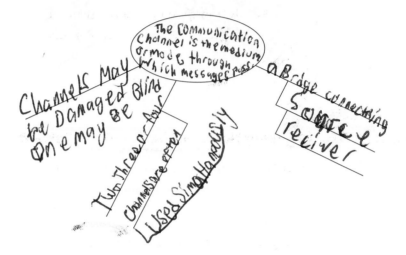

2. *Phishing* is a computer term for the act of tricking people into revealing information like passwords and credit card numbers. People who "phish" set up seemingly legitimate websites and e-mail addresses. Then they send out e-mail messages that request information for some official purpose. In this way, online scam artists "fish" for details they can use for criminal activities. For example, in the early phishing attacks in the mid-1990s, con artists posing as AOL staff members sent messages to potential victims to ask them to "verify your account" or "confirm billing information." Once victims replied and sent back their AOL passwords, the con artist could use the accounts for illegal purposes. This type of phishing scheme with its request for confirmation or verification of an existing account is probably still the most popular form of fraud.

Phishing is the act of tricking people to give them passwords.

People phish to get vr websites and email Addresses

They send emails to people Confirm information?

Con Artists posing as AoI verify your receipt Confirm Billing information

Cause and Effect

The **cause and effect** pattern is crucial to every academic subject. That's because it answers two of the most central questions in our lives: (1) Why did this happen and (2) What are the results of this event having occurred? In longer readings, writers might tackle both ends of the relationship, cause and effect. In paragraphs, they often focus more heavily on one end of that relationship than the other, for instance:

The category word *disadvantages* in the underlined topic sentence is already a clue that the author is focusing on the results of a particular action, in this case "home schooling."

Major and minor details 3–7 all focus on the disadvantages, or effects, of home schooling.

[1]A great deal has been said and written about the advantages of home schooling for students. [2]*But perhaps not enough has been said about home schooling's disadvantages.* [3]The first and most obvious disadvantage of home schooling is that local schools lose per-pupil funding from the state. [4]Even worse, parents who have lost faith in their schools do not support increases in property taxes, which are an important source of funds for a school's operating budget. [5]Another disadvantage has to do with quality. [6]Parents who home school their kids tend to be committed,* affluent,* and articulate.* [7]When these parents withdraw their voices, talents, and involvement, public schools suffer, and their overall quality deteriorates.

---

*committed: dedicated.
*affluent: well-off.
*articulate: well-spoken.

In this paragraph, the supporting details specify the disadvantages (or effects) that can result from home schooling. Yet, as you probably suspected, the cause and effect pattern does not always focus mainly on effects. It can also spotlight causes. Here's an example where the underlined topic sentence announces the focus on causes rather than effects:

The major details— sentences 2, 4, and 6—all identify individual causes of shyness.

The minor details— sentences 3 and 5— add specifics about the causes.

¹<u>Shyness has several causes.</u> ²Unfamiliar social situations are probably the most common cause. ³For example, a person who isn't shy with friends may become clumsy and awkward with strangers. ⁴Meeting someone higher in status is another cause of shyness. ⁵Students, for instance, often become tongue-tied in the presence of their professors. ⁶Then, too, being the focus of attention can cause shyness, even in people who normally feel comfortable in social situations.

Purpose and Pattern

Despite the difference in emphasis—one on effects, the other on causes—the two sample paragraphs shown above were organized by the same pattern. They did not, however, both have the same purpose. The first paragraph was designed to persuade readers that home schooling was not an especially good idea. To that end, the author cited the disadvantages. The second was meant to inform readers about the various causes of shyness. There was no attempt, however, to make one cause seem more important than the others.

Descriptions of cause and effect are very common in informative writing. This is particularly true when causes are emphasized. But often, when effects are the focus, the writer's purpose can shift to persuasion. The effects are used, as they are in the sample paragraph, to discourage a particular action or attitude. Whenever you encounter paragraphs that emphasize the effects that follow from a cause, ask yourself if the author's purpose has shifted to persuasion.

⊶ READING KEYS

- ◆ Paragraphs relying on the cause and effect pattern explain how one event led to or produced another.
- ◆ The cause and effect pattern may focus on causes, effects, or a mix of both.
- ◆ Paragraphs that emphasize effects are often linked to a persuasive purpose.

Clues to the Pattern

Topic sentences like the following are typical of the cause and effect pattern.

1. Some situations are likely to create stress in almost anyone.

2. The war had a terrible effect on the children.

3. Researchers have identified several causes of insomnia.

Transitions That Signal Cause and Effect ◆	as a result because consequently for this reason	hence in response to in the final outcome	thanks to therefore thus

Cause and effect paragraphs are also likely to contain one or more of the following verbs, or action words.

Verbs That Link Cause and Effect ◆	affect bring about cause change contribute create determine	generate increase inspire instigate introduce lead to make happen	produce reduce result in set off stimulate trigger

◯━ READING KEYS

◆ Verbs like *generate*, *increase*, *determine*, and *produce* are clues to the cause and effect pattern, as are transitions like *therefore*, *thus*, and *consequently*.

◆ The strongest clue to the cause and effect pattern is a topic sentence that says one event led to or produced another.

What You Should Take Away from the Pattern

Make sure you have a clear understanding of the general cause and effect relationship described in the topic sentence. For example, in the two sample paragraphs on pages 360–61, you need to understand that (1) home schooling has some significant disadvantages and (2) shyness has more than one cause. When you have a clear understanding of the general cause and effect relationship described, it's easier to remember the specifics about the causes and/or effects mentioned in the reading.

Diagramming Cause and Effect

Outlining cause and effect passages may well become your note-taking format of choice. However, consider using cause and effect diagrams to supplement or even replace your outlines. Diagrams like the following are effective because they help you visualize the relationship you are trying to master:

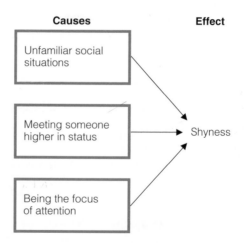

Diagrams like this next one are especially useful if you need to sort out a cycle of causes and effects, where an effect becomes the cause of yet another effect.

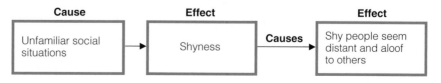

◆ **EXERCISE 7**   **Connecting Cause and Effect**

DIRECTIONS   Read each paragraph, making sure to look closely at the underlined topic sentence. Then answer the questions that follow.

EXAMPLE   [1]For years, the highest number of what doctors call "repeated motion injuries" occurred mainly among workers in meat factories who chopped meat from dawn to dusk. <u>[2]The arrival of computers that can fit on a desk, however, changed all that, and office workers now suffer just as much from repeated motion injuries.</u> [3]Aches in the hands, back, and neck are among the most common complaints. [4]Numb fingers and wrist pain are also common, so much so that surgery is sometimes required. [5]According to doctors who treat these complaints, the human body wasn't designed to be in the same position for hours on end. [6]If it is, pain and injury are often the unpleasant results.

1. Fill in the boxes to identify the cause and effect relationship described in the topic sentence.

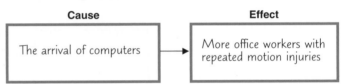

Cause		Effect
The arrival of computers	→	More office workers with repeated motion injuries

2. Do any verbs suggest the cause and effect pattern? ___yes___

   If so, identify the verb or verbs. _____changed_____

3. Do transitions suggest the cause and effect pattern? ___no___

   If so, what are they? __None of the above.__

EXPLANATION   The topic of the paragraph is "repeated motion injuries." This is the subject repeatedly referred to. The topic sentence tells us that the arrival of computers in business caused office workers to join the ranks of those suffering from repeated motion injuries. The verb *changed* signals the cause and effect pattern. However, there are no transition clues.

1. [1]Several studies indicate that laughter produces some positive side effects. [2]It appears, in fact, that laughter can increase creativity. [3]In one study, two groups of college students were asked to take a problem-solving test. [4]One group watched several television

comedies before taking the test. [5]The other group watched more serious dramas and newscasts. [6]Test results showed that the students who laughed at the television comedies came up with better solutions. [7]Studies of teachers, nurses, and computer programmers have arrived at similar conclusions.

1. Fill in the boxes to identify the cause and effect relationship described in the topic sentence.

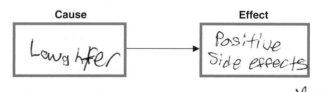

Cause → **Effect**

Cause: Laughter

Effect: Positive Side effects

2. Do any verbs suggest the cause and effect pattern? *Yes*

   If so, what are they? *Increase*

3. Do any transitions suggest the cause and effect pattern? *yes*

   If so, what are they? *came up*

2. [1]As late as 1950, only 7 percent of American women dyed their hair. [2]The current figure is about 75 percent. [3]The question is, What brought about this change? [4]The answer is fairly straightforward. [5]Thanks to the hair color company Clairol, women changed their attitude toward dyeing their hair. [6]In the 1950s, Clairol launched a nationwide campaign. [7]The campaign featured the slogan "Does she or doesn't she? [8]Only her hairdresser knows for sure." [9]The ads also included an attractive woman accompanied by a child. [10]The ads, with their emphasis on motherhood, were meant to suggest that even respectable women dyed their hair. [11]Clairol's ad campaign was a spectacular success. [12]As a result, sales of Clairol's products increased dramatically. [13]By the 1960s, almost 70 percent of American women colored their hair.

1. Fill in the boxes to identify the cause and effect relationship described in the topic sentence.

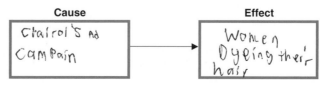

Cause → **Effect**

Cause: Clairol's Ad Campain

Effect: Women Dyeing their hair

2. Do any verbs suggest the cause and effect pattern? _yes_

   If so, what are they? _Changed_

3. Do any transitions suggest the cause and effect pattern? _yes_

   If so, what are they? _thanks to_

IDIOM ALERT: Tar with the same brush

The idiom *tar with the same brush* suggests that someone is guilty of the same fault, crime, or error as someone already accused or proved to be guilty, for instance, "Now that they have discovered the errors made by the teacher, critics want to tar her students with the same brush." The expression probably comes from the practice of brushing tar on sheep to indicate that they belonged to the same flock.

◆ Comparison and Contrast

In our daily lives, we frequently compare and contrast two objects, people, or events. When we **compare**, we look for similarities: "The twins both like contact sports." When we **contrast**, we look for differences: "However, one twin is a computer geek, while the other has a hard time using a cell phone."

As you might expect, comparison and contrast thinking is not limited to casual conversation. Writers also compare and contrast. Sometimes they mainly highlight differences:

Typically for this pattern, the author opens by identifying the two different topics.

Sentences 2–4 focus on state courts.

Sentences 5 and 6 look at federal courts.

The emphasis is on the differences between the two.

The last sentence introduces a similarity.

[1]There are two kinds of courts in the United States, state and federal. [2]State courts have broad jurisdiction, or range of authority. [3]Thus most of the cases individuals are likely to be involved in are tried in a state court. [4]State courts try crimes like traffic violations, robberies, broken contracts, murder, and family disputes. [5]Federal courts have jurisdiction in cases that involve the Constitution or by authorization of Congress. [6]Federal courts hear cases that involve the constitutionality of a particular law, the laws and treaties of the United States in relation to other countries, maritime law, bankruptcy, and copyright. [7]There are cases where both federal and state courts have jurisdiction and the parties involved can choose to go to either state or federal court.

Sometimes they stress similarities:

> Baseball greats Jackie Robinson and Hank Greenberg had much in common. Both, for example, endured insults and abuse from fans and other players. Upon becoming the first African-American Major League baseball player in 1947, Jackie Robinson suffered racist attacks so hateful he came close to having a breakdown. The Jewish Hank Greenberg, who became a legend while playing for the Detroit Tigers, had similar experiences. He was the target of anti-Semitic slurs so mean he vowed to physically retaliate* against those who tormented him. Yet the abuse the two men endured forged a friendship, and each man identified with and admired the other. Robinson was deeply moved by Greenberg's support of him. Greenberg, for his part, wrote in his autobiography that Robinson was a "special person." Both stars continued to fight bigotry even after they stopped playing baseball. Greenberg worked as the general manager of the Cleveland Indians, a team that hired a significant number of African-American players. Robinson not only contributed to the desegregation of baseball, he also worked hard to raise money for other civil rights causes.

And sometimes they do both:

The main idea here is implied. Despite performing at the same level as white soldiers, black soldiers in the Union Army were discriminated against.

[1]During the Civil War, black and white soldiers in the Union Army fought equally hard. [2]Black soldiers, however, received less pay. [3]While many white soldiers were getting thirteen dollars a month, black soldiers were getting only seven. [4]Officially, both black and white soldiers could become officers. [5]But in reality, few black soldiers were ever allowed to become officers.

○━ᴎ READING KEY

◆ Paragraphs based on the comparison and contrast pattern may mention both similarities and differences. However, they can also focus solely on one or the other.

Clues to the Pattern

The most obvious clue to this organizational pattern is the presence of two different topics. Paragraphs organized around this pattern are also

---

*retaliate: respond in kind.

likely to include a topic sentence that practically shouts to readers: "This pattern is comparison and contrast." Consider as examples two of the topic sentences you have already encountered.

1. There are two kinds of courts in the United States, state and federal.

2. Baseball greats Jackie Robinson and Hank Greenberg had much in common.

Keep in mind, too, though, that comparison and contrast patterns of organization often let the similarities and differences speak for themselves. This is illustrated in the third sample paragraph, where the reader supplies the main idea implied by the similarities and differences between black and white soldiers in the Union Army.

Whenever you encounter a paragraph like this one, where the main idea is not stated in a topic sentence, you have to supply one. No serious writer ever compares and contrasts specific details for no reason. There has to be a stated or implied main idea lurking in the paragraph.

Additional clues to this pattern are transitions like the ones listed in the following two boxes.

Transitions That Signal Similarities or Comparison ◆	along the same lines also by the same token in like fashion in like manner	in much the same way or manner in the same vein just like likewise similarly

Transitions That Signal Reversal or Contrast ◆	actually but despite these differences however in contrast	in reality instead of just the opposite nevertheless nonetheless on the contrary	on the one hand on the other hand rather unlike whereas yet

Pattern and Purpose

Like the cause and effect pattern of organization, the comparison and contrast pattern also turns up a good deal in persuasive writing. This makes sense since one way a writer tries to convince is to tell readers how two people or positions are different or similar and then make those specific differences or similarities the basis for proving that one person or position is better or worse than another. Thus topic sentences like the following are also likely to be the point of an argument. (For more on arguments, see Chapter 9.)

1. Supporters are inclined to tell us that e-books are far superior to print books, but despite the obvious differences between the two, e-books and print books deliver content in surprisingly similar ways.

2. Anyone who thinks Lady Gaga is a musical revolutionary should look at some early Madonna videos, which make it clear that Madonna did it all before.

3. Movies and novels have tended to portray the outlaw Billy the Kid as a hot-tempered bad boy whose lethal ways with a gun made him a menace to society, but the reality of the Kid's life had little to do with these fictions.

⟁ READING KEYS

◆ Paragraphs based on comparison and contrast *always* have two topics.
◆ The topic sentence is often a dead giveaway to the comparison and contrast pattern because it tells you that two topics are generally alike or unalike.
◆ References to similarities and differences are often a sign that the writer is trying to persuade readers to share a particular opinion. When you see an author mentioning differences and similarities, make sure you understand the purpose as well as the pattern.

What You Should Take Away from the Pattern

You definitely need to know exactly what two topics are under discussion. You also need to decide if the author has focused on both similarities and differences or has favored one over the other. Make sure, too, that you have a clear grasp of the main idea developed by the similarities and differences. Don't assume that the similarities and differences are an end in themselves. They are not. They're there to support a larger point. Your job is to figure out what that point is.

If there are minor details that clarify similarities or differences, be sure to evaluate them. Would you understand the difference or similarity without the additional example or tidbit of information offered in the minor detail? If the answer is yes, then you don't need to store that bit of information in memory or record it in your notes. But if the difference or similarity is clear to you only if you connect it to, say, an example, then you need to remember that minor example.

0━┓ READING KEY

◆ Transitions like *similarly* and *in contrast* can often signal the presence of the comparison and contrast pattern. So, too, can verbs such as *differ*, *contrast*, and *resemble*.

Charting Similarities and Differences

When you encounter the comparison and contrast pattern in your reading, consider making a chart of the similarities and/or differences. The chart will give visual support to the meaning of the word. For an example, look at the chart following this next paragraph.

Psychologist Carl Rogers is known for his description of two kinds of people, the noxious and the nourishing. The noxious like to criticize. They are quick to find fault with others (not so much with themselves). It's best to see them in small doses or avoid them altogether. Spend too much time with them and you might believe the negative messages they consistently offer. That's a sure way to damage your self-esteem. Nourishing people, *in contrast*, are more inclined to focus on your strengths rather than weaknesses. Make a mistake and they say something positive, like "There's always next time." Spend significant time with nourishing people and you are likely to feel more confident and secure about your abilities. The exact opposite is likely to happen if you spend a lot of time with a noxious personality.

Main Idea The psychologist Carl Rogers made a distinction between noxious and nourishing people.

Noxious	Nourishing
criticize and find fault	optimistic and positive
difficult to be around	make others feel good about themselves
A person can lose self-esteem by accepting the words of the noxious.	Being around them builds self-esteem.

◆ EXERCISE 8   Understanding the Comparison and Contrast Pattern

DIRECTIONS   Read each paragraph. Then circle the correct letter and fill in the blanks to answer the questions that follow.

EXAMPLE   In general, Americans and Spaniards have very different responses to a bullfight. When Americans watch a bullfight, they usually wonder why the matador would want to risk his life. Spaniards, in contrast, imagine the excitement of controlling the bull and displaying courage in the face of death. Few Americans see beauty in the matador's movements. Spanish spectators, however, are trained to understand and appreciate his every twist and turn. They cheer the matador who executes his movements with grace and skill. They just as readily boo the one who lacks the appropriate grace and training. Most American spectators are just the opposite. They focus more on the bull than the matador. Outnumbered by the matador and his banderilleros, or assistants, the bull is often pitied by American spectators. This attitude usually tries the patience of Spanish spectators.

1. This paragraph

    a. compares two topics.

    (b.) contrasts two topics.

    c. compares and contrasts two topics.

2. What two topics are compared and/or contrasted?

    Topic 1: Americans at a bullfight

    Topic 2: Spaniards at a bullfight

3. What is the main idea of the paragraph?

    a. Few Americans understand why bullfighting is so popular in Spain.

    b. It's impossible for people to overcome their cultural differences.

    (c.) Americans and Spaniards often react quite differently to a bullfight.

    d. The Spaniards don't see bullfighting as a sport; it's an art.

4. List any similarities mentioned.

    none

    List any differences mentioned.

    (1) Americans don't understand why the matador takes the risk, while Spaniards appreciate the matador's control. (2) Americans don't see the beauty, while Spaniards understand and judge each movement. (3) Americans focus more on the bull than on the matador.

5. Do any transitions suggest the use of a comparison and contrast pattern? ___yes___

    If so, what are they? in contrast; however; Most American spectators are just the opposite

EXPLANATION   The differences mentioned in this paragraph are specific examples of the topic sentence: "In general, Americans and Spaniards have very different responses to a bullfight." No similarities are mentioned. The transitions *in contrast* and *however* are clues to this pattern. Another clue is the phrase "different responses" in the topic sentence.

1. Outwardly, sleepwalking and sleeptalking seem to be different sleep disturbances. Sleepwalkers are capable of walking down stairs or, for that matter, out of doors, all the while remaining fast asleep. Sleeptalkers, in contrast, stay still, but they effortlessly carry on long conversations. To be sure, little of what they say makes any sense. Yet despite the differences, there are some similarities between the two sleep disturbances. During their waking hours, neither sleepwalkers nor sleeptalkers remember what happened the night before. Also, both disturbances appear to be hereditary, or to run in families.

   1. This paragraph
      a. compares two topics.
      b. contrasts two topics.
      (c.) compares and contrasts two topics.

   2. What two topics are compared and/or contrasted?

      Topic 1: _Sleepwalkers_

      Topic 2: _Sleeptalkers_

   3. What is the main idea of the paragraph?
      a. Sleepwalking is dangerous because the sleepwalker can walk outside while still fast asleep.
      b. Many people suffer from sleep disturbances that interfere with daily life.
      (c.) Sleepwalking and sleeptalking appear to be very different sleep disturbances, but they actually share some similarities.
      d. Sleepwalking and sleeptalking are both hereditary.

   4. List any similarities mentioned.

      They don't remember what happened the night before. Both disturbances appear to be hereditary or to run in families.

List any differences mentioned.

Sleepwalkers tend to walk and sleeptalkers tend to stay still

5. Do any transitions suggest the use of a comparison and contrast pattern? *yes*

If so, what are they? *Despite the Differences there are some similarities.*

2. During robotic surgery, a human surgeon operates a robot that repairs damage to the patient's body. *Robosurgery*, as the procedure has come to be known, has improved upon conventional surgery in several ways. First, robosurgery is almost bloodless. Conventional surgery often requires patients to get blood transfusions due to blood loss. In robosurgery, however, the robot's instruments and cameras enter the patient's body through tiny incisions, causing far less trauma to the body and reducing the need for transfusions. Second, robotic surgeons can do things human surgeons can't. For example, the use of robots eliminates any trembling in fingers. Also, robots can work with precision on a scale barely visible to the human eye. Finally, robosurgery results in far fewer post-operative complications. Cardiac bypass patients, for instance, who were operated on with the help of robots spent an average of only two to eight days in the hospital. In comparison, conventional bypass patients stayed an average of six to eight days.

1. This paragraph
   a. compares two topics.
   b. contrasts two topics.
   c. compares and contrasts two topics.

2. What two topics are compared and/or contrasted?
   Topic 1: *Robotic Surgery*
   Topic 2: *Conventional Surgery*

3. What is the main idea of the paragraph?
   a. Robots are becoming common in all fields of medical care.
   b. Human surgeons can do things robots could never master.
   c. Robosurgery has dramatically shortened hospital stays.
   d. Robosurgery has some advantages over the more traditional surgical procedures.

4. List any similarities mentioned.

None

List any differences mentioned.

1: bloodless
2. Robotic Surgens candoth ings that human surgeons
3. fewer Postoperative complications cant

5. Do any transitions suggest the use of a comparison and contrast pattern? No

If so, what are they? None

Classification

Writers who use the **classification** pattern divide a larger group into smaller categories. Then they define and describe each category, as the author of the following passage has done:

Typically for this pattern, the underlined topic sentence announces the method of classification.

The individual categories in this pattern are named and highlighted.

Burns can be classified according to their causes. **Thermal** burns are those caused by flames or extreme heat. Such heat can result from fire, steam, hot liquid, or a hot object. **Light** burns are caused by light sources or by ultraviolet light from the sun. **Radiation** burns are those produced by nuclear sources such as bombs. **Electrical** burns are caused by electrical current and lightning. **Chemical** burns, as their name suggests, are caused by corrosive* chemical substances that contact the skin.

Here the general topic is "burns." The topic sentence tells readers that burns can be classified, or broken down, into smaller, more specific categories, based on their causes.

*corrosive: gradually and steadily destructive by means of a chemical reaction.

Classification versus Simple Listing

Classification and simple listing are similar in that the order of events in real time plays no role in how supporting details are organized. The key difference between the two patterns is usually the topic sentence. Classification topic sentences announce that some larger group can be categorized into smaller subgroups, which account for *all* members of the larger group: "Our society recognizes five kinds of power."

Simple listing, in contrast, does not suggest that the paragraph takes into account all members of some larger group. In other words, there could be other individual people, events, or experiences left unaccounted for, as in the following example: "A number of Supreme Court decisions have changed our society in dramatic and profound ways." This topic sentence does not suggest that the paragraph will take into account *all* Supreme Court decisions that have profoundly influenced society. Instead, it will take into account some of them, based on the author's sense of their significance. Keep this difference in mind when asked to identify patterns of organization in the tests that end this chapter.

○━╖ READING KEY

♦ Writers using the classification pattern identify, describe, and often name the smaller subgroups that make up a larger whole.

Clues to the Pattern

Next to the sequence of dates and events, the classification pattern is probably the easiest to recognize. This is a good thing because classification is a very common textbook pattern in subjects such as biology and business. Especially in textbooks, the pattern almost always begins with a topic sentence identifying the larger group being subdivided and the number of categories created—for instance, "There are five categories of power," "Managers use three types of interviews when seeking employees," and "Low-cost housing can be divided into four different groups."

What Should You Take Away from the Pattern

Once you spot the classification pattern, make sure you know exactly what larger group is being subdivided. Get a clear grasp, too, of how many subgroups there are. Review the characteristics of each one. If names are included, you need to know them as well.

Classification Charts

If you want to remember the information from a paragraph based on classification, consider making a chart that shows the number of categories and the characteristics of each. Many students find that "charting" the categories makes the subgroups of the classification clearer and more memorable. Here's an example to get you started.

Burns can be classified according to their causes.

Thermal Burns	Light Burns	Radiation Burns	Electrical Burns	Chemical Burns
caused by flames or other extreme heat	caused by light sources or sunlight	produced by nuclear sources like bombs	caused by electrical current and lightning	caused by corrosive chemicals

⊶🗝 READING KEYS

- ◆ Classification is one of the easiest patterns to spot because the topic sentence usually announces that a large group can be divided into smaller subgroups.
- ◆ Classification topic sentences frequently identify the method used to create the categories.
- ◆ Classification paragraphs always describe each category mentioned in the topic sentence.

◆ EXERCISE 9   Understanding the Classification Pattern

DIRECTIONS   Read each paragraph. Then answer the questions that follow.

EXAMPLE   Prisons are classified into three main types, according to their security level. The most restrictive type is the close-security prison. Close-security prisons usually consist of single cells. Each cell has its own sink and toilet. Inmates' movements are severely limited and supervised by the prison staff. The entire facility is surrounded by a double fence that is watched or patrolled by armed guards. In some cases, inmates are confined to their cells twenty-three hours a day. The second type of prison is referred to as a medium-security facility. In medium-security prisons, inmates can leave their cells a little more. But they are housed in secure dormitories. Armed guards usually watch over a double fence surrounding the prison. Minimum-security prisons are the third type. Inmates assigned to this kind of facility pose the least safety threat. Thus, they are housed in dormitories patrolled by corrections officers. A single fence encloses the facility. The fence is not patrolled by armed guards. Many inmates of minimum-security prisons leave the grounds on a regular basis during the day to participate in work programs. They return to prison at night.

1. What larger group is divided into smaller subgroups or categories?

prisons

2. How many subgroups are mentioned? ___3___

3. Name and describe each subgroup.

1. Close-security prisons consist of single cells. Prisoners are closely watched. Their movements are limited; some inmates stay in their cells 23 hours a day.

2. Medium-security prisons give prisoners more freedom of movement, but prisoners are watched over by armed guards who patrol a double fence.

3. Minimum-security prisons house the least dangerous prisoners. Inmates live in dormitories controlled by corrections officers.

—There are no armed guards.

Many inmates leave the grounds for work.

EXPLANATION   Notes on this paragraph should describe the three main types of prisons mentioned in the topic sentence.

1. Shopping centers come in three different types. One is the neighborhood shopping center, which serves customers who usually live within a two- or three-mile radius.* This type usually contains a grocery store, drugstore, gas station, and one or more fast-food restaurants. The community shopping center draws its customers from a much wider area. It usually includes one or two department stores and specialty stores that sell products not available in neighborhood shopping centers. The third type is the regional shopping center. This shopping center, usually called a "mall," generally targets

———————————
*radius: a bounded range of activity or influence.

at least 150,000 customers. It contains large department stores and many specialty stores, along with restaurants and movie theaters.

1. What larger group is divided into smaller subgroups or categories?

   Shopping Centers

2. How many subgroups are mentioned? _3_

3. Name and describe each subgroup. If no names are included, just describe each separate category.

   1. Neighborhood Shopping center. two to three mile radius.
   2. Community shopping Center. Department stores and specialty stores.
   3. Regional Shopping center. Mall.

2. In an article titled "Some Character-Types Met with in Psycho-Analytic Work (1916)," Sigmund Freud, the founder of psychoanalysis,[†] classified his patients into three groups, based on their attitude toward life. The first group Freud described were those who considered themselves exceptions to all rules and requirements imposed by the outside world. If told that they needed to make a sacrifice or accept an undesirable situation, they responded that they did not. In their mind, they were not ordinary human beings. They were exceptional. The second group consisted of those who seemed to have been destroyed by success. They functioned perfectly well while working toward a goal, but as soon as they came close to achieving it, they started to get anxious and ill. The third group included the patients who were plagued by guilt. Oddly enough, what relieved them of guilt was committing a crime.

[†]psychoanalysis: a theory of the mind and its workings developed in the early twentieth century.

1. What larger group is divided into smaller subgroups or categories?

    Patients

2. How many subgroups are mentioned? _3_

3. Name and describe each subgroup. If no names are included, just describe each separate category.

    1. exeptions-Did no thave to follow Rules.

    2. Destroyed By success, close to Goals they felt Anxious and ill.

    3. Plauged by guilt, commited a crime to get rid of it.

ROUNDING UP THE KEYS

Here is a list of all the reading keys introduced in the chapter. Use them to review for the test on page 390. If a particular reading key doesn't make sense on its own, go back to the page where it appeared and review the section preceding it.

READING KEYS: Time Order—Process

- ◆ Writers use the process pattern to explain how something functions, develops, or occurs in real time. (p. 335)
- ◆ If the topic itself is a process and most of the sentences in the passage describe individual stages or steps, you are most likely dealing with the process pattern. (p. 335)
- ◆ Words like *steps*, *stages*, or *phases* in the topic sentence are typical of the process pattern. (p. 335)
- ◆ In the process pattern, the topic sentence often announces the type and number of major details. (p. 335)
- ◆ When dealing with the process pattern, make sure you can identify the process described and list each step in the right order. (p. 335)

READING KEYS: Time Order—Sequence of Dates and Events

- ◆ Dates and events introduced in the order in which they occurred in real time are a surefire clue to the sequence of dates and events pattern. (p. 342)
- ◆ Passages or readings using this pattern are likely to focus on three kinds of topics: (1) a particular segment of time, considered unusual or extraordinary; (2) a person's life or career; or (3) the events leading up to or following a significant historical event. (p. 342)
- ◆ The dates and events that give this pattern its name are always significant. However, don't automatically ignore the supporting details that lack dates. Evaluate them to see if they contribute anything to the main idea. (p. 343)

READING KEYS: Simple Listing

- ◆ In the simple listing pattern, the author chooses the order of details. The order is not part of the content as it is with process or sequence of dates and events patterns. (p. 348)

- ◆ The biggest clue to the simple listing pattern is the ease with which the supporting details can be moved around without creating confusion. (p. 348)
- ◆ A topic sentence that includes a category word like *characteristics*, *symptoms*, *studies*, etc., is also a common element of this pattern. (p. 348)
- ◆ In the simple listing pattern, a category word in the topic sentence often tells readers what they need to know. (p. 348)

O—╥ READING KEYS: Definition

- ◆ Textbook writers using the definition pattern often put the key term in boldface and follow it with a brief definition. Frequently, there's also an example or two illustrating the term being defined. (p. 354)
- ◆ The definition pattern may also explain how a word came into being, how it differs from related terms, or how the word has been misapplied or misused. (p. 354)

O—╥ READING KEYS: Cause and Effect

- ◆ Paragraphs relying on the cause and effect pattern explain how one event led to or produced another. (p. 361)
- ◆ The cause and effect pattern may focus on causes, effects, or a mix of both. (p. 361)
- ◆ Paragraphs that emphasize effects are often linked to a persuasive purpose. (p. 361)
- ◆ Verbs like *generate*, *increase*, *determine*, and *produce* are clues to the cause and effect pattern, as are transitions like *therefore*, *thus*, and *consequently*. (p. 362)
- ◆ The strongest clue to the cause and effect pattern is a topic sentence that says one event led to or produced another. (p. 362)

O—╥ READING KEYS: Comparison and Contrast

- ◆ Paragraphs based on the comparison and contrast pattern may mention both similarities and differences. However, they can also focus solely on one or the other. (p. 367)
- ◆ Paragraphs based on comparison and contrast *always* have two topics. (p. 369)
- ◆ The topic sentence is often a dead giveaway to the comparison and contrast pattern, because it tells you that two topics are generally alike or unalike. (p. 369)

◆ References to similarities and differences are often a sign that the writer is trying to persuade readers to share a particular opinion. When you see an author mentioning differences and similarities, make sure you understand the purpose as well as the pattern. (p. 369)

◆ Transitions like *similarly* and *in contrast* can often signal the presence of the comparison and contrast pattern. So, too, can verbs such as *differ*, *contrast*, and *resemble*. (p. 370)

READING KEYS: Classification

◆ Writers using the classification pattern identify, describe, and often name the smaller subgroups that make up a larger whole. (p. 376)

◆ Classification is one of the easiest patterns to spot because the topic sentence usually announces that a large group can be divided into smaller subgroups. (p. 377)

◆ Classification topic sentences frequently identify the method used to create the categories. (p. 377)

◆ Classification paragraphs always describe each category mentioned in the topic sentence. (p. 377)

IDIOM ALERT: Tongue in cheek

This expression means that something is being said humorously rather than with a serious intent. No one knows for sure where it came from. One theory is that it comes from the habit nineteenth-century actors had of sticking their tongue into their cheek to keep from laughing on stage at the wrong moment. Another theory is that it refers to an eighteenth-century practice of making funny, mocking faces by putting one's tongue in one's cheek. In any case, the expression now means, don't take me seriously as in, "I told him, tongue in cheek, to solve all his marital problems by getting a divorce."

Ten More Words for Your Academic Vocabulary

1. **accelerate:** speed up

   The momentum for a change in the civil rights laws *accelerated* in the 1950s as African Americans staged public protests against racism.

2. **conformity:** tendency to follow or imitate the behavior of others

   When social psychologists talk of *conformity*, they specifically refer to the tendency of people to change their perceptions, opinions, and behavior in ways that are consistent with group norms. (Sharon S. Brehm, Saul Kassim, and Steven Fein, *Social Psychology*, 6th ed., p. 230.)

3. **precedent:** pattern or example that influences similar events

   The Supreme Court justice Oliver Wendell Holmes set a *precedent* when he argued for limiting free speech only in the face of an immediate danger.

4. **contemporaries:** people living in the same time period

   In the eighteenth century, New Englanders lived longer and raised larger families than their *contemporaries* in England. (Adapted from Paul S. Boyer et al., *The Enduring Vision*, 7th ed., p. 65.)

5. **predominate:** rule, overshadow

   Throughout the novel, an antiwar theme *predominates*; thus the ending is a surprise.

6. **hypothesis:** theory not yet proved by evidence

   Their *hypothesis* is that the language we have at our disposal affects what we are capable of thinking about.

7. **urban:** related to the city

   United in their efforts to improve their surroundings, the members of the community worked hard to create a central meeting place and a large *urban* garden.

8. **ironic:** meaning the opposite or reverse of what is said or expressed; the opposite of what was expected occurring.

   (1) Looking at the pile of paperwork on his desk, the deputy chief said with an *ironic* smile, "Nothing like a little paperwork to brighten up the day." (2) It's *ironic* that a man who said he didn't like dogs now has three of them.

9. **assumption:** a belief or idea that is taken for granted without asking for evidence

   The jurors' mistaken *assumption* was that eyewitness testimony could be trusted.

10. **incidence:** frequency, rate of something undesirable

    The *incidence* of sexually transmitted diseases is on the rise among the elderly.

◆ EXERCISE 10   Making Academic Vocabulary Familiar

DIRECTIONS   Each sentence uses a more conversational or simpler version of the words listed below. At the end of the sentence, fill in the blank with the more academic word that could replace the underlined word or phrase in the sentence.

incidence	predominately	conformity	urban	precedents
assumption	accelerated	hypothesis	ironically	contemporary

1. Before going into the courtroom, a good lawyer knows the previous rulings for similar cases. _precedents_

2. It's a rare teenager who will go against the group and strike out on his or her own; being like everyone else is simply part of being a teenager. _conformity_

3. In the run-up to the Iraq War in 2003, the population was primarily pro-war but that sentiment changed with the passage of time.
   predominately

4. The government's refusal to acknowledge the course of the disease only speeded up the spread of the disease. _____*accelerated*_____

5. When Alfred Wegener first put forth his still unproven theory that, at one time, the continents had been joined together, he was laughed at and called a lunatic. But Wegener was eventually proven correct. _____*hypothesis*_____

6. A person born in the same time frame of painter Salvador Dalí and filmmaker Luis Buñuel, the great Spanish poet Federico García Lorca was brutally murdered because he championed democracy in a time of dictatorship. _____*contemporary*_____

7. The generally accepted belief is that fingerprint evidence can't lie; but as evidence, fingerprints are coming under increasing attack. _____*assumption*_____

8. To call attention to the terrible starvation the Irish were enduring during the 1720s, the poet and essayist Jonathan Swift wrote an article called "A Modest Proposal," in which he argued, while implying the opposite, that the Irish, since they had nothing to eat, should consider eating their young. When the British and Irish alike took him seriously, Swift was furious. _____*ironically*_____

9. The photographer specialized in city landscapes. _____*urban*_____

10. When the frequency of cases of swine flu began to increase, people began to panic. _____*incidence*_____

DIGGING DEEPER The Origins of Cinco de Mayo

Looking Ahead The patterns of organization described in this chapter aren't limited to paragraphs. They can and do appear in longer readings as well. As you read the selection that follows, try to identify the different patterns used to organize the content.

1   At one time, the holiday known as Cinco de Mayo (May 5) was celebrated primarily in Mexico. It was also celebrated in U.S. cities with a large Mexican population. More recently, however, American businesses, aware of the market possibilities, have begun to promote the holiday more heavily than ever before. As a result, many people now celebrate Cinco de Mayo without quite knowing why. Yet the story behind the holiday is a proud one and deserves to be told.

2   By 1821, Mexico had finally gained independence from Spain; yet the country was not allowed to enjoy peace after throwing off the Spanish yoke. Instead, there were political takeovers and wars, including the Mexican-American War (1846–1848) and the Mexican Civil War (1858–1861). During this chaotic* period, the Mexican government accumulated a number of debts to Spain, England, and France. All three countries began demanding payment. France, however, decided to use the debts as an excuse to expand its empire.

3   In 1862, France invaded the Gulf of Mexico and marched toward Mexico City. Along the way, French troops encountered some strong resistance. The Battle of Puebla on the fifth of May left French forces stunned and in retreat. Led by General Ignacio Zaragoza Seguin, a small, poorly armed band of Mexican soldiers defeated a well-outfitted French army of more than 6,500 soldiers. The Mexican victory in the Battle of Puebla is remembered to this day in the celebration known as Cinco de Mayo.

4   Unfortunately, Mexico's triumph was short lived. Upon hearing of the Puebla defeat, the French emperor immediately sent 30,000 more soldiers to Mexico. One year later, in 1863, the French army took over Mexico City. The emperor's nephew, Archduke Maximilian of Austria, was installed as the ruler of all Mexico. However, Maximilian had no popular support. In less than three years, he was executed by the leaders of Mexico's revolution, and the French were driven out of the country. To this day, many historians insist that the Mexican triumph on Cinco de Mayo fueled the fight against

---

*chaotic: confusing, unsettling.

Maximilian and France. The Mexican population—soldiers and civilians alike—was convinced that since a miraculous victory had happened once, it could happen again, and that belief helped maintain the fighting spirit needed to drive out the invaders.

Sharpening Your Skills

DIRECTIONS   Answer the following questions by filling in the blanks or circling the letter of the correct response.

1. Overall, what two patterns organize the reading?

   (a.) time order and cause and effect
   b. classification and comparison and contrast
   c. cause and effect and simple listing
   d. definition and comparison and contrast

2. What's the main idea of paragraph 2?

   Cinco de Mayo did not end all of their Problems or give them independence.

3. What's the main idea of paragraph 3?

   The mexican victory in the Battle Puebla is remembeed to this day as Cinco de Mayo.

4. What's the main idea of paragraph 4?

   Maximilian was appointed and soon after executed by the leaders of mexico's revolution.

5. What's the main idea of the entire reading?

   The history of Cinco de mayo.

6. What type of transition opens paragraphs 1 to 3?

   Cause and effect transitions as a result

7. What type of transition opens paragraph 4?

   _____ Unfortunately _____

8. The first sentence of paragraph 4 is

   a. an introductory sentence.
   b. a topic sentence.
   c. a transitional sentence.

9. Which of the following is a major supporting detail?

   a. More recently, however, American businesses, aware of the market possibilities, have begun to promote the holiday more heavily than ever before (paragraph 1).
   b. In 1862, France invaded the Gulf of Mexico and marched toward Mexico City (paragraph 3).

10. In paragraph 1 the claim that at one time Cinco de Mayo was celebrated mainly in Mexico is a

    a. major detail.
    b. minor detail.

▶ **TEST 1**   **Reviewing the Key Points**

DIRECTIONS   Write the name of the organizational pattern being described in the blank following each description.

1. This pattern comes into play when a writer wants to explain how one thing led to another. It's likely to have transitions such as *thus*, *therefore*, and *consequently* along with verbs like *triggered*, *produced*, and *created*.

   Cause and effect

2. This pattern is used when the writer wants to show readers how two topics do or do not resemble one another. It's likely to have transitions such as *similarly*, *likewise*, and *from the opposite point of view*.

   Compairison and contrast

3. This is the pattern of choice when the writer wants to show readers the chain of events that comprises, or makes up, the career of someone famous. It's likely to include transitions like *in the following year*, *after the decade ended*, and *in the fall of 2012*.

   Sequence of dates and events time order

4. This is the pattern that writers are likely to use when they want to explain how something works or functions. Transitions such as *first*, *second*, *next*, and *finally* often appear in this pattern.

   Process; time order

5. Writers use this pattern to tell readers how some larger group can be broken down into smaller subgroups.

   Classification

6. This pattern turns up when order in time is not significant and writers just want to identify factors, symptoms, or parts.

   Simple Listing

To correct your test, turn to page 588. If one or more of your answers is incorrect, re-read the Rounding Up the Keys section of the chapter to find out where your mistake might be.

▶ TEST 2   **Recognizing Patterns and Topic Sentences**

DIRECTIONS   Read each topic sentence. Then circle the letter of the pattern suggested by the topic sentence.

1. German and English grammar differ a great deal; in English, the order of the words is important, but in German, it is much less so.

    a. simple listing

    b. definition

    c. cause and effect

    d. comparison and contrast

2. Many Middle Eastern cultures encourage public expressions of grief.

    a. time order

    b. definition

    c. cause and effect

    d. simple listing

3. In the simplest of terms, an earthquake is a trembling of the ground.

    a. time order

    b. definition

    c. cause and effect

    d. comparison and contrast

4. In superficial ways, movies and television are alike, but as mass media they differ enormously.

    a. time order

    b. definition

    c. cause and effect

    d. comparison and contrast

5. Becoming addicted to alcohol is a slow, step-by-step process.

    a. time order

    b. definition

    c. cause and effect

    d. simple listing

6. The philosopher John Locke had a powerful influence on America's rebellion against England.

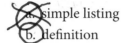

a. ~~simple listing~~

b. definition

c. cause and effect

d. comparison and contrast

7. Most people have three categories of friends, and the categories seldom overlap.

a. definition

b. cause and effect

c. comparison and contrast

d. classification

8. The history of television goes back a good deal longer than many people realize.

a. time order

b. definition

c. simple listing

d. comparison and contrast

9. Thinking about the United States before and after September 11, 2001, is like pondering the fate of two different countries.

a. definition

b. cause and effect

c. comparison and contrast

d. classification

10. There are three main non-volcanic types of mountains.

a. definition

b. cause and effect

c. comparison and contrast

d. classification

▶ TEST 3 　　　　　**Recognizing Patterns of Organization**

DIRECTIONS　　Circle the appropriate letters to identify the primary pattern in each paragraph. Circle all clues to the pattern you select.

1.　Many words in English are derived from the names of people, real and imaginary. The word *sandwich*, for instance, originated with the Earl of Sandwich, who liked to gamble so much, he didn't have time to eat. Anxious not to miss a moment away from the gaming tables, he ordered that a piece of meat between two pieces of bread be brought to his chair, and, thus, the sandwich was born. Similarly, the cardigan sweater is named for the seventh Earl of Cardigan, who liked to sport collarless sweaters with buttons down the front. The word *echo* is yet another example of an eponym. It originated with the story of Echo, a figure from Greek mythology, who used constant chatter to distract Hera, the Queen of the Heavens, from her husband's flirtations. When Hera figured out what was going on, she punished Echo by taking away her powers of speech and allowing her to only repeat the words of others. *Forsythia*, the yellow flowers announcing the coming of spring, were also named for a person. They were named for William Forsyth, the eighteenth-century superintendent of the British Royal Gardens, who introduced the flowers to Great Britain.

　　a. simple listing
　　b. definition
　　c. cause and effect
　　d. classification

2.　Wildly energetic singer La Lupe was once considered the Queen of Latin Soul, but she died poor and forgotten. In 1962, she moved from Cuba to New York, where she soon became famous as a soloist. During the 1960s and 1970s, she sold millions of records, performed in Carnegie Hall, and appeared on several television shows. In 1965 and 1966, New York's Latin press named her Singer of the Year. La Lupe fascinated her fans with her frenzied behavior on stage. Flinging her body around the stage, she threw her wigs, shoes, clothing, and jewelry into the audience. In the 1980s, however, misfortune struck. Her husband became mentally ill; she suffered a back injury; and bad business deals ruined her financially. By the late 1980s, the Queen of Latin Soul was living on welfare and had spent time in homeless shelters. In the last few years of her life, she recorded only a few pieces of Christian music. La Lupe died in 1992 at age 53.

(a.) time order
b. comparison and contrast
c. classification
d. cause and effect

3. People seeking to overcome problems with alcohol can either get help from Alcoholics Anonymous or take part in the Moderation Management treatment program. The two programs share a similar format, but their numbers, target group, guidelines, and level of acceptance differ. Both programs consist of free instructional meetings for participants. However, Moderation Management offers chapters in only fourteen states. Alcoholics Anonymous programs can be found all over the country. Alcoholics Anonymous is available to all problem drinkers, regardless of the severity of their disease. In contrast, the Moderation Management program is designed for mild to moderate problem drinkers only. The two programs' guidelines differ, too. Alcoholics Anonymous stresses that problem drinkers must refrain from drinking all alcohol. Moderation Management, however, sets a weekly quota of drinks for participants. Men are limited to fourteen drinks a week, and women are limited to nine. Finally, the two programs' level of acceptance differs significantly. Alcoholics Anonymous, an established program begun in 1935, is widely accepted and rarely criticized. The newer Moderation Management program, created in 1994, has its critics. They charge that its methods do not permit alcoholics to recover from their disease.

a. time order
b. simple listing
c. definition
(d.) comparison and contrast

4. If your country were to institute a draft, men could still apply to the Selective Service System for an exemption.* The Selective Service System classifies men who are exempt according to their particular

---

*exemption: being freed from something required.

circumstances or beliefs. One category of exemptions includes those who serve as religious clergy. Another category applies to individuals who need a hardship deferment.* Someone in this group must prove that military service would cause his family hardship, perhaps because he is the sole supporter or caregiver. A third category is that of the conscientious objector. This group includes people who oppose military training or service because of their moral or religious beliefs. One subcategory of conscientious objectors opposes only training or service requiring the use of arms. These men can fulfill their service obligation in a noncombat position. The other subcategory of conscientious objectors opposes all military positions, both combatant and noncombatant. If approved for exemption, these individuals usually still serve by being placed in jobs that help national interests. Yet another group of men who sometimes qualify for exemption includes aliens* or those who are citizens of two countries at the same time.

a. definition

b. cause and effect

c. comparison and contrast

d. classification

5. A **hospice** is a special program for the terminally ill. Hospices may be housed in medical centers, but they can also exist on their own. Hospice care neither hastens nor postpones death. Simply put, the goal of hospice is to improve the quality of life for those who are dying. A trained staff, supportive volunteers, pleasant surroundings, and a sense of community all help patients cope with anxiety about death. Relatives and friends, even pets, are all allowed to visit a hospice resident at any time. Patients at a hospice make their own decisions about medical treatment and the use of drugs. If they wish, they can reject both. But they can also receive drugs for pain control if they choose. Within the hospice setting, life goes on for the dying.

a. time order

b. simple listing

c. definition

d. cause and effect

*deferment: official postponement of military service.
*aliens: citizens of another country.

▶ **TEST 4**　　　**Recognizing Patterns of Organization**

DIRECTIONS　Circle the appropriate letter to identify the primary pattern in each paragraph.

1. Hetty Howland Green, known as the "Witch of Wall Street" for her skill at picking stocks, devoted her entire life to saving money. In 1834, Hetty was born to a wealthy family who, nevertheless, lived very simply. In 1865, at the age of thirty-one, Hetty inherited $10 million after her father and an aunt died. Two years later, Hetty married Edward Green, but she and her husband agreed to keep their finances separate. For almost fifty years until her death, Hetty built her fortune by investing in railroad stocks, government bonds, and mortgage loans. At the same time she earned the *Guinness Book of World Records* title of "World's Most Miserly Female," Hetty lived in poor housing, dressed in shabby clothes, ate cheap food, and got medical care free at charity clinics. By 1900, when the average family income was $500 a year, Hetty Green's income was $7 million a year. When she died in 1916 at age 81, her estate was worth more than $100 million. Nonetheless, her name had become a synonym for *miser.*

   a. time order
   b. simple listing
   c. definition
   d. cause and effect
   e. comparison and contrast

2. A *prayer labyrinth** is an ancient aid for meditation, but it's being revived by modern spiritual seekers. Unlike a maze—a network of pathways built with high boundaries such as walls or bushes—a labyrinth is laid out with stones, bricks, or paint, usually in a circular pattern that winds toward the center. To use the labyrinth, one simply walks along the path, concentrating on thoughts and prayers. This is how prayer labyrinths were used by some North American peoples such as the Hopi. European Christians also built them during the Middle Ages. Today, there are more than 650 labyrinths in the United States alone, many of them at Episcopal or Catholic parishes.

---

*labyrinth: a complicated structure of interconnected passages.

a. time order

b. simple listing

c. definition

d. cause and effect

e. classification

3. Schools have implemented several strategies to combat the problem of bullying among students. The most successful schools have begun by establishing firm anti-bullying policies. They have educated teachers, staff, students, and parents about bullying behaviors; as a result, everyone is able to recognize bullying when it occurs. In addition, the schools have established clear consequences for bullying and posted this information so that potential bullies will be aware of the risks involved. Schools successful at reducing bullying have also encouraged the reporting of bullying incidents. For example, some schools have set up a "bully hotline" or a "bully box," where people can submit information. Such reporting systems expose problems and identify situations that require the intervention of school officials. Finally, schools committed to getting rid of bullying behaviors have changed the environment in order to reduce opportunities for bullying. They have begun monitoring unsupervised areas like restrooms. They have also tried to reduce the amount of time students spend in less supervised areas. In addition, some schools have also taken steps to separate specific bullies from their victims. In most cases, these initiatives have led to a significant decrease in bullying incidents.

a. time order

b. simple listing

c. definition

d. cause and effect

e. comparison and contrast

4. The United States Coast Guard classifies personal flotation* devices (PFDs) into five different types. Type I PFDs are offshore life jackets that are either inflatable or made of buoyant* material. Preferred in all situations, this type is absolutely necessary in remote or rough waters. The type I jacket tends to be bulky. However, it's the best type

---

*flotation: floating.
*buoyant: capable of floating.

of flotation device for non-swimmers or for someone who is unconscious. That's because it keeps a person turned face-up. Type II PFDs are also inflatable or made of buoyant materials. These life vests are less bulky than type I PFDs. The type II PFD is appropriate for calm or near-shore waters where there's a good chance of a speedy rescue. Type III PFDs are flotation aids of various styles of vests and jackets. They do not prevent the wearer from going face-down in the water, though. Thus they are best for general boating activities in waters where rescue will be quick. Type IV PFDs are throwable devices, such as floating rings and cushions that a person can hold onto until rescue. They should be used only in calm water with heavy boat traffic where help is always nearby. Type V PFDs are made for special conditions or activities. They are not intended for general use. This class of PFDs includes canoe and kayak vests, boardsailing vests, and work vests for commercial vessels, among others.

   a. time order
   b. simple listing
   c. definition
   d. cause and effect
   e. classification

5. Boxing is a brutal and violent sport; nonetheless, many women are still willing to climb into the ring. Some of them participate because of the financial rewards. Not only do female boxers make money for each fight, but the most successful of them also earn money for endorsing commercial products. Other women, like female boxer Laila Ali, are more interested in becoming famous and want to become celebrities. Still others thirst for respect and equality. They want to prove that women, far from being the weaker sex, can be as tough as men. And some simply like the excitement of participating in the sport. As boxer Trina Ortegon put it, "I've never done anything else that's given me such an adrenaline rush."

   a. time order
   b. simple listing
   c. definition
   d. cause and effect
   e. classification

▶ **TEST 5**   **Recognizing Patterns of Organization**

DIRECTIONS   Circle the appropriate letter to identify the primary pattern in each paragraph.

1. Among the various ways corporations can distribute authority, decentralized and centralized organization stand out as two particularly popular and very different methods. With decentralized organization, management tries to spread authority across various levels of the organization. Coca-Cola is a good example of this type of organization. In the past, for instance, all decisions, even those affecting Coke abroad, had to be approved by its Atlanta, Georgia, office. Because this method of decision making cost a good deal of time, Coca-Cola has now decentralized authority and allowed local executives around the world to make decisions. A centralized organization, in contrast, does not even attempt to distribute authority among the various organizational levels. On the contrary, centralized organizations work hard to keep authority restricted to the upper levels of management. Many large companies are based on a centralized method of organization, where decision making stays at the highest level of management and decisions are then passed down to the lower levels. Kmart Corporation and McDonald's are examples of centralized organization.

   a. time order
   b. simple listing
   c. definition
   d. cause and effect
   e. comparison and contrast
   f. classification

2. Progressive muscle relaxation is a technique for relieving stress. The technique goes like this. Once or twice a day, lie down on a soft surface. Then start squeezing and releasing the muscles of each body part. Begin with the right hand. Make a fist and give a good, firm squeeze for three to five seconds. Then go completely limp for ten to twenty seconds. Focus on how the muscles in the hand feel during a state of relaxation. Next, squeeze and release the muscles of the right arm. Repeat this process with the left hand and arm. Move on to the shoulders, shrugging them toward the ears. Then squeeze the jaw

and facial muscles. Continue by moving down the body, concentrating on the chest muscles, the abdominal and back muscles, and then the hips and buttocks. Finally, squeeze and release the muscles down each leg, from the thighs to the calves to the feet. With each session, you'll gain more awareness of muscle tension and how to relieve it.

a. time order

b. simple listing

c. definition

d. cause and effect

e. comparison and contrast

f. classification

3. Bred for their ability to do work for their human owners, working dogs can be divided into four basic categories. *Search and rescue dogs* are used to locate people who are missing, lost, or dead. They are essential to rescue efforts after earthquakes, tornados, or avalanches, but they also track criminals on the run and locate human remains. As their name implies, *police dogs* are used by the police force to keep watch over suspects found at the scene of a crime. They also help in the detection of bombs, explosives, and firearms. Police dogs used in the detection of drugs are specially trained to pick up the scent of narcotics on people and objects. *Assistance and service dogs* help physically or mentally disabled persons in their everyday activities. The most commonly known assistance and service dogs are those used to guide people who are partially sighted or blind. In this category are also dogs trained to hit buttons or push wheelchairs in emergency situations. Unlike assistance and service dogs, *therapy dogs* do not necessarily perform any specific tasks. Their main role is to be a comforting presence. These dogs are used to help specific patient populations such as the aged, ailing children, and those with severe phobias, or fears that have no basis in reality.

a. time order

b. simple listing

c. definition

d. cause and effect

e. comparison and contrast

f. classification

4. There are many theories about the functions of sleep. For example, one theory claims that the major function of sleep is to conserve energy. Another argues that the hunger mechanism is suppressed during sleep, and we sleep in order to conserve food supplies. That means that sleep is a protective mechanism developed early in human evolution. Then there is the theory that because we are most vulnerable, or open to threat, when it's dark, sleep forces us to withdraw from the world and renders us less likely to become a tasty meal for nocturnal animals. Some sleep researchers argue that sleep gives the brain a chance to reorganize and store the information gathered during the day. Apart from those theories, there is also the common belief that sleep helps the body renew its energy.

   a. time order

   b. simple listing

   c. definition

   d. cause and effect

   e. comparison and contrast

   f. classification

▶ **TEST 6** **Recognizing Patterns of Organization**

DIRECTIONS Circle the appropriate letter to identify the primary pattern in each paragraph.

1. When the famous civil rights activist Rosa Parks died in October 2005, she was mourned across the nation. Parks had helped ignite the civil rights movement in December 1955 when she refused to give up her bus seat to a white rider. Parks insisted that she would rather go to jail than be treated with such contempt, and her stubborn refusal encouraged civil rights supporters, black and white, to rally to her cause. Most important, her arrest resulted in a 381-day boycott of the bus system by the black community in Montgomery, Alabama. Not surprisingly, Rosa Parks's heroic action is reported in almost every history book, and it is usually assumed that she was the first black person to take such a stand. But in fact, she was not. In March 1955, fifteen-year-old Claudette Colvin[†] had taken the very same stand, but her act of rebellion has only recently been celebrated. In March 1955, Colvin was told by the driver of her bus that she and her three friends had to give up their seats. The three friends did as they were told. Colvin refused. Unlike Parks, Colvin had had no training in passive resistance and no involvement in the civil rights movement. All she had were her defiance and her courage. Although they did not look like much when she was arrested and taken to jail, they proved to be powerful weapons. With three other women who had been similarly treated, Colvin went to court with future Supreme Court Justice Thurgood Marshall representing the four women. Their legal action resulted in a 1956 Supreme Court ruling, which labeled the segregated bus system unconstitutional. Perhaps because of her age, Colvin's contribution was generally ignored until December 2005 when the Smithsonian opened a traveling exhibit dedicated to honoring Claudette Colvin and other unsung heroes of the civil rights movement.

   a. time order
   b. simple listing
   c. definition
   d. cause and effect

[†]Claudette Colvin is now a retiree living in the Bronx, a borough of New York City.

    e. comparison and contrast

    f. classification

2. By the 1890s, class conflict was evident in practically every area of city life, from mealtime manners to popular entertainment and recreation. As new immigrants flooded the tenements and spilled out into neighborhood streets, it became impossible for native-born Americans to ignore the newcomers' strange religious and social customs. In addition to ethnic differences, there were also class differences. Often poor and from peasant or working-class backgrounds, the immigrants from southern and eastern Europe took unskilled jobs and worked for low wages. The slums and tenements in which they lived had high rates of disease. Middle- and upper-class Americans often responded by moving to fashionable avenues or suburbs and by treating the new arrivals as if they were inferior.

   (Paul Boyer et al., *The Enduring Vision*, 5th ed. © Cengage Learning.)

    a. time order

    b. simple listing

    c. definition

    (d.) cause and effect

    e. comparison and contrast

    f. classification

3. The late, great paintings of Jackson Pollock and Mark Rothko could not be more different. Pollock's are nervous, edgy webs of lines that seem ready to careen off the canvas at any moment, while Rothko's are smooth, peaceful slabs of color that suggest, as the artist meant them to, a world of quiet and calm. However, the two men, considered by many to be among America's greatest artists, did have one thing in common: Fame seemed to bring them nothing but misery. The more famous they became, the more self-destructive they grew. When a *Life* magazine article brought Pollock to the public's attention, he became, almost overnight, the art world's first big superstar. A brawling drunk, Pollock was a tough guy who could make great art, and his fans were fascinated by the seeming contradiction. Painfully embarrassed by his success, which he both craved and shunned, Pollock started drinking around the clock. In 1956, only an hour away from his home, he wrapped his car around a tree and

404 ◆ Chapter 7 Recognizing Patterns of Organization

died instantly. Rothko became famous more slowly, but success took the same toll. The more people recognized his work, the more the shy, overweight Rothko over-ate and swallowed pills washed down with alcohol. In 1970, at the height of his fame, Rothko slashed the veins in his arms and bled to death in his studio.

a. time order

b. simple listing

c. definition

d. cause and effect

e. comparison and contrast

f. classification

4. **Stress** is the body's reaction to unusual demands (physical, environmental, or interpersonal). Stress is particularly acute in the military. As one researcher wrote in 2008, "U.S. soldiers in Iraq can find stress deadlier than the enemy." Stress is often accompanied by irritability, high blood pressure, and depression. Stress is a process rather than a state. For example, a person will experience different levels of stress throughout a divorce. There are, after all, different levels of stress involved in admitting that one's marriage is over, telling the children, leaving the family residence, getting the final decree, and seeing one's ex. These events are not all equally stressful. Getting the final decree, for instance, is probably a good deal less stressful than admitting the marriage is over (Adapted from David Knox and Caroline Schacht, *Choices in Relationships*, 10th ed. © Cengage Learning.)

a. time order

b. simple listing

c. definition

d. cause and effect

e. comparison and contrast

f. classification

5. Conflict can be divided into three categories based on the level of intensity. For instance, in a low-intensity conflict, those involved do not usually seek to destroy one another; instead, they interact in a way that helps resolve the conflict. Where to go for dinner, for example, would be classified as a low-intensity conflict. In a

medium-intensity conflict, winning, rather than compromise, ends the conflict. Competing with a friend to be captain of a sports team is an example of a medium-intensity conflict. In a high-intensity conflict, the goal is to seriously wound or destroy the other person or party. An angry divorce or a war are examples of a high-intensity conflict. (Adapted from Terry Kwai Gamble and Michael W. Gamble, *Contacts*. Boston: Allyn and Bacon, 2004, p. 325.)

a. time order
b. simple listing
c. definition
d. cause and effect
e. comparison and contrast
f. classification

♦ **TEST 7** **Enlarging Your Academic Vocabulary**

DIRECTIONS Circle the letter of the sentence that uses the opening word correctly.

1. **accelerate**

   a. Because the senators could not *accelerate* key provisions of the law, they overwhelmingly voted against it.

   b. The best way to *accelerate* a flu is by staying in bed and drinking plenty of water.

   c. Shifting to a lower gear allows you to *accelerate* faster when you drive a car with a manual transmission.

2. **conformity**

   a. Traditional societies tend to place a high value on *conformity*— being different from the group is not encouraged.

   b. The committee was in such total *conformity*, it could not agree on whether to approve the chairperson's report.

   c. Some physical *conformities* in children can be traced back to bad nutrition and lack of medical care.

3. **precedent**

   a. If elected officials want to avoid even the suspicion of being corrupt, they should not accept *precedents* from their constituents.

   b. She cut her remarks short because she agreed with everything the *precedent* speaker had said.

   c. He attributed his strong sense of justice to the *precedent* set by his parents.

4. **contemporary**

   a. Since the shows aired *contemporary*, they competed for the same viewers.

   b. The painters were *contemporaries*, but differed greatly in the way in which they approached their art.

   c. If a problem is addressed in a *contemporary* manner, it's harder to solve because so many of the solutions are out of date.

5. **predominate**

   a. In the first presidential debate, economic issues *predominated*.

   b. Some parents *predominate* large parts of their estate to their children during their lifetime.

   c. There are people who claim to be able to *predominate* winning lottery numbers.

6. **hypothesis**

   a. A *hypothesis* is an exaggerated thesis.

   b. After getting caught cheating on his taxes, the candidate should not be so *hypothetical* about her opponent's record.

   c. Scientists often proceed by formulating a *hypothesis* and then looking for evidence that does or does not support it.

7. **urban**

   a. *Urban* renewal is a process that aims at bringing new life to run-down neighborhoods.

   b. The author cuts an *urban* figure in his three-piece suit, two-tone shoes, and fedora.

   c. People *urban* to Boston are easy to recognize by their accent.

8. **ironic**

   a. The governor got into trouble because his *ironic* remarks were taken at face value.

   b. The one-cent coin shows an *ironic* image of President Lincoln.

   c. Even adults may appear at Halloween parties in *ironic* costumes.

9. **assumption**

   a. Teachers start with the *assumption* that their students are willing to learn.

   b. In order to hide her modest background, she put on many of the *assumptions* associated with the rich.

   c. The *assumption* of fluids is recommended for a cold.

10. **incidence**

a. The attack on Fort Sumter was the *incidence* that started the Civil War.

b. There is no *incidence* that a full moon increases madness in people.

c. All over the world, clean water and covered sewers dramatically lower the *incidence* of infectious diseases.

Mixing and Matching Organizational Patterns

8

IN THIS CHAPTER, YOU WILL LEARN

● why writers often combine patterns.

● which patterns are most likely to appear together.

● why combining patterns is practically essential in longer readings.

"People seek out patterns to help make sense of information."[1]

At this point, you can identify the six patterns of organization often used by writers. Now let's take that knowledge a step further to work more on longer readings that mix, or combine, patterns.

Pure versus Mixed Patterns

Whether a writer uses a pattern of organization in its pure form or mixes it with others depends on one thing: the main idea. Imagine, for instance, that you're writing a paragraph for a health class. You've been assigned to describe the different types of vegetarians. The main idea could be expressed in a topic sentence like this: "There are four different types of vegetarians." As that topic sentence suggests, the supporting

---

[1]Additional discussion of patterns can be found on http://faculty.washington.edu/ezent/impo.htm, which is also the source of this quotation.

details will fall neatly into a straightforward classification pattern. Take a look:

> There are four different kinds of vegetarians. **Semi-vegetarians** don't eat red meat. They do, however, consume fish, chicken, eggs, milk, and cheese. **Lacto-ovo vegetarians** will consume eggs, milk, and cheese, but they won't eat fish or chicken. **Lacto-vegetarians** will drink milk and eat cheese, but they don't eat eggs or any animal meat. **Vegans** eat no animal flesh or products at all. They eat only fruits, grains, and vegetables.

There's no need for mixing patterns in this paragraph. The main idea can be fully explained through classification.

Now consider the main idea expressed in this topic sentence: "According to economists, there are four different types of unemployment, each with its own specific cause." Do you think that main idea could be developed solely by the classification pattern? You're right: It couldn't. This time around, the author's main idea requires two patterns: classification *and* cause and effect.

> According to economists, there are four different types of unemployment, each with its own specific cause. The first type of unemployment is **seasonal**. Workers in certain industries—such as agriculture, resorts, and retail—are subject to fluctuating demands for their services because of peak and off-peak times in these industries. This type of unemployment is regular, predictable, and relatively short-term. The second type of unemployment is referred to as **frictional**. It is caused by school and college graduates seeking jobs for the first time and by workers changing jobs. These people usually remain unemployed for just a short time while they seek a position. A third type of unemployment is **structural**, caused, for example, by the use of new machinery, such as robots, that can perform simple repetitive tasks. Workers displaced by structural changes often experience long-term unemployment while seeking a job that matches their skills and salary expectations. The last type of unemployment is **cyclical**. This kind is produced by the overall business cycle. Cyclical unemployment increases in recessions;* it decreases during growth periods.

In this case, the main idea has two essential parts. It tells us that (1) there are four different types of unemployment, and (2) each of

---

*recessions: periods of economic downturn.

those types has its own cause. Because of its content, the main idea needs the support of two patterns rather than one.

🔑 READING KEY

◆ The main idea determines the patterns a writer will use. It follows, then, that the main idea is also the best clue to the patterns present in the reading.

> ### IDIOM ALERT: Short shrift
>
> In the Middle Ages, *short shrift* was a brief penance given to a person condemned to death so that the individual could be forgiven for his or her sins. Over time, though, being given *short shrift* came to mean "being given little or no attention," as in the following sentence: "The superintendent was given a list of teacher grievances, but he typically gave it *short shrift*."

VOCABULARY EXTRA

The word *frictional* on page 410 offers a good example of the way words can take on very specialized meanings when used in an academic context. The most common meaning for *frictional* is "relating to the rubbing of one object or surface against another." But that meaning changes dramatically in the context of discussions about unemployment, where *frictional* refers to job changing.

◆ EXERCISE 1   Recognizing Patterns in Paragraphs

DIRECTIONS   Read each passage. Then indicate the pattern or patterns present by circling the appropriate letter or letters. *Note*: Keep in mind that the main idea is the best clue to the pattern or patterns an author will use.

EXAMPLE   One way to classify burns is by their degree of severity. **First-degree burns** are those that affect only the outer layer of skin. They are the most common and least serious type of burn. Although they are red and painful, they do not produce blisters. First-degree burns usually heal on their own in two to five days and leave no scars. A **second-degree burn** occurs when the first layer of skin is burned through, and the second layer is damaged as well. These burns are red, produce blisters, and are very painful. However, they usually heal within three weeks and leave little scarring. The worst type of burn is a **third-degree burn**. This kind of burn damages all of the skin's layers. If the skin's nerve endings are not destroyed, these burns cause a great deal of pain. As third-degree burns heal, they create thick scars. Skin grafting is sometimes necessary to correct the damage.

a. time order
b. simple listing
c.) definition
d.) cause and effect
e. comparison and contrast
f.) classification

EXPLANATION   This paragraph creates categories by referring to the degree of burn severity. Because the severity of a burn is also the effect, the writer needs two patterns: classification *and* cause and effect, with both patterns being equally important. The author also needs the definition pattern to define each kind of burn.

1. By all indications, crows are very, very smart creatures. They are also quite sociable. In fact, there are numerous reports of crows making regular visits to people they have taken a shine to. However, what ever charms crows may possess, history records numerous superstitions related to crows. Most of those superstitions suggest that crows, unlike bluebirds, who are consistently associated with good tidings, bring bad luck. In early New England, for instance, it was believed that two crows flying together was a sign of bad things to come. In Europe, it was thought that crows that didn't make noise were plotting with the devil. The French even had a saying suggesting that evil priests would, after death, turn into crows. The Greeks said "Go to the crows" in the same way we might say "Go to the devil." In parts of England, people used to carry an onion to ward off crows in much the same way people in horror movies carry garlic to keep away vampires. Perhaps the biggest indication of how crows were viewed comes from the superstition that a dead crow in the road brought good luck.

  a. time order

  b. simple listing

  c. definition

  d. cause and effect

  e. comparison and contrast

  f. classification

2. A computerized pool-monitoring system called *Poseidon* is helping lifeguards save people from drowning. The system works like this: First, cameras are installed in the walls of the pool. The cameras monitor the bottom of the pool and transmit images to a computer. The computer then analyzes these images for signs of swimmers in trouble. When it sees images of objects that are sinking or have sunk, it sends a signal to a waterproof pager worn by the lifeguard. The pager alerts the lifeguard to possible trouble. He or she can then dive in to help the victim. To be sure, lifeguards already save many people from drowning. The purpose of the Poseidon system is to increase the speed of those rescues, thereby saving more swimmers from potential harm. Poseidon's supporters also believe it will prevent the severe brain damage that can occur when a swimmer is deprived of oxygen for too long.

  a. time order

  b. simple listing

  c. definition

  d. cause and effect

  e. comparison and contrast

  f. classification

3. Because soccer is still not nearly as popular as baseball and football are in the United States, we have yet to experience what is routine for fans of the sport around the world—soccer violence. Bigger fans of women's soccer than men's, Americans generally think of a soccer match as a time to cheer for their team and get together with friends. But in other countries, soccer is a serious and sometimes deadly pastime. One of the first outbreaks of soccer violence was recorded in 1985 when a match in Belgium ended with thirty-nine people dead. But if anything the trend seems to be growing, especially in countries where people are divided over political issues. As

Unlike soccer fans from many other countries, South Koreans still know how to just enjoy a soccer game.

chances of a peace settlement between Israelis and Palestinians have dwindled, pressure is being placed on the Israeli soccer federation to find a way to calm the violence between Israeli and Palestinian teams, fans, and clubs. The situation is even worse in Egypt now that the dictator Hosni Mubarak has been driven out of office. Those who hated him and those who supported him meet and do battle on the soccer field and in the stands. In 2012, when an anti-Mubarak team played in Port Said, where the former president of Egypt still has supporters, seventy-four people died in a clash between political enemies.

a. time order
b. simple listing
c. definition
d. cause and effect
e. comparison and contrast
f. classification

4. Men and women react differently to widowhood. In general, those who were most dependent on their partners during the marriage report the biggest increase in self-esteem in widowhood. That's largely because they have learned to do the tasks formerly done by their partners. Widows are at higher risk of dying themselves soon

after their partner, either by suicide or natural causes. They are also at higher risk for depression. Some people believe that the loss of a wife presents a more serious problem for a man than the loss of a husband for a woman. This may be because a wife is often a man's only close friend. It also may be that men are usually unprepared to live out their lives alone. Older men are also often ill equipped to handle such routine and necessary tasks as cooking, shopping, and keeping house. Then, too, they may become emotionally isolated from family members when a wife is no longer there to keep family members connected. (Adapted from Robert V. Kail and John C. Cavanaugh, *Human Development*, 5th ed. © Cengage Learning.)

a. time order
b. simple listing
c. definition
d. cause and effect
e. comparison and contrast
f. classification

5. For the last one hundred years, advertisers have both shaped and reflected American society's ideas about femininity. In the postindustrial revolution era of the 1890s through 1920, advertisements were filled with pictures of beautiful, devoted mothers, all of whom bought products that made their homes comfortable, attractive, and safe. The decade of the 1920s, however, was known as the Jazz Age. Women in ads from that time openly longed for glamour, youth, and sex appeal. Homemakers were not highly visible. By the 1930s, when America was in the grip of economic Depression, advertisers' message to women was, "Looking good can defeat financial hardship." After America's entry into World War II in 1941, women were needed in the workplace. As a result, ads featured women like Rosie the Riveter,[†] because women were needed to serve their country. With the war over, women in the 1950s were encouraged to again focus on homemaking. But the 1960s and 1970s brought political change and challenged traditional notions of femininity. Quick to respond to a cultural shift, ads from these decades portrayed women using beauty and household products in order to discover

[†]Rosie the Riveter: a popular figure in a World War II campaign designed to encourage women to become factory workers.

their identity. By the 1980s and 1990s, the women in advertisements were decidedly feminist: confident, career-oriented, and successful. But, as always, they remained beautiful. Today's advertising message remains much the same. Women are told they can have it all as long as they wear the right clothes and makeup.

a. time order
b. simple listing
c. definition
d. cause and effect
e. comparison and contrast
f. classification

VOCABULARY EXTRA

Although we now use the word *cynic* to describe someone who mistrusts the motives of others, the original Cynics (there's another eponym for you) were Greek philosophers who believed that striving for virtue was the essential goal in life. Unfortunately, in their pursuit of virtue, Cynics often pointed out the faults of others. Thus, the word came to mean "suspicious and critical of others."

Combining Patterns in Longer Readings

If paragraphs need to combine patterns, so, too, do longer readings. In fact, while paragraphs frequently rely on a single pattern, longer readings seldom do. Thus, it makes sense for readers to be on the lookout for two or more patterns when a reading extends beyond a single paragraph.

For an illustration of patterns combined in longer pieces of text, read the selection that follows. Look closely at the stated main idea, which in longer readings is called the **thesis statement**, because the main idea may require several sentences to be fully expressed or stated. Like the topic sentence, the thesis statement sums up the point of a longer reading.

Try to identify the patterns used to clarify and explain the main idea expressed in the underlined thesis statement shown on page 417. As always the main idea offers a clue. However, in longer readings so too does the title. The title is often a clue to the organizational patterns used. It's also a clue to the main idea.

It Pays to Imitate Mother Nature

The title suggests positive effects of imitating Mother Nature, so perhaps cause and effect is in play.

Note the presence of the word *ways*. It suggests simple listing.

Here are the first two examples of the way nature can help meet human needs.

Now comes the third way.

In the description of how the lotus stays clean, you can see hints of the process pattern.

In paragraph 6, the writer makes fuller use of the process pattern, so consider whether or not you need to remember the steps described.

Probably not, since the key word is *ways*; all the reader wants is to be able to explain the "ways" humans mimic nature.

1   Biomimicry comes from *bios*, meaning "life," and *mimesis*, meaning "to imitate." It is a fairly new science that studies nature for ways to answer the needs of humans. According to author and biomimicry expert Janine Benyus, nature has already invented many processes and products far superior to what humans have created. Benyus says that animals, plants, and microbes are the "consummate* engineers." They have discovered through trial and error what works and what doesn't. Most important, they have figured out what *lasts*.

2   Two examples of biomimicry are the airplane and the telephone. The Wright brothers studied birds to learn how they fly. Inventor Alexander Graham Bell imitated the human tongue and eardrum to create his original telephone speaker and receiver.

3   Velcro is another famous example of biomimicry. One summer day in 1948, Swiss inventor George de Mestral took his dog for a hike. They both returned from their walk covered in burrs. De Mestral studied one of the burrs under his microscope and discovered it was covered with tiny hooks. The hooks grabbed the loops in the fabric of the clothing and stuck.

4   From studying the burrs, De Mestral got the idea to develop a hook and loop fastener made of nylon. He called it Velcro, a combination of the words *velour* and *crochet*. In 1955, he patented his design. Today, of course, Velcro is a multimillion-dollar company.

5   Yet another example of a product conceived through biomimicry is a house paint called Lotusan. This paint mimics the self-cleaning properties of the lotus flower's leaves. German botanist Dr. Wilhelm Barthlott discovered this process when he noticed that a lotus leaf is covered with tiny points. When a speck of dirt lands on the leaf, it perches atop those points. Then, as water flows over the leaf, it easily picks up the dirt and carries it away. Lotusan is guaranteed to stay clean for five years without washing.

6   In the world of biomimicry, another major goal is to recreate spider silk. This substance is five times as strong as steel, yet remains light and elastic. Thus researchers are studying how spiders spin silk. So far, they know only that spiders first eat and digest insects for protein. Glands in the spider's body then add water to the proteins to create a wet solution. When the spider squirts this wet solution through a tiny opening, the soluble* proteins turn into an insoluble fiber, a strand of silk. This last step of the process is the secret scientists hope to be able to unlock and duplicate.

*consummate: best, most perfect.
*soluble: capable of being dissolved.

The main idea here is expressed in the first two sentences of the reading, which make up the thesis statement. We can paraphrase that thesis statement like this: "Scientists use biomimicry to create new products modeled on the natural world." If you look over the remaining paragraphs in the reading, you'll see the author uses four different organizational patterns to make that point: (1) simple listing to identify the products mimicking the natural world, (2) definition to explain what biomimicry is, (3) sequence of dates and events to describe its development, and (4) process to describe how spiders spin silk.

O─╥ READING KEYS

◆ When a reading extends beyond a paragraph, expect a combination of patterns rather than a single one.

◆ In longer readings, the sentence or sentences expressing the main idea are called the *thesis statement.*

◆ **EXERCISE 2   Titles and Patterns**

DIRECTIONS   What organizational pattern or patterns would you predict based on the thesis statements that follow?

1. Obesity in infants can be detected in babies as young as six months. However, it's only recently that doctors have begun to understand its causes.

   a. comparison and contrast

   b. cause and effect

   c. time order

Children as young as six months can be classified as obese.

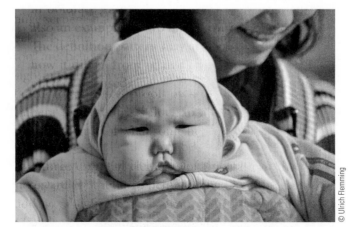

© Ulrich Flemming

2. According to the Big Bang Theory, the universe began in an instant as energy moved outward from a single point.

    a. cause and effect
    b. time order
    c. classification

3. Drugs are usually grouped into several different categories depending on how they affect the body.

    a. cause and effect
    b. time order
    c. classification

4. Stem cells self-renew. They divide and produce more stem cells. For that reason, researchers believe that stem cells hold the secret to creating new body parts that can replace those that are damaged or diseased.

    a. definition
    b. time order
    c. cause and effect

5. The Kurds of Iraq are a stubborn and determined minority, who inhabit parts of Iraq, Syria, and Turkey. Despite centuries of attempts to enslave them, they refuse to give up their independence. The Kurds survived even Saddam Hussein's attempt to annihilate them with poison gas.

    a. cause and effect
    b. time order
    c. definition

Kurdistan, home of the Kurds, includes parts of Iraq, Syria, and Turkey.

© Ulrich Flemming

6. Charles Darwin and Alfred Wallace discovered the theory of evolution at about the same time. But they arrived at it in vastly different ways.

   a. cause and effect

   b. comparison and contrast

   c. classification

Patterns and the Implied Main Idea

In the next reading, the main idea is implied: "Started thousands of years ago by Greece's King Iphitos, the Olympic Games continue to this day; but although some similarities remain, the modern Olympics differ a good deal from the original." Notice now how the author uses three patterns—comparison and contrast, sequence of dates and events, and classification—to develop that point.

Just a glance at the title and opening paragraph should suggest a time order pattern tracing a sequence of events.

The dates and events continue but now you're learning about why the games were revived, meaning cause and effect is coming into play.

The topic is splitting into two, so start thinking about comparison and contrast.

Notice all the time order transitions

The Olympic Games: Past and Present

1   Around 824 BCE, Greece's King Iphitos began a movement to establish what became the Olympic Games. As a result of Iphitos's efforts, the first Olympic Games were held in Greece in 776 BCE. Thereafter, they occurred every four years as a part of a religious festival, a period when all fighting and hostilities within the Greek world ceased. These ancient games continued for twelve consecutive centuries. In 394 CE, they were abolished by the Byzantine emperor Theodosius.

2   In 1896, the games were officially revived by avid* sportsman Pierre de Fredy, the Baron de Coubertin, who believed that sports could bring together nations from all over and thereby encourage world peace. Coubertin organized a meeting in Paris in 1894. There, an international group of delegates planned the first modern Olympic Games. These games took place in Athens in 1896. The games have occurred every four years since, except for the years during World Wars I and II.

3   Until 1924, only the Olympic Summer Games existed. Not until 1924 did the first Olympic Winter Games take place in France. Before that, the figure skating and ice hockey competitions were part of the Summer Games. Beginning in 1924, though, these sports joined others, such as skiing and bobsledding, to become the Winter Games. Now, Olympic sports are classified as either a summer or winter event. The Olympic Summer Games

---

*avid: enthusiastic.

that start both sentences and paragraphs. That means time order has to be a significant pattern in this reading.

Notice here how the reading is starting to emphasize then and now. So again, start looking for points of comparison and contrast.

include, among others, sports such as baseball, basketball, boxing, diving, field hockey, gymnastics, soccer, and track and field. The Olympic Winter Games include alpine skiing, biathlon, bobsled, cross-country skiing, curling, figure skating, ice hockey, luge, Nordic combined, ski jumping, snowboarding, and speed skating.

4 Over time, the Winter Games have added many new sports that were not part of the original games. But the Summer Games, too, have expanded to include many more sports than were part of the ancient events. Like the original Olympic Games, the modern games include boxing, running, jumping, discus, and javelin. However, the modern games incorporate many newer sports, too. There are now thirty-seven major sport categories—from archery to yachting—and two hundred medal events for the Olympic Summer and Winter Games.

5 Not surprisingly, the games have grown from a one-day affair to one that lasts sixteen days each time it is held. Yet despite those changes, some important similarities between the ancient and modern games remain. For one thing, both the past and present games have inspired young athletes to strive to be the best in their sports. Also, both past and present games continue to draw many different nations together in the spirit of peaceful competition.

Once you recognize the patterns present in a reading, it's time to decide which of those patterns are essential to explaining the main idea. If you know that, you're in a much better position to decide what's important information and what's not.

Deciding What's Important

In the Olympics reading, the comparison and contrast pattern is central to developing the author's main idea, which stresses differences and similarities between the Olympics past and present. Thus, it's important to know how the ancient and modern games are similar or different. However, the dates and events pattern is also important. After all, the main idea focuses on changes taking place over time. Therefore, the order of events over time is critical to understanding how the Olympics have changed or stayed the same.

The classification pattern introduced in paragraph 3 is probably the least significant pattern. It doesn't contribute all that much to the main idea. After all, it's possible to understand how the games developed and evolved without knowing exactly which activities are part of the

Summer Games and which ones belong to the Winter Games. In fact, you can generally rely on common sense to figure out which activities make up the Summer Olympics and which ones the Winter Olympics.

It's Always the Thought That Counts the Most

As the previous example showed, *the importance of a pattern depends on its relationship to the main idea*. Yes, one reading may consist of several patterns. But that doesn't mean that every element of each pattern carries equal weight. If a pattern is central to explaining the main idea, pay special attention to the information related to the pattern. If a pattern does *not* contribute much to the main idea, it doesn't deserve the same degree of attention.

To see a specific example of how the various patterns in a reading are not all equally significant, read the following selection. As you read, ask yourself these two questions: (1) What patterns of organization does the author use and (2) Which patterns are central to developing the main idea?

The Placebo Effect

1   The word *placebo* is a centuries-old term that is derived from the Latin phrase for "I shall please." The word entered medical terminology in the nineteenth century to describe a medicine or procedure administered to please or calm, rather than cure, a patient. There are two types of placebos: inert (or inactive) placebos and active placebos. Inert placebos do not cause any action within the body. Active placebos do have effects of some kind, but they are not specific to the disease for which they are given.

2   Placebos are used in clinical trials[†] designed to test the effectiveness of a particular treatment. In clinical trials, some participants in the study get real treatment, and some get a placebo. None of the participants knows what he or she is getting. In this way, researchers can test the benefits of a drug or procedure. Yet, astonishing as it may seem, some clinical trials have shown that patients who are given placebos—active or inert—often seem to improve. For example, in one trial testing the worth of a specific surgical procedure, doctors anesthetized all the subjects. But in half of them, the physicians did no more than nick the skin. They performed no surgery, whereas they actually operated on the other half of the group. As it turns out, both groups claimed to feel better after "surgery."

Thesis Statement

[†]clinical trials: studies of a drug or treatment that are based on direct observation.

3   In another study of 2,000 heart attack patients suffering from irregular heartbeat, the death rate was cut in half for both those who took the real drug *and* those who took the placebo. Similarly, studies of pain-relief drugs have shown that some patients who take a placebo experience maximum relief one to two hours after treatment. In other words, they have exactly the same reaction as patients who actually received the real drug. In another study, 70 percent of depressed patients improved after a few weeks even when they received only a placebo. This phenomenon has come to be known as the *placebo effect*.

4   Why does this placebo effect occur? Researchers believe that expectations play a central role. People who expect to improve are more likely to do just that. Another cause of the placebo effect may well be the kind of medical care that patients receive while participating in a study. Just like patients who get the real drug, patients who take a placebo are immersed* in a healing environment. This environment includes caring, responsive doctors and nurses, regular examinations, and many opportunities to discuss their illness and courses of treatment. Some psychologists believe that this nurturing, or caring, atmosphere promotes recovery, regardless of whether treatments are real.

5   Therefore, researchers wonder if the use of placebos could eventually lead to reductions in the dosage of actual medications. In other words, a patient in pain might be first treated with a placebo. If it worked, the real medication would not be prescribed. Substituting placebos for actual medication could result in lower costs and fewer side effects for patients. Of course, the medical community must first resolve the ethical dilemma involved in the use of placebos. If doctors tell patients they are prescribing a placebo, the placebo effect is lost. If doctors tell patients that a placebo is real medicine, however, they are being dishonest. Despite these ethical questions, some scientists still believe that placebo treatments could benefit those who suffer from illnesses for which there is no other treatment.

(Source of studies: Walter A. Brown, M.D., with Barbara Severs, "Placebos: Fooling the Body to Heal Itself," *USA Today Magazine*, July 1999, pp. 32–33.)

In this selection, the author needs three different patterns to develop the thesis statement. She clearly needs the definition pattern to make sure readers understand what a placebo is. However, cause and effect is the most essential pattern. That's because the message or main idea

---

*immersed: completely covered or involved.

of the reading revolves around a cause and effect relationship that, if diagrammed, would look like this:

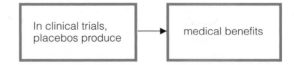

There is also a comparison and contrast pattern in paragraph 1. It's here that the author contrasts active and inert placebos. However, this pattern is the least significant because the reading suggests that placebos of both types have had some kind of healing effect. The difference between active and inert placebos doesn't seem to play much of a role in that outcome.

⊶ READING KEYS

◆ Once you identify the patterns used in a reading, identify the elements of each one. Then decide how many of those elements are essential to the main idea. These are the ones to store in your memory or record in your notes.

◆ The importance of a pattern depends on its relationship to the main idea.

◆ EXERCISE 3   Recognizing Patterns in Longer Readings

DIRECTIONS   Read each selection and look closely at the underlined thesis statement. Then circle the letters of the patterns present. There might be two, three, or even four.

EXAMPLE

Saving Our Children

Two dates in the opening paragraph are a strong signal that time order will play a role in this reading.

Notice as well the two topics and the use of the word *similar*. These are clues to comparison and contrast at work.

1   The fates of Adam Walsh and Amber Hagerman were tragically similar. Both were small children when they were kidnapped and murdered. In 1981, when Adam was six years old, a stranger abducted him from a department store in Florida. Sixteen days later, he was found dead, and his killer was not identified until 2008.[†] In 1996, nine-year-old Amber went out to ride her bicycle around her Texas neighborhood and vanished. Four days later, she, too, was found dead. The person who killed Amber was never brought to justice.

[†]According to Florida police, it wasn't new evidence that finally solved the case. It was a re-analysis of preexisting evidence. The loss of his son turned the boy's father, John, into an advocate of missing children. He co-founded the National Center for Missing & Exploited Children.

2   From these and other abductions, police learned that speed is essential in rescuing a kidnapped child. According to the Justice Department, three out of every four victims are killed within three hours of being taken. Consequently, parents, law enforcement officials, and organizations that advocate for children worked together to create two systems for responding quickly when a child is abducted. Code Adam, named after Adam Walsh, is a notice distributed throughout the building from which a child has disappeared. An Amber Alert is a notice to the general public about a kidnapped child. AMBER is not only the system's namesake but also an acronym for America's Missing Broadcast Emergency Response.

3   A Code Adam alert attempts to prevent an abduction from being completed in a public place like a store. If a parent or guardian reports a missing child to an employee or official on the premises, a five-step sequence is set in motion. The first step involves developing a detailed description of the missing child. Next, the person in charge uses the public address system to page everyone in the building and announces a "Code Adam" followed by the child's description. This alert signals the building's employees to initiate the third step. Designated employees go to the building's exits and begin monitoring everyone who leaves. At the same time, most of the other employees begin searching the premises for a child resembling the description. If the child is not found within ten minutes, someone calls the police. The fourth step depends upon who is with the child when he or she is found. If the child is alone and unharmed, he or she is reunited with the parent or guardian. If the child is with someone other than the parent or guardian, employees try to prevent that person from leaving without putting themselves, other staff members, or customers in danger. In the fifth and final step, the incident is concluded by a "Code Adam cancelled" announcement on the public address system.

4   If the Code Adam fails or if the child is abducted from some place other than a building, police issue an Amber Alert after confirming that the child has been abducted and hasn't run away. Next, they determine whether the child is in danger of being harmed or killed. Then, they produce descriptions of the child, the suspected abductor, and the suspect's vehicle. Finally, they distribute a notice to the public via television, radio, the Internet, and electronic highway signs. This notice includes details about the child's description and abduction location. The public is asked to immediately report any sighting of the child or abductor.

5   Both systems have successfully recovered many abducted children. The Code Adam program, which is now in place in thousands of stores across the country, has also foiled numerous child abductions.

Cause and effect starts to enter the picture when the author begins to explain how the right system can prevent an abduction.

Here you have a definition of a key term, *Code Adam*.

To describe how the system works, the author has to explain a sequence of steps.

The phrase "five-step sequence" is a dead giveaway to this pattern, as are phrases like "the first step."

Here again, transitions like *next, then,* and *finally* suggest that sequence of steps plays a big role.

(a.) time order

b. simple listing

(c.) definition

(d.) cause and effect

(e.) comparison and contrast

f. classification

EXPLANATION   In this case, the author needs four different patterns to develop the main idea. The time order pattern is essential for telling the stories of Adam and Amber and for explaining how the two response systems work. The definition pattern is needed to clearly state what the terms *Code Adam* and *Amber Alert* mean. The cause and effect pattern explains why the two systems were created and, in the final paragraph, the results of implementing them. Comparison and contrast is important only to point out a few similarities between Adam and Amber, so it's the least important of the four patterns.

1. Kwanzaa

1   Kwanzaa is a nonreligious African-American celebration. It takes place from December 26 to January 1 each year. The name Kwanzaa comes from the Swahili phrase "*matunda ya kwanza*," which means "first fruits." This festival originated in ancient Egypt and Nubia, when African people gathered to celebrate the harvest. Since then, the holiday has been observed by numerous African kingdoms and tribes, both large and small. In 1966, the celebration was introduced to America by civil rights activist Dr. Maulana Karenga, professor and chair of the Department of Black Studies at California State University at Long Beach. Since then, Kwanzaa has spread across the United States, becoming a mainstream African-American holiday tradition.

2   Dr. Karenga conceived of this celebration in the context of the Black Liberation Movement of the 1960s. He hoped it would encourage African Americans to reconnect with their African heritage. He also hoped the holiday would strengthen community and family ties. Dr. Karenga believed Kwanzaa celebrations would promote the values that encourage personal and professional achievement. For this reason, Kwanzaa rituals in America emphasize seven principles: unity, self-determination, collective work and responsibility, cooperative economics, purpose, creativity, and faith.

3   During the seven-day Kwanzaa celebration, participants devote one day to each of these seven principles. Observers, often wearing traditional African clothing, gather together each evening. They greet each other with

the phrase "*Habari gani*," which is Swahili for "What's new?" The answer is the Swahili word for the principle of the day. Then participants light one or more of seven candles in a special candelabra called a kinara. Each candle represents one of the seven principles. Next, participants discuss how that day's principle affects their lives. The ritual may also include the exchange of small gifts; a meal of traditional African foods; and musical performances, dances, or poetry readings. The evening ends with the participants calling out "*Harambee*" (Swahili for "let's all pull together") seven times. On the final night of the holiday, friends and relatives join in a feast called the *Karamu*.

4   Those who participate in Kwanzaa say they cherish the opportunity to remember and reflect upon their past and to set goals for their future. They like the celebration's emphasis on family and community, noting that the rituals leave them with a positive feeling of black pride. Kwanzaa is a cultural holiday, not a religious one, so most people observe it in addition to Christmas. However, Kwanzaa is also viewed by many in the black community as an antidote to the increasingly commercial Christmas season.

a. time order
b. simple listing
c. definition
d. cause and effect
e. comparison and contrast
f. classification

2. Unions and the Government

1   Unionization in state and local government developed and flourished in the 1960s and 1970s, some thirty years after the heyday of private-sector unionism. During the 1960s, the number of public-employee union members more than tripled. Why the sudden growth? In retrospect, several reasons are apparent.

2   First, the rise of unionism in government was spurred by the realization by state and local employees that they were underpaid and otherwise maltreated in comparison to their counterparts in the private sector who had progressed so well with unionization and collective bargaining. Second, the bureaucratic and impersonal nature of work in large government organizations encouraged unionization to preserve the dignity of the workers. A third reason for the rise of state and local unionism was the employees' lack of confidence in many civil service systems. Not only were pay and benefits inadequate, but grievance processes were controlled by

management, employees had little or no say in setting personnel policies, and "merit" selection, promotion, and pay often were fraught with management favoritism. Fourth, public employees got caught up in the 1960s' fervor of social change. They saw other groups in American society winning concessions from government authorities and they decided to join in.

3   Perhaps most important, the growth of unions in government was promoted by a significant change in the legal environment of labor relations. The rights of public employees to join unions and bargain collectively with management were guaranteed by several U.S. Supreme Court rulings, state legislation, local ordinances, and various informal arrangements that became operative during the 1960s and 1970s. Wisconsin was the first state to permit collective bargaining for state workers, in 1959. Today, forty-two states specifically allow at least one category of state or local government employees to engage in collective bargaining. (Ann Bowman and Richard Kearney, *State and Local Government*, 5th ed. © Cengage Learning.)

a. time order
b. simple listing
c. definition
d. cause and effect
e. comparison and contrast
f. classification

WEB QUEST/CLASS ACTION

What percentage of the population belonged to a union in the mid-1950s? What percentage is unionized today? Come to class prepared to discuss the trend in union membership and perhaps explain why you would or would not join a union.

35 Percent in the mid 50s
11.1 Percent today

Problably Not

◆ **Common Combinations**

There's no strict rule as to how organizational patterns combine. In fact, they can combine in any number of ways. However, some combinations are more likely to occur than others. If, for example, you encounter a reading organized around dates and events, check to see if the cause and effect pattern is also present. These two patterns are likely to appear together. For an illustration, look at the following reading. Note how the sequence of dates and events pattern combines with cause and effect to develop the underlined thesis statement.

The Legacy of P. T. Barnum

1   In the nineteenth century, Phineas Taylor (P. T.) Barnum made a name for himself as a showman while almost single-handedly transforming the taste of the American public—and not necessarily for the better.

2   Born in 1810, Barnum, the son of a wealthy businessman, launched his entertainment career when he was just 25. It was at that point that he took under his wing an elderly black woman named Joice Heth. Heth claimed to be 166 years old. She also claimed to have been George Washington's nurse. Whether or not Barnum believed her story, he billed her as a "living mummy" and made himself a small fortune.

3   After his success with Heth and similar attractions—like the three-foot-tall man Tom Thumb—Barnum bought his own museum in 1841. He packed it with oddities like the skeleton of a mermaid—probably a fish tail attached to a monkey's skeleton—and made the museum into a national attraction. And there were more successes to come. In 1881 Barnum joined James A. Bailey to form a three-ring traveling circus that became the "Barnum & Bailey Greatest Show on Earth."

4   Barnum died only ten years after launching the circus tour. But by that time he had changed the face of American entertainment. More than anyone else, P. T. Barnum had whetted* the public's appetite for the sensational. He had titillated* his audiences with bearded ladies, pretzel-limbed contortionists, and the conjoined twins Chang and Eng. Even when some of Barnum's so-called freaks of nature, like the gorilla-man dressed in a fur suit, turned out to be frauds, the public applauded and called for more.

In this reading, the sequence of dates and events pattern is necessary to trace some key events in Barnum's career. But the cause and effect pattern is also necessary because Barnum's successful career (the cause) powerfully influenced public taste (the effect).

---

*whetted: stimulated.
*titillated: excited.

As you might expect, the two patterns in the Barnum reading are not the only two that readily combine. Here are some other common combinations:

Patterns That Frequently Combine
◆

Time Order with Cause and Effect

Time Order with Definition

Cause and Effect with Simple Listing

Cause and Effect with Comparison and Contrast

Classification with Comparison and Contrast

Knowing that classification and comparison and contrast are likely to team up doesn't mean they always go hand in hand. Still, if you recognize the classification pattern, it's smart to be on the lookout for signs of comparison and contrast. The faster you recognize which patterns are present, the quicker you can make decisions about what's important and what's not.

⊶ READING KEY

◆ If you spot a pattern that commonly combines with another pattern, check to see if the other pattern is present. That way, you can speed up the process of deciding what's important.

ROUNDING UP THE KEYS

Here is a list of all the reading keys introduced in the chapter. Use them to review for the test on page 440. If a particular reading key doesn't make sense on its own, go back to the page where it appeared and review the section preceding it.

READING KEY: Pure versus Mixed Patterns

◆ The main idea determines the patterns a writer will use. It follows, then, that the main idea is also the best clue to the patterns present in the reading. (p. 411)

READING KEYS: Combining Patterns in Longer Readings

◆ When a reading extends beyond a paragraph, expect a combination of patterns rather than a single one. (p. 418)

◆ In longer readings, the sentence or sentences expressing the main idea are called the *thesis statement*. (p. 418)

READING KEYS: Deciding What's Important

◆ Once you identify the patterns used in a reading, identify the elements of each one. Then decide how many of those elements are essential to the main idea. These are the ones to store in your memory or record in your notes. (p. 424)

◆ The importance of a pattern depends on its relationship to the main idea. (p. 424)

READING KEY: Common Combinations

◆ If you spot a pattern that commonly combines with another pattern, check to see if the other pattern is present. That way, you can speed up the process of deciding what's important. (p. 430)

Ten More Words for Your Academic Vocabulary

1. **prototype:** original, first, or ideal model from which other similar forms are developed or copied

   For the Wright brothers, birds in flight were the original *prototypes* for the airplane.

2. **generate:** produce or create

   In less than two days, the architect was able to *generate* the first set of sketches for the competition, but he wasn't sure he could keep up the pace.

3. **harmony:** agreement in feeling or opinion, a pleasing arrangement of parts; in music, a simultaneous combination of tones that are pleasing to the ear

   (1) There was little *harmony* at the conference since everyone there wanted to win the same software contract. (2) At the turn of the nineteenth century, composers began rejecting *harmony* in favor of music marked by the clashing of tones.

4. **predator:** an animal who survives by taking the lives of other creatures; a person or organization that exploits others for personal or corporate benefit

   (1) The zoo was not about to combine *predators* with non-*predators*. (2) Wells Fargo was one of the banks accused of *predatory* lending that led to the mortgage crisis of 2008.

5. **syntax:** word order

   English *syntax* relies heavily on the subject-verb sentence pattern.

6. **lucid:** having or showing the ability to think, speak, or write clearly

   As soon as they got to a lower altitude, the hiker became *lucid* and was able to explain how she got stranded.

7. **deprivation:** experiencing a lack of things that are considered physical or emotional necessities

   When they arrived in Kingstown, South Africa, they could not believe how cheerful people were in the midst of extreme *deprivation*.

8. **collaboration:** working together in a group or as partners; to cooperate with those who are considered enemies

   (1) For several different reasons, schools are currently stressing activities that require *collaboration*. (2) During World War II, French women accused of *collaboration* with the Nazis had their heads shaved.

9. **confiscate:** take over or seize by means of authority

   After she hadn't made a car payment for six months, the repo man came to her house and *confiscated* her car.

10. **tangible:** capable of being seen or touched

    When the Internal Revenue Service went after the actor for back taxes, the first thing they did was confiscate his *tangible* assets—his cars, houses, furniture, and jewelry.

◆ **EXERCISE 4**   **Making Academic Vocabulary Familiar**

   DIRECTIONS   Each sentence uses a more conversational or simpler version of the words below. At the end of the sentence, fill in the blank with the more academic word that could replace the underlined word or phrase in the sentence.

prototype	harmony	syntax	deprivation	confiscate
generate	predatory	lucid	collaborative	tangible

1. The diplomat's English was almost perfect; only occasionally did the odd word order of his sentences reveal that he was Hungarian rather than American. ___Syntax___

2. The engineer's description of his new machine impressed the company owners, but they wanted to study the basic model before they went any further with contract negotiations. ___Prototype___

3. The anger in the room was so intense, it was almost <u>capable of being touched</u>. _tangible_

4. <u>Fraudulent</u> lending practices are designed to make the borrower default on a loan so that the lender can take over the borrower's assets. _~~confiscate~~ predatory_

5. Once the patient was taken off the medication, his speech was as <u>clear and understandable</u> as it had been prior to hospitalization. _Lucid_

6. The children were proud of their <u>working together as a group</u>. _Collaborative_

7. In the wake of the hurricane, the once thriving community experienced severe <u>hardship</u>. _deprivation_

8. Many museums are being forced to return artwork that <u>was taken over</u> by the Nazis during World War II. _Confiscate_

9. The senator's comment on rape <u>produced</u> a flood of angry emails from people all over the country. _Generated_

10. What surprised everyone was the fact that the cat and mouse were living in <u>a state of complete friendship and agreement</u>. _harmony_

DIGGING DEEPER The *Kursk's* Tragic End

Looking Ahead The *Kursk* was a Russian submarine that disappeared into the sea. For a while, there was hope that the crew could be rescued. But time ran out.

1 On the morning of Saturday, August 12, 2000, the nuclear submarine *Kursk* was engaged in naval exercises deep in the Barents Sea just off the coast of Norway. Suddenly, at 11:28 a.m., the *Kursk* was ripped apart by two explosions that sent the ship plummeting even deeper into the Barents' murky waters. The commander of Russia's northern fleet, Admiral Vyacheslav Popov, knew immediately that there had been explosions in the area where the *Kursk* was located. Still, he did not investigate the ship's whereabouts. Instead, he put rescue vessels on immediate alert. Then, strangely, he waited more than eleven hours to dispatch them. During that time, Popov made no attempt to establish radio contact with the sunken sub. As a result, it took almost a full day for the submarine to be discovered lying at the bottom of the sea. Apparently following the admiral's example, navy spokespeople did not announce that a mishap had taken place until two days after the ship's sudden slide into the deep.

2 Normally, the bottom of the Barents is a dark and silent place. Yet, in the first few days after the *Kursk's* descent, there were some hopeful sounds. Electronic listening devices used in the rescue effort picked up what seemed to be the *tap, tap, tap* of a hammer knocking on a pipe. Rescuers assumed that a sailor still alive on the sub was trying to make contact. A nearby vessel even claimed to have picked up the message "SOS … water." But by Wednesday, August 16, no more sounds came from the *Kursk*. It was only at this point that the Russian government asked Norway and Britain for help. Three days later, on August 19, a week after the ship went down, fully equipped rescue teams arrived from both countries. Tragically for the more than 100 men trapped inside the doomed submarine, help had come too late.

3 In the first days following the tragedy, Russia's state-controlled televised news desperately tried to convince the families of those on board the *Kursk*, as well as the general public, that every possible rescue effort was being made. Yet, at the same time, newspaper journalists were boldly insisting that international help should have been requested immediately. Even worse, headlines like "Whose Honor Is Sinking in the Barents Sea?" suggested that the Russian government had refused to ask for help out of a misguided sense of pride. If the government couldn't save the ship on its own, it may have been unwilling to make that admission to the world.

4   As a result of the newspaper coverage of the *Kursk*'s horrible plight, grief and outrage swept the country. Everyone wanted answers to the same two questions: Why had the *Kursk* dropped to the bottom of the Barents in the first place? Why hadn't the Russian government immediately asked for international help in the rescue attempt? The questions grew louder and angrier when it became obvious that both navy and government officials had been lying all along. Navy officials had claimed that radio communication had been established and that cables dropped from the surface were providing the ship with both electricity and oxygen. Neither claim was true. Russia's president, Vladimir Putin, who had been on vacation when the ship went down, insisted that everything that could be done was being done. Yet that was clearly not the case.

5   Even after the *Kursk* was fully lifted from the bottom of the Barents in 2001, both questions remained unanswered. Some experts believed fuel leaks aboard the *Kursk* ignited the explosions that sent crew members to their doom. Others pointed out that two of the soldiers in charge of the *Kursk*'s torpedoes were recent graduates of submarine courses. Thus, the explosions may have resulted from human error. One scenario suggested that crew members tried to expel a missile that failed to fire as expected. Instead, it remained inside its torpedo tube and exploded on board. That explosion then generated the second.

6   There's also more than one possible answer as to why the Russian government did not ask for help sooner. One explanation is that several important members of Russia's military were old-style cold warriors.[†] They might well have feared that bringing in outsiders could reveal state secrets to the West—the cardinal sin of cold-war thinking. Some Moscow analysts openly wondered if members of the old guard had kept the details of the disaster from President Putin himself. Otherwise, there is no satisfactory explanation as to why Putin first discussed the crisis some three days after the *Kursk* had sunk. Moreover, when Putin finally acknowledged the *Kursk*'s plight, he made a terrible mistake. He appeared on television looking tanned and relaxed. Wearing a white, open-necked golf shirt, he acted like a man still on vacation. This is hardly the image a president wants to convey when speaking to the public about a national tragedy. The suspicion is that Putin may not have been aware of how bad the situation really was. Navy commanders may have kept him in the dark, just as they did the general public. Sadly, their secrecy seems to have only perpetuated a dangerous and potentially tragic situation.

[†]cold warriors: During the 1950s, these were the people who believed that the United States and the Soviet Union were ready to go to war at any moment.

7 In the fall of 2003, just three years after the *Kursk* tragedy, severe weather damaged another Russian nuclear submarine and sent it hurtling to the bottom of the Barents Sea. Rescuers who arrived on the scene were able to rescue one crew member. They found another one already dead and floating in the cold sea water. On the sea floor, seven crew members were trapped in the sub. Like the sailors on the *Kursk*, their rescue was impossible.

8 There was a difference, though; this time, officials spoke out about the causes of the tragedy. Russia's navy chief, Admiral Viktor Kravchenko, complained that during ship operations "all the imaginable safety rules were broken." Even the Russian defense minister, Sergei Ivanov, blamed those in charge for their "frivolous Russian reliance on chance, that everything will be okay."

9 For those who know anything about Russia's submarines, it's clear that everything is not okay. Russia's fleet of nuclear-powered submarines is in such disrepair that many of them lie in port. However, they can't be destroyed because the necessary funds aren't available for their demolition. Russian officials, however, do seem to have learned one lesson: When a potential tragedy threatens lives, call for help.

10 In 2005, a mini-submarine became trapped off Russia's coast and would have sunk without assistance. In response, Russian officials called for foreign assistance, and a British remote-controlled vehicle rescued all seven crew members. Although the outcome was a happy one, the Russian newspaper *Rossiyskaya Gazeta* asked a key question, "Where is the underwater technology the navy solemnly promised to get into shape after the *Kursk*?" Both the paper and the public are still waiting for an answer.

Sharpening Your Skills

DIRECTIONS Answer the following questions by filling in the blanks or circling the letter of the correct response.

1. What's the implied main idea of the entire reading?

 a. The *Kursk* tragedy was the result of human error, although the Russian government was slow to admit that fact.

 b. The tragic fate of the *Kursk* and other Russian submarines suggests the Russian navy is in terrible shape, with more accidents likely to follow.

    c. The tragedy of the *Kursk* proves what the world has known all along: The Russian navy is too poor to adequately equip and staff its ships.

    d. Vladimir Putin's reputation will never recover from his mismanagement of the *Kursk* tragedy.

2. Overall, which two patterns organize the reading?

    a. comparison and contrast *and* classification

    b. process *and* comparison and contrast

    c. sequence of dates and events *and* cause and effect

    d. cause and effect *and* definition

3. Based on the context, how did you define the word *plummeting* in paragraph 1?

    Falling

4. Based on the context, how did you define the word *mishap* in paragraph 1?

    Accident

5. Use an online or a print dictionary to explain where the Barents Sea got its name.

    An Explorer that Discovered the Sea.

6. Explain why Vladimir Putin's appearance (paragraph 6) was "hardly the image a president wants to convey when speaking to the public about a national tragedy."

    he was tanned and Relaxed he had a Golf shirt.

7. In paragraph 3, the headline "Whose Honor Is Sinking in the Barents Sea?" is a supporting detail that illustrates what main idea?

   a. Russian journalists boldly challenged the official version of events and suggested that the government had been at fault.

   b. Like newspapers in the United States, Russian papers were intent on stirring up interest in a potential government scandal.

   c. Journalists everywhere like headlines that stir up controversy.

   d. Russian journalists exposed the truth about the navy's substandard ships and equipment.

8. What pattern of organization is at work in paragraph 4?

   a. comparison and contrast

   b. cause and effect

   c. time order

   What transitional clue to the pattern appears in the paragraph?

   as a result

9. In your own words, what's the main idea of paragraph 5?

   the weapons were not handled safely.

10. Beginning in paragraph 7, what point does the author imply about the tragedy that befell the *Kursk*?

    they waited too long to call for help and the explosions were the cause of poor weapon handling.

▶ **TEST 1**   **Reviewing the Key Points**

DIRECTIONS   Answer the following questions by filling in the blanks or circling the correct response.

1. What determines the patterns a writer uses?

   _____ *the main Idea* _____

2. What is the reader's best clue to determining the pattern or patterns of organization used by the writer?

   _____ *the MainIdea* _____

3. *True* or ⟨*False.*⟩ Single paragraphs are likely to combine patterns, but longer readings tend to rely on one pattern.

4. ⟨*True*⟩ or *False.* Some patterns are more likely to combine than others.

5. *True* or ⟨*False.*⟩ If a reading contains several patterns, all the patterns are equally important.

6. When you take notes on a reading that contains several patterns, how can you determine which ones are essential to your notes?

   Consider What the contribute to the main Idea.
   The Patterns most essential for explaining the main idea
   are the ones most essential to your notes

To correct your test, turn to page 588. If one or more of your answers is incorrect, re-read the Rounding Up the Keys section of the chapter to find out where your mistake might be.

▶ **TEST 2**　　　**Recognizing Patterns in Paragraphs**

DIRECTIONS　Circle the appropriate letter or letters to identify the pattern or patterns of organization in each paragraph.

1. Most people know that lack of sleep causes irritability and increases the risk of accidents while driving. However, researchers are finding evidence that long-term lack of sleep also weakens the body's immune system. Inadequate sleep may also be contributing to America's rising rates of diabetes and obesity. There is even new evidence that too little sleep on a regular basis may increase the risk of breast cancer. Furthermore, chronic lack of sleep affects the metabolism and secretion of hormones, producing striking changes that resemble advanced aging. Cheating on sleep for just a few nights may even harm brain cells.

   a. time order
   b. simple listing
   c. definition
   d. cause and effect

2. The juvenile justice system has been evolving since the 1600s. Before the seventeenth century, society viewed children as miniature adults. Kids were held to the same standards of behavior as adults, so the justice system punished them as adults. In the seventeenth century, though, European church and community leaders managed to convince the rest of society that children were a distinct group, weaker and more innocent than adults. As a result, young offenders began to be judged against different, age-related standards. By the eighteenth century, English common law considered children under fourteen to be incapable of having criminal intentions. Reflecting that belief, the first juvenile court was established in America in 1899. For the next hundred years, the juvenile justice system focused on reforming rather than punishing young offenders. Today, however, in the aftermath of numerous violent crimes committed by juveniles, many people are taking a harsher position. They want young lawbreakers referred to criminal courts and tried as adults.

   a. time order
   b. simple listing
   c. cause and effect
   d. classification

3. **Astrobiology** is a controversial new science that concerns the search for life in outer space. Astrobiologists study meteorites, which are fragments of rocks that have come from outer space. Researchers examine these rocks for evidence of life. For example, in 1996, excited NASA scientists found evidence of bacteria fossils in a meteorite that originated on Mars. The building blocks of protein—the basis of life—have been discovered in other meteorites. In addition to examining rocks that hit earth, astrobiologists are also interested in sending orbiters or probes to other planets and moons to search for evidence that life exists elsewhere.

    a. simple listing
    b. definition
    c. cause and effect
    d. comparison and contrast

4. English explorer Captain Robert F. Scott tried with a team of four other men to be the first to reach the South Pole in Antarctica. Not only were Scott and his team beaten by another team, but they also lost their lives on their journey back to base camp. Scott's party reached the South Pole on January 17, 1912, only to find that Norwegian Roald Amundsen had arrived there a month before. Two days later, Scott and his companions headed for home. In early February, one of the men became ill because of malnutrition and injuries. He died on February 17. On March 17, another man, suffering from frostbite, also died. On March 20, the remaining three members of the team set up their final campsite just eleven miles from a depot containing food and heating oil. Tragically, a blizzard trapped the men in their tent. Scott, who was suffering from painful frostbite, recorded his final journal entry on March 29. Soon after, he and his two companions froze to death.

    a. time order
    b. simple listing
    c. definition
    d. cause and effect

5. Organizations use a variety of public relations tools to convey messages and construct an image. Written messages in the form of brochures, company magazines, annual reports, and news releases are

one form of public relations tools. But spoken messages are important as well, and organizations rely on the spoken along with the written word to get their point across. They also use corporate-identity materials, such as business cards, logos, signs, and stationery. Event sponsorship is another public relations tool. It involves a company paying for all or part of a special event, such as a sports competition, concert, festival, or play. A good example of event sponsorship was Ben & Jerry's sponsorship of the "Pint for Pint" program that helped the Red Cross boost blood donations. Those who donated a pint of blood to the Red Cross got a free pint of ice cream. Increasingly, organizations are using the Internet for public relations through blogs and social-networking sites. (Adapted from William M. Pride, Robert J. Hughes, and Jack R. Kapoor, *Business*, 8th ed. © Cengage Learning.)

a. simple listing
b. definition
c. cause and effect
d. classification

▶ **TEST 3** **Recognizing Patterns in Paragraphs**

DIRECTIONS Circle the appropriate letter or letters to identify the pattern or patterns of organization in each paragraph.

1. Many automotive experts claim that synthetic motor oil is better than natural petroleum oil. The most important differences between the two are related to vehicle performance, cost, and convenience. Synthetic oils increase an engine's performance and overall length of life because they are better than petroleum-based oils in several ways. Synthetic-based oils are better at protecting the engine from high temperatures. They flow more easily in cold temperatures, and they also prevent deposits from forming. In addition, synthetic oils reduce friction and wear more effectively than petroleum oils do. Also, the cost of synthetic oils is the same as or less than the cost of petroleum oil. Though a quart of synthetic oil can cost several dollars more than the same amount of petroleum oil, synthetic oil is changed much less often than petroleum oil. Generally, synthetic oils last two to three times longer than petroleum oils. Thus, their longer life offsets their higher price. Furthermore, the reduced number of oil changes offered by synthetic oils results in greater convenience for car owners. Some oil manufacturers even suggest that the vehicle owner change synthetic oil every 25,000 miles, as opposed to every 3,000–5,000 miles for petroleum oils.

   a. simple listing
   b. definition
   c. cause and effect
   d. comparison and contrast
   e. time order

2. University of Virginia professor E. Mavis Hetherington has studied the effects of divorce on children. Her research has turned up some interesting similarities and differences between children of divorced parents and children with intact* families. According to Dr. Hetherington, only 10 percent of children from intact families appeared to have emotional problems. However, 25 percent of children with divorced parents experienced depression or antisocial

---

*intact: complete, unbroken.

behavior in school. Yet almost the same percentage of children in each group said they felt close to their biological mothers: Seventy percent of children in divorced families and 80 percent of children in intact families claimed to enjoy a good relationship with their moms. Perhaps most interesting, Dr. Hetherington found that a majority of children with divorced parents find divorce to be both acceptable and understandable. Seventy percent of young people with divorced parents said that divorce is acceptable, even if children are involved. In contrast, only 40 percent of children in intact families approved of divorce.

a. time order

b. simple listing

c. definition

d. cause and effect

e. comparison and contrast

3. **Electronic waste**, also known as "e-waste" and "e-trash," describes worn-out, broken, or obsolete computers, cell phones, videocassette recorders, and television sets that people throw out. Less than 10 percent of e-waste is recycled, so it now accounts for 1 percent of trash in the United States. As a result, it's becoming a problem for local governments all over the country. City and county officials are worried about the high cost of collecting and dumping e-waste in their crowded landfills. Already, California and Massachusetts have banned computer monitors from being dumped in the states' landfills and incinerators. Environmental groups, too, are concerned about the impact of e-waste. They fear that the lead, mercury, and other hazardous substances in electronic devices will leak into the soil and water. Overexposure to these toxins can cause serious health problems. For example, the lead that shields the user of an electronic device from radiation could seep into the groundwater. Lead poisoning can result in kidney, nervous system, and reproductive system damage.

a. time order

b. simple listing

c. definition

d. cause and effect

e. comparison and contrast

4. The two major branches, or types, of Islam are Sunni and Shia. Sunni Muslims account for 90 percent of Islam's followers. They accept the first three spiritual leaders who succeeded Muhammad, the religion's central prophet. This group believes community leaders should be chosen by election. The majority of Muslims in Egypt, Saudi Arabia, Syria, Jordan, Lebanon, Turkey, and Indonesia are Sunni Muslims. Also, most of America's African-American converts to Islam follow the Sunni traditions. Shiite Muslims account for about 10 percent of Muslims in the world today, mostly in Iran and Iraq. These Muslims accept only the fourth spiritual leader to follow Muhammad, rejecting his first three successors. Shiites believe their community leader is both a religious and a political authority, who can be appointed only by divine command. They tend to be more strict than Sunni Muslims in their religious practices. They are also more restrictive in their dietary rules and views on women.

   a. time order
   b. simple listing
   c. definition
   d. comparison and contrast
   e. classification

5. Fashion magazines love giving girls and women advice about beauty. They've been doing that since the mid-nineteenth century when the first beauty magazines were published. Unfortunately, much of that advice for cultivating beauty has ranged from silly to dangerous. Women were once told, for instance, that cutting their eyelashes would make them grow. In fact, cutting one's eyelashes only makes them short and stubby; it doesn't make them grow. As if that advice weren't bad enough, it was also suggested that women should put petroleum jelly on their lashes and then sprinkle coal dust over the lashes to make them appear darker and fuller. What that advice probably did was to give the women who followed it severe eye infections. In the past, women were also advised to take small doses of arsenic to whiten their skin. Although it's true that arsenic produces pale skin—considered extremely desirable in the nineteenth century—it's also true that arsenic builds up in the body and can cause death. In the past, women were also told that a dark tan was both attractive and good for the skin. Women who followed

that advice ended up with leathery, lined skin if they were lucky, and with skin cancer if they weren't.

a. definition
b. simple listing
c. cause and effect
d. classification
e. comparison and contrast

▶ **TEST 4**   **Recognizing Patterns in Paragraphs**

DIRECTIONS   Circle the appropriate letter or letters to identify the pattern or patterns of organization in each paragraph.

1. An **antibiotic** is a chemical substance that destroys microorganisms in the body without harming the body itself. Produced by bacteria and fungi, antibiotics are now routinely used to treat a wide variety of illnesses. Discovered in 1928 by Alexander Fleming, penicillin was the first antibiotic. Then, in the early 1940s, researchers learned how to produce the antibiotic in commercial quantities to treat wounded World War II soldiers. In the 1950s and 1960s, scientists discovered many new classes of antibiotics and developed some of them for use against a broad range of microorganisms. Other antibiotics targeted specific kinds of bacteria. Unfortunately, far too many doctors and patients started turning to antibiotics for a quick cure. As a result, the medical community is now concerned about the growth of new drug-resistant bacteria. These bacteria no longer respond to the current crop of antibiotics. There are signs that existing antibiotics are proving less effective at treating serious diseases such as tuberculosis and strep infections.

   a. time order
   b. simple listing
   c. definition
   d. cause and effect
   e. comparison and contrast
   f. classification

2. In 1978, an underwater diver named Gerald Klein discovered the remains of a ship while diving in Biscayne National Park. Klein removed some items from the wreck, and, in 1979, he filed a claim with the district court in Florida, where the park is located. Believing that the items, dating back a century, were valuable, Klein asked to keep what he had taken or, at the very least, to receive a salvage award for his efforts. Salvage awards are monies paid for the rescue of property lost at sea, and the awards were created to encourage acts of rescue and salvage. To Klein, keeping the items or being rewarded for their discovery seemed the fair and obvious outcome for his efforts. Not so, said the district court in 1979 under the rule

of Judge C. Clyde Atkins. As a result, Klein ended up appealing his case to the state of Florida, where in 1985 he lost again. The judges, however, did not all agree, and they filed widely dissenting opinions. One judge found that because the United States was "the owner of the land on and/or in which the shipwreck is located, it owns the shipwreck." In his view, Klein had ignored legitimate property rights. Another argued that because Klein had removed the articles, which, it was assumed, would have been found eventually, he had actually done more harm than good, making it more difficult to trace the original ownership of both the ship and its contents. But another judge took a completely different position. He argued that the "plaintiff performed a highly valuable service simply by locating the shipwreck, and should be compensated accordingly." Unfortunately for Klein's estate—by 1985 Gerald Klein had died—this was a minority decision, and his widow was denied any claim to the ancient ship and its contents. (Source of case details: www.karlloren.com/ healthinsurance/p12.htm; http://philtrupp.com/smith.htm.)

a. time order
b. simple listing
c. definition
d. cause and effect
e. comparison and contrast
f. classification

3. A growing number of Europeans and Americans who need serious medical care but cannot afford the price of it in their own country are traveling to India for medical treatment. Private Indian hospitals offer first-rate medical care at a price that foreign patients and well-off Indians can afford. Thus, when Robin Steeles of Alabama needed to have the mitral valve of his heart repaired, he flew halfway around the world to Bangalore, India, to have his surgery. After the mitral valve was repaired, Steeles recuperated quickly. The same is not true, however, for 150 Indian laborers who were ill during the same time Steeles was hospitalized. They died because the public hospitals where they were brought after drinking illegally brewed liquor could not provide adequate treatment. Many of the victims needed expensive medical equipment to help them breathe and keep the poison from overwhelming their system. The public hospitals,

however, had neither the staff nor machines to keep the men alive. It's tragic but true that India has a dual health care system: There's superb private care for those who can afford it and the bare minimum of treatment for those who cannot. (Source of information: Somini Sengupta, "Royal Care for Some of India's Patients, Neglect for Others," *New York Times*, June 1, 2008, p. 3.)

   a. time order

   b. simple listing

   c. definition

   d. cause and effect

   e. comparison and contrast

   f. classification

4. Having seen elephants only occasionally in a zoo or on a movie screen, most people don't realize how different Asian and African elephants really are. African elephants are the much bigger and heavier of the two. They are the ones with huge, floppy ears. Asian elephants, in comparison, have much smaller ears. They also have shorter tusks and smoother skin. The skin of the African elephant is wrinkled and thicker. In terms of personality, African elephants have been known to display a nasty temper while Asian ones are said to be more docile and trainable. The two animals also differ in their trunks. The African elephant has two finger-like pieces of skin at the end of its trunk. These two "fingers" help elephants pick up small objects, like peanuts, from the ground. Asian elephants have only one finger at the end of their trunks, not two. When it comes to the threat of extinction, it's the African elephant whose roamable habitat has been steadily reduced by the spread of farming and building and whose numbers have dramatically diminished in the last two decades.

   a. time order

   b. simple listing

   c. definition

   d. cause and effect

   e. comparison and contrast

   f. classification

5. Depending on how the skin has been broken or punctured, there are six different types of wounds: abrasions, incisions, lacerations, punctures, avulsions, and amputations. With an abrasion, the top layer of the skin is rubbed or scraped off against a rough surface like a piece of rope or carpet. Because the wound from an abrasion is large and open, the chance for infection is higher. Incisions are made by sharp instruments like knives, razors, or glass. Of the six wounds, incisions are the least likely to become infected because the blood flowing from an incision washes away infection-causing bacteria. Laceration wounds, such as those made by a dull knife, are jagged and deep and involve a good deal of tissue damage. This makes it likely for lacerations to be followed by an infection. Puncture wounds are also caused by objects that penetrate the body's tissue, but they leave a smaller surface opening. Puncture wounds are made by nails, needles, wire, and bullets, all of which are likely to carry bacteria that lead to infection. Avulsion wounds result when tissue is forcibly torn from the body, producing heavy bleeding. Avulsion wounds are typical of the wounds that occur in auto accidents. In some cases, it is possible to surgically reattach the torn tissue. With amputation wounds, entire limbs are accidentally torn from the body when, for instance, a finger or hand gets caught in a piece of machinery.

a. time order
b. simple listing
c. definition
d. cause and effect
e. comparison and contrast
f. classification

◆ **TEST 5**   **Recognizing Mixed Patterns in Longer Readings**

DIRECTIONS   Circle the appropriate letter or letters to identify the pattern or patterns of organization in the following readings.

1. Norman Rockwell's Rising Reputation

1   For most of his professional career, painter and illustrator Norman Rockwell (1894–1978) was treated as something of a stepchild by the established art world. The public loved his portraits of small-town life. Art critics, however, considered Rockwell's work technically good but creatively worthless. For them, he was the "King of Kitsch."[†] In their eyes, Rockwell shamelessly tried to satisfy the public's desire to see the world through rose-colored glasses. Rockwell's critics claimed his work lacked the mystery and subtlety of great art. But in the end, Rockwell may have the last laugh. As is so often the case with artists despised during their lifetimes, a new generation of art critics has begun to reevaluate the work of Norman Rockwell.

2   Like many artists, Rockwell showed a gift for drawing early on. By the age of eighteen, he was already supporting himself working as an illustrator. In 1916, when he was only twenty-two years old, Rockwell created his first cover for the weekly magazine *Saturday Evening Post*. He would go on to create a total of 800 covers for popular magazines. Of those 800 covers, more than 300 were for the *Post*. Clearly hungry for Rockwell's vision of the world, people couldn't seem to get enough portrayals of happy families eagerly anticipating Thanksgiving turkey, kids paddling in swimming holes, or little girls contentedly cradling their dolls. As the United States and Europe slid into first an economic depression and then a brutal war, Norman Rockwell assured his public that the world was still a sane, safe, and fairly simple place.

3   It's not surprising, then, that Rockwell's work has often been compared to that of his contemporary, Walt Disney, the creator of Mickey Mouse and countless animated films. Disney was a big fan of Rockwell's. Judged by their work, both men seemed to have had a similar view of the world. While Rockwell painted what he described as "life as I would like it to be," Disney offered up a cartoon world where animated characters effortlessly survived every threat to health and happiness.

4   Naturally, Rockwell's link to Disney made him seem even more suspicious to members of the art world. Because of it, he was viewed as an entertainer rather than an artist. Probably for that reason, the Museum of Modern Art never once included Rockwell in exhibitions devoted to

---
[†]kitsch: corny and sentimental.

modern art. Respected museums generally didn't think Rockwell was fit to be seen alongside "real" artists.

5   Given his treatment at the hands of art critics, Rockwell might have been happy to learn that the current crop of critics does not necessarily share the old views. Biographer and art critic Laura Claridge, for example, insists that Rockwell has much in common with the great seventeenth-century Dutch painter Jan Vermeer (1632–1675). Claridge insists that Rockwell, like Vermeer, gave ordinary objects and settings a spiritual meaning. In Rockwell's paintings, families seated around the dinner table may have suggested more than life's simple pleasures. They represented a heroic determination to create a safe haven* in a world gone mad from hunger and war. Such interpretations may seem strained to those used to dismissing Rockwell as a popular hack. Nevertheless, these interpretations are more frequent than ever before. If the current trend persists, Norman Rockwell's work may finally end up hanging in the great museums of the world.

a. time order
b. simple listing
c. definition
d. cause and effect
e. comparison and contrast
f. classification

2. "Moonshine" Lives On

1   The manufacture of the strong country whiskey known as moonshine, hooch, and white lightning began in the Appalachian Mountains in the 1700s. Scots-Irish immigrants arriving in America brought with them their recipes for brewing sugar and yeast into a powerful drink. Unfortunately for those involved in moonshining, the United States began taxing liquor in 1781. To avoid paying these taxes, descendants of those original Scots-Irish settlers began making their spirits in secret after dark. From this night-time necessity, the term *moonshining* was coined.

2   The practice of moonshining continued throughout the Civil War and beyond. It particularly thrived during the 1930s, when Prohibition[†] laws forbade the selling of alcohol. In the 1960s and 1970s, even legalized liquor

---

*haven: place of rest and safety.
[†]Prohibition: the period (1920–1933) when the Eighteenth Amendment forbade the manufacture and sale of alcohol.

sales in southern cities did not put an end to the home brews. On the contrary, even today, some southern towns—for example, New Prospect, South Carolina, and Dawsonville, Georgia—celebrate their moonshining heritage with annual festivals. Many southerners still keep a bottle under the sink. At the same time, though, federal and state alcohol-control agents are cracking down on bootleg whiskey makers. In 2001, agents wrapped up Operation Lightning Strike, an eight-year series of raids that put twenty-seven major moonshiners out of business.

3   The government is persistent about eliminating moonshine for several reasons. First, moonshiners don't pay taxes. They wouldn't even consider it, and the U.S. government does not smile on tax evasion. Then, too, the large-scale manufacture of moonshine often leads to other crimes, such as money laundering.[†] In addition, bootleg whiskey can be a health hazard. Moonshiners have used old truck radiators as stills,[*] and some brewers get their water from creeks that cattle walk through. As a result, moonshine has sometimes been contaminated with dangerous toxins, such as radiator fluid and lye. The production process can also accidentally create wood alcohol, which can cause blindness if drunk.

4   Despite these health concerns, though, there has been a market for moonshine in both the South and the North for more than 300 years. People like bootleg liquor because it's cheap. A gallon jug of home brew is 50 percent alcohol, yet it costs only $20 to $30 per gallon. That's half the price of legal whiskey. Over the centuries, moonshine has also been one of the most valuable trading goods for poor rural southerners. In an odd way, moonshine also enjoys a certain mystique.[*] Those who make it often consider themselves to be daredevil descendants of Robin Hood. They see themselves as unwilling to bow their heads to the rule of an unjust law. Furthermore, many people believe the illegal brew tastes better than commercial liquors.

a. time order
b. simple listing
c. definition
d. cause and effect
e. comparison and contrast
f. classification

[†]money laundering: using illegally earned money in a noncriminal enterprise so that the money appears to be legally earned.
[*]still: apparatus for purifying liquids such as alcohol.
[*]mystique: mystery.

▶ **TEST 6** **Recognizing Mixed Patterns in Longer Readings**

DIRECTIONS Circle the appropriate letter or letters to identify the pattern or patterns of organization in the following readings.

1. **"Hybrids" Make Good Sense**

1 The Toyota Prius and Honda Insight are gasoline-and-electric-powered cars called "hybrids." They work by getting power from both a gasoline engine and an electric motor. First, the car's batteries feed power to the electric motor. This motor gets the car moving. Then, when the car's speed reaches fifteen miles per hour, the gasoline engine takes over. This engine begins sending power to a generator. In turn, the generator feeds power to the electric motor and the batteries. As the car continues to accelerate, the batteries send power to the electric motor, which increases the gasoline engine's performance. Finally, as the car slows down, the electric motor transfers energy from the spinning axles and uses it to recharge the batteries.

2 Relying on two sources of energy—gasoline and electricity—results in amazing fuel efficiency. In the city, both cars average sixty miles per gallon. Consequently, owners of these cars realize big savings at the gas pump. Someone who switched to a hybrid car from a small car like a Honda Civic would save about $500 a year on fuel. Someone who switched to a hybrid from a car less fuel-efficient than the Civic would save even more.

3 Because hybrid cars use so much less fuel than traditional cars, they could help reduce or even eliminate America's dependence on foreign oil. If everyone in this country drove a hybrid, we would need fewer barrels of oil per year. Hybrids would allow us to take care of our own energy needs. We would no longer have to buy fuel from other countries.

4 Hybrids also produce a third positive effect: They are much less damaging to the environment than traditional cars. They do not emit as many polluting gases. They also generate only half of the carbon dioxide released by other cars. Cars that produce less of that particular gas could help slow or even stop global warming. Given the benefits of hybrid cars, the public needs to pressure automakers into producing more of them at cheaper prices. If hybrids were more affordable, more people would buy them, and the whole world would reap the reward of cleaner air.

a. time order
b. simple listing
c. definition

d. cause and effect

e. comparison and contrast

f. classification

2. The Sinking of the *Andrea Doria*

1   The *Andrea Doria*, named after one of Italy's great sea captains, was among the fastest ships in the world when she made her maiden voyage in January 1953. Just three and a half years later, though, she collided with the *Stockholm* and sank to the bottom of the sea.

2   The last voyage of the *Andrea Doria* began on July 17, 1956, in Genoa, Italy. After stops in Cannes, Naples, and Gibraltar, the ship headed out to sea on July 20 for what would have been her fifty-first crossing to New York City. She carried 1,134 passengers and 572 crew members. The voyage was routine until July 25. On that day, dense fog formed off the Massachusetts coast, so the captain reduced the ship's speed. At 9:30 p.m., the *Andrea Doria*'s crew noticed a blip on the radar screen. That blip was the *Stockholm*, a Swedish passenger liner that had left New York at 11:31 that morning. It was seventeen miles away, but the two ships were headed directly toward each other. Heeding the signal, the captain of the *Andrea Doria* ordered a change of course. Then, during the next hour and a half, the *Andrea Doria*'s crew continued to monitor the radar and make adjustments to their own course. Tragically, crew members misinterpreted the radar information. A little after 11:00 p.m., crews on each ship could see the other vessel's lights through binoculars. The *Andrea Doria*'s crew blew the foghorn, but the two captains' attempts to evade each other had actually resulted in a collision course. At 11:11 p.m., about fifty miles south of Nantucket Island, the *Stockholm* crashed into the side of the *Andrea Doria*.

3   The impact ripped open the *Andrea Doria*'s steel hull. A number of luxury cabins and a garage containing automobiles were demolished. The ship's fuel tanks were ruptured, and water began pouring in. The *Stockholm* reversed its engines and pulled back. But the *Andrea Doria*'s deep gash was a mortal wound. Within a minute, the ship began to lean as seawater continued to flood into the hole. Engineers aboard the *Andrea Doria* could find no way to stop the flooding, so the captain ordered the crew to begin loading passengers aboard lifeboats. He also sent out a distress signal. Several ships responded and began heading to the scene. The French passenger liner *Ile de France* and the freighter *Cape Ann* were the first two ships to arrive, at about 2:00 a.m. Along with the *Stockholm*, these ships rescued about 1,600 of those aboard the *Andrea Doria*. Fifty-two people were killed

in the collision. At 9:45 a.m. on July 26, the *Andrea Doria* capsized.* At 10:09 a.m., eleven hours after being hit, she was swallowed by the sea.

4   Today the *Andrea Doria* lies 230 feet below the ocean's surface, where she is a favorite destination of scuba divers. The first divers descended just one day after the ship sank. A month later, *Life* magazine sent a team of diver-photographers to bring back pictures and artifacts from the ship's watery grave. The dive is dangerous because the water is deep. Divers can stay for only twenty minutes, and then they must decompress carefully for ninety minutes on their way back to the surface. The interior of the 700-foot-long ship is also vast and dark, so divers can get disoriented while inside. During the summer of 1998 alone, three divers died while exploring the wreck. Despite the danger, though, divers are attracted to the hunt for treasure aboard the doomed liner.

a. time order
b. simple listing
c. definition
d. cause and effect
e. comparison and contrast
f. classification

---

*capsized: overturned.

▶ TEST 7   **Recognizing Mixed Patterns in Longer Readings**

> **DIRECTIONS**   Circle the appropriate letter to identify the pattern or patterns. Then answer the question about what's important in the reading.

1.   The Difference Between Data and Information

data   numerical or verbal descriptions that usually result from some sort of measurement

1   Many people use the terms *data* and *information* interchangeably, but the two differ in important ways. **Data** are numerical or verbal descriptions that usually result from some sort of measurement. (The word *data* is plural; the singular form is *datum*.) Your current wage level, the amount of last year's after-tax profit for Hewlett Packard Computers, and the current retail prices of Honda automobiles are all data. Most people think of data as being numerical only, but they can be non-numerical as well. A description of an individual as a "tall, athletic person with short, dark hair" certainly would qualify as data.

information   data presented in a form that is useful for a specific purpose

2   **Information** is data presented in a form useful for a specific purpose. Suppose that a human resources manager wants to compare the wages paid to male and female employees over a period of five years. The manager might begin with a stack of computer printouts listing every person employed by the firm, along with each employee's current and past wages. The manager would be hard-pressed to make any sense of all the names and numbers. Such printouts consist of data rather than information.

3   Now suppose that the manager uses a computer to graph the average wages paid to men and to women in each of the five years.... The result is information because the manager can use it for the purpose at hand—to compare wages paid to men with those paid to women over the five-year period. When summarized in the graph, the wage data from the printouts become information.

4   Large sets of data often must be summarized if they are to be useful, but this is not always the case. If the manager in our example had wanted to know only the wage history of a specific employee, that information would be contained in the original computer printout. That is, the data (the employee's name and wage history) already would be in the most useful form for the manager's purpose; they would need no further processing.

5   The average company maintains a great deal of data that can be transformed into information. Typical data include records pertaining to personnel, inventory, sales, and accounting. Often each type of data is stored in individual departments within an organization. However, the data can be used more effectively when they are organized into a database. A

database   a single collection of data stored in one place that can be used by people throughout an organization to make decisions

database is a single collection of data stored in one place that can be used by people throughout an organization to make decisions. Today, most companies have several different types of databases. Often the data and information necessary to form a firm's databases are the result of business research activities. (William M. Pride, Robert J. Hughes, and Jack R. Kapoor, *Business*, 8th ed. © Cengage Learning.)

1.   a. time order
   b. simple listing
   (c.) definition
   d. cause and effect
   (e.) comparison and contrast
   f. classification

2.   Based on the pattern or patterns you chose, what should your notes on the reading record?

   how to tell how Data and information are different and Alike.

2.   **Grievance Procedures**

grievance procedure   a formally established course of action for resolving employee complaints against management

1   A **grievance procedure** is a formally established course of action for resolving employee complaints against management. Virtually every labor contract contains a grievance procedure. Procedures vary in scope and detail, but they may involve all four steps described below.

2   **Original Grievance**   The process begins with an employee who believes that he or she has been treated unfairly, in violation of the labor contract. For example, an employee may be entitled to a formal performance review after six months on the job. If no such review is conducted, the employee may file a grievance. To do so, the employee explains the grievance to a **shop steward**, an employee elected by union members to serve as their representative. The employee and the steward then discuss the grievance with the employee's immediate supervisor. Both the grievance and the supervisor's response are put in writing.

shop steward   an employee elected by union members to serve as their representative

3   **Broader Discussion**   In most cases the problem is resolved during the initial discussion with the supervisor. If it is not, a second discussion is held. Now the participants include the original parties (employee, supervisor, and steward), a representative from the union's grievance committee, and the firm's industrial-relations representative. Again, a record is kept of the discussion and its results.

4 **Full-Scale Discussion** If the grievance is still not resolved, a full-scale discussion is arranged. This discussion includes everyone involved in the broader discussion, as well as all remaining members of the union's grievance committee and another high-level manager. As usual, all proceedings are put in writing. All participants are careful not to violate the labor contract during this attempt to resolve the complaint.

arbitration the step in a grievance procedure in which a neutral third party hears the two sides of a dispute and renders a decision

5 **Arbitration** The final step in a grievance procedure is arbitration, in which a neutral third party hears the grievance and renders a binding decision. As in a court hearing, each side presents its case and has the right to cross-examine witnesses. In addition, the arbitrator reviews the written documentation of all previous steps in the grievance procedure. Both sides may then give summary arguments and/or present briefs. The arbitrator then decides whether a provision of the labor contract has been violated and proposes a remedy. The arbitrator cannot make any decision that would add to, detract from, or modify the terms of the contract. If it can be proved that the arbitrator exceeded the scope of his or her authority, either party may appeal the decision to the courts. (William M. Pride, Robert J. Hughes, and Jack R. Kapoor, *Business*, 8th ed. © Cengage Learning.)

1. a. time order
   b. simple listing
   c. definition
   d. cause and effect
   e. comparison and contrast
   f. classification

2. Based on the pattern or patterns you chose, what should your notes on the reading record?

   how to define a Grievance Procedure and List the steps.

▶ TEST 8 — **Enlarging Your Academic Vocabulary**

DIRECTIONS   Circle the letter of the sentence that uses the opening word correctly.

1. **prototype**

   a. The mathematician Alan Turing is credited with creating the *prototype* for our modern computers.

   b. He was the typical *prototype* man who couldn't stand having a woman for a boss.

   c. Her *prototype* did not indicate what she had been doing for the last five years, and for the interviewer that was a warning signal.

2. **harmony**

   a. The house was *harmonious* because the pets fought as much as the people who lived there did.

   b. The current lack of *harmony* between the two brothers was apparent to everyone who knew them from happier days.

   c. Right before the curtain opened, he strapped his *harmony* around his neck.

3. **predator**

   a. She went to the animal shelter in the hopes of finding a *predator* that she could bring home to cheer up her ailing child.

   b. Her parole officer kept on *predatoring* her about her unexplained absences because he was convinced they were drug related.

   c. Unlike their prey, *predators* have eyes in the front of their head so that spotting and attacking their victims is easier.

4. **syntax**

   a. *Syntax* is the root of all evil.

   b. If you *syntax* your paper before turning it in, you will be more inclined to get a higher grade.

   c. The speaker's *syntactical* patterns suggested that English was not his first language.

5. **generate**

   a. His *generating* the same word three times for emphasis was a source of annoyance to his listeners.

   b. The manager's new office practices *generated* a flood of paper.

   c. His clothes were so tattered and worn, he looked like a complete *generate*, but he was actually both smart and hard-working.

6. **lucid**

   a. Thanks to her new wardrobe, the young actress was more *lucid* than ever before.

   b. As a novelist, the author was intentionally hard to understand, but as an essayist, few writers were more *lucid* than she.

   c. The detective stared at the *lucid* footprint and wondered what human could have a foot that big.

7. **tangible**

   a. The sounds of the bells in the distance were already *tangible* to the ear.

   b. There was a *tangible* red mark on the victim's left arm.

   c. His ex-wife was coming in an hour to collect all of her *tangibles*, and he didn't want to be there when she arrived.

8. **collaboration**

   a. Everyone knew that the report was a *collaborative* effort, but only one member of the group got credit for writing it.

   b. The government had sent him an official *collaboration*, which he could not ignore.

   c. After winning the prize for best independent film, everyone involved got together for a huge *collaboration*.

9. **deprivation**

   a. Years of *deprivation* had made him remarkably strong and fit.

   b. In the aftermath of the war, everyone except the very wealthy experienced extreme *deprivation*.

   c. After much *deprivation*, the members of the committee came to an agreement.

10. **confiscate**

   a. No one could understand why the board had chosen someone so incompetent to *confiscate* over the meeting.

   b. When police arrest drug dealers, they *confiscate* their cars and use them as police force vehicles.

   c. No one without an entry code could get within the *confiscates* of the estate.

Analyzing Arguments

IN THIS CHAPTER, YOU WILL LEARN

- how to tell the difference between fact and opinion.
- how to analyze arguments in persuasive writing.
- how to evaluate those arguments.
- how to identify tone.

"Persuasion is often more effective than force."
—Aesop[1]

Chapter 7 talked about the way certain kinds of patterns can be clues to a persuasive purpose. This chapter returns to the subject of persuasive writing. At this point, we'll take a close look at arguments. They are the cornerstone of persuasive writing.

No Opinion, No Argument

Writers with a persuasive purpose want their readers to think or act in a certain way. To that end, they are likely to give readers an **argument**. That doesn't mean they will get in a dispute with them. It does mean that writers intent on persuasion will give their readers an opinion and tell them, in a variety of ways, why they should share it.

---

[1]Supposedly, Aesop was a teller of stories with a moral, or lesson, who lived around the sixth century BCE.

Arguments will vary in content and form. But at the most basic level, a written argument always has two parts:

1. The opinion the author wants you to share or at least seriously consider.

2. The supporting evidence selected to make you think, "Why that makes a good deal of sense. Having read this, I'm inclined to share that point of view."

There can also be a third element. Writers often address, or speak to, the opposition in order to tell readers why those who disagree are wrong. However, that third element is not always present in a written argument. What is always there is the opinion the authors want readers to share or consider and the evidence, or justification, for that opinion. Those are the two elements of an argument that we will be focusing on in this chapter.

Because the writer's opinion is the core or heart of the argument—it's the reason why the author writes in the first place—let's start there. If you are going to analyze an argument, you need to be clear on what opinions are and how they differ from another key element of many written arguments, facts.

> ▶ **SHARE YOUR THOUGHTS**
> How is it possible for persuasion to be more powerful than force? After all, with force, you can just tell someone, "Do as I say or I'll shoot you." Was Aesop engaging in wishful thinking? Or did he have a point? Please explain.

READING KEYS
- At the heart of every argument is an opinion that the author wants readers to share or at least seriously consider.
- Readers who want to understand persuasive writing need a clear grasp of the opinion or perspective being promoted.
- They also need to determine what kind of support the author offers readers in an effort to make them consider sharing the opinion.
- In addition to an opinion and the support for that opinion, writers also frequently address the opposition. They explain, that is, why those who disagree are wrong or misguided.

VOCABULARY EXTRA

Aesop's stories are usually, and more correctly, called "fables." Although the intent was to instruct adults in how to behave in an ethical way, the figures in the stories were always animals. It's the use of animals that defines the term *fable*. Fables are also different from myths, which don't necessarily make any moral point. Myths are more likely to tell you how something began. Thus, there are myths about the origins of echoes, flowers, the seasons, and even the entire world. The meaning of the word *myth*, however, has expanded over time, and it's now commonly used to refer to a story that isn't true.

Opinions versus Facts

To analyze arguments, readers have to know the difference between facts and opinions; the next few pages will explain these differences.

Opinions

Opinions are personal views about the world and its workings. Opinions are the result of an individual's experiences, upbringing, and education. They are even linked to personality. A person who doesn't like controversy is likely to form opinions that line up nicely with traditional, or long-standing, points of view. A person who thoroughly enjoys a heated argument is likely to take precisely the stand that will provoke disagreement.

While it's true that the same opinion can be shared by many people, you'll never find unanimous agreement on any single one. Just consider the following. They are all statements of opinion. They are, therefore, all subject to disagreement:

1. Sarah Palin would make a great, first female president.
2. Rush Limbaugh is a hypocritical windbag.
3. Health care is the right of every U.S. citizen.
4. Elephants are the smartest animals on earth.

Don't tell a cat lover that elephants are smarter than cats.

© Ulrich Flemming

Because these are all statements of opinion, not everyone would agree with them. For instance, there are people who would grow pale with fright at the thought of Sarah Palin becoming president. Similarly, there are those who would turn red with anger at hearing Rush Limbaugh labeled a "windbag." And many Americans think that health care is something every individual should pay for, while cat lovers might well challenge elephants' supremacy in the brains department. In other words, the four statements listed above are opinions. Therefore, they have the following characteristics:

Statements of Opinion
♦

1. cannot be considered *true* or *false*.
2. can only be labeled *valid* or *invalid*, *sound* or *unsound*, *informed* or *uninformed*, depending on the amount and type of support offered.
3. cannot be *verified*, or checked for accuracy, with outside sources such as newspaper records and trained experts.
4. often use *connotative*, or emotionally charged, language.
5. are affected by a writer's personality, background, and training.
6. frequently use words that make comparisons such as *more*, *better*, *most*, and *least*.
7. are likely to make value judgments suggesting that some action or event has a positive or negative effect, e.g., *great*, *wonderful*, *horrible*, *failure*, *triumph*, and *disaster*.
8. are often introduced by verbs and adverbs that suggest doubt or possibility, such as *appears*, *seems*, *apparently*, *probably*, *potentially*, and *possibly*.

Facts

Unlike opinions, **statements of fact** aren't affected by the background, experience, or education of the person holding the opinion. Factual statements describe people, places, and events in the same way no matter who is making the statement. Facts make no value judgments.

Statements of Fact

◆

1. can be verified for accuracy through turning to experts, reference works, and public records.
2. can be labeled *true* or *false*, *accurate* and *inaccurate*.
3. rely on denotative, or unemotional, language.
4. are not shaped or affected by a writer's personality, background, or training.
5. frequently use numbers, statistics, dates, and measurements.
6. name and describe but do not evaluate.

⊶ READING KEYS

◆ Opinions are ideas or beliefs about the world that are shaped by background, experience, and education. Thus they can't be verified, or checked for accuracy.

◆ Facts are not affected by the background or experience of the person who states them. Thus they can be verified for accuracy and can be labeled *true* or *false*.

IDIOM ALERT: Sacred cow

In parts of India, cows have a religious significance and are viewed as sacred. Thus they are objects of respect, even worship. That view of holy or sacred cows is the origin of the idiom *sacred cow*, which refers to a belief or an institution so widely viewed with respect that people get upset if someone criticizes it. Here's an example of how the idiom is used: "For those who worship the economist Milton Friedman, belief in the free market is a *sacred cow*. A hint of government intervention in the marketplace sends Friedmanites into a tizzy."

VOCABULARY EXTRA

There's a big difference between holding a strong opinion and being *opinionated*. People who are opinionated often believe that their opinion is the only one that matters. But it's possible to hold a strong opinion and still listen to opposing points of view. In fact, that's what most of us strive for.

◆ EXERCISE 1   Separating Fact from Opinion

DIRECTIONS   Label each statement *F* (fact) or *O* (opinion).

EXAMPLE

_____F_____ a. The longest game in the history of *Monday Night Football* lasted four hours and ten minutes.

_____O_____ b. The movie *The Hunger Games* was even better than the book.

EXPLANATION   Statement *a* is a fact. Its accuracy can be verified against reference works like *The World Almanac and Book of Facts.* Any statement that can be verified as *true* or *false, correct* or *incorrect,* is bound to be factual. Statement *b* is an opinion. There is no way to check every reader's opinion of the movie *The Hunger Games.* Nor is it possible to survey every single person who saw the film.

_____F_____ 1. The term *brain freeze* refers to a pain in the temples that comes on after eating something frozen.

_____F_____ 2. Bears usually hibernate for a period of three to five months.

_____F_____ 3. Nurses who have three years of advanced training in anesthesia are allowed to give anesthesia without a doctor's supervision.

 4. Making tobacco companies pay for the damage caused by cigarettes is a superb form of justice.

5. *Fifty Shades of Grey* is nothing but disgusting soft porn.

_____O_____   6. Parents whose children participate in organized sports have a responsibility to model good sportsmanship on the sidelines.

_____F_____   7. The collected letters of John Adams and Thomas Jefferson[†] reveal that Adams wrote two letters to every one of Jefferson's.

_____O_____   8. Smokers in this country are treated like second-class citizens.

_____O_____   9. Women who say they don't want children are challenging one of society's sacred cows: All women have a maternal instinct.

_____F_____   10. The first zoo opened its doors in 1874.

Fact and Opinion Aren't Always Divided

It would be easier to determine when an author is introducing a fact versus an opinion if they always stayed separated. But they don't. Sometimes, often in fact, writers mix the two together. Take, for example, these next two statements. Which one is pure fact and which one is a mix of fact and opinion?

1. Attorney Morris Dees, the co-founder of the Southern Poverty Law Center, used the courts to effectively destroy the power of the Ku Klux Klan.

2. When attorney Morris Dees, the co-founder of the Southern Poverty Law Center, took the Ku Klux Klan to court, he won a $7,000,000 judgment against the Klan.

If you said that the first statement was partially an opinion and the second a pure fact, you are correct. Dees did win a huge judgment against the Klan. In fact, the award set a precedent. That's a fact. You can check it in any number of places.

_____

[†]Adams was the country's second president, Jefferson the third.

As a result of that win, it's been argued that Dees's financial victory effectively stopped the Klan's ability to function. But the key word in that sentence is *argued*. People don't generally argue over facts. The word *argued* is in the sentence because not everyone agrees Dees stopped the Klan from functioning. In other words, implicit in the word *destroy* is an opinion, or value judgment. Before you accepted it as a valid, or trustworthy, opinion, you would need to see some support for that claim.

Members of the Ku Klux Klan were free to terrorize those men and women its members considered inferior, until civil rights lawyer Morris Dees sued the KKK and won.

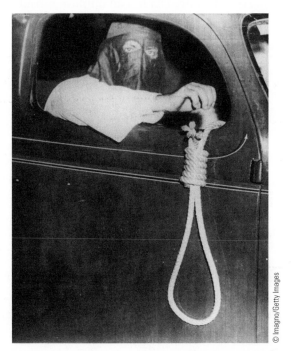

Statements like sentence 1 need to be part of an argument that provides evidence for the claim. Yet they often appear in writing meant mainly to inform. It's not that the writer means to trick you (although once in a while that might be the case). It's more that writers of all kinds, including textbook writers, find it hard to keep their opinions out of their words. The opinions just sneak in without the writers noticing. This only becomes a problem if readers don't notice either.

That's why it's so important for readers to be aware when facts and opinions mix. If they do mix within the context of an argument, where the writer provides evidence for the point of view mixed in with the facts, no problem. But if the writer provides both within the context of writing meant mainly to inform, for instance, in a textbook, then you need to sift out opinion from fact. You shouldn't just unthinkingly absorb opinion along with the facts provided.

Particularly when you read writing meant to persuade, look carefully at the language. Are there words that reveal an opinion mixed in with facts? If there are, then make sure you don't take in the opinion with the facts. Withhold judgment until you know more.

🔑 READING KEY

◆ Facts and opinions don't always remain separate. Sometimes what appears to be pure fact has an opinion mixed into the language used.

◆ EXERCISE 2   Recognizing When Opinion and Fact Mix

DIRECTIONS   Read each statement. Then label each one *F* (fact), *O* (opinion), or *B* (both).

EXAMPLE

___B___   a. A jury justly convicted a pair of dog owners of murder when the owners' dogs attacked and killed someone.

___F___   b. *Songs for Japan* is a 2011 album made to benefit the survivors of the disaster caused by a tsunami that washed away entire towns.

EXPLANATION   Statement *a* doesn't just tell you that a jury convicted two dog owners of murder. With the word *justly*, it also tells you how to feel about that conviction. Statement *b*, however, limits itself to what happened and when. There's no attempt to evaluate the action.

    1. In his book *Blink*, writer Malcolm Gladwell correctly asserts that snap judgments deserve more respect.

    2. The Supreme Court ruled that the Americans with Disabilities Act does not require companies to alter assembly lines in order to suit disabled workers.

    3. If there were full employment in this country, street gangs would disappear from the urban landscape.

    4. The Chinese government sentenced Christian pastor Gong Shengliang to death for the supposed "crime" of practicing Christianity.

_B_   5. Oddly enough for a state so liberal, Massachusetts has the lowest divorce rate in the nation.

_B_   6. A federal judge has ruled that fingerprinting, a respected tool of crime fighting, has never been proven to be sci-entifically valid.

_B_   7. Photographer Robert Frank's book *The Americans* was first published in France because no American pub-lisher wanted it.

_B_   8. In a stunning blow to campaign reform, the Supreme Court ruled that corporate contributions to political campaigns did not require limits.

_F_   9. For close to 15 percent of the U.S. population, Spanish is the mother tongue.

_F_   10. The record weight for a black bear is 880 pounds.

Getting to the Point of the Argument

Whenever you are reading a newspaper editorial, letter to the editor, journal article, or any other text where the purpose is persuasion, you need to look for the point of the author's argument. You need, that is, to determine what opinion is being put forth for your acceptance or con-sideration. Take, for example, the following reading.

The title is a big clue to the opinion being developed.

Consider which of these sentences are facts and which are opinions.

Don't Confuse Animal Hoarders with Animal Lovers

1   [1]A self-proclaimed animal lover, Audrey Weed took in every stray animal she could find until neighbors' complaints brought the police to her door, and Weed had to give up her pets. [2]Many read about Weed's story and reacted with immediate sympathy, "How sad that she had to give up her pets," they sigh. [3]But sympathy for Weed is a mistake since she is doing a good deal more harm than good, and what she really needs is medical treatment.

Paragraph 2 offers a factual report of the

2   [1]When the police arrived at Weed's Florida home, they found it over-run with cats and dogs. [2]Some of the animals in the house were painfully

situation. Facts are a way of convincing readers that the author's position is the right one.

Paragraph 3 gives us more facts and a quote from someone with expertise, or knowledge, about animal hoarding.

thin and mangy. [3]A number were dead. [4]When the police opened Weed's freezer, they found over sixty dead cats. [5]Clearly, Weed wasn't the animals' caretaker—if she had been, the animals would have been in better shape and still alive. [6]She was someone who suffered from psychological illness. [7]She was afflicted by the compulsion to hoard animals.

3   [1]According to Gary Patronek at the Center for Animals and Public Policy at Tufts University, "animal hoarding" is a serious psychological malady. [2]Although no one knows for sure what causes it, the disorder mainly affects women who grew up in abusive or neglectful family situations, where animals were the only source of affection. [3]As adults, the victims compulsively collect pets even if they cannot possibly care for them. [4]Ironically, animal hoarders, because they cannot provide for the animals they adopt, usually end up doing the animals significant harm. [5]Certainly, four similar raids conducted on homes not far from Weed's confirm that point of view. [6]Of the 201 cats and dogs confiscated, only 90 of those animals were healthy enough to be adopted. [7]The rest had to be destroyed.

Although the author starts off with a factual description of events, the third sentence in the first paragraph offers up an opinion. If you are feeling sorry for people like Audrey Weed, stop right now. She is hurting the animals she collects, not helping them. We can tell this is the core opinion of the argument because everything else in the reading offers us proof for this position.

⊙Ⓣⓘ READING KEYS

◆ Arguments usually open with the opinion they want readers to share. Be on the lookout for places in the opening paragraphs where the author ends the factual description and introduces an opinion.

◆ Sometimes the writer will introduce the facts and lead up to the opinion, which appears closer to the end of the reading.

◆ The opinion that forms the core of the argument will always be further supported by the paragraphs that follow or build up to it. The opinion that gets support is the one central to the argument.

◆ There may be other opinions in the reading, but if they don't get developed further, they are not being put forth for your consideration. They are there to support the point of the argument.

> **WEB QUEST/CLASS ACTION**
>
> Use your favorite search engine to read up on animal hoarding. Be prepared to answer any or all of the following questions in class. Is animal hoarding restricted to any particular economic class of people? Are there different degrees of the illness? Did the reading you just finished accurately describe the typical background of an animal hoarder?

[handwritten: No, Different Degrees yes Yes,]

◆ EXERCISE 3   Identifying the Central Opinion

DIRECTIONS   Read each passage. Underline the opinion being argued.

1. Myths of the Hunter

1 Hunters hotly defend their right to kill wildlife. However, the reasons they offer to justify their "sport" are nothing but self-serving myths. Hunters claim, for instance, that they pursue and shoot animals for meat. The Humane Society of the United States does not support this claim. The society's research shows that only 25 percent of hunters say they kill animals for the meat. A large number, 43 percent, say they kill purely for recreation. In America, most hunters are not killing to put food on the table for their families. They kill animals because they enjoy it.

2 Hunters would also like us to believe that they help to control wildlife populations. However, the majority of animal species—both those that are hunted and those that are not—rarely become overpopulated. When left alone, Nature herself corrects species overpopulation. She doesn't require the bloodthirsty help of hunters. Claiming to be doing an animal a favor by shooting it is another flimsy reason offered by those who love the hunt.

3 Yet hunters don't gun for weak, sick animals—the ones most likely to succumb in a harsh winter. Instead, they aim for the large, strong, trophy* animals, despite the fact that these are the ones that would be least likely to starve to death. Finally, hunters want us to believe that they know what they're doing. But if they do, how is it that they accidentally kill or injure thousands of people every year? They also wound or kill livestock and family pets. During hunting season, the woods aren't safe for anyone. Thanks to hunters on the prowl, hikers and campers must fear for their lives if they want to enjoy the outdoors.

---

*trophy: prize.

2. Jailing the Ailing

1 Pulmonary tuberculosis is a bacterial infection that usually attacks the lungs but can spread to other organs. If left untreated, it's deadly. In its active form, it is also highly contagious. That's why mandatory treatment is sometimes necessary when a patient is reluctant to follow the necessarily strict medical regime. What's not necessary, however, is what happened to Armando Rodriguez of Stockton, California. Rodriguez was arrested for failing to take his medication and he will probably do jail time.

2 Rodriguez has pulmonary tuberculosis and knows he needs to take medication. But on two occasions he failed to do so because he had been drinking the night before and knew medication does not mix well with liquor. Rodriguez made the mistake of telling a nurse in the public health system about his missed treatments. As a result, a warrant for his arrest was issued, and if convicted, he could spend up to a year in jail.

3 While criminal prosecution of tuberculosis patients who fail to take medications is rare, it does happen. But the truth is, it does no long-term good. If a patient who fails to take medication gets jailed for it, what happens when that person gets released. If the disease recurs after treatment—and in a small percentage it does—and the person again fails to take medication, he or she will probably keep it a secret. The stage is then set for further contagion. Punishment with a prison term is not the answer when it comes to dealing with patients who are irresponsible about taking their medication. Being irresponsible is a character flaw. It's not a crime.

◆ Locating Support for the Author's Opinion

If someone told you that drinking green tea was a more effective way to treat illness than any other traditional medication, you would undoubtedly ask that person, "What makes you say that?" or "Is there research to support that opinion?" or "Where did you hear that?" It's doubtful that you would just throw out any cold medications you had in your medicine cabinet. You also wouldn't refuse to take antibiotics just because someone had announced that those treatments were worthless compared to drinking green tea.

It's precisely this skeptical, or doubtful, attitude that will serve you well when reading persuasive writing. Once you grasp the opinion put forth, you need to ask, "Where's the support for that opinion? What kind of evidence is the author using in an effort to convince me?"

To answer these questions, you should start looking for the different kinds of evidence writers offer in an effort to persuade. Although the support can vary according to the opinion being expressed, these are some of the most common ways writers say to readers, "Here's why you should agree with me."

Types of Evidence	Some Examples
1. Reasons relevant, or related, to the opinion	*Opinion*: Dress codes in high school need to be strictly enforced with stiff penalties for ignoring them. *Reason*: Students wearing the same outfit can't get into unhealthy competition over fashion.
2. Facts that make the author's opinion seem trustworthy	*Opinion*: Sometimes the use of force is the only way to bring peace. *Fact*: The Serbian attacks on Kosovo only ended when NATO and the United States initiated bombing strikes of the Yugoslavian invaders.[†]
3. Studies and statistics that support the author's point of view	*Opinion*: A hybrid classroom combining an instructor's expertise with customized technological support is the most effective method of teaching mathematics to children. *Study*: A 2009 study at Carnegie Mellon University showed that students taught with a hybrid approach consistently out-performed students taught with more traditional instructional methods.
4. Expert opinion that echoes the author's point of view	*Opinion*: Promoting whale watching as a spiritual experience is not as ridiculous as some people have claimed; people have long connected animals to spiritual understanding. *Expert opinion*: As the anthropologist Eric Foundry points out in his book, *Animal Ancestors*, humans have a history of making animals embody the desires of the human spirit.
5. Examples that illustrate the author's claim	*Opinion*: Zero tolerance of drugs, weapons, and sexual harassment in school is a great idea in theory and a perfectly terrible one in practice. *Examples*: How ridiculous is it for a five-year-old boy in a Maryland elementary school to get suspended for pinching a little girl on the buttocks? Add to that idiotic affair, the high school kids who were reprimanded for handing out candy canes because candy canes can be sharpened and used as weapons!

[†]The timing described here is correct. What's often disputed is how effective the bombing was in bringing *long-term* peace.

6. Personal experience of the writer

Opinion: Asking young children to memorize poems is a terrific way to make them fall in love with language.

Personal experience: I've always heard that memorization was a poor educational tool, but teaching my fifth graders to memorize poems showed me how wrong I was.

The Audience Influences the Support

Like any other kind of supporting detail, the evidence in an argument can take different forms depending on the point being argued. However, it can also shift with the author's idea or sense of the audience.

For instance, if the writer has written a letter to the editor of a local, neighborhood newsletter, he or she might cite his or her personal experience as evidence that the current system of trash disposal is much worse than the editor seems to think. However, if the writer were responding to an article in a national newspaper and pointing out the article's flaws, he or she would probably offer studies and statistics as proof and avoid personal experience.

⊶ READING KEY

◆ The audience influences the kind of support a writer chooses. Some audiences are more prone to respond to personal experience used as evidence. Others would need factual evidence to decide in favor of the author's point of view. When deciding what kind of support to use, the writer has to think about his or her audience.

Reducing an Argument to the Bare Bones

In persuasive writing, the title is frequently a clue to the opinion the author wants you to share. At the very least, it will identify the topic under discussion. As soon as you read the title then, start asking yourself what opinion, or point of view, about that topic the writer wants you to consider or share.

Once you think you have identified the opinion, start asking yourself, "What does the author do to encourage my willingness to share or at least consider that opinion?" For practice, read the following argument. When you finish, use the blank lines at the end to (1) identify the opinion the author wants you to share and (2) explain how the author tries to make readers say, "Yes, having read this, I'm inclined to agree or at the very least I'm willing to call this opinion informed."

Zero Tolerance *Is* the Answer

What does the title suggest? Why is the word *is* italicized?

1   Thankfully, many schools across the nation are finally deciding to enforce "zero tolerance" policies that dictate harsh, automatic punishments for students who bring drugs or weapons to school. Some mistakenly criticize these policies as too rigid and unreasonable. However, the current zero tolerance policies are both effective and fair. Schools must keep them in place, despite pleas from soft-hearted parents.

2   With zero tolerance policies in effect, students know that they will be expelled and placed in another school if they bring guns or illegal drugs to campus. As a result, most choose to refrain from breaking the rules, making schools safer places for everyone.

3   If schools did not have zero tolerance policies in place, their halls would be filled with students carrying guns, selling drugs, and fighting. No one would be able to learn a thing in the resulting chaos. Maintaining a tough stance on serious infractions is not only effective but also much fairer than previous policies. In the past, school discipline has been arbitrary* and inconsistent. Zero tolerance, however, is based solely on behavior and not on other factors, such as the student's race, past record, or relationships with school employees. Therefore, it is more equitable, or just.

4   Establishing a universal zero tolerance policy also protects schools against lawsuits. Parents are less likely to sue schools for not keeping their children safe. Furthermore, parents of children who violate the rules cannot claim that their kids are victims of discrimination.

What opinion is being argued?

Zero Tolerance is being argued About and tough Disapline.

What kind of evidence does the author provide?

Children Bringing Guns Drugs and Weapons to School.

---

*arbitrary: determined by chance.

In your own words, list the reasons, examples, etc., that the author uses to support her position:

> Schools Would not be a Safe Place
> Every body Would Start fighting
> The Parents Would Sue the schools
> for Children bringing Guns
> Drugs and Weapons to school,
> The Schools Would Be closed
> Because of that society

Any time you are dealing with an argument, reduce it to its basic elements: (1) the point being argued, (2) the evidence provided to convince, and (3) if any, the response to opposing points of view. Arguments are easier to evaluate once the original text has been pared down to the underlying pieces that comprise, or go into, it.

🔑 READING KEYS

◆ Once you know what opinion the author is arguing in favor of, try to determine what methods the author uses to convince you of his point of view.

◆ Reducing an argument to its basic elements, i.e., opinion and support, is the first step to evaluating it.

◆ If a writer also responds to an opposing point of view, add that to the list of pieces comprising the argument. Then evaluate the response along with the opinion and support.

◆ EXERCISE 4   Analyzing Arguments

DIRECTIONS   Read each selection and answer the questions that follow.

EXAMPLE

The title should raise the question, What happens when kids refuse to grow up?

When Kids Refuse to Grow Up

1   Parents who don't make children responsible for their actions are doing their kids a grave disservice. They are all but guaranteeing that their children won't develop a strong character. Over-protectiveness in parents may

even lead to what's called "Peter Pan Syndrome," or the unwillingness to give up childhood.

2   Professor Humbelina Robles Ortega from the University of Granada is an expert in emotional disorders, and she argues that "Peter Pan Syndrome" is a direct result of over-protective parents. A similar argument has been made closer to home by clinical psychologist Wendy Mogel in her book *The Blessing of a Skinned Knee*. In interviews, Mogel talks about college administrators who refer to some students as "tea cups," because they are so emotionally fragile. From Mogel's perspective, such students have missed out on the toughening up of character children need if they are going to succeed as adults.

The author introduces the first expert who echoes the opening opinion and offers evidence for it.

3   Author and child psychologist Dan Kindlon says that parents who always protect their children from the consequences of their actions are shortchanging their kids. By covering for their kids' mistakes or keeping them from unpleasant situations, they are inhibiting their children's character development. A father who inconveniences himself by retrieving an item his child forgot at school loses an opportunity to help that child develop a sense of personal responsibility. Likewise, parents who don't want their teenagers to work during the summer or after school rob teens of a chance to develop a work ethic.

Paragraph 3 introduces another expert. He offers a specific reason why overprotecting kids leads to the Peter Pan Syndrome.

4   Obviously there are parents who don't want to get this message. They think that sparing their children every difficulty and hardship is the right thing to do. However, their need to protect their children from every slight may have its origin in little more than guilt. As two-income families have grown, children spend less time with their parents, and their parents feel like they are shortchanging them. To make up for that, they tend to go overboard making their children's life easier and, in their minds, happier. But as the work of people like Ortega, Mogel, and Kindlon suggests, the end result is not happiness. It's an inability to grow up.

In paragraph 4, the author addresses a likely objection by saying that parental overprotectiveness grows out of guilt and leads to a negative result.

1. In your own words, what opinion is being argued in this reading?

Parents make a big mistake if they over-protect their children. They are creating kids who don't want to be adults.

2. How many experts does the author cite in support of the opinion being promoted? ___3___

3. Which of these reasons is given to support the author's opinion?

    a. Children who are over-protected think they are entitled to happiness.

    b. Children who are over-protected are inclined to blame everyone else for their mistakes.

    (c.) Children who never have to acknowledge mistakes or fix errors don't develop a strong character or sense of responsibility.

4. What two specific examples of over-protective behavior are given in support of the opinion?

    a. the father who takes the time to pick up whatever it is the child forgot

    b. the parents who don't want their kids to work over the summer

1. Nutella's Dubious Health Benefits

1   In 2012, two mothers won a lawsuit against Ferrero, the makers of the hazelnut spread Nutella. The plaintiffs claimed that Nutella had advertised the chocolate spread as a healthy breakfast alternative when it clearly isn't. They were correct, of course, and Ferrero's advertising did suggest that Nutella on bread was a healthy breakfast choice. As a result of the mothers' victory, any consumer who purchased Nutella in the last five years can get reimbursed for up to five jars of Nutella. The total settlement amounted to a whopping $3.5 million.

2   While Ferrero had no business describing the spread as healthy—there are eleven grams of fat in every two tablespoons—the success of this consumer lawsuit may do serious damage to consumer rights. It will encourage what has become a nationwide effort to limit consumers' ability to take corporations to court. Supporters of tort reform, as this effort is called, would like to limit the rights of consumers to take their grievances to court. Unfortunately, those who don't want consumers to have the right to sue corporations for damages can now cite the Nutella payout as another example of why letting the courts evaluate consumer complaints is a bad idea. They can point to the Nutella award as another instance of individuals using the courts for personal profit rather than to advance consumer protections or right a wrong.

3   When the judgment became public, letters to the editor across the country were almost unanimously against the award. Most of them followed the lead of columnist Dennis Rockstroh of the *Mercury News*, who said, "For crying out loud everyone, read the labels or have someone read

them to you." Yes, Ferrero did use misleading advertising and they got caught. But parents should rely more on reading the ingredients clearly printed on the label than on the advertisers' commercials. And if they fail to do so, they shouldn't turn to the court to make up for their mistake. In the end, that behavior will fuel efforts to promote tort reform, and we will all suffer by losing our ability to fight back when a company or corporation shortchanges or injures the consumer.

1. In your own words, what opinion is being argued in this reading?

    The consumer has to Be more Responsible and (oad the ingredients.

2. Which of these reasons is given to support the author's opinion?

    a. Ferrero clearly lied in its advertising of Nutella spread.
    b. Parents should read labels in order to determine if a product is good for their children to consume.
    c. The judgment against Ferrero is going to encourage the demand for tort reform.

3. What does the reference to Dennis Rockstroh illustrate?

    Personal Responsibility.

4. Does the last paragraph continue the reasoning begun previously or offer a new reason for the author's opinion?

    They talked about losing The comany Short Changes or injures the Consumer.

2. When Justice Is Not Served

1 In 2011, the state of Texas executed Milton Mathis for murder. He had killed two people and critically injured a third. However, according to multiple tests administered by the Texas Department of Corrections, Mathis's IQ was somewhere in the low sixties. This is way below what most states recognize as mild retardation. Mathis was a killer, but given his level of mental functioning, it's hard to believe that he knew the consequences of his actions.

2   The prosecution argued that Mathis wasn't mentally retarded but street smart and gaming the system. This is a matter of interpretation, which is another way of saying it's a matter of opinion. Opinion should not play a role when a human being's life is at stake. Any time a prisoner takes several IQ tests, both on paper and in interviews, and fails them, that prisoner should not be executed, no matter how vile his or her crime.

3   People with extremely low IQs who commit crimes cannot fully understand the nature of their actions or the moral implications of those actions. This means that imposing the death penalty on them violates the Eighth Amendment of the Bill of Rights, which prohibits cruel and unusual punishment. Then, too, it is important to remember that people suffering from severe mental retardation often lack impulse control. Even if they could grasp the consequences of their actions, they may be emotionally and physiologically unable to control themselves. Thus, it's not fair or just to take their lives when they never possessed the ability to restrain the behavior they are being punished for.

1. In your own words, what opinion is being argued in this reading?

   Mathis committing a Crime when he had a low IQ.

2. Which of these reasons is given to support the author's opinion?

   a. People with a low IQ who commit crimes cannot fully understand the nature of their actions, making the death penalty especially cruel and unfair.

   b. People with a low IQ who commit crimes have already been punished enough by having a limited understanding of the world.

   c. People with a low IQ who commit serious crimes have often been abused as children and are therefore not responsible for their crimes.

3. Where and how does the author respond to the opposition?

   In Paragraph 2 he says that the prisoner shouldn't be executed no matter how serious A Crime.

4. What example does the author offer in support of the opinion put forth?

Milton Mathis Committing a hush Crime.

3. An Unproductive Policy

1 Some schools believe it's a good idea to have children repeat kindergarten if their academic performance is weak. However, there are some good reasons not to hold back kids who struggle in school.

2 One reason is the educational leap children often experience toward the end of their kindergarten year. A child who struggles throughout kindergarten may very well make up his or her lack of progress at the end of kindergarten, over the summer, or even during first grade. Another reason is that making a child repeat a grade doesn't necessarily remedy the original weakness or difficulty that kept the child from being promoted in the first place.

3 Teacher and educational consultant Sandra Rief, the author of *Ready . . . Start . . . School!*, counsels against having children repeat kindergarten. She says, "Children who are held back may do better at first, but many fall behind again if their areas of weakness haven't been addressed." Being held back also carries a social stigma, or negative label, which can give children a sense of inferiority. Children who are teased by their peers for being held back begin to dislike school. If teachers insist on holding kindergarteners back, they should prepare themselves for soaring dropout rates as these kids fall behind, become frustrated, and start thinking they can't learn.

(Source of quotation: Vicky Mlyniec, "Should Your Child Repeat Kindergarten?" *Parents*, February 2002, pp. 137–38.)

1. Paraphrase the opinion that is argued in this reading.

Children Being Droppedout or Repeating A Grade in School.

2. Which of these reasons is given to support the author's opinion?

a. Children who are held back never recover from the shame of the experience.

b. Studies show that children who are held back are more likely to quit school early.

c. Children who do poorly in kindergarten often make big improvements in the following year.

3. Why is Sandra Rief mentioned?

Because She's a teacher and Educationl Consultant

4. Why does the author use the phrase "social stigma"?

That Children are being Shamed inschool.

IDIOM ALERT: Nanny state

Nannies are caretakers for children. Because of its association to child care, the word *nanny* has been attached to the word *state* or *government* as a term of criticism. Implicitly, it criticizes governments that intervene in the lives of their citizens. The expression has strictly negative connotations. It was once only popular in other countries, but has now made its way to our shores and is turning up quite frequently. In 2010, Sarah Palin called Pennsylvania a "nanny state" for its attempts to limit the consumption of sweets in the schools.

Evaluating the Evidence

Once you have identified the support the author uses to convince, you also have to consider how good it is. There are, after all, good and bad arguments. Some people put forth an opinion and provide reasons that are relevant, or directly related to the opinion promoted. Others are so **biased**, or convinced their point of view is the correct one, they don't spend enough time trying to convince others. Thus, it's up to you, the reader, to evaluate the kind of evidence each author offers you.

Although there are many ways to evaluate arguments, we'll only go over two of the most basic and most necessary questions you need to ask about the evidence in an argument.

1. Are the reasons, facts, and examples relevant?

2. Do the experts have the right background and experience?

Spotting Irrelevant Reasons, Examples, and Facts

Once you have reduced the author's argument to its bare bones, it's easier to see if the author's reasons are clearly and directly related to the opinion. In the paragraph that follows, for example, the author provides an example. The example is meant to illustrate the reason for the opinion proposed: Like the relatives of crime victims, defendants' relatives should also be heard. However, neither the example nor the implied reason it represents has any bearing on the opinion.

> In many states, the relatives of victims have the right to speak at the trial of the person convicted. But there are times when the families of defendants need the right to speak as well. In 2010, Karen Blackwon was appealing a murder conviction and her stepmother wanted to speak on her behalf. The judge told her no. But the judge was wrong to do so. Blackwon's stepmother is eighty-two years old and sick with pancreatic cancer. She should have the right to speak in court.

Break this argument down to its basic elements, and it looks something like this:

Opinion: Like crime victims, defendants deserve the right to be heard in court.

Example: Karen Blackwon's appeal

Implied reason: The stepmother should have been heard because she was seriously ailing.

While the example is relevant to the opinion expressed, the reason it implies isn't. It's possible to argue that relatives of a defendant should be heard because they might be able to explain the causes of the defendant's behavior. But the stepmother being ill doesn't in any way explain why defendants' relatives have the right to be heard in court. That would, after all, exclude the testimony of all healthy relatives.

Questions to Ask About Relevance
◆

1. Is the author's supporting evidence appealing to your emotions or your logic?
2. Are the facts cited up-to-date?
3. Do the facts and reasons presented prove what the author suggests they do?

4. Do you have enough information about the facts to know how they relate to the opinion?

5. Do the reasons differ from the opinion, or do they restate it in different words?[†]

6. Is there a clear connection between the reasons given and the opinion stated?

7. Do you know enough about the facts used and the figures cited to be sure they support the author's opinion?

Checking the Experts

When the names of people are used to support an opinion, check to see how they are identified. The people used to support an opinion should have knowledge of the situation or event described. They should also have the background and training to evaluate it. Being famous isn't enough. Alec Baldwin may be an excellent actor. But that doesn't mean he understands the roots of the financial crisis that rocked the country in 2008. If the author you're reading quotes him, or any other celebrity, to support the opinion being proposed, look elsewhere for information on the subject.

Similarly, if the author tells you that Dr. Paul Miller believes exercises training the right side of the brain are an excellent way to develop more flexible thinking and greater creativity, check to see how Dr. Miller is identified in the reading.[2] If he isn't, see if you can find him on the Web. Dr. Miller may have gotten his degree in dentistry and teamed up with a company more interested in your money than your creativity.

Questions to Ask of the Experts
◆

1. Does the author give you background about the person providing supposedly expert opinion?

2. Does the expert used to support the opinion expressed have anything to gain by having that idea generally accepted?

3. Is there an indication that the person quoted has written about the subject or studied it in-depth?

[†]This form of reasoning is called *circular argument*.
[2]Although the different sides of the brain do have different functions, there is remarkably little hard evidence that the brain can be "trained" to become more creative. Yet books and courses on this subject were once very popular.

4. Is the expert's training and experience in the subject up-to-date? Or is the expert someone who knew a lot about the situation or issue described a long time ago but whose information may well be out of date?

5. Is the expert used to support the author's opinion known solely as a celebrity rather than an expert in the field being discussed?

IDIOM ALERT: Writing on the wall

According to the Bible, mysterious writing on the wall signaled the fall of the Babylonian Empire. Now when we talk about writing on the wall, we mean that it's obvious a particular train of events is going to occur, and it probably won't be good. "When the soldiers were assigned to train the local police force, the writing was on the wall; soon they would be leaving and turning over security to local law enforcement. The result would be chaos."

⌐ READING KEYS

♦ Whatever facts, reasons, or examples the author provides in support of his or her opinion, make sure you evaluate them for relevance.

♦ Be sure you can explain how the facts, reasons, and examples are related to the opinion being expressed. Don't be distracted by emotional appeals or facts that are meaningless without more specific explanation.

♦ If other people are cited to support the author's opinion, make sure you know why they are considered knowledgeable enough to be called experts.

♦ Ignore celebrity endorsements unless the topic under discussion has to do with being a celebrity.

♦ If someone cited as an expert is introduced only as doctor or professor without any information about what their degree is in or where they work, double-check their names on the Web to discover their credentials, i.e., their experience and training.

♦ EXERCISE 5   Evaluating Arguments

DIRECTIONS   Read each selection. Then answer the questions that follow by circling the letter of the correct answer or writing in the blanks.

EXAMPLE

When the System Works, Don't Fix It

Here's the reason we don't need legislation: The food industry regulates itself.

Note the heel image used to suggest the unfairness of it all.

1   It's true that consumers have been faced with several food scares over the last few years. Peanut butter has been tainted by salmonella, melon and lettuce by listeria. Mad cow disease has now been found in some of our cows and *E. coli* on our spinach. Yet none of these scares merits the kind of regulation and legislation our government has been throwing at the problem. We have enough legislation protecting our food supply. In 2010, President Obama signed into law yet another piece of legislation designed to regulate the food industry. This time it's the Food Safety and Modernization Act, a huge set of regulations and restrictions that puts the food industry under the heel of the federal government in a way unheard of before this.

2   Yet the U.S. food supply is, in general, one of the safest in the world. Those who put food on our table do not want to face angry consumers who will sue them for improper handling and preparation of food. Thus they maintain the highest safety standards willingly. They don't need a nanny government looking over their shoulders, slowing down production, and undoubtedly raising the cost of the food we eat.

1. What opinion does the author want readers to share or consider?

The food industry needs no additional legislation to protect our food supply. What we already have is too much.

2. What is the reference to the Food Safety and Modernization Act supposed to suggest to readers?

a. The federal government has responded effectively to the recent food scares.

b. Governments always want to produce legislation that has a long, fancy title but in the end, changes nothing.

c. This new legislation was even worse than what came before in terms of burdening the food industry.

3. What's missing from the discussion of the Food Safety and Modernization Act that readers would need to know to evaluate it as evidence?

what the legislation actually does to protect the country's food supply

4. Does this statement provide effective support for this opinion? "Those who put food on our table do not want to face angry consumers who will sue them for improper handling and preparation of food. Thus they maintain the highest safety standards willingly."

No. It could, but it would need some factual evidence. Otherwise, all you have is

an opinion supporting another opinion.

EXPLANATION   In the author's mind, the fact that a big piece of legislation regulating the food industry was passed in 2010 proves the point of the argument: We have enough legislation protecting the food supply; we don't need more. But unless you know what the legislation does, you don't know if it "puts the food industry under the heel of the federal government." (Note how imagery is used to imply the excessive nature of the regulation.) Nor do you know how effectively it protects the food supply. While this fact *could be* relevant to the author's argument, it hasn't been developed enough for you to take it as adequate evidence.

1. Our Guns Are in Control

1   Anyone who believes that law-abiding citizens should have the right to own a gun needs to call his or her representatives immediately. Our government should know that we do not require any more gun-control legislation. We already have 20,000 gun control laws in the United States.[3]

2   Yet now in the aftermath of the Gabrielle Giffords[4] shooting, members of state and federal government are again talking about stricter gun legislation. Everyone knows where this will lead. By the time the government is through, no one will be able to buy a handgun for protection or a rifle for hunting. Even gun clubs will be outlawed. Target practice will be severely punished with stiff fines, even jail time. Supposedly, the laws controlling the purchase of guns are designed to ensure that guns don't fall into inappropriate hands. But the truth is, these laws are supported by people who believe that no one should have guns. They don't even want honest citizens to keep a gun for their own protection.

---

[3]Actually, this figure has not withstood the test of research, and it seems to be more fiction than fact. See http://www.brookings.edu/es/urban/publications/gunbook4.pdf.
[4]In 2011 Arizona Rep. Gabrielle Giffords was the target of a shooting, which left her seriously injured.

1. What opinion does the author want readers to share or consider?

   They want us not to own Guns for Protection.

2. What is the reference to 20,000 gun control laws supposed to suggest to readers?

   a. Liberal legislators try to make themselves popular with their supporters by restricting gun use.

   b. If we have this many laws controlling the use of guns, then that must be enough. *(circled)*

   c. Gun control legislation has a two-hundred-year-long history, and people have been making laws against using guns for years.

3. Is that figure an effective and relevant piece of evidence?

   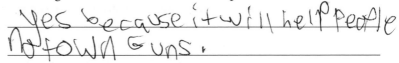
   Yes because it will help people to own Guns.

4. Does this reason provide effective support for the author's opinion? "By the time the government is through, no one will be able to buy a handgun for protection or a rifle for hunting."

   yes and to Let People not buy Guns.

2. Re-thinking the Role of Standardized Testing

1 In 2002, George W. Bush signed No Child Left Behind, a school reform plan that has left the nation's school systems in shambles. Yet for some reason, many educational reformers remain enthusiastic about the assumption on which No Child Left Behind is based: Standardized testing can accurately measure what a child has learned.

2 Standardized testing, with its emphasis on multiple-choice questions that can be scored electronically, does have a place in education. But high standardized test scores are being treated as the crown of educational success. Nothing else really counts except those test scores. A student might have improved classroom communication skills, become a better essay writer, and

developed more self-confidence. But if you can't test those improvements with an instrument that can be machine scored, they don't exist.

3   Terrified of losing their jobs and having their schools close down, many teachers have seen the writing on the wall and started teaching to the test. Not surprisingly, they have been encouraged by their equally terrified administrators, who know that low scores can mean a school gets shut down. This fear of what low test scores will bring about quite naturally dampens all spontaneous discussion as kids focus only on what might be on the test.

4   If teaching to the test doesn't work, a few teachers and administrators have gone even further and tampered with the exam results. In 2011, teachers in Atlanta were caught up in a cheating scandal that ended with forty-one teachers resigning or retiring. By 2012, the same thing was happening in Philadelphia, where one in five schools was investigated for tampering with test scores. Accusations of score inflation have been leveled in other cities, including Houston, New York, Detroit, and Washington, D.C.

5   Even Michelle Rhee, former chancellor of Washington D.C.'s public schools and current promoter of standardized testing as a way of evaluating educational achievement, has been accused of manipulating test scores to indicate gains students in the schools did not really make. As educational historian and former supporter of No Child Left Behind, Diane Ravitch has argued, "No Child Left Behind has created a culture in which people will do anything to keep their jobs," and keeping their jobs, at least currently, means making sure that students do well on standardized tests. Nothing else matters. It doesn't take an educational historian to know that this is a very limited view of educational accomplishment.

1. What opinion does the author want readers to share or consider?

The no Child Left Behind Reform Plan makes people do things to keep their Jobs.

2. What two reasons does the author provide in support of that opinion?

Atlanta was caught up cheating. Philadelphia was investigated.

3. The author introduces Diane Ravitch as a source of expert opinion. What are Ravitch's qualifications?

an Educationalhistorian

Does she qualify as an expert on the subject? *yes*

4. What is the author doing in this sentence? "Standardized testing, with its emphasis on multiple-choice questions that can be scored electronically, does have a place in education."

a. stating the opinion that ties the pieces of the argument together

b. providing evidence for that opinion

c. responding to those who might disagree

◇ Word Choice and Tone

"I spend a great deal of time thinking about the power of language—the way it can evoke an emotion, a visual image, a complex idea or a simple truth. As a writer, language is the tool of my trade...."

—novelist Amy Tan, from her essay "My Mother's English"

In an attempt to persuade their readers, writers are careful to provide supporting evidence such as solid reasons, good examples, and experienced experts. But writers have another powerful tool of persuasion at their disposal as well. They have the power of language to sway the opinions of their readers.

Can you say, for example, what this sentence from an essay on page 518 suggests about the author's point of view? "The book spells out what has become increasingly apparent to *most thoughtful observers*: The more time we spend online, the less we interact with real people and the less we want to." Do you see that by saying that another author's opinion is shared by "most thoughtful observers," the writer suggests that those who disagree aren't all that thoughtful?

What about the image of the crown in the following sentence? What does the implied comparison to a crown suggest about test scores: "But high standardized test scores are being treated as the crown of educational success." Do you see that the comparison suggests how test scores are ruling educational practice?

To see the effect word choice can have, take this sentence from the reading on page 479: "In the past, school discipline has been arbitrary and inconsistent." What would happen if you changed the adjectives *arbitrary* and *inconsistent* to "flexible and personalized." That phrase still means that the discipline varied. But now the connotations, or associations, are positive rather than negative. Thus readers might view schools that *don't* practice zero tolerance in a more approving way, precisely because they aren't so consistent in how they discipline students.

When Tone Becomes Recognizable

Sometimes writers use only a few words to nudge readers in the direction they want them to go. But sometimes they go beyond just a few words to give the entire reading a certain **tone**, or attitude, much like the tone or attitude you hear when someone speaks to you.

If you've ever read a piece of writing and thought to yourself, "Boy, he really loves life" or "She really knows what she's talking about," then you've responded to the writer's tone. When the writer is successful at creating tone, readers react in a way that makes them side with the writer's point of view. Here, for instance, the author's tone is so deeply felt and so passionate on the subject of family, it's all but impossible to disagree with him:

> I have come to believe that family goes far beyond a child's eyes looking like her mother and father's, or a child having the same mannerisms as her parents (which we do, in fact, have). It is more than a name or the number of bedrooms in a home. I have come to believe that family is about love and struggle and adapting. That there are many different types of family and they evolve—2.5 kids and a white fence, single parent families, those involving incarceration, illness or a combination of all these—family is a wide term with plenty of room for interpretation. (Lee Herrick, "What Is This Thing Called Family?" In *Visions Across the Americas*, 7th ed., J. Sterling Warner and Judith Hilliard, eds. Boston: Wadsworth Publishing, p. 222.)

Not everyone would agree with this author. Many people have much stricter notions of what family entails. However, some of those who disagree might well be swayed by the passion in the author's tone. And that's exactly what tone is expected to do. It's meant to make even a reluctant reader think, "Well, he might have a point."

Creating Tone

Like the power of words, the effect of tone is something of a mystery. It's hard to pin down precisely how a writer creates it. In the passage above, some of the tone—its feeling and directness—comes from the author's repetition of the phrase "have come to believe." It also comes from the author's willingness to be specific. When he says there are many different types of families, he offers examples of the people the term must include, "single parent families, those involving incarceration, illness, or a combination of all these."

But however writers create tone—the chart on page 497 describes some of the devices they use—as a reader you need to be aware of its presence. It shouldn't influence or affect you unknowingly. You don't want to be sweet-talked or bullied into accepting an opinion you don't really share.

Whenever you sense the writer is trying to persuade you to share an opinion, look carefully at the language and consider its effect on you. Are there only a few words and phrases designed to influence your thinking? Or has the author given you the sense of a person behind the words, one who speaks to you in a tone meant to convince.

Look over the list of words describing tone. These are some of the tones a writer might create with words, in the hope of persuading the reader.

Words That Describe Tone ♦		
admiring	doubtful	proud
amazed	enthusiastic	puzzled
angry	friendly	regretful
anxious	humorous	respectful
arrogant	insulted	rude
breezy	insulting	sarcastic
bullying	ironic (saying the	self-pitying
cautious	opposite of what	serious
challenging	is intended)	shocked
comical	neutral	skeptical
confident	nostalgic (longing	solemn
critical	for a past time)	spiteful
curious	objective	sympathetic
cynical	outraged	worried
determined	passionate	
disgusted	patriotic	

A Writer's Toolbox for Tone

Word choice is crucial to tone. It encourages different reactions in readers and reveals the author's point of view. Of the sentences on the right, which one suggests the writer thinks PETA does good work?

Example: "People in PETA are devoted to the cause of animal rights" versus "People in PETA are obsessed by the cause of animal rights."

Figurative language that implicitly or explicitly makes comparisons can lighten tone and make it comical or turn it more serious. Where is the figurative language in each of the two sentences shown here on the right?

Example: "My father's death left a hole in my heart that never completely healed" versus "Getting the U.S. Senate to agree on anything these days is like trying to herd a bunch of ornery cats."

Allusions, or references to other people and events, are critical to tone, and like word choice they tell you a lot about the author's point of view and the tone he or she is trying to convey. In this case, the allusion to the whistle blower Frank Serpico puts Lohse in a positive light. Imagine if he were compared to Judas from the Bible.

Example: "Andrew Lohse is a college student who blew the whistle on fraternity hazing at Dartmouth and, like Frank Serpico, the cop who wouldn't accept police corruption as part of his job description, Lohse is paying heavy dues for telling the truth."

Reporting personal experience with a conversational style can create a sincere tone. Writers know that readers are inclined to trust authors who reveal personal failings as part of an effort to convince.

Example: "Like most people, I indulge myself in small falsehoods and still think of myself as an honest person. Sure I lie, but it doesn't hurt anything. Or does it?" (Stephanie Ericsson, "The Ways We Lie," in *Visions Across the Americas*, ed. J. Sterling Warner and Judith Hilliard, p. 181.)

Writers intent on persuasion are especially careful about their word choice. They choose words that will incline readers to accept or at least consider their opinion.

Sometimes writers include only a few words chosen to influence readers. But sometimes the entire reading, from choice of pronouns to imagery and sentence length, encourages the reader to infer a particular feeling or attitude from the author's words.

Word choice, allusions, imagery, and personal anecdotes are just a few of the ways writers create a tone.

Recognizing Tone

DIRECTIONS   Read each passage and identify the tone you hear in the author's choice of words.

EXAMPLE

The word *legendary* encourages readers to see Gutiérrez in a positive light.

Notice the phrase "no Christian with a conscience," which suggests those not in support of liberation theology are also not serious Christians.

The allusion to Jesus is meant to stress the level of the sacrifice.

The Meaning of Liberation* Theology*

Archbishop Oscar Romero, executed by right-wing thugs in El Salvador, was probably the most famous practitioner of liberation theology. But it was the legendary Gustavo Gutiérrez who, in the 1960s and 1970s, gave the movement its meaning and momentum. Believing that no Christian with a conscience could ignore the cries of the poor, Gutiérrez campaigned for committed Christian action in response to the poverty and pain of the millions barely earning a living in Third World countries.

Many heard Gutiérrez's call. And many followed his teachings. It became commonplace, especially in Latin America and the Caribbean, for priests and nuns to take part in trade union politics and community organizations. These acts of courage got them targeted as a threat to the government. Sometimes, they ended up dead as a result. From the perspective of these Catholic workers, it was sinful to pray for people's souls while ignoring their need for food, shelter, and simple dignity. Living, and often dying, in service to the poor, liberation theologians have become the true disciples of Jesus.

(a.) admiring

b. sarcastic

c. friendly

d. neutral

---

*liberation: setting free.
*theology: study of religion.

EXPLANATION   The language throughout emphasizes the positive and widespread effect of Gutiérrez's writing.

USDA Might Not Be the Bank of Choice

So if you had to pick the best bank to get a mortgage from, whom would you pick? Would you pick big, bad Bank of America routinely criticized for its mortgage practices of the past decade and the focus of numerous protests? Or would you be more inclined to choose the less known and certainly less criticized U.S. Department of Agriculture's Rural Housing Service (USDA)? You would probably opt for the latter rather than the former, right?

Well if you did, you would be making a mistake. For a while, Bank of America seemed to be the embodiment of folk singer Woody Guthrie's claim that some men rob you with a six gun while others do it with a fountain pen. Bank of America's banking practices during the country's financial meltdown have been called everything from "disorganized" to "corrupt." Bank of America, however, may have taken to heart all of the criticism leveled at it. Prodded by the U.S. government, the bank, along with five other big banks, has set up a mortgage modification program, which is designed to lower interest payments for mortgage holders who got into debt. For many the program is a lifesaver.

The USDA specializes in mortgages for people living in isolated areas and has generally flown under the radar when it comes to public criticism of its banking practices. Perhaps that's the reason it has not tried to help those who hold mortgages with them.

At seventy-one, Charles Ward of Nelsonville, Ohio, is an illustration of what that means in concrete terms. Ward fell behind in his mortgage in the fall of 2011. His wife was fighting lung cancer and his medical bills were going through the roof. Scrambling for money and counting on a tax refund, he only got more bad news from his bank. His lender, the USDA, had confiscated his tax refund for failure to make his mortgage payments. It had also taken out money from his Social Security payments.

As the *Wall Street Journal* has correctly pointed out in a headline, "The USDA Is a Tough Collector When Mortgages Go Bad," and it's not interested in helping those who have defaulted on their mortgages. Next time you hear someone complaining about the Bank of America, you might also want to mention the USDA, which has a take-no-prisoners attitude when it comes to getting paid. (A more detailed discussion of the USDA versus big banks can be found in the May 25, 2012, issue of the *New York Times*.)

a. comical
b. critical
c. friendly
d. neutral

Pueblo Architects

One doesn't have to be an architectural historian to admire the adobe architecture of the Pueblo Indians from the Southwest. Pueblo dwellings made of adobe, or red clay, are esteemed by even the most modern of architects and engineers. They are the perfect marriage of form and function.

In addition to their spare and simple beauty, what makes the adobe dwellings so impressive is their ability to "air condition" a house without using electrical equipment. During hot days, walls made of adobe absorb the heat generated by the sun and release that heat slowly during cool nights, thus warming the house when it's necessary. When a new day breaks, the walls have given up their heat and are now cold enough to cool the house during the hot day. Then they warm up again at night.

This cycle goes on day after day. The walls absorb heat during the day and cool off during the night. Thus the houses themselves are always capable of responding to outside temperatures. The Pueblo Indians did not go to architecture school. But they were and are natural architects. Using no technology except the human brain, they figured out exactly how thick the adobe walls needed to be to make the cycle work consistently and efficiently for decades.

Built to meet the demands of a desert environment, adobe architecture cools the air in daytime and warms it during the night.

a. curious

b. disturbed

c. approving

d. neutral

Brides on Demand

Every year more men search print and online ads looking for women to marry—the right kind of women, that is. Russian, Eastern European, and Asian women are in particularly hot demand. They are popular because they are famous for pampering the men they love.

Or at least that's what the men who search for brides overseas like to think—that the women whose flights or ship passage they have bought and paid for must really love them. It never occurs to these egomaniacs that the women, who often come from notoriously poor countries, are willing to put themselves up for sale because they are desperate to escape the circumstances of their lives. No, these gentlemen prefer to think that they are living out the fairy tale depicted in the movie that gave Julia Roberts her start, *Pretty Woman*. In the movie, the heroine starts out interested only in money but ends up falling in love with the man who has it. It's a nice thought, but most of these guys looking overseas for wives bear no resemblance to Richard Gere in his prime.

Naïve enough to marry women they barely know, men who "order" their wives from overseas are usually shocked and surprised when the women don't remain forever grateful. After a two-year probation period, the women can legally stay in the United States. Thus it's no surprise that marriages begun on a less than promising basis—she's got looks; he's got cash—don't have a long shelf life. Yet the husbands are routinely astonished when the wives abandon their marriages. But what did these men think? Did they really believe that women from poor countries don't want personal independence? They do not deserve our sympathy. The time when men were masters of the household is gone. Men should just accept it and prepare to treat women as their equals.

a. comical

b. sarcastic

c. friendly

d. neutral

Just3 Exercises

Rounding up the keys:

Here is a list of all the reading keys introduced in the chapter. Use them to review for the test on page 513. If a particular reading key doesn't make sense on its own, go back to the page where it appeared and review the section preceding it.

At the heart of every argument is an opinion that the author wants readers to share or at least seriously consider. (p. 465)

Readers who want to understand persuasive writing need a clear grasp of the opinion or perspective being promoted. (p. 465)

They also need to determine what kind of support the author offers readers in an effort to make them consider sharing the opinion. (p. 465)

In addition to an opinion and the support for that opinion, writers also frequently address the opposition. They explain, that is, why those who disagree are wrong or misguided. (p. 465)

Opinions are ideas or beliefs about the world that are shaped by background, experience, and education. Thus they can't be verified, or checked for accuracy. (p. 468)

Facts are not affected by the background or experience of the person who states them. Thus they can be verified for accuracy and can be labeled *true* or *false*. (p. 468)

Facts and opinions don't always remain separate. Sometimes what appears to be pure fact has an opinion mixed into the language used. (p. 472)

Arguments usually open with the opinion they want readers to share. Be on the lookout for places in the opening paragraphs where the author ends the factual description and introduces an opinion. (p. 474)

Sometimes the writer will introduce the facts and lead up to the opinion, which appears closer to the end of the reading. (p. 474)

The opinion that forms the core of the argument will always be further supported by the paragraphs that follow or build up to it. The opinion that gets support is the one central to the argument. (p. 474) There may be other opinions in the reading, but if they don't get developed further, they are not being put forth for your consideration. They are there to support the point of the argument. (p. 474)

The audience influences the kind of support a writer chooses. Some audiences are more prone to respond to personal experience used as evidence. Others would need factual evidence to decide in favor of the author's point of view. When deciding what kind of support to use, the writer has to think about his or her audience. (p. 478) Once you know what opinion the author is arguing in favor of, try to determine what methods the author uses to convince you of his point of view. (p. 480) Reducing an argument to its basic elements, i.e., opinion and support, is the first step to evaluating it. (p. 480) If a writer also responds to an opposing point of view, add that to the list of pieces comprising the argument. Then evaluate the response along with the opinion and support. (p. 480)

Whatever facts, reasons, or examples the author provides in support of his or her opinion, make sure you evaluate them for relevance. (p. 489) Be sure you can explain how the facts, reasons, and examples are related to the opinion being expressed. Don't be distracted by emotional appeals or facts that are meaningless without more specific explanation. (p. 489) If other people are cited to support the author's opinion, make sure you know why they are considered knowledgeable enough to be called experts. (p. 489) Ignore celebrity endorsements unless the topic under discussion has to do with being a celebrity. (p. 489) If someone cited as an expert is introduced only as doctor or professor without any information about what their degree is in or where they work, double-check their names on the Web to discover their credentials, i.e., their experience and training. (p. 489)

Writers intent on persuasion are especially careful about their word choice. They choose words that will incline readers to accept or at least consider their opinion. (p. 498)

Sometimes writers include only a few words chosen to influence readers. But sometimes the entire reading, from choice of pronouns to imagery and sentence length, encourages the reader to infer a particular feeling or attitude from the author's words. (p. 498)

Word choice, allusions, imagery, and personal anecdotes are just a few of the ways writers create a tone. (p. 498)

Ten More Words for Your Academic Vocabulary

dilemma: a situation in which a choice has to be made between two possibilities, with neither possibility being a good one

The president was facing a serious *dilemma*. If he didn't pass the new mining legislation, his environmental supporters would despise him. But if he passed it, his opponents were going to say he destroyed jobs and should not be re-elected.

proximity: nearness in space, time

Proximity seems to be one of the key elements in forming a friendship.

altruistic: inclined to think of others before one's self

When it comes to their children, many parents tend to be highly *altruistic*.

convergence: a state in which different people, things, or conditions come together and meet or combine

The automobile manufacturer claimed that the car embodied the *convergence* of style, safety, and value.

homogeneous: similar, alike

Populations in European countries are more *homogeneous* than the population of the United States, where people of many different ethnic backgrounds have come together in one country.

heterogeneous: different, dissimilar

The committee was a very *heterogeneous* group, which unfortunately led to much conflict.

replicate: make an exact copy of something, repeat, reproduce

Because it had not *replicated* the previous conditions of the event, the study was not solid evidence for the author's claims.

obligation: an act that is required from a moral or financial standpoint

Having been lucky enough to find a wonderful foster parent when he was young, the doctor felt a moral *obligation* to do the same for someone else.

administer: to oversee or manage; to be responsible for giving out or supplying anything from justice to medicine

(1) After the arts editor got the grant, she was determined to *administer* the poetry program herself. (2) The medical team arrived thirty days later to *administer* the vaccine against hepatitis.

susceptible: easily influenced or affected; inclined or likely to be infected by a disease

(1) Like most celebrities, she was *susceptible* to flattery and that made her easy to manage. (2) During the flu epidemic, it was clear that the very young and very old were especially *susceptible*.

Exercise 6 Making Academic Vocabulary Familiar

DIRECTIONS Each sentence uses a more conversational or simpler version of the words listed below. At the end of the sentence, fill in the blank with the more academic word that could replace the underlined word or phrase in the sentence.

~~dilemma~~ ~~altruistic~~ ~~homogeneous~~ ~~replicate~~ ~~administer~~
~~proximity~~ ~~convergence~~ ~~heterogeneous~~ ~~obligation~~ ~~susceptible~~

1. <u>Closeness</u> to the university was one of the reasons the house wasn't on the market for very long. _Proximity_

2. The <u>coming together</u> of three different storms produced a "perfect storm" that destroyed boats and lives. _Convergence_

3. The new president was faced with a decision that left her no good options. _Dilemma_

4. The CEO's son did not have the right personality to take over his father's chair as head of the board. He was always thinking of others before himself, and that kind of character couldn't survive his father's world. _Altruistic_

5. The young mothers were lining up with their babies so that the doctors could give the vaccine to the screaming infants. _Administer_

6. Having clawed his way to the top on his own, the oil baron John D. Rockefeller didn't feel any need to help anyone else. _Obligation_

7. When people started to arrive at the protest of the new bank fees, the organizer was surprised at how different all the arrivals were. _heterogeneous_

8. No scientific claim should be believed until it can be repeated under the same circumstances. _Replicate_

9. The people living in the apartment building were, professionally at least, remarkably similar: They were all single, in their thirties, and working at the university. _homogeneous_

10. His father had smoked the entire time his mother was pregnant with him. Decades later, he wondered if that had made him an easy target when it came to lung disease. _Susceptible_

Archbishop Oscar Romero

This reading reintroduces Archbishop Oscar Romero, mentioned on page 498. As you read, apply what you have learned about detecting purpose, tone, and bias.

On March 24, 1980, Archbishop Oscar Romero stood in the pulpit of a chapel in El Salvador while, outside, from a car across the street, an assassin took aim. As Romero was finishing his sermon, a bullet pierced him in the heart, silencing once and for all one of Latin America's most compassionate and influential voices.

Just three years before, Romero had been a most unlikely martyr. A predictable, orthodox, timid bookworm, Romero wasn't expected to make any waves. After all, he had criticized clergy who argued that God's abundance was for everyone, not just for the very rich. He had spoken out against "liberation theology" and its notion that wealth should be spread around to feed, clothe, and shelter *all* of God's people. Naturally, El Salvador's conservative upper classes considered him a safe choice. Their soft-spoken new archbishop would surely work with them to maintain the status quo.

They were wrong. At first, Romero had no intention of challenging his country's ruling elite. Then, a priest named Rutilio Grande was ambushed and killed. Grande was murdered for publicly insisting that wealthy landowners' dogs ate better than the families who worked those landowners' fields. He had also supported peasants' right to organize farm cooperatives. For daring to speak up for the poor, he was killed in cold blood.

Romero went to see the corpses of Grande and the old man and seven-year-old boy murdered with him. From there, he went to a church packed with local peasants. That night, he stood before the terror-stricken faces of his congregation while their eyes silently pleaded for his help. Suddenly, Romero realized that liberation theology had it right: No true Christian could turn his back upon the poor and suffering. His voice firm with new resolve, he urged his audience to become the "masters and protagonists of their own struggle for liberation."

He couldn't—and didn't—promise them that the atrocities would cease. In war-torn El Salvador, 3,000 people were killed every month. Corpses sometimes lay in the streets and were tossed onto garbage dumps and into streams. Two hundred of the people Romero had addressed in that country church would be dead within a year, along with 75,000 others. While violence ripped the country apart, rich and powerful Salvadorans refused to acknowledge that many of their countrymen went to bed hungry night after night.

But Romero refused to close his eyes to the suffering of his people. Every week, in his Sunday sermon, he pleaded with those in power to stop the vicious repression of anyone questioning their authority. Above all, he called for an end to social and economic inequality. All the while, he assured those who believed in him that the church would not be silent no matter how dangerous the situation became.

Away from the pulpit, he begged for help from the international community. Appealing to President Jimmy Carter, he asked the United States to end its annual $1.5 million in aid. The money, he said, was being used to hurt the very people it was meant to help. But his letters were ignored. Even the Salvadoran bishops, with only one exception, turned their backs on him.

Although Romero knew he was alone in his fight, he continued to speak out. Despite death threats, he defied those in power who demanded his silence. Romero knew the price for such defiance would be high, but he was ready to pay it. "I am bound, as a pastor, by divine command," he said, "to give my life for those whom I love, and that is all Salvadorans, even those who are going to kill me."

For his enemies, the last straw was Romero's public criticism of the Salvadoran military. The day before he was murdered, Romero accused the army of violating God's law against killing. Then, he encouraged the soldiers to mutiny: "No soldier is obliged to obey an order that is contrary to the will of God." His sermon, which was broadcast throughout the country, was punctuated by thunderous applause. But the next day, Romero was dead, probably killed by a soldier's gun.

In 2000, on the twentieth anniversary of Romero's death, thousands of people marched through the streets of El Salvador to honor Romero's memory. The men and women of El Salvador had not forgotten the man they called the "people's saint." (Sources of figures and quotations: The Romero Society, www.romerosociety.org/index.htm; James R. Brockman, "The Spiritual Journey of Oscar Romero," www.spiritualitytoday.org/spir2day/904242brock.html; "Remembering the Assassination of Archbishop Oscar Romero," www.creighton.edu/CollaborativeMinistry/romero.html.)

DIRECTIONS   Answer the following questions by filling in the blanks or circling the letter of the correct response.

Based on the context, how would you define *orthodox* in paragraph 2?

a. unreliable

b. traditional

c. rebellious

d. fierce

Based on the context, how would you define *resolve* in paragraph 4?

a. determination

b. puzzlement

c. joy

d. defeat

Based on the context, how would you define *protagonists* in paragraph 4?

a. enemies

b. friends

c. heroes

d. defeatists

Which statement best expresses the main idea of paragraph 2?

a. Romero hid his rebellious spirit behind the mask of a bookworm.

b. Romero's heroism was unexpected.

c. Romero did not ever come to accept liberation theology.

d. Romero originally expected to earn great wealth in his new office.

What cause and effect relationship is implied in paragraph 4?

the Killing caused him to speak up.

What's the implied main idea of the entire reading?

how the Archbishop spoke up for El Salvadorans.

Three of the sentences in paragraph 9 are connected by which type of transition?

a. contrast
b. time order
c. cause and effect
d. comparison

How would you describe the author's tone?

a. doubtful
b. quietly supportive
c. admiring
d. slightly suspicious

What is the author's purpose?

to Let PeoPle Know not to Kill PeoPle Who didn't Deserve to Die.

Based on the reading, how do you think the author would react to the idea of naming a bridge or a building in honor of Archbishop Romero?

he would SuPPort it.

♦ **TEST 1** **Reviewing the Key Points**

DIRECTIONS Answer the following questions.

1. What are the three basic elements of an argument?

   The opinion being put fourth for consideration. The author's support for that opinion and the Response for that opposition.

2. Of the three elements, which one is not always present?

   The Response for the opposition.

3. What's the difference between a fact and an opinion?

   Opinions are beliefs or beliefs about the world that are Shaped by background, experience, and Education. Thus they can't be verified or checked for Accuracy. Facts are not affected by the background or experience of the person who states them. Thus They can be verified for accuracy and can be labeled true or false.

4. How does a writer mix opinion in with a factual statement?

   The language used can imply a value judgement.

5. Why is reducing an argument to its bare bones a good thing to do?

   When the argument is pared Down it is easier to evaluate the support offered for the opinion.

6. Whatever kind of support the author uses, readers should always evaluate it for what? relevance

7. If the author mentions people that support his or her argument, what do you need to know about the people mentioned?

   Why they are considered Knowledgeable about the subject and whether they have anything to gain from Supporting the authors opinion.

8. If someone in the reading is referred to as doctor or professor without further explanation, what should you do?

Check the web for background information. Find out what the person's training and experience consist of.

9. Does every persuasive reading develop a particular tone? Please explain.

No Sometimes the writer only uses a few words to influence the reader.

10. What are some of the devices writers use to create tone?

Word choice, allusions, figurative language, imagery, and Personal anecdotes.

To correct your test, turn to page 588. If one or more of your answers is incorrect, re-read the Rounding Up the Keys section of the chapter to find out where your mistake might be.

▶ TEST 2 **Distinguishing Between Fact and Opinion**

DIRECTIONS Read each statement. Then label it *F* (fact), *O* (opinion), or *B* (both).

_F_ **1.** Putting a sky marshal on each of 30,000 flights per day is impractical and unrealistic.

_B_ **2.** The annual Consumer Electronics Show showcases thousands of new cutting-edge gadgets.

_O_ **3.** The ability to manage one's emotions is an essential ingredient of effective leadership.

_O_ **4.** If you don't eliminate poverty and homelessness, you can't decrease the crime rate.

_F_ **5.** Today, Americans' life expectancy has increased to seventy-eight years, thirty years longer than the outlook for their ancestors living in 1900.

_B_ **6.** A defective O-ring caused the tragic explosion of the space shuttle *Challenger* on January 28, 1986.

_B_ **7.** An astonishing 61 percent of all Americans are overweight.

_F_ **8.** The largest Indian land claim in U.S. history was the $247.9 million a judge ordered the state of New York to pay the Cayuga Indians in 2001.

_B_ **9.** Many European and Asian countries have a better organ donation system than does the United States: Unless an individual objects to being an organ donor, he or she is considered to be one.

_O_ **10.** America is the world's mightiest power—militarily, economically, politically, and culturally.

▶ **TEST 3**   **Distinguishing Between Fact and Opinion**

DIRECTIONS   Read each statement. Then label it *F* (fact), *O* (opinion), or *B* (both).

_B_   **1.** Alan Mathison Turing (1912–1954) was an English mathematician whose brilliant career was senselessly destroyed when it was discovered that he was a homosexual.

_F_   **2.** A carcinogen is any agent that increases the chances of a cell becoming cancerous.

_F_   **3.** During World War I, Chile remained neutral.

_O_   **4.** Home shopping networks encourage viewers to engage in mindless consumerism.

_F_   **5.** Although most people don't realize it, eyewitnesses to crimes are extremely unreliable.

_O_   **6.** The music of rapper 50 Cent is offensive and disgusting.

_F_   **7.** A new species of land mammal has been discovered in the forests of Vietnam.

_F_   **8.** The pop singer Michael Jackson died in 2009 at the age of fifty.

_O_   **9.** When he pardoned the fugitive financier Marc Rich, William Jefferson Clinton disgraced his presidency.

_F_   **10.** The Japanese mushrooms called *maitake* sometimes grow as big as footballs.

▶ **TEST 4**   **Analyzing Arguments**

DIRECTIONS   Read each selection and answer the questions that follow.

1. PETA's Scare Tactics

1   We members of the National Poultry Producers Association support and always strive for the humane treatment of animals. Like animal rights groups such as People for the Ethical Treatment of Animals (PETA), we are concerned about animal welfare and are careful to avoid any form of animal cruelty.

2   However, there is a basic difference between us and groups like PETA. While it's understandable that some people object to eating meat on ethical grounds, PETA's anti-animal products campaigns go too far in attempts to win converts. This is especially true of their ads discouraging children from eating meat.

3   Although the organization's campaign coordinator Matt Rice has claimed, "We would never use shock tactics with children; it wouldn't be right," this is exactly what the organization has done. In reality, Rice's organization aims some of its most ghastly campaigns directly at kids.

4   In 2004, for example, PETA announced its plan to distribute "Buckets of Blood" to children outside middle schools and KFC fried chicken restaurants. These "toys"—which might well horrify an adult, let alone a vulnerable child—included a bloody plastic chicken and a caricature of a blood-splattered Colonel Sanders threatening a frightened bird with a butcher knife. Because those campaigns were harshly criticized for scaring children, they were quickly abandoned only to be replaced by new ones that were just moderately better.

5   One of the 2011 campaigns introduced around Thanksgiving featured what can only be called a "turkey dog." The creature had a dog's head and a turkey's body. The caption for the ad was "Kids, if you wouldn't eat your dog, why eat a turkey? Go Vegan." While some parents claimed their children found the ads funny, others said their children refused to participate in any Thanksgiving celebrations as a result. (Source of quotation: *Animal News*, December 12, 2004, p. 26.)

1. Paraphrase the opinion that is argued in this reading.

The Poultry People are arguing about peta's meat scare tatics.

2. What reason does the author offer in support of the opinion expressed?

> *The Author talks about Various scare tatics.*

3. What two examples provide evidence for the author's opinion?

> *a blood splattered colonel and a body Plastic Chicken.*

4. Matt Rice is quoted in order to

   a. support the author's opinion.

   b. answer an opposing point of view that expresses support for PETA.

   c. illustrate that PETA's claims about their campaigns are not true.

5. What tone do you hear in this reading?

   a. neutral

   b. critical

   c. solemn

   d. insulting

2. Living Life Online

1   In 1995, MIT professor Sherry Turkle published a book called *Life on the Screen*. In it, she celebrated the freedom of spending time communicating on the Web. On the Web, extolled Turkle, you could be anyone you wanted to be. Sick of being a timid and fearful mouse in real life? No problem. On the Web, you could present yourself as an assertive social lion, complete with a lion as your avatar.

2   But like so many early Web enthusiasts, Turkle has changed her mind. Her new book *Alone Together* sums up the writer's current and more pessimistic message in the subtitle: *Why We Expect More from Technology and Less from Each Other*. As always, Turkle is an astute observer of society's trends, and she is particularly on point in *Alone Together*. The book spells out what has become increasingly apparent to most thoughtful observers: The more time we spend online, the less we interact with real people and the less we want to.

3 According to a study conducted by the marketing company, Lightspeed Research, heavy social media users spend most of their time in cyberspace rather than engaging with real people. That suggests that heavy users of social media can't be very skilled at interpreting face-to-face signals, whether they are facial expressions or physical gestures. They just don't have enough experience in real-world relationships. In turn, that lack of real world experience makes real friends harder to come by or at least hold on to. As the novelist Stephen Marche pointed out in his 2012 *Atlantic* cover story, "Is Facebook Making Us Lonely," "the more connected we become, the lonelier we are."

4 Marche's description of people who don't know how to connect when they actually have to look at one another fits perfectly with the results of Sherry Turkle's interviews. At one point in her book, she talks to several young people who are uncomfortable speaking on the phone in times of crisis. For them, communicating by phone requires too much emotional effort. Texting is easier. That way they aren't confronted by any emotional response that requires a thoughtful reaction on their part.

5 Life online can be conducted via brief messages and emoticons. Thus it's easy to see why it becomes preferable to relate to an avatar rather than a real person. With a real person, things can get messy. If you get into an argument with your best friend, face-to-face, over dinner, that argument might turn into a blow up. As a result, you might not speak for days. Plus there's the sticky problem of having to work out what went wrong. Unfortunately, that kind of problem between friends probably can't be resolved by a smiley face, which is one reason why some people prefer life online.

1. Paraphrase the opinion that is argued in this reading.

Life online is Getting People to not communicate in Real life

2. Why is Sherry Turkle's new book mentioned?

 a. The author uses it in order to respond to an opposing point of view.

 b. It supports the author's point of view.

 c. The author wants to persuade people to read Turkle's book.

3. Why is Stephen Marche mentioned?

he thinks that online social media is Getting in the way of talking face-to-face.

4. What does the study from Lightspeed Media say?

People who spend more time online Become less sociable to other people.

What does the author say the study means?

People are spending too much time on technology.

5. What tone do you hear in this reading?

a. neutral

b. supportive

c. worried

d. insulting

◆ **TEST 5**   **Evaluating Arguments**

DIRECTIONS   Read each selection and answer the accompanying questions.

1. ### For Some Mail Order Brides, It Really Is "Till Death Do Us Part"

1   Historically, the label "mail order bride" was attached to women who published their desire to find a man and get married. A century ago, the women posting the ads might well be from the same country as the men who answered them. But today, the situation has changed. Nowadays, women usually marry men from other countries. Usually those countries are better off financially than the countries in which the women reside.

2   For precisely that reason, the women who publish their availability for marriage online or in newspapers have been the butt of nasty and degrading jokes. They are considered gold diggers, pure and simple. It's assumed that the women are looking for men with open checkbooks. They want men who are established and who can take care of them financially.

3   But, in fact, in some countries, women aren't looking for open checkbooks. They really are looking for husbands. This is true, for instance, of Russia, where marriageable men are in short supply. That lack of male suitors leaves Russian women looking elsewhere for someone to marry.

4   In Russia, it's no shame for women to make their desire for marriage known abroad. The women want families and children. Thus, they post their ads in an attempt to find men with whom they can have a family. From the women's point of view, it's a practical solution to a serious social problem.

5   Another incorrect assumption is that mail order brides leave their husbands once they have U.S. citizenship. In general, they don't. The United States Citizenship and Immigration Services (USCIS) says that "marriages arranged through [mail order bride] services would appear to have a lower divorce rate than the nation as a whole. Yes, some mail order brides are only interested in their husband-to-be's bank account. But that's most certainly not true of all the women who look overseas for a husband, and it would be nice if these women weren't subjected to crude jokes and even cruder stereotyping. The situation is just not that simple. (See http://listverse .com/2010/02/17/top-10-facts-about-mail-order-brides/ for the quotation and more facts about mail order brides.)

1. In your own words, what opinion is the focus of the author's argument?

   People ordering Brides online
   So men can be Married.

2. What reason does the author give in support of that opinion?

   Crude assumptions and the
   Butt of nasty and Degrading Jokes.

3. What example of that reason does the author supply?

   Newspaper and online ads,

4. Are the reason and example relevant to the author's opinion? Please explain.

   yes Because it's not right
   to Joke around selling Advertisment
   in the newspaper for men.

5. The tone of this reading is

   (a.) disgusted.
   b. sarcastic.
   c. sympathetic.
   d. neutral.

2. Robots in Our Future

1   For decades, the study of robotics, the branch of technology focused on the creation of robots, was a subject that seemed to have more influence on science fiction than practical life. Because they so often mimicked human or animal form, robots were seen as amusing gadgets. But what practical purpose could they serve?

2   As it turns out, the answer to that question is that robots can fulfill a host of practical functions. Before long, robots will be an indispensable part of our daily lives. If there's an oil spill, for instance, robot fish will determine the extent of the environmental damage. Robotic fish contain

sensors that do an on-the-spot chemical analysis. They eliminate the need to take samples and send them off to a laboratory for analysis.

3   Although their price range is still in the hundreds of thousands, afford-able robotic housekeepers are only about a decade away. The robotic device known as PR2 can already fold laundry, move furniture, set a table, and bake a batch of cookies. Developers are convinced that with a few more years, housekeeper robots will help keep our homes in order at an affordable price.

4   In May 2012, researchers met in Sweden as part of the Robot-Era Project, which is focused on using robots to care for the elderly. Robots that can provide a shoulder to lean on or an arm to hold groceries already exist. The goal now is to make them affordable, so that nursing homes, except for the very sick, are no longer necessary. The Japanese have taken the idea of using robots to aid the aging a step further. They have robotic skeletons that can be strapped on to the body in order to make weak limbs functional again.

5   Two researchers in robotics in New Zealand are really thinking ahead. Ian Yeoman and Michelle Mars of the Victoria Management School in Wellington, New Zealand, have written a paper titled "Robots, Men, and Sex Tourism." In it, they describe how robot prostitutes could be made to look so desirable they could replace the human kind. In the not-too-distant future, robot prostitutes will provide sex without guilt or disease. They will also help end the crime of illegal sex trafficking, which in recent years has been soaring.

6   As robotics researchers continue to apply their knowledge to practi-cal uses, there will be few social problems that can't be eliminated or at least partially solved through the use of robots. Hollywood with its movies about robots gone mad got it all wrong. Robots aren't going to destroy civilization. They are going to build it.

1. In your own words, what opinion is the focus of the author's argument?

    how Robots are building our future

2. Is the robot PR2 relevant to the author's opinion? Please explain.

    yes, it does everything a normal person does only much faster.

3. Are the robots that can care for the elderly relevant to the author's opinion? Please explain.

No Dogs can do this Job, not Robots.

4. Are the descriptions of robot fish and claims from the researchers in New Zealand relevant to the author's opinion? Please explain.

Yes The fish would help the enviroment.

What about the reference to the conference in Sweden?

Same as Question 3.

5. The tone of this reading is

a. ironic.

b. sarcastic.

c. enthusiastic.

d. neutral.

▶ **TEST 6**   **Enlarging Your Academic Vocabulary**

DIRECTIONS Circle the letter of the sentence that uses the opening word correctly.

1. **dilemma**

   a. What people call a "win-win situation" always indicates a *dilemma*.

   b. No *dilemma* in the world could force politicians to concede an election they had won.

   (c.) I'm facing a real *dilemma*: I saw my best friend's wife kissing another man at a party; I want to tell my friend so he knows he is married to a cheat, but if he finds out his wife is cheating on him, it will break his heart.

2. **proximity**

   (a.) Because of the *proximity* of several universities, the bookstore has survived.

   b. The comedian was able to do a very good *proximity* of the president.

   c. A vote by *proximity* is a vote cast on somebody else's behalf.

3. **altruistic**

   (a.) In an *altruistic* impulse after winning the lottery, he dedicated half of his prize to cancer research.

   b. *Altruistic* people would never consider giving to charity.

   c. The candidate had a strong *altruistic* streak, and his obvious greed had angered many of his previous supporters.

4. **convergence**

   a. Known for her lively *convergence*, the actress was a frequent guest at talk shows.

   (b.) The success of what came to be known as the World Wide Web resulted from the *convergence* of two trends: The decreasing prices for personal computers and the increasing availability of easy-to-use web browsers on those computers.

   c. The two friends started to really *converge* when both fell in love with the same woman and ceased to speak to one another.

5. **homogeneous**

(a.) Some historic towns enacted tough zoning laws in order to preserve the *homogeneous* look of their buildings, which were not supposed to vary much.

b. Some analysts consider the invasion of Iraq a *homogeneous* political blunder.

c. In last night's interview, the singer presented himself from his most *homogeneous* side.

6. **heterogeneous**

a. A *heterogeneous* marriage is one between a man and a woman.

(b.) The new menu shows the chef's ability to blend very *heterogeneous* cuisines.

c. Once the opening niceties were dispensed with, the debate turned *heterogeneous* within minutes.

7. **replicate**

(a.) A programmer who wants to debug a piece of software has to be able to *replicate* the errors that have been observed.

b. The paper submitted by the student was *replicate* with typos and grammatical mistakes.

c. The other member of the team looked like a *replicate*, but he was actually human.

8. **obligation**

(a.) For many, a dinner invitation leads to an *obligation* to return the favor.

b. People who insist on a strict separation between church and state demand the *obligation* of "under God" from the Pledge of Allegiance.

c. The photographer had a keen eye for the *obligations* of the natural world.

9. **administer**

    (a.) The teacher *administered* his duties with a fierce efficiency that won him little affection from the children he taught.

    b. They wanted to get married and needed an *administer*.

    c. At the town meeting, speaker after speaker *administered* the committee not to accept the proposed budget.

10. **susceptible**

    a. The most *susceptible* part of the law will not survive a review by legal experts.

    b. Customers entering the premises were presented with a hot towel and a *susceptible* filled with fragrant water.

    (c.) When the speaker claimed that rich people in high office are less *susceptible* to bribery, several members of the audience laughed out loud.

Combining Your Skills

As the title of this section suggests, this is your chance to combine all the skills you mastered in Chapters 1 through 9. The questions accompanying the following readings give you additional practice on everything from using context clues to analyzing arguments.

◆ **READING 1**   # The Seven-Day Anti-Procrastination Plan

Dave Ellis

Looking Ahead   Many college students procrastinate, or put off, doing their assignments until the very last minute. And guess what? Students who wait until the last minute often don't do their best work. Author Dave Ellis describes seven sound tips for managing time and breaking the procrastination habit.

Word Watch   You probably know most of the words in the reading. The ones you don't know can mostly be defined from context. The words that follow, however, cannot be fully understood from either context or analysis of word parts. For this reason, their meanings are supplied here. Look them over before you begin reading.

> **irregular verbs (5):** verbs that do not follow the usual rules for forming the past tense— for example, *ring, rang, rung*
>
> **legitimately (6):** rightfully
>
> **immersion (7):** sinking into; submerging
>
> **ponder (9):** consider or think about
>
> **imminent (9):** immediate, just about to happen

Reading Tip   The author has lots of specific suggestions for improving how you manage time. Paraphrase those suggestions in the margins of your text.

1   Here are seven strategies you can use to eliminate procrastination. The suggestions are tied to the days of the week to help you remember them.

Monday: Make It Meaningful

2   What is important about the job you've been putting off? List all the benefits of completing it. Look at it in relation to your goals. Be specific about the rewards for getting it done, including how you will feel when the task is complete.

Tuesday: Take It Apart

3   Break big jobs into a series of small ones you can do in 15 minutes or less. If a long reading assignment intimidates you, divide it into two-page or

three-page sections. Make a list of the sections and cross them off as you complete them, so you can see your progress.

Wednesday: Write an Intention Statement

4 Write an Intention Statement on a 3 × 5 card. For example, if you can't get started on a term paper, you might write, "I intend to write a list of at least 10 possible topics by 9 p.m. I will reward myself with an hour of guilt-free recreational reading." Carry the 3 × 5 card with you or post it in your study area where you can see it often.

Thursday: Tell Everyone

5 Announce publicly your intention to get it done. Tell a friend you intend to learn 10 irregular* French verbs by Saturday. Tell your spouse, roommate, parents, and children. Include anyone who will ask whether you've completed it or who will suggest ways to get it done. Make the world your support group.

Friday: Find a Reward

6 Construct rewards carefully. Be willing to withhold them if you do not complete the task. Don't pick a movie as a reward for studying biology if you plan to go to the movie anyway. And when you legitimately* reap your reward, notice how it feels. You might find that movies, new clothes, or an extra hour on the bicycle are more fun when you've earned them.

Saturday: Settle It Now

7 Do it now. The minute you notice yourself procrastinating, plunge into the task. Imagine yourself at a mountain lake, poised to dive. Gradual immersion* would be slow torture. It's often less painful to leap. Then be sure to savor the feeling of having the task behind you.

Sunday: Say No

8 When you keep pushing a task into the low-priority category, reexamine the purpose for doing it at all. If you realize you really don't intend to do something, quit telling yourself that you will. That's procrastinating. Just say NO! Then you're not procrastinating, and you don't have to carry around the baggage of an undone task.

9 If you are going to procrastinate, there are three good reasons why you should do it consciously. First of all, if you recognize that you are

procrastinating, you can decide if you really, really do want to put things off. After all, if you choose to procrastinate, you can also choose not to. Consciously thinking about the process of procrastination is also important. In effect, you need to think like a scientist and observe what you are doing and why. Ponder* the question of why you might be postponing important tasks. Second, consider the consequences of postponing. Seeing the cost of procrastination clearly may just help you kick the habit. And finally, ask yourself straight out if procrastination actually works in your favor. Some people really do thrive under pressure, and if you do your best work when you are pushing hard against an imminent* deadline, you may be one of those people. (Dave Ellis, *Becoming a Master Student*, 12th ed. © Cengage Learning.)

Combining Your Skills

DIRECTIONS   Answer the following questions by circling the appropriate letter or filling in the blanks.

Main Idea   1. In your own words, what's the main idea of the entire reading?

how to make yourself stop procrastinating.

2. The main idea is

(a.) stated.

b. implied.

Inference   3. In paragraph 3, the author tells readers what to do if they feel intimidated by a long reading assignment. But he doesn't say why someone would feel intimidated. What's your guess, or inference?

They would feel stressed out by Reading too much.

4. In paragraph 4, the author tells you to post your Intention Statement where you can see it. Why do you think this would be important?

So you can Remember where it is.

5. In paragraph 5, the author encourages those who would kick the procrastination habit to "publicly" announce what they expect to get done. Again, he doesn't say why this should work. What is your guess, or inference?

it Would helP your modoVation

Analyzing Language

6. What category word is central to this reading?

Procrastinating.

Organizational Patterns

7. What is the primary organizational pattern in this reading?

time order and Step by Step.

Supporting Details

8. What phrase in the first sentence of paragraph 9 provides you with a huge clue to the supporting details?

three good reasons.

Purpose

9. The author's purpose is to

(a.) describe techniques for time management.

b. convince readers that managing time is really possible.

Tone

10. How would you describe the author's tone?

a. friendly and natural

(b.) serious and formal

c. neutral

Share Your Thoughts

Procrastination has often been linked to fear of failure. Explain what you think might be the connection between the two.

PeoPle are afraid they're going to Lose

Thinking Through Writing

Start your paper by explaining which of the seven tips in the reading is the best. Be sure to explain how you arrived at your decision. Conclude by describing the tip you personally consider the *least* useful or valuable. Again, make sure to give the basis for your opinion.

best reward—cause it makes you want to think that you earned

worst say no cause you can do more things that way

◆ READING 2 **Culture, Subcultures, and the Marketplace**

William M. Pride and O. C. Ferrell

Looking Ahead The following excerpt offers definitions for the terms *culture* and *subculture*. It also describes how companies analyze the needs and desires of three different American populations in order to promote their products.

Word Watch You probably know most of the words in the reading. The ones you don't know can mostly be defined from context. The words that follow, however, cannot be fully understood from either context or the analysis of word parts. For this reason, their meanings are supplied here. Look them over before you begin reading.

> **per capita (3):** per person
> **designations (5):** places
> **demographic (5):** identifying characteristics of populations
>
> **retailer (9):** someone involved in direct selling to consumers
> **vignettes (11):** pictures

Reading Tip Just a glance at the headings tells you that the reading is going to describe three separate subcultures—African American, Hispanic, and Asian American.

culture The accumulation of values, knowledge, beliefs, customs, objects, and concepts of a society

1 **Culture** is the accumulation of values, knowledge, beliefs, customs, objects, and concepts that a society uses to cope with its environment and passes on to future generations. Examples of objects are foods, furniture, buildings, clothing, and tools. Concepts include education, welfare, and laws. Culture also includes core values and the degree of acceptability of a wide range of behaviors in a specific society. For example, in U.S. culture, customers as well as businesspeople are expected to behave ethically.

2 Culture influences buying behavior because it permeates our daily lives. Our culture determines what we wear and eat and where we reside and travel. Society's interest in the healthfulness of food affects food companies' approaches to developing and promoting their products. Culture also influences how we buy and use products and our satisfaction from them. In the U.S. culture, makers of furniture, cars, and clothing strive to understand how people's color preferences are changing.

3 Because culture determines product purchases and uses to some degree, cultural changes affect product development, promotion, distribution, and pricing. Food marketers, for example, have made a multitude of changes in their marketing efforts. Thirty years ago, most U.S. families ate at least two meals a day together, and the mother spent four to six hours a day preparing those meals. Today more than 75 percent of women between ages 25 and 54 work outside the home, and average family incomes have risen considerably. These shifts, along with scarcity of time, have resulted in dramatic changes in the national per capita* consumption of certain food products, such as take-out foods, frozen dinners, and shelf-stable foods.

4 When U.S. marketers sell products in other countries, they realize the tremendous impact those cultures have on product purchases and use. Global marketers find that people in other regions of the world have different attitudes, values, and needs, which call for different methods of doing business as well as different types of marketing mixes. Some international marketers fail because they do not or cannot adjust to cultural differences.

subculture A group of individuals whose characteristics, values, and behavioral patterns are similar within the group and different from those of people in the surrounding culture

5 A culture consists of various subcultures. A **subculture** is a group of individuals whose characteristics, values, and behavioral patterns are similar within the group and different from those of people in the surrounding culture. Subcultural boundaries are usually based on geographic designations* and demographic* characteristics, such as age, religion, race, and ethnicity. U.S. culture is marked by many different subcultures. Among them are West Coast, teenage, Asian American, and college students.

6 Within subcultures, greater similarities exist in people's attitudes, values, and actions than within the broader culture. Relative to other subcultures, individuals in one subculture may have stronger preferences for specific types of clothing, furniture, or foods. Research has shown that subcultures can play a significant role in how people respond to advertisements, particularly when pressured to make a snap judgment. It is important to understand that a person can be a member of more than one subculture and that the behavioral patterns and values attributed to specific subcultures do not necessarily apply to all group members.

7 The percentage of the U.S. population consisting of ethnic and racial subcultures is expected to grow. By 2050, about one-half of the U.S. population will be members of racial and ethnic minorities. The U.S. Census Bureau reports that the three largest and fastest-growing ethnic U.S. subcultures are African Americans, Hispanics, and Asians. The population growth of these subcultures interests marketers. Businesses recognize that to succeed, their marketing strategies will have to take into account the values, needs, interests, shopping patterns, and buying habits of various subcultures.

African American Subculture

8   In the United States, the African American subculture represents 12.4 percent of the population. Like all subcultures, African American consumers possess distinct buying patterns. For example, African American consumers spend more money on utilities, footwear, children's apparel, groceries, and housing than do white consumers. The combined buying power of African American consumers is projected to reach $1.1 trillion by 2012.

9   Like many companies, Procter & Gamble Company has hiked its marketing initiatives that are aimed at the African American community, spending $52.5 million last year. By including African American actors in its ads, the company believes it can encourage a positive response to its products, increasing sales among African American consumers while still maintaining ties with white consumers. Many other corporations are reaching out to the African American community with targeted efforts. Walmart, for example, has adjusted the merchandising of 1,500 stores located in areas with large black populations to include more products favored by African American customers, such as ethnic hair-care products and large selections of more urban music offerings. The retailer* has also included more African American actors in its advertising campaigns. Another retailer, Target, launched a yearlong campaign called "Dream in Color" to celebrate diversity. The campaign included numerous Martin Luther King Day events, guest appearances by poet Dr. Maya Angelou, free posters for schools, and a unique online curriculum to provide access to historical and contemporary African American poets. McDonald's launched 365BLACK, a program that celebrates black history all year-round. The following year, it introduced 365BLACK Awards, which honor African Americans for their outstanding achievements.

Hispanic Subculture

10   Hispanics represent nearly 15 percent of the U.S. population, and their buying power is expected to reach $1.2 trillion by 2012. When considering the buying behavior of Hispanics, marketers must keep in mind that this subculture is really composed of nearly two dozen nationalities, including Cuban, Mexican, Puerto Rican, Caribbean, Spanish, and Dominican. Each has its own history and unique culture that affect consumer preferences and buying behavior. They should also recognize that the terms *Hispanic* and *Latino* refer to an ethnic category rather than a racial distinction. Because of the group's growth and purchasing power, understanding the Hispanic subculture is critical to marketers. Like African American consumers, Hispanics spend more on housing,

groceries, telephone services, and children's apparel and shoes. But they also spend more on men's apparel and appliances, while they spend less than average on health care, entertainment, and education.[†]

11   To attract this powerful subculture, marketers are taking Hispanic values and preferences into account when developing products and creating advertising and promotions. For example, a growing number of retailers, including Walmart, are promoting the Hispanic holiday of Three Kings Day on January 6 in markets with a significant concentration of Latino consumers. American Airlines has launched a Spanish-language advertising campaign to encourage more Latinos to fly across the country during the holiday. The *destinó* campaign, which includes ads on television, radio, online, and out-of-home, includes vignettes* showing Latinos' lives to illustrate how the airline can help them fulfill their destinies.

Asian American Subculture

12   The term *Asian American* includes people from more than 15 ethnic groups, including Filipinos, Chinese, Japanese, Asian Indians, Koreans, and Vietnamese, and this group represents 4.4 percent of the U.S. population. The individual language, religion, and value system of each group influences its members' purchasing decisions. Some traits of this subculture, however, carry across ethnic divisions, including an emphasis on hard work, strong family ties, and a high value placed on education. Asian Americans are the fastest-growing U.S. subculture. They also have the most money, the best education, and the largest percentage of professionals and managers of all U.S. minorities, and they are expected to wield $670 billion in buying power by 2012.

13   Marketers are targeting the diverse Asian American market in many ways. Kraft, for example, learned from marketing research that its Asian American customers were not interested in having "Asian" products from Kraft but rather in learning how to use well-known Kraft brands to create healthy Western-style dishes. Targeting immigrant mothers trying to balance between Eastern and Western cultures, the company therefore launched a new ad campaign in Chinese and Mandarin—the two most commonly spoken Asian dialects—and offered samples and demonstrations in Chinese as well as a website with recipes and healthy tips. Retailer JCPenney likewise used an advertising campaign to tout its competitive prices to Chinese and Vietnamese women, particularly during cultural holidays. (William M. Pride and O. C. Ferrell, *Marketing*, 15th ed. © Cengage Learning.)

[†][By 2020,] Hispanics will become the largest ethnic group in the United States.

Combining Your Skills

DIRECTIONS   Answer the following questions by circling the appropriate letter or filling in the blanks.

Main Idea

1. Which statement best expresses the main idea of the entire reading?

    a. Businesses are well aware that their marketing campaigns in the United States must take into account the needs and desires of the influential subcultures that make up the U.S. population.

    b. If marketers do not address the fact that the Hispanic subculture is made up of nearly two dozen different nationalities, they are unlikely to do well marketing to its members, who have unique preferences depending on their origins.

    c. Marketers have probably been most successful at targeting the Asian-American community.

    d. Ethnic and racial subcultures in the United States are expected to grow dramatically, and, by 2050, about one-half of the U.S. population will belong to a racial or ethnic minority.

Supporting Details and Paraphrasing

2. How would you paraphrase the authors' definition of *culture*?

    racial and ethnic groups of people

    _____

    _____

3. In your own words, what makes a group a subculture?

    If they're from different countries

    _____

    _____

4. The authors say in paragraph 8 that African Americans spend more money on utilities and footwear than white Americans do. This supporting detail is used to develop which main idea?

    a. African Americans are more concerned with appearances than white Americans are.

    b. African Americans are more willing to spend money than white Americans are.

c. There is evidence of distinct purchasing patterns among African-American consumers.

d. Targeted by banks, African Americans were encouraged to take subprime mortgages even if they qualified for mortgages with a better rate.

Sentence Sense 5. In paragraph 9, the references to Procter & Gamble and Walmart are illustrations of which phrase from the opening sentence?

a. many companies

b. marketing initiatives

c. African-American community

Inference 6. In paragraph 10, the authors say that marketers have to keep in mind that the Hispanic culture in the United States is actually composed of two dozen nationalities. But they don't say why marketers have to keep that in mind. What inference do they expect readers to draw?

So they know what to buy

Supporting Details 7. In paragraph 11, the *destinó* campaign is used to make what point?

to reach their goals

Patterns of Organization 8. Which of the following patterns does *not* organize the reading?

a. definition

b. comparison and contrast

c. simple listing

d. cause and effect

e. classification

Supporting Details 9. In paragraph 12, the authors point out that Asian Americans, like Hispanic Americans, come from many different ethnic groups. However, the authors also suggest that Asian Americans, *unlike* Hispanic Americans, are

a. uninterested in having products that are Asian.

b. less affected by their differences in ethnic origin.

c. not affected at all by religious differences.

d. not being targeted by marketers.

Purpose **10.** How would you describe the authors' purpose?

a. The authors are describing the ways in which marketers target specific subcultures to sell products.

b. The authors are arguing that the targeting of subcultures to market products is unethical.

Share Your Thoughts In paragraph 6, the authors make a point of saying how important it is to understand that "the behavioral patterns and values attributed to specific subcultures do not necessarily apply to all group members." Why do you think the authors make it a point of mentioning this fact? What are they concerned about? *So people dont know what to expect*

Thinking Through Writing Write a few paragraphs discussing whether marketers should or should not target products to specific subcultures. State your opinion in the opening paragraph. Then give at least one reason (two is better) why you hold that opinion.

shouldn't do that
— because its more better to learn new things
— that way they know what to buy and what not to buy

◆ **READING 3**   # What Makes a Hero?

Ted Tollefson

Looking Ahead   Author Ted Tollefson believes that the heroic character can be defined. Read to see if his description of a hero matches yours.

Word Watch   You probably know most of the words in the reading. The ones you don't know can mostly be defined from context. The words that follow, however, cannot be fully understood from either context or analysis of word parts. For this reason, their meanings are supplied here. Look them over before you begin reading.

> **orator** (1): speaker
>
> **zest** (3): excitement, enthusiasm
>
> **catalysts** (4): people or substances that cause a change
>
> **charismatic** (4): possessed of personal magnetism or charm
>
> **universal** (5): common to all people
>
> **tutelage** (5): teaching, education
>
> **disdained** (5): disliked, disregarded
>
> **unbridled** (7): uncontrolled
>
> **purveyors** (7): people who hand out or give out something
>
> **grandiose** (9): grand, great
>
> **pious** (9): saintly
>
> **naïveté** (9): innocence
>
> **collage** (10): a picture created out of pieces from other pictures

Reading Tip   As you read, keep asking yourself how you would define a hero if you were to write an essay similar to this one. List some key traits of a hero in the margins of the reading. Think, too, about people who do or do not match Tollefson's description.

1   For several years, a picture of Warren Spahn of the Milwaukee Braves hung on my closet door, one leg poised in midair before he delivered a smoking fastball. Time passed and Spahn's picture gave way to others: Elvis, John F. Kennedy, Carl Jung,[†] Joseph Campbell,[†] Ben Hogan.[†] These heroic images

---

[†]Carl Jung (1875–1961): Swiss psychologist.
[†]Joseph Campbell (1904–1987): a collector of myths who was heavily influenced by Carl Jung.
[†]Ben Hogan (1912–1997): one of the greatest golfers in the history of the game.

have reflected back to me what I hoped to become: a man with good moves, a sex symbol, an electrifying orator,* a plumber of depths, a teller of tales, a graceful golfer. Like serpents, we keep shedding the skins of our heroes as we move toward new phases in our lives.

2   Like many of my generation, I have a weakness for hero worship. At some point, however, we all begin to question our heroes and our need for them. This leads us to ask: What is a hero? Despite immense differences in cultures, heroes around the world generally share a number of traits that instruct and inspire people.

3   *A hero does something worth talking about.* A hero has a story of adventure to tell and a community who will listen. But a hero goes beyond mere fame or celebrity. *Heroes serve powers or principles larger than themselves.* Like high-voltage transformers, heroes take the energy of higher powers and step it down so that it can be used by ordinary mortals. *The hero lives a life worthy of imitation.* Those who imitate a genuine hero experience life with new depth, zest,* and meaning. A sure test for would-be heroes is what or whom do they serve? What are they willing to live and die for? If the answer or evidence suggests they serve only their own fame, they may be celebrities but not heroes. . . .

4   *Heroes are catalysts* for change.* They have a vision from the mountaintop. They have the skill and the charm to move the masses. They create new possibilities. Without Gandhi,[†] India might still be part of the British Empire. Without Rosa Parks[†] and Martin Luther King Jr., we might still have segregated buses, restaurants, and parks. It may be possible for large-scale change to occur without charismatic* leaders, but the pace of change would be glacial, the vision uncertain, and the committee meetings endless.

5   Though heroes aspire to universal* values, most are bound to the culture from which they came. The heroes of the Homeric Greeks wept loudly for their lost comrades and exhibited their grief publicly. A later generation of Greeks under the tutelage* of Plato disdained* this display of grief as "unmanly."

6   Though the heroic tradition of white Americans is barely three hundred years old, it already shows some unique and unnerving features. While most traditional heroes leave home, have an adventure, and return home to tell the story, American heroes are often homeless. They come out of nowhere, right what is wrong, and then disappear into the wilderness.

[†]Mohandas Gandhi (1869–1948): Indian leader who used nonviolent disobedience to gain India's independence from Great Britain.
[†]Rosa Parks (1913–2005): African-American Rosa Parks refused to give up her bus seat to a white man in 1955. In doing so, she helped ignite the civil rights movement.

Throughout most of the world, it is acknowledged that heroes need a community as much as a community needs them.

7   And most Americans seem to prefer their heroes flawless, innocent, forever wearing a white hat or airbrushed features. Character flaws—unbridled* lust, political incorrectness—are held as proof that our heroes aren't really heroes. Several heroes on my own list have provided easy targets for the purveyors* of heroic perfectionism.

8   The ancient Greeks and Hebrews were wiser on this count. They chose for their heroes men and women with visible, tragic flaws. Oedipus'† fierce curiosity raised him to be king but also lured him to his mother's bed. King David's unbounded passion made him dance naked before the Ark *and* led him to betray Uriah so he could take Bathsheba for his wife.

9   American heroes lack a sense of home that might limit and ground their grandiose* ambitions. American heroes avoid acknowledging their own vices, which makes them more likely to look for somebody else to blame when things go wrong. Our national heroes seem to be stuck somewhere between Billy Budd† and the Lone Ranger:† pious,* armed cowboys who are full of energy, hope, and dangerous naïveté.*

10   Here are some exercises to give you insights into your own ideas about heroes and villains:

1. Draw a time line with markings every five years in your life. For each era, name an important hero (male or female). Identify three core qualities each stands for. Look at the overall list for recurring qualities. Who or what do your heroes serve?

2. Make a list of enemies, the people who really push your buttons. For each, specify three qualities that make your blood boil. Now look for recurring qualities. What emerges is your "shadow," parts of yourself that you fear, loathe, and therefore loan to others. What does your shadow know that you don't?

3. Make a collage* of your heroes, leaving room for their tragic flaws and holy vices. (Ted Tollefson. "What Makes a Hero?" From "Is a Hero Really Nothing But a Sandwich?" by Ted Tollefson as appeared in *Utne Reader*. May/June 1993, pp. 102–3. Reprinted by permission of the author.)

---

†Oedipus: the hero of a Greek tragedy who was determined to know the secret of his birth. When he found it out, he was so horrified that he blinded himself.

†Billy Budd: a character from a short story by Herman Melville. Young Billy is so innocent he arouses the hatred of the ship's cynical master-of-arms, John Claggart.

†Lone Ranger: the white-hatted hero of a television western.

**Combining
Your Skills**

DIRECTIONS Answer the following questions by circling the appropriate letter or filling in the blanks.

Main Idea **1.** Which paragraph introduces the main idea of the entire reading?

    a. paragraph 1

    b. paragraph 2

    (c.) paragraph 3

2. Which statement accurately paraphrases the main idea of the entire reading?

    a. In different stages of our lives, we need different heroes on whom to model ourselves.

    (b.) No matter where they come from or what their era, heroes are likely to share similar traits that are admired and imitated by others.

    c. All too often, Americans confuse celebrities with heroes.

    d. There are many differences between American and European heroes.

Sentence
Relationships **3.** In paragraph 3, what relationship binds these two sentences together? "A hero has a story of adventure to tell and a community who will listen. But a hero goes beyond mere fame or celebrity."

    a. cause and effect

    (b.) agreement and modification

    c. time order

Drawing
Inferences **4.** Based on what the author says in paragraph 3, which inference is appropriate?

    a. He thinks the words *heroes* and *celebrities* mean the same thing.

    (b.) He thinks heroes should not be confused with celebrities.

    c. He believes Americans have replaced European royalty with celebrities.

**Main Ideas
in Paragraphs**

5. Gandhi, Rosa Parks, and Martin Luther King Jr. are illustrations of which main idea?

    a. Heroes always suffer for their beliefs.

    (b.) Heroes bring about change in the world.

    c. Heroes are made, not born.

    d. Ordinary people are capable of great heroism.

6. What's the main idea of paragraph 6?

    a. Generally, heroes leave home and return to tell the story of their adventures.

    b. American heroes often feel homeless.

    (c.) Although it's only a few centuries old, the American heroic tradition already has some disturbing traits.

    d. Heroes almost always disappear into the wilderness and return completely transformed.

**Patterns of
Organization**

7. Which organizational pattern links paragraphs 7 and 8?

    a. sequence of events

    (b.) comparison and contrast

    c. cause and effect

    d. classification

8. What is the primary pattern of organization for the entire reading?

    Comparing and Contrasting

    What word or phrase in the thesis statement strongly suggests the presence of this pattern?

    but a hero goes beyond Mere fame.

**Understanding
Figurative
Language**

9. In paragraph 1, what simile—comparison using *like* or *as*—does the author use to convey the point that we have different heroes at different points in our lives?

    Like Serpents, We continue to shed the skin of our heroes to shape newfaces in our lives.

Analyzing Arguments 10. The author of this reading tries to convince you of what point?

he is trying to convince What a hero is and What the differences the American And European heroes have.

What kind of evidence does he offer to prove that point?

a. expert opinion

b. reasons

c. examples

d. studies and statistics

Share Your Thoughts The author lists his heroes. Who are your heroes? Do they fit the author's description? How are they similar or different? Do you think you are capable of being a hero? Why or why not? *Yes I have my Mum as My hero And my Doctors to save my kidney.*

Thinking Through Writing Write an essay in which you define the characteristics of a hero. Begin with a brief description of someone you consider heroic. Then describe the characteristics that make that person a hero to you.

Note: Your hero doesn't have to be a famous person; he or she just has to be someone you admire.

My hero would be the doctors At CHOP. because they gave me a new kidney And saved it When I was on new medicine.

◆ **READING 4**   **Taylor's Miracle**

Rick Bragg

Looking Ahead   Taylor Touchstone was ten years old when he got lost for four days in the Florida swamp near his home. Author Rick Bragg describes Taylor's miraculous journey through the dark and deadly swamp waters, where four men had already died when they got lost.

Word Watch   You probably know most of the words in the reading. The ones you don't know can probably be defined from context. The words that follow, however, cannot be fully understood from either context or the analysis of word parts. For this reason, their meanings are supplied here. Look them over before you begin reading.

---

autistic (1): being the victim of a disorder that causes problems with communication, behavior, and social interaction

glints (4): small flashes of light

neurological (5): having to do with the brain

manifests (5): reveals, shows

coddling (9): spoiling, treating like a baby

redundant (15): repetitious, repetitive

hypothermia (17): abnormally and dangerously low body temperature

---

Reading Tip   As you read the article, try to answer this question. What helped Taylor survive?

1   Taylor Touchstone, a 10-year-old autistic* boy who takes along a stuffed leopard and pink blanket when he goes to visit his grandmother, somehow survived for four days lost and alone in a swamp acrawl with poisonous snakes and alligators.

2   He swam, floated, crawled and limped about 14 miles, his feet, legs and stomach covered with cuts from brush and briars that rescuers believed to be impassable, his journey lighted at night by thunderstorms that stabbed the swamp with lightning.

3   People in this resort town on the Gulf of Mexico say they believe that Taylor's survival is a miracle, and that may be as good an explanation as they will ever have. The answer, the key to the mystery that baffles rescue workers who have seen this swamp kill grown, tough men, may be forever

lost behind the boy's calm blue eyes. "I see fish, lots of fish," was all Taylor told his mother, Suzanne Touchstone, when she gently asked him what he remembered from his ordeal in the remote reservation on Eglin Air Force Base.

4   Over the years, Taylor may tell her more, but most likely it will come in glints* and glimmers of information, a peek into a journey that ended on Sunday when a fisherman found Taylor floating naked in the East Bay River, bloody, hungry but very much alive. He may turn loose a few words as he sits in the living room, munching on the junk food that is about the only thing his mother can coax him to eat, or when they go for one of their drives to look at cows. He likes the cows, sometimes. Sometimes he does not see them at all, and they just ride, quiet.

5   Taylor's form of autism is considered moderate. The neurological* disorder is characterized by speech and learning impairment, and manifests* itself in unusual responses to people and surroundings.

6   "I've heard stories of autistic people who suddenly just remember, and begin to talk" of something in the far past, Mrs. Touchstone said. "But we may never know" what he lived through, or how he lived through it, she said. His father, Ray, added, "I don't know that it matters." Like his wife and their 12-year-old daughter, Jayne, Mr. Touchstone can live with the mystery. It is the ending of the story that matters.

7   Still, they have their theories. They say they believe that it is possible that Taylor survived the horrors of the swamp not in spite of his autism, but because of it. "He doesn't know how to panic," Jayne said. "He doesn't know what fear is." Her brother is focused, she said. Mrs. Touchstone says Taylor will focus all his attention and energy on a simple thing—he will fixate on a knot in a bathing suit's drawstring—and not be concerned about the broader realm of his life.

8   If that focus helped him survive, Mrs. Touchstone said, then "it is a miracle" that it was her son and not some otherwise normal child who went for a four-day swim in the black water of a region in which Army Rangers and sheriff's deputies could not fully penetrate. He may have paddled with the gators, and worried more about losing his trunks.

9   "Bullheaded," said Mrs. Touchstone, who is more prone to say what is on her mind than grope for pat answers. Instead of coddling* and being overly protective of her child, she tried to let him enjoy a life as close to normal as common sense allowed.

10   Taylor's scramble and swim through the swamp, apparently without any direction or motive beyond the obvious fact that he wanted to keep in motion, left him with no permanent injuries. On Wednesday, he sat in his living room, the ugly, healing cuts crisscrossing his legs,

and munched junk food. "Cheetos," he said, when asked what he was eating. But when he was asked about the swamp, he carefully put the plastic lid back on the container, and left the room. He did not appear upset, just uninterested.

Lifelong Swimmer at Home in Water

11   Taylor has been swimming most of his life. In the water, his autism seems to disappear. He swims like a dolphin, untiring.

12   His journey began about 4 p.m. on Aug. 7, a Wednesday, while he and his mother and sister were swimming with friends in Turtle Creek on the reservation lands of the Air Force base. Taylor walked into the water and floated downstream, disappearing from sight. He did not answer his mother's calls. An extensive air, water and ground search followed. It involved Army Rangers, Green Berets, marines, deputies with the Okaloosa County Sheriff's Department and volunteers, who conducted arm-to-arm searches in water that was at times neck-deep, making noise to scare off the alligators and rattlesnakes and water moccasins, and shouting Taylor's name.

13   He is only moderately autistic, Mrs. Touchstone said, but it is possible that he may not have responded to the calls of the searchers. At night, when it was nearly useless to search on foot, AC-130 helicopters crisscrossed the swamp, searching for Taylor with heat-seeking, infrared tracking systems. In all, the air and ground searchers covered 36 square miles, but Taylor, barefoot, had somehow moved outside their range. "The search area encompassed as much area as we could cover," said Rick Hord of the Sheriff's Department. "He went farther."

14   It was not just the distance that surprised the searchers. Taylor somehow went under, around or through brush that the searchers saw as impassable. Yet there is no evidence that anyone else was involved in his journey, or of foul play, investigators said.

15   Apparently, Taylor just felt compelled to keep moving. Members of his family say they believe that he spent a good part of his time swimming, which may have kept him away from snakes on land. The nights brought pitch blackness to the swamp, and on two nights there were violent thunderstorms. "Lightning would have penetrated his shell," Mrs. Touchstone said. "I think it may have kept him moving," she said, and that might have been a blessing. Certainly, said his mother and doctors who treated the boy, he was exhausted. "Do you really think God would strike him with lightning?" she asked. "Wouldn't that be redundant?"*

16   Somewhere, somehow, he lost his bathing suit. His parents said he might have torn them, and, concentrating on a single blemish, found them unacceptable. Mrs. Touchstone compared it to a talk she once heard by an autistic woman who had escaped her shell, who told the audience that most people in a forest see the vastness of trees, but she might fixate on a spider web.

17   On the third day of Taylor's journey, Mrs. Touchstone realized that her son might be dead. For reasons she could not fully explain, she did not want to see his body recovered. It would have been too hard to see him that way. Even though Taylor is physically fit and strong, friends and relatives knew that this was the same terrain that in February 1995 claimed the lives of four Rangers who died of hypothermia* while training in swampland near here.

18   Instead, about 7 a.m . . . . a fisherman named Jimmy Potts spotted what seemed to be a child bobbing in the waters of the East Bay River. Mr. Potts hauled him into his small motorboat. Later that day, Taylor told his momma that he really liked the boat ride. In the hospital, he sang, "Row, Row, Row Your Boat."

Mother Encourages Son's Independence

19 Mrs. Touchstone lost Taylor at a Walmart, once. "That was bad," she said. He ran out of Cheetos once and hiked a few blocks, alone, to get some. The police found him and brought him home. He decided once that the floor in the grocery store needed "dusting"—he likes to dust—and he got down on the floor and began dusting the grimy floor with his fingers.

20   But he has never lived in a prison of over-protectiveness. Even though his mother says there are limits to how much freedom he can realistically have and how much so-called normal behavior she can expect from him, she decided years ago that the only way he could have anything approaching a normal life—in some ways, the only way she herself could have one—was to let him go swimming, visit neighbors, take some normal, childlike risks.

21   He is prone, now and then, to just walk into a neighbor's house. Once, he went into the kitchen of a neighbor, opened the refrigerator, took out a carton of milk, slammed it down on the counter and stood there, expectantly. The woman called Mrs. Touchstone. "What should I do?" the woman asked. "Well," Mrs. Touchstone said, "I'd pour him a glass of milk."

22   The fact that Taylor is not completely dependent on his parents, that he is not treated like an overgrown infant, that he is allowed to swim on his own and roam the aisles of the Walmart and raid the neighbors' refrigerators, may have helped him survive when he was all alone in the swamp, his family believes. His father offered this explanation: "That's all his mom. I was overly protective."

23   The phenomenon of his journey has prompted teachers at his school to consider changes in the study plan for autistic or handicapped students. One teacher told Mrs. Touchstone that they would stress more self-reliance.

24   Mrs. Touchstone, who jokingly calls herself "Treasurer for Life" for the Fort Walton chapter of the Autism Society of America, said her son's journey should clarify, in some people's minds, what autism is. "I want every inch of that swamp he crossed to count for something," she said. For now, life is back to normal. He screamed when he was forced to take his medicine, which is not so unusual for a 10-year-old. "We've got a little autism in all of us," Mrs. Touchstone said.

25   Taylor has always been something of a celebrity in his neighborhood, so his mother does not expect much to change after his ordeal. There was a sign outside his school that just said, "Welcome Home," and many people have called or written to tell her how relieved they are. One elderly neighbor wrote to tell Mrs. Touchstone how relieved she was that "our child" was home safe.

26   Mrs. Touchstone will not waste time wondering, at least not too much, about her son's strange trip. She can live with the notion of a miracle. "I guess God was looking for something to do," she said. "I guess he looked down and said, 'Let's fix things up a little bit.'" ("Autism No Handicap, Boy Defies Swamp" by Rick Bragg from *The New York Times*, August 17, 1996. Copyright © 1996 The New York Times Co. All rights reserved. Reprinted by permission.)

Combining Your Skills

DIRECTIONS   Answer the following questions by circling the appropriate letter or filling in the blanks.

Sentence Relationships

1.   What relationship links these two sentences together: "'I've heard stories of autistic people who suddenly just remember, and begin to talk' of something in the far past, Mrs. Touchstone said. 'But we may never know' what he lived through, or how he lived through it, she said."

    a. time order
    b. agreement and modification
    c. cause and effect

2. What relationship does Mrs. Touchstone imply in these two sentences from paragraph 15? "'Lightning would have penetrated his shell,' Mrs. Touchstone said. 'I think it may have kept him moving.'"

   a. time order

   b. agreement and modification

   c. cause and effect

Main Idea 3. Which statement most effectively sums up the main idea of the entire reading?

   a. Taylor Touchstone's experience in a deadly swamp is a perfect illustration of an everyday miracle that proves the existence of god.

   b. Oddly enough, being autistic may well have saved Taylor Touchstone's life when he was lost for four days in a dangerous swamp.

   c. Taylor touchstone inherited his gritty spirit from his equally strong-willed and determined mother.

   d. Being a celebrity has not gone to Taylor Touchstone's head; he remains the same as he was before becoming famous.

Supporting Details 4. What word in paragraph 7 offers a clue to the major details?

   Theroies

Organizational Patterns 5. Which two organizational patterns are central to this reading?

   a. comparison and contrast

   b. cause and effect

   c. time order

   d. simple listing

Drawing Inferences 6. The word *shell* is used twice in relation, once in relation to Taylor (15) and once in relation to a woman who is also autistic (16). What does that word suggest to you about autism? What does it do to its victims?

   His Shyness Autistic Children are shy. Their Shyness makes them impenetrable.

7. In paragraph 15, what does Mrs. Touchstone imply when she asks these two questions: "'Do you really think God would strike him with lightning?' she asked. 'Wouldn't that be redundant?'" Why would Taylor being struck by lightning while lost in the swamp be redundant?

She was already afraid That he might Die.

8. Which statement do you think Mrs. Touchstone would agree with wholeheartedly?

a. "God moves in a mysterious way. His wonders to perform." William Cowper

b. "God is dead." Friedrich Nietzsche

c. "I think that God, in creating man, somewhat overestimated his ability." Oscar Wilde

d. "To be a Christian means to forgive the inexcusable because God has forgiven the inexcusable in you." C. S. Lewis

9. What from the reading led you to choose that quotation?

it was A Miracle.

Purpose 10. What is the writer's purpose?

a. to tell you about Taylor's experience
b. to make you admire Taylor and his family

Please explain your answer.

Because it was how he survived a swamp for four days And got rescued By a fisherman And Taken Back Home.

Share Your Thoughts Do you think Ted Tollefson, the author of reading 3, would consider Taylor a hero? Why or why not? yes Because taylor was a hero,

Thinking Through Writing Write a paper in which you describe how Mrs. Touchstone's attitude toward her son either helped him or hurt him. Or, if you wish, explain how her attitude toward Taylor did both. Use statements or quotations from the reading to help prove your point.

She Helped him
Get through the
swamp on his own,

◆ **READING 5**   # Unhealthy Eating Behaviors

Dianne Hales

Looking Ahead   At one time or another, everyone eats too many candy bars or doesn't eat enough protein. Because we are busy, we don't pay much attention to how, and, above all, why we eat. But this reading from a textbook titled *An Invitation to Health* suggests that perhaps we should.

Word Watch   You probably know most of the words in the reading. The ones you don't know can, for the most part, be defined from context. The words that follow, however, cannot be fully understood from either context or the analysis of word parts. For this reason, their meanings are supplied here. Look them over before you begin reading.

compulsively (2): uncontrollably, involuntarily

potentially (2): in the future, possibly

nutrition (7): the study of the food necessary for good health

misconceptions (7): mistaken thoughts, misunderstandings

Reading Tip   Because the reading covers several unhealthy eating patterns, make sure you know the definition and symptoms of each one. Because the author stresses that the roots of unhealthy eating are complex, underline carefully those passages that explain how the behavior gets started.

1   Unhealthy eating behavior takes many forms, ranging from not eating enough to eating too much too quickly. Its roots are complex. In addition to media and external pressures, family history can play a role. Researchers have linked specific genes to some cases of anorexia nervosa and binge eating, but most believe that a variety of factors, including stress and culture, combine to cause disordered eating.

2   Sooner or later, many people don't eat the way they should. They may skip meals, thereby increasing the likelihood that they'll end up with more body fat, a higher weight, and a higher blood cholesterol level. They might live on diet foods but consume so much of them that they gain weight anyway. Some even engage in more extreme eating behavior: Dissatisfied

with almost all aspects of their appearance, they continuously go on and off diets, eat compulsively,* or binge on high-fat treats. Such behaviors can be warning signs of potentially* serious eating disorders that should not be ignored.

Unhealthy Eating in College Students

3 College students—particularly women, including varsity athletes—are at risk for unhealthy eating behaviors. Researchers estimate that only about a third of college women maintain healthy eating patterns. Some college women have full-blown eating disorders. Others develop "partial syndromes" and experience symptoms that are not severe or numerous enough to make a diagnosis of anorexia nervosa or bulimia nervosa. Distress over body image increases the risk of all forms of disordered eating in college women.

4 In a survey at a large, public, rural university in the mid-Atlantic states, 17 percent of the women were struggling with disordered eating. Younger women (ages 18 to 21) were more likely than older students to have an eating disorder. In this study, eating disorders did not discriminate. They affected women of different races, religions, athletic involvements, and living arrangements (living on or off campus, with boyfriends, roommates or family).

5 Although the students viewed eating disorders as both mental and physical problems and felt that individual therapy would be most helpful, all said that they would first turn to a friend for help. Women in sororities are at slightly increased risk of an eating disorder compared with those in dormitories. Loneliness has also emerged as a risk factor for eating disorders in college women.

Extreme Dieting

6 Extreme dieters go beyond cutting back on calories or increasing physical activity. They become preoccupied with what they eat and weigh. Although their weight never falls below 85 percent of normal, their weight loss is severe enough to cause uncomfortable physical consequences, such as weakness and sensitivity to cold. Technically, these dieters do not have anorexia nervosa, but they are at increased risk for it.

7 Extreme dieters may think they know a great deal about nutrition,* yet many of their beliefs about food and weight are misconceptions* or myths. For instance, they may eat only protein because they believe complex carbohydrates, including fruits and whole-grain breads, are fattening.

8   Sometimes nutritional education alone can help change these eating patterns. However, many avid dieters who deny that they have a problem with food may need counseling (which they usually agree to only at their family's insistence) to correct dangerous eating behavior and prevent further complications.

Compulsive Overeating

9   People who eat compulsively cannot stop putting food in their mouths. They eat fast and they eat a lot. They eat even when they are full. They may eat around the clock, rather than at set mealtimes, often in private because of embarrassment over how much they consume.

10   Some mental health professionals describe compulsive eating as a food addiction that is much more likely to develop in women. According to Overeaters Anonymous (OA), an international 12-step program, many women who eat compulsively view food as a source of comfort against feelings of inner emptiness, low self-esteem, and fear of abandonment. The following behaviors many signal a potential problem with compulsive overeating:

- **Turning to food when depressed** or lonely, when feeling rejected, or as a reward.
- **A history of failed diets** and anxiety when dieting.
- **Thinking about food** throughout the day.
- **Eating quickly** and without pleasure.
- **Continuing to eat** even when no longer hungry.
- **Frequently talking about food** or refusing to talk about food.
- **Fear of not being able to stop eating** after starting.

11   Recovery from compulsive eating can be challenging because people with this problem cannot give up entirely the substance they abuse. Like everyone else, they must eat. However, they can learn new eating habits and ways of dealing with underlying emotional problems. An OA survey found that most of its members joined to lose weight but later felt the most important effect was their improved emotional, mental, and physical health. As one woman put it, "I came for vanity, but stayed for sanity."

Binge Eating

12   Binge eating—the rapid consumption of an abnormally large amount of food in a relatively short time—often occurs in compulsive eaters. The 25 million Americans with a binge-eating disorder typically eat a

larger than ordinary amount of food during a relatively brief period, feel a lack of control over eating, and binge at least twice a week for at least a six-month period. During most of these episodes, binge eaters experience at least three of the following:

- **Eating much more rapidly** than usual.
- **Eating until they feel uncomfortably full**.
- **Eating large amounts of food** when not feeling physically hungry.
- **Eating large amounts of food throughout the day** with no planned mealtimes.
- **Eating alone** because they are embarrassed by how much they eat and by their eating habits.

13   Binge eaters may spend up to several hours eating, and consume 2,000 or more calories worth of food in a single binge—more than many people eat in a day. After such binges, they usually do not do anything to control weight, but simply get fatter. As their weight climbs, they become depressed, anxious, or troubled by other psychological symptoms to a much greater extent than others of comparable weight.

14   Binge eating is probably the most common unhealthy eating behavior. An estimated 8 to 19 percent of obese patients in weight loss programs are binge eaters.

15   If you occasionally go on eating binges, use the behavioral technique called *habit reversal* and replace your binging with a competing behavior. For example, every time you are tempted to binge, immediately do something—text message a friend, play solitaire, check your e-mail—that keeps food out of your mouth. If you binge twice a week or more for at least a six-month period, you may have binge-eating disorder, which can require professional help. Short-term talk treatment either individually or in a group setting, has proven most effective for binge eating. (Adapted from Diane Hales, *An Invitation to Health*, 10th ed. © Cengage Learning.)

**Combining
Your Skills**   **DIRECTIONS**   Answer the following questions by circling the appropriate letter or filling in the blanks.

Surveying   1.   Based on the title of this reading, what should you be looking for while you read?

how People are eating Unhealthy.

2. The opening paragraph introduces three kinds of category words, all of which can be used to guide your reading. What are those three category words?

unhealthy, Variety and Disordered

Sentence Relationships 3. In the last sentence of the first paragraph, the author starts off by saying what about eating disorders?

It's caused by a variety of factors.

But the train of thought in the sentence then switches to say what about unhealthy eating behaviors?

Stress and Culture.

What relationship unites the parts of that sentence?

Combined Pattern.

4. In paragraph 2, what's the relationship between the two parts of this sentence? "Some even engage in more extreme eating behavior: Dissatisfied with almost all aspects of their appearance, they continuously go on and off diets, eat compulsively, or binge on high-fat treats."

The Second Part of the Sentence explains The first Part of the sentence.

Main Idea 5. Which statement best expresses the overall main idea of this reading?

a. There is more than one kind of unhealthy eating behavior, but only one is really dangerous, and that's binge eating.

b. There are several different kinds of unhealthy eating behaviors, and none of them should be ignored.

c. Unhealthy eating behaviors cannot be treated as a phase that kids are going through; on the contrary, unhealthy eating is the first indication of a serious emotional problem that might well lead to anorexia nervosa, also known as the starvation disease.

d. Compulsive overeating is typical of college students, who are likely to overeat due to anxiety.

6. Which statement best expresses the main idea of paragraph 11?

(a.) People who engage in compulsive eating almost never change their behavior, largely because it's impossible to give up food.

b. Compulsive eating is one of the unhealthy eating behaviors that can be enormously improved through group therapy.

c. Compulsive eating usually begins in childhood, and once it takes root as a consistent habit, it is all but impossible to alter.

d. People who eat compulsively can change their eating habits and find other ways of dealing with the emotional origins of their overeating.

Organizational Patterns **7.** What's the overall pattern of the entire reading?

Working on Problems in the first part of the reading the explaing solutions in the end.

Paraphrasing **8.** In your own words, describe how "habit reversal" mentioned in paragraph 15 can help binge eating.

Playing Video Games and Playing On the IPad can help with Binge eating.

Analyzing Arguments **9.** What evidence does the author use to prove the claim that female college students are at high risk for eating problems?

Because of a Survey at a university

Do you think the evidence is adequate to the claim? *Yes* Please explain your answer.

Because it will Help Women in college Stop their eating Disorders.

Fact and Opinion **10.** Read the following statement from paragraph 10: "Some mental health professionals describe compulsive eating as a food addiction that is much more likely to develop in women." Based on this sentence, would you say the claim that food addictions are more likely develop in women is a factual statement? _Yes_ Please explain your answer.

Because more women are more likley to get hungrier than men should.

Share Your Thoughts The reading repeatedly suggests that eating problems stem from emotional problems. Why do you think so many people handle their problems by consuming food? What's the connection between our emotions and our diet? _People are eating because not Because they're hungry But are ons medi that them_

Thinking Through Writing Use the Web to read about Overeaters Anonymous. Then write a paper explaining why people who compulsively overeat are likely (or not likely) to benefit from this kind of group support.

Over eaters Anonymous is a Twelve-step Program for People with Problems relat to food including, but not Limited to, Compulsive overeaters; Those with binge eating disorders, bulimics and anorexics; Anyone with a Problematic Relationship with food is welcomed. OA's third tradition states that the only requirement for membershipes is a desire to stop eating compulsively.

◆ **READING 6** **Look at My Scars**

Mary Elizabeth Williams

Looking Ahead Illness and injury can change the way we look at the world. Perhaps more significantly, they can change the way the world looks at us. The author of the following reading, who has survived a bout with skin cancer that has left her with scars that can't be disguised or removed talks about what it's like when your scars can't be covered up.

Word Watch You probably know most of the words in the reading. The ones you don't know can, for the most part, be defined from context. The words that follow, however, cannot be fully understood from either context or the analysis of word parts. For this reason, their meanings are supplied here. Look them over before you begin reading.

> **qualms (2):** worries, hesitations
>
> **winced (4):** make an involuntary movement of distress or unease
>
> **indelible (5):** incapable of being removed
>
> **psoriasis (6):** a disease of the skin that causes severe flaking and dryness
>
> **lesion (6):** an abnormality of tissue
>
> **exquisiteness (13):** extreme beauty

Reading Tip Read to answer the question the title evokes, "Why would you want to look at someone's scars?" Why is that important for both you and the person you are looking at?

1 Do I freak you out?" she had asked.

2   It was the kind of question adults rarely pose. But Abigail (a pseudonym, like some other names in this piece) is 8, and she doesn't have any qualms* about being direct. The person she was asking, my daughter Beatrice, likewise didn't hesitate in her reply.

3   Abigail is new to our school this year. She is in every way a typical second-grader, except that she was born without a left hand. It's a trait that makes her undeniably noticeable, and so, sometimes, people ask questions. Sometimes Abigail has questions of her own. Sometimes, when you're different, you want to know.

4   When Bea told me what Abigail had inquired about a few weeks ago, I'd winced* a little, wondering how my child had answered. Had she passed whatever test Abigail was giving? I know how frank Bea can be, how she walks behind me when we're out in public, checking whether the shiny, taut expanse of bare skin on my scalp is visible. "Mom, your bald spot," she'll say when we're in a restaurant, fussing with locks to try to hide the five-centimeter circle where, a year and a half ago, I had surgery to remove cancer.

5   I know that Abigail's question haunts many of us who are physically different, in ways both small and large, either by birth or circumstance. It plagues my friend with accident scars on his legs, who's already nervous about summertime and exposing his flesh at the beach this year. Maybe it's a small yet indelible* birthmark on the chin. Or it's a big burn. Or a missing limb. Does this make you want to look, or want to look away? Do we make you uncomfortable? Do we freak you out?

6   "It's a thing that has to get explained," says Natalie, a New York executive who's had three serious melanoma surgeries and lives with ongoing psoriasis* lesions.* "For me, the anticipation of that is hard. I think people want to distance themselves from someone who's had a traumatic event. Somehow you wind up having to reassure them that you're not contagious, that they'll be OK."

7   Though she tries to be "very open about my illness, because I want people to get it," Natalie admits she has nevertheless "some really upset moments" of unasked for attention. "I once had someone literally cross the road to ask what was wrong with my legs," she says. "I was feeling really proud of myself for being brave enough to wear the skirt. And this woman came along and destroyed it." She adds, however, "I don't feel sorry for myself, and I don't wear this as a badge. I just want to be looked at as the successful, independent woman I am—but I understand that some people can't do it."

8   It's true that some people can't, and there's loss in there. I used to have a friend who liked taking pictures of his buddies, including me—right up until my diagnosis and my relatively minor disfigurement. Then he never took another photograph of me again. I wonder if I freaked him out.

9   My friend Frank, a West Coast entrepreneur, understands. A few years ago, Frank had radical surgery for bladder cancer that left him with what he calls a "Guinness Book of World Records scar" that starts at his sternum, loops around, and ends at his pubic bone. He also has a partial hernia that leaves him, in his word, "lumpy" under a shirt.

10   "I get a lot of people staring. I'm used to it," he says. "It usually doesn't bother me. I'm just a little self-conscious when people are peeking out the corner of their eyes in the locker room." And, he recalls, "one time my wife and I were at Caesar's Palace lying out in the super-bright, crystal-clear Vegas sun, and this woman next to us asked, 'What happened to your stomach?' She was pretty horrified when I told her." He's still sometimes horrified himself. "I look at myself every morning, and I think of all the horrible shit that I've been through because of this disease," he tells me. But when he looks in the mirror, he also sees a mark of survival. "I'm working out and riding my bike to train, and if that doesn't tell you how I'm doing, go ahead and ask me. I don't think I look that bizarre. I think I look like a guy who's had major abdominal surgery."

11   As Frank knows, when you've been through something life-altering, the first person you have to get to accept your look is yourself. "The first time I saw myself afterward, I thought, *That looks very interesting*," says Johan Otter. Johan is a master of understatement. Seven years ago, Johan was hiking with his daughter in Glacier National Park when he was mauled by a grizzly bear. His scalp was torn off; his eye was clawed. He had to wear a halo brace for 12 weeks and go through multiple grafts and surgeries to recover. And then, he says, he had to learn to "push through" his first time out in public again.

12   "You get used to it," he says. Besides, he jokes, "I never have a bad hair day." Otter admits he can still be somewhat surprising to strangers. "Once at Costco this woman said, 'Oh my God, what happened to your head?'" he recalls. But though he admits, "I'm a vain person just like anybody else," Otter says that "I'm always extremely proud of my scars. When you go through something like this, people see you with your true self. You learn that what matters is what's inside."

13   It's not always easy in our perfection-driven culture—where a weight gain of five pounds can be treated as a life crisis and toothpaste brands wage war on dingy teeth and a "puffy face" means you're no longer considered "pretty"—to believe that within battle scars and what others would call abnormalities, there is a raging, painful exquisiteness.* It's often hard to feel the sideways glances and puzzled stares. But it's harder still to be overlooked entirely, to feel like the remnants of the trials we've endured are the things that make others unable to look at us. We want to be looked at not with pity, not with fear, not with morbid curiosity. Simply with clear and open eyes.

14   So when Bea told me her friend Abigail wanted to know if she was freaking her out, I hoped Bea had answered honestly. More than that, I

hoped she answered kindly. I hoped she didn't pretend she'd never noticed Abigail's missing hand, or changed the subject altogether. "What did you say?" I asked her nervously. "I told her no," she shrugged. "I said, 'Why would I be freaked? I love you.'" And then I exhaled.

15   I know life for Abigail—and Natalie and Johan and Frank and everybody else wounded or scarred or born different—is more complicated than that. The things that make us stand out in the crowd define us in a million little ways. They can remind us of the most dramatic, heroic moments of our lives, and of every small indignity and cruelty that has happened since. But what Bea and Abigail got to in the span of one recess period was that life isn't about seeing past each other's imperfections. It's about being unafraid to look at them directly. Because that's where the love is—in the cracks and the sufferings and the challenges. Life isn't flawless. But it can be very, very beautiful. That day at recess, Bea told me, she had kissed Abigail, right on the place where her arm stops at the wrist. And they played together until the bell rang, and it was time to go back to class. ("Look at My Scars" by Mary Elizabeth Williams from Salon.com, April 2012. This article first appeared in Salon.com, at http://www.Salon.com. An online version remains in the Salon archives. Reprinted with permission.)

Combining Your Skills

DIRECTIONS   Answer the following questions by circling the appropriate letter or filling in the blanks.

Main Idea   1. Where does the author introduce the main idea of this reading?

     a. the beginning

     (b.) the middle

     c. the end

What paragraph do you think sums up the main idea of the entire reading?

_____Paragraph 13._____

2. Why do you think the author uses a single question as her introduction?

to get People interested in other People with Different Challanges

3. What does the author want readers to believe or think after reading what she wrote?

   a. If people you love have physical imperfections, pretend you don't see them so they will not feel embarrassed.

   b. Don't look away from people scarred by illness or disease; instead accept the scars as marks of both their heroism as well as their suffering.

   c. People who have been marked by disease or injury may get over their wounds or their illness, but they never recover from the indignity they suffer at the hands of other people.

   d. Intense physical suffering makes or breaks a person's character.

Analyzing Arguments

4. What kinds of support does the author use to prove her point?

   a. reasons

   b. studies

   c. examples

   d. expert opinion

Drawing Inferences

5. Why do you think Bea kissed her friend Abigail right where "her arm stops at the wrist"?

   to remind ABigail that Everybody's Different.

6. Why does the author say at the end of paragraph 14, "And then I exhaled"?

   to Be Relieved and happy.

7. In paragraph 12, Frank jokes, "I never have a bad hair day." What's the literal point of his joke?

   his hair is Still Perfect even after the Bear Attacked him.

8. But what else is he communicating about himself and his attitude toward life?

That he is Different and Special after the Bear Attack.

9. In what paragraph does the author explain the two sides of being someone who is scarred or disfigured? __13__ In your own words, what are the two sides?

Listen to the Song Beautiful By christina Agruliara and you Will get used to that Song.

Tone 10. Why do you think the author tells you about her own experience? What does it contribute to her tone?

    a. anger

    b. unhappiness

    c. sincerity

    d. frustration

Share Your Thoughts If you had gone through what Johan Otter, the man who was mauled by a grizzly, did, do you think you would be able to make jokes as he does? *No* What do you think of his attitude toward his experience? *he is not Being reasonable he Should Be happy that h is Dif*

Thinking Through Writing The author talks about our "perfection-driven culture." Write a paper in which you take the phrase and either agree or disagree with what it suggests. Is it a gross exaggeration? If so, how might you argue your claim? What examples could back up your point? Or do you think it's true, that we demand physical perfection from ourselves and others? If that's what you think, provide examples or reasons that prove your claim.

People with Scars and cuts Scraps and Scabs Shoud Show their True Colours.

◆ **READING 7**   **Influences**

Sherman Alexie

Looking Ahead   The reading in Chapter 1 described how the arrival of white settlers in the West proved a tragedy for Native Americans. This poem, by acclaimed writer Sherman Alexie, who is himself Native American, focuses not on the past but on the present.

Reading Tip   Read the poem slowly, line by line, figuring out what each line adds to the previous one in much the same way you do with sentences. Poems don't necessarily have one main idea. Often they focus on several, weaving them together to describe an experience that readers can feel through the words. That experience, however, will only come to life if the reader is prepared to infer the author's meaning.

1   We waited in the car
    outside the bar
    my sisters and I
    "for just a couple drinks"
5   as we had heard it
    so many times before
    as Ramona said
    like all Indian kids
    have heard
10 before
    from their parents, disappeared into the smoke and laughter of a reservation tavern, emerging every half-hour with Pepsi, potato chips, and more promises. And, like all Indians have learned, we never did trust those promises. We knew to believe something when it happened,
15 learned to trust the source of a river and never its mouth. But this is not about sadness. This is about the stories
    imagined
    beneath the sleeping bags
    between starts
20 to warm up the car
    because my parents trusted me
    with the keys.
    This is about the stories
    I told my sisters

25   to fill those long hours, waiting outside the bar, waiting for my mother,
my father to knock on the window, asking Are you warm enough? Are
you doing all right? We'll be out soon, okay? Sometimes, we refused to
open the locked doors for our parents, left them to gesture wildly and
make all of us laugh because there was nothing else left to do. But this

30   is not about sadness. This is about the stories
I created
how I built
landscapes and imaginary saviors.
Once, I dreamed a redheaded woman

35   gave her name and weight and told my sisters
she would rescue us
from our own love
for this mother and father who staggered from the bar always five minutes before closing, so they could tell us later At least we left before last

40   call. But we did love them, held tightly to their alcoholic necks and arms
as we drove back home, stole the six-pack they bought for the road and
threw it out the window, counted mile markers and coyotes standing
on the edge of the road. But this is not about sadness. This is about the
stories, those rough drafts

45   that thundered the walls
of the HUD[†] house
as my sisters and I lay awake
after we finally arrived home
and listened to my mother and father dream

50   breathe deep
in their sleep, snore
like what you might want me to call drums
but in the reservation dark
it meant we were all alive

55   and that was enough. ("Influences" from "First Indian on the Moon" by Sherman Alexie.

Copyright © 1993 Sherman Alexie. Reprinted by permission of Hanging Loose Press.)

[†]HUD: U.S. Department of Housing and Urban Development, the government organization that is responsible for awarding grants to create affordable housing for Native
Americans.

Combining   DIRECTIONS   Answer the following questions by circling the appropri-
Your Skills   ate letter or filling in the blanks.

Main Idea   **1.** How would you say the speaker of this poem views his parents?

    a. He hates them for leaving him and his sisters alone while they go into a bar to drink, and he cannot forgive them no matter how hard he tries.

    (b.) He loves his parents so much he can't see them as having any flaws.

    c. He knows his parents aren't behaving like responsible parents, but he also knows they love him and his sisters.

2. What is the role of "stories" in this poem?

how he was telling about him and his sisters waiting in the car.

Inferences   **3.** Why does the author emphasize this point about promises? "And, like all Indians have learned, we never did trust those promises. We knew to believe something when it happened, learned to trust the source of a river and never its mouth."

    a. Parents like the speaker's make and break promises all the time, so their children pay no attention to what they say.

    (b.) Throughout history Indians have been lied to and promises don't impress them. It's the promise becoming reality that matters.

    c. Indians believe that words will always deceive, so it makes no sense to listen to what anyone says. The person is always lying.

4. Why do you think the author calls his stories "rough drafts."

he's been waiting for his parents in the car with his sisters.

5. Where can the "landscapes and imaginary saviors" mentioned in line 23 be found?

They could be found in the car.

6. Why do the children throw the six-pack out the window?

They were trying to help their parents to stop drinking the six pack.

7. What sense do you get of how the parents view the speaker in the poem?

They were ignoring him and Drinking six packs

8. What is the evidence for your inference?

They gave him a lot of responsibility to handle the car on his own.

9. What does the pronoun _it_ refer to in line 38?

the stories meant they were all alive

What effect did it have on the children?

They felt that they were growing up

Tone 10. How would you describe the author's tone?

a. angry and filled with fury

b. sad and despairing

c. cool and unemotional

d. resigned but hopeful

Share Your Thoughts The Digging Deeper reading in Chapter 1 describes what happened to Native Americans as white settlers moved westward. What connection can you make between that historical description and Sherman Alexie's poem? _The settlers and Native Americans did not get along in Digging deeper and the poem,_

Thinking Through Writing Use the Web to find and read these four poems by Sherman Alexie: "Good Hair," "How to Write the Great American Indian Novel," "Poverty of Mirrors," and "What the Orphan Inherits." Read the poems several times each. If possible, read and discuss them with a friend. Then write a few paragraphs in which you explain at least one key theme or idea that runs through these works. Use quotations from the poems to illustrate what you say about the idea or experience they suggest to you.

The Native Americans felt that They did not Belong with the wh[i]... Settlers And were put into The US Department of housing and urban Develop...

Answer Key: Reviewing the Key Points

Chapter 1, Getting into a Textbook State of Mind, p. 45

1. F
2. T
3. F
4. F
5. T
6. F
7. F
8. F
9. F
10. T

Chapter 2, More on Words and Meaning, p. 85

1. F
2. F
3. T
4. F
5. F
6. T
7. T
8. F
9. F
10. T

Chapter 3, Understanding Sentence Relationships, p. 145

1. relationships that connect the sentences
2. a number of different ways
3. specific illustrations
4. False
5. admit that something is true or believed; revise, challenge, or modify the general statement
6. an event led to or caused another event

7. two topics are different
8. point out how two topics are alike
9. cause of another
10. dates and events; the steps in a process

Chapter 4, Identifying Topics, Main Ideas, and Topic Sentences, p. 207

1. It's the person, place, idea, event, or thing the writer is discussing.
2. It's the central point or message the writer wants to make about the topic.
3. Topic sentences are general sentences that sum up the point of the paragraph.
4. (1) The topic sentence is among the most general sentences in the paragraph. (2) It introduces an idea that is developed by the other sentences in the paragraph. (3) It answers the question, What's the point of this paragraph?
5. They can appear anywhere.
6. The first sentence is very likely the topic sentence.
7. The second sentence is likely the topic sentence.
8. They bulge at the mid-point of the paragraph.
9. They express the main idea of that paragraph and the main idea of the entire reading.
10. Turn the topic sentence into a question and see how well it gets answered by the remainder of the paragraph.

Chapter 5, Working Together: Topic Sentences and Supporting Details, p. 271

1. misinterpretation or misunderstanding; supporting details
2. False
3. make the main idea clear and convincing
4. the main idea
5. False

6. alter the meaning with the words
7. (1) to further explain major details
   (2) to add emphasis
   (3) to add a colorful fact or detail
8. explain a major detail
9. True
10. reasons, advantages, goals, studies, programs, categories, groups
11. I mean this, not that.
12. indention; relationships
13. False
14. True
15. bare bones; major or minor details essential to understanding it

Chapter 6, Drawing Inferences About Implied Main Ideas, p. 317

1. Nothing in the paragraph should contradict the main idea you inferred.
2. Look at the evidence that's given and decide what it suggests.
3. They should both sum up the paragraph.
4. Logical inferences keep readers and writers on the same track, while illogical inferences draw the reader away from the writer's actual train of thought.
5. The main ideas readers infer have to rely most heavily on the author's words.

Chapter 7, Recognizing Patterns of Organization, p. 390

1. cause and effect
2. comparison and contrast
3. sequence of dates and events; time order
4. process; time order
5. classification
6. simple listing

Chapter 8, Mixing and Matching Organizational Patterns, p. 440

1. the main idea
2. the main idea
3. False
4. True
5. False
6. Consider what they contribute to the main idea. The patterns most essential to explaining the main idea are the ones most essential to your notes.

Chapter 9, Analyzing Arguments, p. 513

1. (1) the opinion being put forth for consideration, (2) the author's support for that opinion, and (3) the response to the opposition
2. the response to the opposition
3. Opinions are ideas or beliefs about the world that are shaped by background, experience, and education. Thus they can't be verified or checked for accuracy. Facts are not affected by the background or experience of the person who states them. Thus they can be verified for accuracy and can be labeled *true* or *false*.
4. The language used can imply a value judgment.
5. When the argument is pared down, it is easier to evaluate the support offered for the opinion.
6. relevance
7. (1) why they are considered knowledgeable about the subject and (2) whether they have anything to gain from supporting the author's opinion
8. Check the Web for background information. Find out what the person's training and experience consist of.
9. No, sometimes the writer only uses a few words to influence the reader.
10. word choice, allusions, figurative language imagery, and personal anecdotes.

Index